Better Homes and Gardens.

KITCHEN
APPLIANCE
COOK BOOK

Library of Congress Catalog Card Number: 79-57482
ISBN: 0-696-00565-4

BETTER HOMES AND GARDENS® BOOKS

Editor: Gerald M. Knox
Art Director: Ernest Shelton
Managing Editor: David A. Kirchner

Food and Nutrition Editor: Doris Eby
Department Head Cook Books: Sharyl Heiken
Senior Food Editor: Elizabeth Woolever
Senior Associate Food Editors: Sandra Granseth,
    Rosemary C. Hutchinson
Associate Food Editors: Jill Burmeister, Julia Martinusen,
    Diana McMillen, Alethea Sparks, Marcia Stanley,
    Diane Yanney
Recipe Development Editor: Marion Viall
Test Kitchen Director: Sharon Stilwell
Test Kitchen Home Economists: Jean Brekke, Kay Cargill,
    Marilyn Cornelius, Maryellyn Krantz, Marge Steenson

Associate Art Director (Managing): Randall Yontz
Associate Art Directors (Creative): Linda Ford,
    Neoma Alt West
Copy and Production Editors: Nancy Nowiszewski,
    Lamont Olson, Mary Helen Schiltz, David A. Walsh
Assistant Art Directors: Faith Berven, Harijs Priekulis
Graphic Designers: Mike Burns, Alisann Dixon, Mike Eagleton,
    Lynda Haupert, Deb Miner, Lyne Neymeyer, Trish Podlasek,
    Bill Shaw, D. Greg Thompson

Editor in Chief: Neil Kuehnl
Group Editorial Services Director: Duane L. Gregg
Executive Art Director: William J. Yates

General Manager: Fred Stines
Director of Publishing: Robert B. Nelson
Director of Retail Marketing: Jamie Martin
Director of Direct Marketing: Arthur Heydendael

KITCHEN APPLIANCE COOK BOOK
Editors: Sandra Granseth, Sharyl Heiken, Elizabeth Woolever
Copy and Production Editor: David A. Kirchner
Graphic Designer: Randall Yontz

Our seal assures you that every recipe in
Kitchen Appliance Cook Book is
endorsed by the Better Homes and Gardens Test
Kitchen. Each recipe is carefully tested for
family appeal, practicality, and deliciousness.

Contents

When time is short, small kitchen appliances can be a tremendous help. In the *Kitchen Appliance Cook Book*, the editors of Better Homes and Gardens have compiled a collection of recipes that let you make the most of them. Now you can use your microwave oven, crockery cooker, skillet, fondue pot, food processor, blender, crepe pan, and wok to turn out more tempting dishes than you ever thought possible. Whether you're planning a meal for the family or a party for friends, save time and work by preparing these delicious appetizers, main dishes, side dishes, and desserts created especially for appliance cooking.

MICROWAVE COOKING

You'll soon discover that a microwave oven is one of the best appliances you can own. In this section there are dozens of tantalizing recipes you'll want to try. Just look through the following pages and take your pick — from appetizers, main dishes, and vegetables to tempting desserts and candies.

counter-top
microwave

The day you brought your microwave oven home was a special occasion. With the owner's manual in hand, you entered the world of micro-cooking. Perhaps boiling water for a cup of coffee or tea was your first experiment. Maybe you cooked bacon, baked a few potatoes, or baked some apples for dessert. Now that you've mastered those tasty beginnings, perhaps you want more timesaving recipes to prepare in this electronic wonder. Look no further. This section of tempting microwave-tested recipes was written with your needs in mind.

how foods cook

You'll use and enjoy your counter-top microwave oven more if you understand how it cooks food and why it's different from conventional methods of cooking.

Conventionally: Your gas or electric oven cooks with hot air, the temperature of which is controlled by a thermostat. The air cooks the surface of the food first, then the heat gradually works its way to the center of the food. By the time the food is heated all the way through, it's also brown on the outside.

By microwave: Your microwave oven cooks food inside and out at the same time. Since food is cooked so much faster, many quick-cooking foods do not brown—unless you use a special browning accessory.

Food cooks directly by means of electromagnetic waves, similar to radio or light waves. These microwaves, traveling in straight lines, bounce off the walls of the oven cavity and are absorbed by the food. They cause the food molecules to vibrate and rub against each other, producing friction and heating all parts of the food simultaneously.

You'll notice that a "standing time" is sometimes specified in a microwave recipe. Letting food stand for a few minutes after microwaving allows for "carry-over" cooking, during which heat spreads throughout the food and equalizes its temperature. To allow for carry-over cooking, it's occasionally necessary to slightly undercook some foods.

Some recipes also ask you to stir mixtures, turn dishes, and/or rearrange foods during cooking. This is because most ovens distribute their microwaves in an uneven pattern, and because the waves lose power as they penetrate foods. Therefore, stirring a mixture helps to distribute the heated food. When stirring isn't possible, turning the dish a quarter- or half-turn is a solution.

While microwaves are *absorbed* by food, they also are *reflected* by metal and *transmitted* by glass, paper, china, pottery, and plastic. That's why it's so important to choose the right containers and utensils for micro-cooking.

micro-cooking utensils

Part of the fun of micro-cooking is the variety of containers you can cook food in. There's no need to completely re-equip your kitchen just because you have a microwave oven. You'll be able to use many items already on your shelves. A basic rule is: glass, paper, and other containers that contain no metal are good. Metal reflects microwaves and prevents food from absorbing them. Some ovens allow a limited use of metal, however, so check your owner's manual for the appropriate dishes to use in your oven.

Also, consider the type of food you'll be cooking and how long the food will be in the oven. Use dishes that withstand high temperatures, especially for foods containing high proportions of fats and sugars. Paper and certain plastic items are fine for short-time cooking and for warming

Oriental Beef Ring
(see recipe, page 29)

Dishes: Glass-ceramic and heat-resistant glass dishes, such as casseroles, baking dishes, bowls, measuring cups, and custard cups are especially good to use in the microwave oven. You will want to use these utensils for foods that reach boiling temperature and for foods that are cooked for a long time. Be sure to use these containers for recipes high in fat or sugar; these foods become very hot in the microwave oven. Some casseroles have covers that can be used as cooking trays for small amounts. You'll find glass measuring cups (especially the 2-cup and 4-cup sizes) are handy for cooking sauces and soups. You can warm beverages right in the cups. China without metallic trim and dinnerware dishes can be used if recommended by the dish manufacturer or if they pass the dish test described in the tip box at right.

Special microwave cookware: Microwave enthusiasts can buy non-metal cookware designed specifically for micro-cooking, including bacon and meat roasting racks, muffin pans, and fluted cake pans. (Follow manufacturer's directions for proper use and care.)

dish test

To find out if a dish is suitable for use in a microwave oven, make the following test. Pour ½ cup cold water into a glass measuring cup. Set the cup inside the dish you want to test. Micro-cook 1 minute.

Use: If the water becomes warm and the dish remains cool (or cool enough to pick up with bare hands), the dish can be used.

Do not use: If the water remains cool but the dish becomes too hot to handle, do not use the dish for micro-cooking.

Paper, wood, and baskets: For short-time cooking and simple cleanup, you can't beat cooking on paper plates, cups, napkins, and paper toweling. Avoid using wax-coated plates, cups, and bowls as cooking containers. The wax melts as the food becomes hot. Wooden utensils and baskets should be used only for very short-time food warming because they will dry out if microwaved too long.

Covers: Covering food helps it heat more evenly and retain moisture at the same time. Covers also keep greasy foods from spattering and eventually clogging your oven's ventilating system. Use all-glass casserole lids or waxed paper, but avoid using plastic wrap. It can swell and then shrink tightly to the dish, creating a steam buildup. (If you do use plastic wrap, always slit it to allow steam to escape.)

microwave safety

Safe use of a microwave oven depends jointly on the oven's manufacturer and its owner.

The manufacturer's responsibility: Federal regulations specify safety features that must be built into microwave ovens.

The owner's responsibility: Even though microwave ovens are built with safety in mind, safe operation also depends on how you care for your oven. Read the owner's manual for operation instructions and special cautions; they may vary from oven to oven.

Examine the oven. If the door doesn't close properly or if there is any damage to the door hinge, latch, or sealing surface, don't operate the oven until it's repaired by qualified service personnel. Don't operate the oven if an object becomes caught in the door, and don't insert objects through the door seal or the oven vents. To ensure safety, don't tamper with the door interlocks or the power cord, and don't lift the oven by the door or door handle.

Keep the oven clean. Frequently clean the cavity, door, and door seal with water and a mild detergent to keep the oven free of food spatters, especially grease.

other safety tips

Do not pop corn in the microwave oven (unless of course a special corn popper is available for your model). The small amount of corn that's used for popping doesn't absorb enough energy to pop. There's an additional problem with containers; a paper bag could catch fire, and a glass dish could break from overheating.

Also, don't cook eggs in their shells or bake potatoes without pricking the skins. Steam pressure can build up inside eggshells and potato skins, causing them to explode.

timings

Several variables affect the cooking times of foods prepared in a microwave oven. For instance, your house voltage may be slightly higher or lower than standard. Other variables are introduced by individual ovens and the types of food cooked in them.

Ovens: Ovens vary from brand to brand and model to model, and also in the amount of cooking power they produce. Therefore, the timings given in these recipes are approximate to allow for all models. (See the tip box for more information on recipe timings.)

recipe timings

The recipes in this book were tested in counter-top microwave ovens operating on a 2,450-MHz (megahertz) frequency. Unless specified otherwise, the high or "cook" power setting was used. The manufacturer's power output rating of the test ovens ranged from 600 to 700 watts. You can find the output power rating of your oven in the owner's manual or on a label affixed to the back of the cabinet.

Ovens under 600 watts: Foods cooked in lower-wattage ovens may need extra cooking time. First, check the food for doneness at the timing given. Then add more time if needed, checking after every 30 seconds to avoid overcooking.

Ovens over 700 watts: Foods cooked in higher-wattage ovens may need less cooking time. Check foods for doneness a little sooner than the timings listed in the recipes.

Food: Micro-cooking times also depend on the characteristics of the food you're cooking. Some things to consider are:

1. Beginning temperature. Foods just removed from the refrigerator take longer to heat than those at room temperature.

2. Size and shape. Small, thin, uniformly shaped food portions will cook faster or more evenly than large, thick, irregularly shaped ones.

3. Density. Porous foods micro-cook faster than more compact and solid foods.

4. Quantity. The more food you cook at one time, the longer it will take. Remember this when you're thinking about doubling a recipe. It's better to cook in smaller batches and repeat the cooking procedure than to cook a large quantity at once.

5. Browning. Certain foods don't brown when micro-cooked. If some people consider this a drawback, it's only because they're so accustomed to seeing foods with a browned appearance. For instance, it would be hard to taste any difference between a microwaved cupcake and one baked conventionally. And if the cupcakes were frosted, you wouldn't see any difference either.

Solutions: Use doneness tests as your guide when micro-cooking. The golden rule for microwave cooking is "cook and look." Learn to judge the degree of doneness for the types of foods you micro-cook often.

If browning is an important part of the recipe, or just important to you, here are some suggestions: brown food under a conventional broiler, brush meats lightly with Kitchen Bouquet, or sprinkle main dishes lightly with paprika. A crumb topping also can enhance a food's appearance. Some ovens have built-in browning units, or browning trays available as accessories.

special uses for the oven

You can use your microwave oven for many cooking tasks normally done on top of the range as well as in your conventional oven. Besides general recipe preparation, other popular uses are the quick reheating of leftovers, take-out foods, and convenience foods, and the speedy thawing of frozen foods.

Leftovers: In these days of stretching the dollar, it's important to use all the food you prepare. The microwave oven helps by making it a snap to turn leftovers into a meal. As a general guideline for reheating cooked food, allow about 1½ minutes for each cup or 8 ounces of cooked food. When warming several different foods on one plate, make sure that the serving portions are similar for even heating. It's a good idea to underheat the food and check the temperature before continuing to cook.

Convenience foods: You'll be able to turn the deli sandwiches you picked up on the way home from work into a hot meal with your microwave oven. Convenience foods are more convenient than ever when heated in the microwave. However, check your owner's manual for the timings of specific foods, and for any limitations on cooking foods sold in foil containers, such as frozen dinners.

converting a recipe favorite

Converting conventional recipes for microwave preparation takes some experimenting. To avoid boilovers, you may need a larger baking dish than specified in the conventional recipe. Start checking food for doneness after approximately one-fourth of the conventional cooking time. Then, continue checking the food often until it's done. You might find a similar recipe in this book to use as a guideline.

Defrosting foods: If you've ever started to prepare dinner only to realize that you'd forgotten to take some food out of the freezer to thaw, you'll really appreciate a microwave oven. Frozen food can be thawed, cooked or heated, and brought to the table in practically no time at all.

Most models have a defrost setting as a built-in feature. If your oven has an automatic defrost, consult your owner's manual for usage instructions and timings.

Defrosting is easy in an oven without an automatic defrost setting, too. Simply alternate cooking and standing times. The standing time allows food temperature to equalize so that the outside doesn't begin to cook before the inside is defrosted.

As a rule of thumb, for every 1 cup or 8 ounces of frozen, cooked food, micro-cook 1 minute and let stand in the oven with the power off for 1 minute. Repeat the cycles until just a few ice crystals remain in the food. For 2 cups or 16 ounces, the cycles should be 2 minutes on, 2 minutes off. Once the food is thawed, micro-heat about 1½ minutes for each cup of food. Follow recipe directions for preparing uncooked frozen food.

Other uses: Not only will you use your oven to prepare entire recipes, you'll also rely on it for small tasks, such as melting butter or chocolate for cooking. You'll get crisp bacon for a bacon-lettuce-and-tomato sandwich by cooking slices between layers of paper toweling in a flat dish. Merely allow 1 to 1½ minutes for one slice, 2½ to 3 minutes for four slices, and about 4½ minutes for six bacon slices. Or, for a quick snack that even the kids can fix, wrap a frankfurter and bun together in a paper napkin and micro-cook in less than a minute.

As you use your microwave oven, you'll undoubtedly find many other uses to streamline everyday food preparation chores. You may even discover a few interesting non-food uses.

appetizers, snacks, & beverages

Peppy Almonds

Pictured on page 13 —

- 2 tablespoons butter *or* margarine
- 1½ teaspoons chili powder
- 1 teaspoon celery salt
- 1 teaspoon Worcestershire sauce
- ½ teaspoon salt
- ⅛ teaspoon cayenne
- 1½ cups whole almonds (8 ounces)

In a 10x6x2-inch baking dish micro-melt the butter or margarine 30 to 40 seconds. Stir in chili powder, celery salt, Worcestershire sauce, salt, and cayenne. Add almonds; stir to coat. Micro-cook, uncovered, about 7 minutes, stirring twice. Cool thoroughly on paper toweling. Makes 1½ cups nuts.

Toasted Pumpkin Seeds

- 2 cups raw unprocessed shelled pumpkin seeds (8 ounces)
- 1 tablespoon cooking oil
- 1½ teaspoons salt *or* 1½ teaspoons seasoned salt *or* 1 teaspoon garlic salt

In a 10x6x2-inch baking dish combine pumpkin seeds, cooking oil, and salt, seasoned salt, or garlic salt. Micro-cook, uncovered, 8 minutes, stirring every 2 minutes. Cool thoroughly on paper toweling. Store in tightly covered container. Makes 2 cups.

Parmesan Nibble Squares

- 2 tablespoons butter *or* margarine
- ⅛ teaspoon garlic powder
- 2 cups bite-size shredded rice *or* shredded corn squares
- ¼ cup grated Parmesan cheese

In a 10x6x2-inch baking dish combine butter and garlic powder. Micro-melt the butter 30 to 40 seconds. Stir in rice or corn squares till coated with butter mixture. Sprinkle with cheese. Micro-cook, uncovered, about 3 minutes, stirring twice. Cool. Makes 2 cups.

Nut Bars

- 2 tablespoons butter *or* margarine
- 1 cup packed brown sugar
- 1 cup chopped nuts
- ⅓ cup all-purpose flour
- ⅛ teaspoon baking soda
- ⅛ teaspoon salt
- 2 beaten eggs
- 1 teaspoon vanilla
  Powdered sugar

In an 8x8x2-inch baking dish micro-melt the butter or margarine 30 to 40 seconds. In mixing bowl thoroughly stir together the brown sugar, chopped nuts, all-purpose flour, baking soda, and salt; stir in beaten eggs and vanilla. Carefully pour nut mixture over melted butter in baking dish; do not stir.

Micro-cook, uncovered, 6 to 6½ minutes or till done, giving dish a quarter-turn after each minute. Cookies will appear moist in the center. Remove from oven; let stand 2 minutes.

Sift powdered sugar over top of cookies. Place waxed paper under wire rack; invert cookies onto rack. Cool. Dust again with powdered sugar. Cut into bars. Makes 24.

Clam Dip

Pictured on page 13 —

- 2 slices bacon
- 1 8-ounce package cream cheese
- ¼ cup finely chopped onion
- 2 tablespoons grated Parmesan cheese
- 2 tablespoons chili sauce
- 2 tablespoons milk
- ½ teaspoon dried basil, crushed
- ¼ teaspoon garlic salt
- ⅛ teaspoon pepper
- 1 7½-ounce can minced clams
  Crackers and vegetable dippers

In a 1-quart casserole place bacon slices between layers of paper toweling. Micro-cook about 2 minutes or till bacon is crisp. Remove bacon and paper toweling; crumble bacon and set aside. Place cream cheese in same casserole. Micro-cook, covered, about 1 minute or just till softened. Blend in onion, grated Parmesan, chili sauce, milk, basil, garlic salt, and pepper. Drain clams. Stir drained clams into cheese mixture. Micro-cook, uncovered, about 3 minutes or till heated through, stirring after each minute. Stir in crumbled bacon. Serve warm with crackers and vegetable dippers. Makes 1⅔ cups dip.

Garlic Bean Dip

Save dishwashing by cooking the bacon and the dip mixture in the same casserole —

- 2 **slices bacon, chopped**
- 1 **8-ounce can red kidney beans, drained**
- ¾ **teaspoon chili powder**
- ½ **teaspoon onion salt**
- ⅛ **teaspoon garlic powder**
  Dash pepper
- ¾ **cup dairy sour cream**
  Corn chips *or* tortilla chips

Place bacon in a 1-quart casserole. Cover with paper toweling. Micro-cook about 2 minutes or till bacon is crisp. Remove bacon and paper toweling, leaving any drippings in casserole.

To bacon drippings in casserole add the drained kidney beans, chili powder, onion salt, garlic powder, and pepper. Mash the beans till smooth; blend with the seasonings and drippings. Micro-cook, covered, about 1 minute or till mixture is heated through. Fold in the dairy sour cream and crisp-cooked bacon. Micro-cook, un-covered, about 2 minutes or just till hot, stirring every 30 seconds. Serve the dip warm with chips. Makes 1¼ cups dip.

Zesty Cheese Dip

Horseradish and mustard add zip —

- 1 **8-ounce package cream cheese**
- 1 **5-ounce jar sharp American cheese spread**
- ⅓ **cup beer**
- 1 **tablespoon snipped green onion tops**
- ½ **teaspoon prepared horseradish**
- ¼ **teaspoon dry mustard**
  Crackers and vegetable dippers

In a 1-quart casserole combine the cream cheese and sharp Ameri-can cheese spread. Micro-cook, covered, about 1 minute or just till softened. By hand, gradually beat in the beer, onion, prepared horse-radish, and dry mustard till smooth. Micro-cook, covered, about 3 to 3½ minutes or till heated through, stirring after each minute. Stir be-fore serving. Serve warm with crackers and vegetables. Makes 1¾ cups.

Taco Chicken Wings

- 1½ **pounds chicken wings (8)**
  Milk
- 2 **tablespoons taco seasoning mix**
- 2 **tablespoons fine dry bread crumbs**

Remove wing tips and discard; separate wings at joints. Dip chicken pieces in milk. Combine seasoning mix and bread crumbs in plastic bag. Add two or three chicken pieces at a time, shaking to coat. Place chicken in a 12x7½x2-inch baking dish. Micro-cook, covered, about 14 minutes or till chicken is done, giving dish half-turns every 4 minutes. Makes 16 appetizers.

Teriyaki Appetizer Meatballs

- 2 **beaten eggs**
- ⅓ **cup milk**
- ⅓ **cup fine dry bread crumbs**
- 2 **tablespoons finely chopped onion**
- ½ **teaspoon salt**
- ⅛ **teaspoon pepper**
- 1½ **pounds ground beef**
- 4 **teaspoons cornstarch**
- 1½ **teaspoons sugar**
- ½ **teaspoon ground ginger**
- ¾ **cup beef broth**
- 3 **tablespoons soy sauce**
- 1 **tablespoon dry sherry**
- 1 **clove garlic, minced**

In mixing bowl combine eggs, milk, crumbs, onion, salt, and pepper. Add beef; mix well. Shape mixture into 48 meatballs; set aside. In a 2-cup glass measure blend cornstarch, sugar, and ginger. Stir in broth, soy, sherry, garlic, and ¾ cup *water*. Micro-cook, uncovered, about 3 to 4 minutes or till hot. Stir. Micro-cook, uncovered, 1 to 2 minutes more or till thickened and bubbly, stirring every 30 seconds. Transfer to blazer pan of chafing dish and place over hot water. Ar-range *24* of the meatballs in a 12x7½x2-inch baking dish. Micro-cook, covered, about 4 minutes or till meatballs are done, rearrang-ing meatballs during cooking. Re-move meatballs from dish with slot-ted spoon and add to hot sauce in chafing dish. Repeat with remain-ing meatballs. Serve with wooden picks. Makes 48 appetizers.

Clockwise from top left: Clam Dip (see recipe, page 11), Hot Buttered Lem-onade (see recipe, page 15), Taco Chicken Wings, and Peppy Almonds (see recipe, page 11).

Scallop Kabob Appetizers

- 1 **12-ounce package frozen scallops (35 to 40)**
- 2 **tablespoons snipped parsley**
- 2 **tablespoons cooking oil**
- 2 **tablespoons lemon juice**
- 2 **tablespoons soy sauce**
- ½ **teaspoon salt**
  Dash pepper
- 12 **slices bacon, cut into thirds crosswise**
- 1 **6-ounce can whole mushrooms, drained**
- 1 **20-ounce can pineapple chunks, drained**

Remove frozen scallops from package. To thaw, place in a 12x7½x2-inch baking dish. Micro-cook, covered, 1½ minutes, stirring twice. Rinse scallops; drain. Combine parsley, cooking oil, lemon juice, soy sauce, salt, and pepper; add scallops. Let stand 1 hour at room temperature, stirring mixture occasionally.

Meanwhile, partially cook bacon by placing two layers of paper toweling in a 12x7½x2-inch baking dish. Add *half* of the bacon; cover with paper toweling. Micro-cook 3½ minutes. Drain on additional paper toweling. Repeat with remaining bacon. Remove scallops from marinade. For each kabob, thread a scallop, mushroom, piece of bacon, and pineapple chunk onto a wooden pick. Place *half* of the kabobs in a 12x7½x2-inch baking dish. Micro-cook, uncovered, for 8 minutes, giving dish a half-turn every 2 minutes and brushing kabobs with marinade. Repeat with remaining ingredients. Serve warm. Makes 35 to 40 appetizers.

Seafood Appetizers

- 1 **4½-ounce can shrimp, drained and mashed, *or* one 6½- or 7-ounce can tuna, drained and flaked**
- ¼ **cup mayonnaise *or* salad dressing**
- 2 **tablespoons chili sauce**
- 1 **tablespoon finely chopped celery**
- 1 **tablespoon finely chopped onion**
- 32 **rich round crackers**

Combine shrimp or tuna, mayonnaise or salad dressing, chili sauce, celery, and onion. Spread about ½ *tablespoon* mixture on *each* cracker. Place *eight* of the appetizers at a time on a paper plate. Micro-cook, uncovered, about 30 seconds or till hot. Trim each appetizer with parsley, if desired. Serve immediately. Makes 32.

Blue Cheese-Stuffed Mushrooms

- 24 **fresh mushrooms, each about 1 inch in diameter (1 pound)**
- 1 **tablespoon butter *or* margarine**
- ⅓ **cup crumbled blue cheese**
- 3 **tablespoons fine dry bread crumbs**
- ¼ **cup snipped parsley**

Remove stems from mushrooms; set caps aside. Chop stems. In a 2-cup glass measure combine butter or margarine and stems. Micro-cook, uncovered, about 2 minutes or till tender; stir once. Stir in cheese and crumbs. Spoon about *1 teaspoon* filling into *each* mushroom cap; sprinkle with parsley. Place *12* of the filled mushrooms in a glass pie plate; micro-cook, covered, about 2 minutes or till hot, turning dish once. Cook remaining mushrooms. Makes 24.

Appetizer Franks

- 1 **8-ounce can tomato sauce**
- ½ **cup water**
- 2 **tablespoons vinegar**
- 1 **envelope spaghetti sauce mix**
- 1 **tablespoon sugar**
- ¼ **teaspoon dry mustard**
- 1 **pound frankfurters, cut into bite-size pieces**

In a 2-quart casserole combine the tomato sauce, water, vinegar, spaghetti sauce mix, sugar, and dry mustard. Stir in franks till coated. Micro-cook, covered, about 7 to 8 minutes or till heated through, stirring twice. Keep warm in chafing dish. Serve with wooden picks. Makes about 36.

Nachos

- 2 **ounces cheddar *or* Monterey Jack cheese**
- 1 **canned mild chili pepper**
- 24 **taco-flavored tortilla chips**
- ½ **cup canned bean dip**

Cut cheese into twenty-four ¾-inch squares, each about ⅛ inch thick. Dice the canned mild chili pepper. Arrange *12* of the taco-flavored tortilla chips on a plate. Top *each* chip with *1 teaspoon* of the bean dip, a piece of chili pepper, and a piece of cheese. Micro-cook, uncovered, about 30 to 45 seconds or just till cheese melts, turning plate several times. Repeat with remaining chips, dip, pepper, and cheese. Makes 24.

Eggnog Special

- 4 cups milk
- ¼ cup sugar
- 1 teaspoon vanilla
- ¼ teaspoon salt
- 2 beaten eggs
- 1 beaten egg yolk
- 1 egg white
- ½ teaspoon vanilla
- 2 tablespoons sugar
  Ground nutmeg

In a 2-quart heat-resistant pitcher or bowl combine milk, ¼ cup sugar, 1 teaspoon vanilla, and salt. Micro-cook, uncovered, about 8 minutes or till hot. Stir. Combine eggs and egg yolk. Gradually stir *1 cup* of the hot mixture into beaten egg mixture. Return to hot mixture. Micro-cook, uncovered, 2 minutes more, stirring once. Beat egg white and ½ teaspoon vanilla till soft peaks form; gradually add the 2 tablespoons sugar, beating to stiff peaks. Pour eggnog into mugs.

Top with small dollops of the egg white mixture. Sprinkle with nutmeg. Makes 8 (4-ounce) servings.

easy instant coffee

Making coffee in the microwave oven is simple. For 8-ounce mugs, combine about 1 teaspoon *instant coffee crystals* with ¾ cup *water* in each mug. Micro-cook just till hot: 1 mug — 1¼ minutes; 2 mugs — 2 minutes; 4 mugs — 3½ minutes.

For larger mugs, combine about 1¼ teaspoons *instant coffee crystals* with 1 cup *water* in each mug. Micro-cook just till hot: 1 mug — 1½ minutes; 2 mugs — 2½ minutes; 4 mugs — 4¾ minutes.

Hot Buttered Lemonade

Pictured on page 13 —

- 2 cups water
- ½ cup sugar
- 6 inches stick cinnamon
- 6 whole allspices
- 4 whole cloves
- ½ cup lemon juice
- 3 tablespoons brandy *or* rum (optional)
  Butter *or* margarine

In a 4-cup glass measure combine water and sugar. For spice bag, place spices in cheesecloth and tie; add to sugar mixture. Micro-cook, uncovered, about 6 to 7 minutes or till boiling. Let stand 30 minutes. Stir in lemon juice. Micro-cook 6 to 7 minutes or till boiling. Remove spice bag. Stir in brandy or rum, if desired. Top *each* serving with *1 teaspoon* butter. Makes 4 (6-ounce) servings.

Coffee Plus

- 2 cups water
- 3 tablespoons instant coffee crystals
- 3 tablespoons coffee liqueur
- 2 tablespoons crème de cacao
- 1 tablespoon brandy
  Whipped cream
- 4 cinnamon sticks (optional)

Combine water, coffee crystals, coffee liqueur, crème de cacao, and brandy. Pour into four coffee cups or mugs. Arrange cups in microwave oven. Micro-cook, uncovered, about 4½ minutes or till liquid is heated through but not boiling. Top each serving with a dollop of whipped cream. If desired, serve with cinnamon-stick stirrers. Makes 4 (4-ounce) servings.

Buttered Cranberry Punch

- 3 cups cranberry-apple juice drink
- ¼ cup packed brown sugar
- ¼ cup orange juice
- 3 tablespoons lemon juice
- 4 inches stick cinnamon
  Butter *or* margarine

In a 1½-quart casserole or heat-resistant pitcher combine the cranberry-apple juice, brown sugar, orange juice, lemon juice, and stick cinnamon. Micro-cook, uncovered, for 8 to 9 minutes or till almost boiling. Remove cinnamon. Serve in mugs. Top *each* serving with about *1 teaspoon* butter. Makes 4 (7-ounce) servings.

main
dishes

Mexican-Style Tuna

¼ cup chopped onion
1 tablespoon butter *or* margarine
1 10-ounce can mild enchilada sauce
1 8-ounce can red kidney beans, drained
1 6½- *or* 7-ounce can tuna, drained and flaked
½ cup shredded sharp American cheese
   Corn *or* tortilla chips, slightly crushed

In a 1-quart casserole micro-cook onion in butter or margarine about 1½ minutes or till tender. Stir in enchilada sauce and the drained kidney beans. Micro-cook, uncovered, about 3 minutes or till mixture is bubbly, stirring once.

Stir in tuna and cheese. Micro-cook about 2 minutes more or till cheese melts and mixture is hot. Serve in bowls; top with slightly crushed corn or tortilla chips. Makes 3 or 4 servings.

Elegant Fish Roll-Ups

2 pounds fresh *or* frozen flounder fillets
   Salt
¼ cup chopped onion
1 tablespoon butter *or* margarine
1 7¾-ounce can salmon, drained, bones and skin removed, and flaked
2 tablespoons snipped parsley
   Dash pepper
3 tablespoons butter *or* margarine
3 tablespoons all-purpose flour
¾ cup chicken broth
¾ cup milk
1 cup shredded Swiss cheese
½ teaspoon paprika

Thaw fish, if frozen (see tip, page 18). Cut and piece fillets together to make eight portions. Sprinkle with salt. Set aside.

In a 4-cup glass measure or bowl micro-cook onion in 1 tablespoon butter about 1½ minutes or till onion is tender. Stir in the salmon, parsley, and pepper. Spread about *3 tablespoons* of the filling over each fillet. Roll up fillets. Place, seam side down, in a 10x6x2-inch baking dish; set aside. In a 4-cup glass measure micro-melt the 3 tablespoons butter about 45 seconds. Stir in flour; stir in broth and milk. Micro-cook, uncovered, 1 minute; stir. Micro-cook 3 to 4 minutes longer or till mixture thickens and bubbles, stirring every 30 seconds. Pour sauce over fish rolls. Micro-cook, uncovered, 8 to 9 minutes or till fish flakes easily when tested with a fork, giving dish a quarter-turn every 2 minutes and spooning sauce over fish each time. Sprinkle fish with cheese and paprika. Micro-cook, uncovered, about 1 minute longer or till cheese melts. Makes 8 servings.

Salmon Logs

1 beaten egg
2 tablespoons milk
1 teaspoon lemon juice
¾ cup soft bread crumbs (1 slice)
2 tablespoons snipped parsley
½ teaspoon instant minced onion
⅛ teaspoon salt
1 7¾-ounce can salmon, drained, bones and skin removed, and flaked
1 tablespoon butter *or* margarine
1 tablespoon all-purpose flour
½ cup milk
¼ cup shredded American cheese

In small bowl combine egg, milk, lemon juice, bread crumbs, parsley, onion, and salt. Add salmon; mix thoroughly. In a glass pie plate shape mixture into two 4x2x1-inch logs. Micro-cook, covered, 3 minutes, giving dish a quarter-turn every minute. Keep hot.

In a 2-cup glass measure micro-melt the butter 30 to 40 seconds. Stir in flour; stir in milk. Micro-cook, uncovered, for 1½ to 2 minutes or till mixture thickens and bubbles, stirring every 30 seconds. Stir in cheese till melted. Place logs on individual dinner plates. Spoon sauce atop. Makes 2 servings.

Sole Provençale

Sole Provençale

6 **fresh or frozen sole fillets**
    (1½ pounds)
Salt
Paprika
¼ **cup chopped onion**
1 **clove garlic, minced**
1 **tablespoon butter or**
    margarine
2 **teaspoons cornstarch**
1 **8-ounce can tomato sauce**
1 **8-ounce can tomatoes, cut up**
1 **3-ounce can sliced**
    mushrooms, drained
½ **cup dry white wine**
2 **tablespoons snipped parsley**
1 **vegetable or chicken bouillon**
    cube, crushed
1 **teaspoon sugar**
Hot cooked rice

Thaw sole fillets, if frozen (see tip, page 18). Sprinkle each fillet with salt and paprika. Roll up fillets. Place, seam side down, in 10x6x2-inch baking dish; set aside.

For sauce, in a 4-cup glass measure or bowl micro-cook the onion and garlic in butter or margarine, uncovered, about 1½ minutes or till onion is tender. Stir in cornstarch. Stir in tomato sauce, *undrained* tomatoes, sliced canned mushrooms, white wine, parsley, vegetable or chicken bouillon cube, and sugar. Micro-cook, covered, about 3 minutes or till sauce is boiling, stirring twice.

Pour sauce over fish. Micro-cook, covered, for 7 to 8 minutes or till fish flakes easily when tested with a fork, giving dish a quarter-turn every 2 minutes and spooning sauce over fish each time. Serve fish and sauce over hot cooked rice. Makes 6 servings.

Halibut Steaks Teriyaki

4 **fresh or frozen halibut steaks**
    (1½ pounds)
¼ **cup teriyaki sauce**
2 **tablespoons lemon juice**
1 **tablespoon cooking oil**
½ **teaspoon dry mustard**
½ **teaspoon ground ginger**
⅛ **teaspoon garlic powder**

Thaw halibut steaks, if frozen. Place halibut steaks in a plastic bag. Combine teriyaki sauce, lemon juice, cooking oil, dry mustard, ground ginger, and garlic powder; pour over halibut steaks in bag. Close bag securely and place bag in pan or bowl. Marinate halibut in refrigerator 3 to 4 hours, turning occasionally. Remove halibut from marinade and arrange steaks in a 12x7½x2-inch baking dish; pour marinade atop. Micro-cook, covered, about 6 minutes or till fish flakes easily when tested with a fork, turning steaks over after 3 minutes. Makes 4 servings.

Seafood-Asparagus Casserole

2 1⅛-ounce packages
    hollandaise sauce mix
1⅓ cups milk
½ cup dairy sour cream
    Dash bottled hot pepper sauce
1 tablespoon butter *or*
    margarine
¾ cup soft bread crumbs (1 slice)
⅛ teaspoon paprika
2 8- *or* 10-ounce packages
    frozen cut asparagus
1 6½- *or* 7-ounce can tuna,
    drained and broken into
    pieces
1 4½-ounce can shrimp, drained
1 hard-cooked egg, sliced

Place hollandaise sauce mix in a 4-cup glass measure; gradually stir in milk. Micro-cook, uncovered, about 4 minutes or till mixture thickens and bubbles, stirring every 30 seconds. Stir in sour cream and bottled hot pepper sauce; set aside. In a small bowl micro-melt the butter 30 to 40 seconds. Toss with bread crumbs and paprika; set aside.

Place blocks of asparagus side by side in a 10x6x2-inch baking dish. Micro-cook, covered, 6 minutes. Separate pieces with a fork. Cook, covered, about 6 minutes or till tender. Drain well on paper toweling. Return asparagus, tuna, and shrimp to the 10x6x2-inch baking dish. Pour hollandaise sauce over all; mix well. Cook, uncovered, 5 to 6 minutes or till hot, giving dish two quarter-turns during cooking. Arrange egg slices atop; sprinkle crumbs over all. Micro-cook 30 seconds. Makes 6 servings.

thawing fish

If your microwave oven has a defrost setting, first place the frozen block of fillets in a shallow baking dish. Then, simply follow the manufacturer's directions for thawing.

If your oven doesn't have a defrost feature, place a 16-ounce block of frozen fish in a baking dish, micro-cook 2 minutes, then let stand 2 minutes. Micro-cook 1 minute; let stand 2 minutes. Again, micro-cook 1 minute; let stand 2 minutes. Then, micro-cook about 30 seconds. (Turn fish over about halfway through defrosting.)

Shrimp a la King

¼ cup chopped green pepper
¼ cup chopped onion
2 tablespoons butter
3 tablespoons all-purpose flour
1 cup milk
1 7-ounce package frozen
    shelled shrimp
1 3-ounce can sliced
    mushrooms, drained
2 tablespoons dry white wine
    Toast

In a 1-quart casserole micro-cook the green pepper and onion in butter, covered, 4 to 5 minutes or till vegetables are tender. Stir in flour, ½ teaspoon *salt*, and several dashes *pepper*. Stir in milk; blend in shrimp and drained mushrooms. Micro-cook, uncovered, 2 minutes; stir. Micro-cook 5 to 6 minutes or till thickened and bubbly, stirring every 30 seconds. Stir in white wine; micro-cook 30 seconds longer. Serve over toast. Serves 6.

Oriental Shrimp

1 7-ounce package frozen
    shelled shrimp (2 cups)
¾ cup chicken broth
1 tablespoon cornstarch
¼ cup sliced green onion
2 tablespoons soy sauce
⅛ teaspoon ground ginger
1 6-ounce package frozen
    pea pods
½ cup sliced water chestnuts
1 small tomato, peeled and cut
    into wedges
    Hot cooked rice

In a 1½-quart casserole micro-cook frozen shrimp in ½ cup *water*, covered, 3½ to 4 minutes or till shrimp are done, stirring twice. Drain; set aside. In same casserole stir chicken broth into cornstarch; stir in onion, soy sauce, and ginger. Micro-cook, uncovered, about 3 minutes or till thickened and bubbly, stirring after each minute. Rinse pea pods in strainer under hottest tap water. Add pea pods to sauce; stir in water chestnuts and shrimp. Add tomato. Micro-cook, covered, about 2 minutes or till hot. Serve over rice. Serves 3 or 4.

Sweet-Sour Turkey

- 1 **cup bias-sliced celery**
- ½ **cup chopped onion**
- 2 **tablespoons butter *or* margarine**
- 1 **15½-ounce can pineapple chunks**
- 1 **cup chicken broth**
- ¼ **cup packed brown sugar**
- ¼ **cup soy sauce**
- 3 **tablespoons cornstarch**
- 2 **cups cubed cooked turkey**
- 3 **tablespoons vinegar**
- 2 **tablespoons lemon juice**
- ¼ **cup toasted slivered almonds Hot cooked rice**

In a 2-quart casserole micro-cook the celery and onion in butter or margarine, covered, about 3 minutes or till vegetables are crisp-tender. Stir in *undrained* pineapple chunks, chicken broth, and brown sugar. Micro-cook, covered, 4 to 5 minutes or till bubbly. Meanwhile, blend soy sauce into cornstarch. Stir into casserole with turkey.

Micro-cook, covered, for 3 to 4 minutes or till sauce is thickened and bubbly, stirring after each minute. Stir in vinegar and lemon juice. Sprinkle toasted slivered almonds atop (see tip, page 34). Serve over rice. Serves 4 or 5.

Turkey-Spinach-Rice Bake

- 1 **10-ounce package frozen chopped spinach**
- ½ **cup chopped onion**
- ½ **cup water**
- ½ **cup Minute Rice**
- 6 **slices bacon**
- 2 **cups cubed cooked turkey**
- 1 **10¾-ounce can condensed cream of mushroom soup**
- ½ **cup dairy sour cream**
- ¼ **cup sliced water chestnuts**
- 2 **tablespoons chopped pimiento**
- ¼ **teaspoon salt**
- 1 **tablespoon butter *or* margarine**
- 1½ **cups soft bread crumbs Paprika (optional)**

In a 1½-quart casserole combine spinach, onion, and water. Micro-cook, covered, 7½ to 8 minutes or till mixture boils; stir to separate spinach. Stir in rice. Let stand, covered, 10 minutes to absorb liquid. Place bacon between layers of paper toweling in a 10x6x2-inch baking dish. Micro-cook 6½ to 7 minutes or till crisp, rearranging bacon once. Crumble bacon; stir into rice mixture with turkey, soup, sour cream, water chestnuts, pimiento, and salt. Place in the 10x6x2-inch baking dish. Micro-cook, covered, about 10 minutes or till hot, turning dish twice. Micro-melt the butter or margarine 30 to 40 seconds; mix with crumbs. Sprinkle atop casserole. Sprinkle with paprika, if desired. Micro-cook 1 minute. Makes 6 servings.

Turkey How-So

- 1 **10¾-ounce can condensed golden mushroom soup**
- ½ **cup water**
- 1 **tablespoon soy sauce**
- 1 **teaspoon instant beef bouillon granules**
- 1 **teaspoon Worcestershire sauce**
- ½ **to 1 teaspoon curry powder**
- ¼ **teaspoon poppy seed**
- 1 **8-ounce can bamboo shoots, drained**
- ½ **cup sliced celery**
- 1 **small onion, cut into strips**
- 1 **small green pepper, cut into strips**
- 1 **3-ounce can sliced mushrooms, drained**
- 2 **cups cubed cooked turkey**
- 1 **3-ounce can chow mein noodles *or* 3 cups hot cooked rice**

In a 2-quart casserole combine soup, water, soy, bouillon granules, Worcestershire sauce, curry, and poppy seed. Stir in bamboo shoots, celery, onion, green pepper, and mushrooms. Micro-cook, covered, about 8 minutes or till celery and onion are crisp-tender, stirring every 2 minutes. Stir in the turkey. Micro-cook, covered, about 4 minutes or till turkey is heated through, stirring twice. Serve over chow mein noodles or rice. Makes 6 servings.

Ginger Peachy Chicken

1 2½- to 3-pound ready-to-cook broiler-fryer chicken, cut up
1 16-ounce can peach halves
2 tablespoons lemon juice
2 tablespoons soy sauce
½ teaspoon ground ginger
1 tablespoon cornstarch

Cut large pieces of chicken in half. Place chicken, skin side up, in a 12x7½x2-inch baking dish. Sprinkle with salt. Drain peaches, reserving ½ cup syrup. Combine reserved syrup, lemon juice, soy sauce, and ginger. Set aside four peach halves. Mash remaining peaches; add to soy mixture. Drizzle over chicken.

Micro-cook, covered, for 20 to 25 minutes or till chicken is tender, rearranging chicken pieces and brushing with sauce after 10 and 15 minutes. Place reserved peaches in baking dish with chicken. Micro-cook, covered, about 1 minute or just till peaches are hot, brushing with sauce. Remove chicken and peaches to serving plate. Skim fat from sauce. Stir 2 tablespoons cold water into cornstarch; stir into juices in baking dish. Micro-cook, uncovered, about 3 minutes or till thickened and bubbly, stirring after each minute. Serve sauce with chicken and peaches. Makes 4 servings.

Chicken Curry

Saffron Rice
½ cup chopped onion
1 clove garlic, minced
1 tablespoon cooking oil
1 2½- to 3-pound ready-to-cook broiler-fryer chicken, cut up
2 tablespoons curry powder
1 tablespoon cornstarch
1 teaspoon salt
½ teaspoon sugar
⅓ cup water
¼ cup milk
1 medium tomato, chopped
Condiments: Indian Chutney, kumquats, peanuts, shredded coconut, thinly sliced green onion

Prepare Saffron Rice. Cover; let stand while preparing chicken.

In a 12x7½x2-inch baking dish micro-cook onion and garlic in oil, uncovered, about 2 minutes or till onion is tender. Cut large pieces of chicken in half. Arrange chicken, skin side up, in baking dish. For sauce, combine curry, cornstarch, salt, and sugar; stir in water and milk. Mix in the tomato; pour over chicken in baking dish. Micro-cook, covered, for 25 to 28 minutes or till chicken is done, turning dish three times and spooning sauce over chicken each time. Before serving, reheat Saffron Rice in casserole by micro-cooking, covered, 2 minutes. Transfer chicken and rice to heated serving containers. Spoon excess fat from sauce. Pour sauce over chicken. Serve with condiments. Serves 4.

Saffron Rice: In a 1-quart casserole dissolve ⅛ teaspoon crushed *thread saffron* in 1½ cups *hot water.* Add 2 tablespoons *butter* and ¼ teaspoon *salt.* Micro-cook, covered, 2½ to 3 minutes or till boiling. Stir in 1½ cups *Minute Rice.*

Indian Chutney

2 apples, peeled, cored, and chopped
½ cup chopped onion
½ cup raisins
⅓ cup vinegar
¼ cup packed brown sugar
¼ cup water
2 tablespoons chopped candied citron
1 teaspoon curry powder
½ teaspoon salt
½ teaspoon ground ginger
⅛ teaspoon ground cloves
⅛ teaspoon ground cinnamon
1 small clove garlic, minced

In a 1-quart casserole stir together apples, onion, raisins, vinegar, brown sugar, water, candied citron, curry powder, salt, ginger, cloves, cinnamon, and garlic. Micro-cook, covered, 5 minutes; stir. Micro-cook 3 minutes. Chill. Makes 1¾ cups.

Easy Chicken Bake

1 2⅜-ounce package seasoned coating mix for chicken
2 tablespoons grated Parmesan cheese
2 tablespoons snipped parsley
4 whole small chicken breasts
¼ cup milk

Place seasoned coating mix for chicken, Parmesan cheese, and parsley in plastic bag. Dip chicken in milk; shake in bag to coat. Place, skin side up, in a 12x7½x2-inch baking dish. Micro-cook, covered, 23 minutes. Uncover; micro-cook about 5 minutes or till done. Makes 4 servings.

Chicken Curry, Saffron Rice, Indian Chutney

Crab-Stuffed Chicken

½ **cup chopped onion**
½ **cup chopped celery**
3 **tablespoons butter or margarine**
1 **7½-ounce can crab meat, drained, flaked, and cartilage removed**
½ **cup herb-seasoned stuffing mix**
5 **tablespoons dry white wine**
5 **whole small chicken breasts, skinned and boned**
   Salt
   Pepper
1 **envelope hollandaise sauce mix**
¾ **cup milk**
½ **cup shredded Swiss cheese**

In bowl micro-cook onion and celery in butter, covered, about 2 minutes, stirring once. Stir in the crab, stuffing mix, and 3 *table-spoons* of the wine. Pound chicken to flatten each breast into an 8x6-inch rectangle. Sprinkle with salt and pepper. Divide stuffing mixture among chicken breasts. Roll up starting with short side; secure with wooden picks. Place in a 12x7½x2-inch baking dish. Sprinkle with pa-prika, if desired. Micro-cook, cov-ered, about 10 minutes or till done, turning dish once. Keep hot. In a 2-cup glass measure blend sauce mix and milk. Micro-cook, uncov-ered, about 2½ minutes or till boil-ing, stirring every 30 seconds. Stir in remaining wine and cheese. Re-move picks from chicken; serve with sauce. Makes 5 servings.

cooking rice

Quick, no-boil rice: In a 1-quart casserole combine 1 cup *wa-ter*, 2 teaspoons *butter*, and ¼ teaspoon *salt*. Micro-cook for 3 to 3½ minutes or till boiling. Stir in 1 cup *Minute Rice*. Cover; let stand 5 minutes. Fluff with fork. Makes 2 cups.

Quick rice that needs boil-ing: In a 1-quart casserole combine 1 cup *Uncle Ben's Quick Rice*, ¾ cup *water*, 2 teaspoons *butter*, and ¼ tea-spoon *salt*. Micro-cook, cov-ered, for 5 to 5½ minutes or till rice is tender and water is absorbed, stirring twice. Makes about 1⅓ cups.

Chicken Livers Peking

1 **tablespoon chopped onion**
1 **tablespoon butter**
8 **ounces chicken livers**
2 **teaspoons cornstarch**
¼ **cup chicken broth**
1 **2-ounce can chopped mushrooms**
1 **tablespoon soy sauce**
⅛ **teaspoon ground ginger**
1 **10-ounce package frozen Chinese-style vegetables**
   Chow mein noodles

In a 1-quart casserole micro-cook onion in butter about 1½ minutes or till tender. Cut large livers in half; add livers to onion mixture, coating well. Stir in cornstarch; then mix in broth, *undrained* mushrooms, soy, and ginger. Place frozen vegeta-bles with sauce atop liver mixture. Micro-cook, covered, 2 minutes. Stir in vegetables. Micro-cook, covered, 6 minutes; stir every 2 minutes. Serve over noodles. Makes 4 servings.

Macaroni and Cheese

For four servings, double all ingredients except the milk (use only 1 cup) —

1½ **cups hot tap water**
½ **cup elbow macaroni**
⅛ **teaspoon salt**
2 **tablespoons chopped onion**
1 **tablespoon butter or margarine**
4 **teaspoons all-purpose flour**
⅔ **cup milk**
½ **teaspoon Worcestershire sauce**
¾ **cup shredded sharp American cheese (2 ounces)**

In a 1-quart casserole combine wa-ter, macaroni, and salt. Micro-cook, uncovered, 7 to 8 minutes or till macaroni is tender, stirring twice. Drain. In same casserole micro-cook onion in butter about 1½ minutes or till tender. Stir in flour, ⅛ teaspoon *salt*, and dash *pepper*. Stir in milk and Worcestershire. Micro-cook, uncovered, 2 to 3 minutes or till thickened and bubbly, stirring every 30 seconds. Stir in cheese till melted. Stir in macaroni. Micro-cook, uncovered, 1 to 2 minutes longer or till bubbly, stirring once or twice. Makes 2 servings.

Pork and Apples with Stuffing

    6   pork cubed steaks (1½ pounds)
    1   envelope brown gravy mix
    ¼   cup packed brown sugar
    1   20-ounce can pie-sliced
        apples
    ¼   cup chopped celery
    2   tablespoons butter *or*
        margarine
    1   teaspoon instant minced onion
    1½ cups herb-seasoned stuffing
        mix
    ¼   teaspoon salt
    ½   cup hot water

Sprinkle pork with salt and pepper; arrange in a 12x7½x2-inch baking dish. Set aside. In bowl combine gravy mix and sugar; break up lumps. Stir in *undrained* apples; spoon over meat.

   In bowl micro-cook celery in butter, covered, about 2½ minutes or till tender. Stir in onion; let stand 2 minutes. Add stuffing mix and salt; toss with the water till moistened. Set aside. Micro-cook steaks, covered, 13 minutes, giving dish a half-turn after 9 minutes. Stir sauce around meat. Sprinkle stuffing over meat. Micro-cook, covered, about 5 minutes longer or till pork is done. Makes 6 servings.

Individual Ham Loaves

    1   beaten egg
    ¾   cup soft bread crumbs (1 slice)
    2   tablespoons chopped onion
    1   teaspoon Dijon-style mustard
    8   ounces ground fully cooked
        ham
    2   tablespoons orange
        marmalade

Combine egg, crumbs, onion, and mustard. Add ham; mix well. In a 9-inch glass pie plate shape mixture into two loaves, about 4½x2½-inches. Micro-cook, covered, 6 minutes, turning plate every 2 minutes. Spread *each* loaf with *half* the marmalade. Micro-cook, uncovered, about 1 minute. Serves 2.

Peach-Glazed Spareribs

    2   pounds pork spareribs
    1   8¾-ounce can peach slices,
        drained
    ¼   cup packed brown sugar
    2   tablespoons catsup
    2   tablespoons vinegar
    1   tablespoon soy sauce
    1   small clove garlic, minced
    ½   teaspoon salt
    ½   teaspoon ground ginger
        Dash pepper

Cut ribs into serving-size pieces. Arrange in a 12x7½x2-inch baking dish. Micro-cook, covered, 15 minutes, rearranging ribs every 5 minutes. Drain off pan juices; rearrange ribs. Meanwhile, sieve peaches or puree in blender container. Stir in remaining ingredients. Pour peach mixture over ribs. Micro-cook, uncovered, about 8 minutes or till ribs are done, brushing sauce over meat and rearranging ribs every 2 minutes. Garnish with parsley and additional peach slices, if desired. Makes 2 servings.

Mushroom-Sauced Eggs

    2   cups fresh mushrooms
        (5 ounces)
    4   teaspoons all-purpose flour
    2   tablespoons butter *or*
        margarine
    ¾   cup milk
    1½ teaspoons Worcestershire
        sauce
    ¾   teaspoon dry mustard
    ½   teaspoon paprika
    ¼   teaspoon salt
    ⅛   teaspoon pepper
        Poached eggs
    2   English muffins, split and
        toasted

Chop mushrooms; sprinkle with flour. In a 1-quart casserole micro-cook mushrooms in butter, covered, about 3½ minutes, stirring after 2 minutes. Stir in milk, Worcestershire sauce, mustard, paprika, salt, and pepper. Micro-cook, uncovered, about 3 minutes or till thickened and bubbly, stirring every 30 seconds. Cover; set aside. Prepare Poached Eggs. Return mushroom sauce to microwave oven and micro-cook, covered, 1 to 2 minutes or till heated through. Place Poached Eggs on muffin halves. Spoon mushroom sauce over. Makes 2 servings.

Poached Eggs: In a 1½-quart casserole micro-cook 2 cups *water* for 5 to 5½ minutes or till boiling. Using 4 *eggs*, break eggs, one at a time, into a cup. With fork or wooden pick, carefully pierce yolk just to break membrane. Slide egg into water. Working quickly, repeat with remaining eggs. Micro-cook, uncovered, for 1½ to 2 minutes or till white is firm.

Ham Rolls with Creamed Onions

Pork and Rice à l'Orange

Use either rib or loin pork chops —

- ½ cup Minute Rice
- ½ cup orange juice
- 2 tablespoons raisins
- 1 tablespoon water
- 2 teaspoons brown sugar
- ¼ teaspoon salt
- ⅛ teaspoon ground cinnamon
- 2 pork chops, cut ½ inch thick (about 5 ounces each)
  Salt
  Pepper
  Paprika

In a 6½x6½x2-inch ceramic baking dish combine the uncooked rice, orange juice, raisins, water, brown sugar, ¼ teaspoon salt, and the cinnamon. Mix well. Place chops atop rice mixture; sprinkle meat with salt, pepper, and paprika. Micro-cook, covered, for 9 to 10 minutes or till chops and rice are done, giving dish a half-turn after 5 minutes. Serves 2.

Mixed Vegetable — Ham Bake

A curry-flavored meat and vegetable main dish —

- 2¼ cups beef broth
- ¾ cup uncooked regular rice
- ½ cup chopped onion
- ⅓ cup chopped green pepper
- ¼ cup chopped celery
- 1 teaspoon curry powder
- 2 cups diced fully cooked ham (10 ounces)
- 1 10-ounce package frozen mixed vegetables

In a 2-quart casserole combine beef broth, rice, onion, green pepper, celery, and curry powder; mix well. Micro-cook, covered, 8 minutes, stirring after 4 minutes. Stir in ham and partially thawed mixed vegetables. Micro-cook, covered, 12 minutes more, stirring every 3 minutes. Transfer mixture to serving bowl. Makes 4 or 5 servings.

Ham and Broccoli Bake

- 2 10-ounce packages frozen chopped broccoli
- ½ cup chopped onion
- 2 tablespoons water
- 2 10½-ounce cans condensed cream of chicken soup
- 1 cup shredded sharp American cheese (4 ounces)
- ½ cup milk
- 3 cups diced fully cooked ham
- 2 cups Minute Rice
- ½ teaspoon Worcestershire sauce
  Parsley (optional)

In a 2½-quart casserole micro-cook the frozen broccoli, onion, and water, covered, about 11 minutes or till vegetables are tender. Stir twice to break up broccoli. Stir in soup, cheese, and milk. Stir in ham, uncooked rice, and Worcestershire. Micro-cook, covered, 10 to 11 minutes, stirring twice. Let stand, covered, for 5 minutes. Stir before serving. Garnish with parsley, if desired. Serves 8.

Ham Rolls with Creamed Onions

A fancy main dish pictured opposite —

- 1 12-ounce package frozen rice with peas and mushrooms
- ½ cup shredded sharp American cheese (2 ounces)
- 8 slices boiled ham (8 ounces)
- 1 9-ounce package frozen onions in cream sauce
- ¾ cup water
- 1 tablespoon butter or margarine
  Parsley (optional)

Cook frozen rice with peas and mushrooms in cooking pouch according to package directions for microwave oven. Transfer contents of pouch to bowl; stir in cheese.

Using ham slices, spoon a scant ¼ cup of the rice mixture on *each* ham slice. Roll up, jelly-roll style. Arrange ham rolls, seam side down, in a 10-inch glass pie plate or a 10x6x2-inch baking dish; set aside while preparing sauce.

In bowl combine frozen onions in cream sauce, water, and butter or margarine. Micro-cook, covered, for 7 to 8 minutes or till onions are tender and sauce is thickened, stirring twice. Micro-cook ham rolls, covered, about 3 minutes or till heated through. Uncover and spoon onions in cream sauce atop; micro-cook, uncovered, about 1 minute longer or till hot. Garnish with parsley, if desired. Makes 4 servings.

Barbecued Ham and Pineapple

- 1 3-pound canned ham
- 1 20-ounce can pineapple slices
- ½ cup chili sauce
- ¼ cup sugar
- 2 tablespoons lemon juice
- 2 teaspoons Worcestershire sauce
- ½ teaspoon chili powder
- 2 tablespoons cold water
- 1 tablespoon cornstarch

Place ham, fat side down, in a 12x7½x2-inch baking dish. Micro-cook, covered, 10 minutes, giving dish a half-turn after 5 minutes. Meanwhile, drain pineapple, reserving syrup. For sauce, combine ¼ *cup* of the syrup, chili sauce, sugar, lemon juice, Worcestershire sauce, and chili powder. Turn ham over. Spoon sauce over ham.

Micro-cook, uncovered, about 10 minutes or till ham is hot, giving dish a half-turn and brushing ham with sauce after 5 minutes. Remove ham from dish; cover with foil to keep warm.

Pour pan juices into a 2-cup glass measure. Add *water* to make 1¼ cups. Stir cold water into the cornstarch. Stir into juices in measuring cup. Micro-cook, uncovered, for 2 to 2½ minutes or till thickened and bubbly, stirring every 30 seconds. Set aside.

Place pineapple slices and remaining pineapple syrup in same 12x7½x2-inch baking dish. Micro-cook, covered, about 3 minutes or till pineapple is hot, turning dish once. Remove pineapple from syrup; brush with a little of the sauce. Place ham on platter. Arrange pineapple around ham. Spoon some sauce over ham and pass remaining. Makes 8 to 10 servings.

Golden-Sauced Franks

Sweet potatoes, pineapple, and frankfurters plus some tasty seasonings make this family main dish both hearty and appealing —

- 2 18-ounce cans sweet potatoes
- 1 15¼-ounce can pineapple chunks
- 1½ pounds frankfurters, cut into 1-inch pieces
- ⅓ cup packed brown sugar
- 2 tablespoons cornstarch
- ½ teaspoon grated orange peel
- ½ cup orange juice
- ¼ cup water
- 2 tablespoons vinegar
- 2 tablespoons chili sauce

Drain potatoes; cut up large pieces and set aside. Drain pineapple, reserving syrup. In a 3-quart casserole combine potatoes, pineapple, and franks; set aside. In a 2-cup glass measure combine the brown sugar and cornstarch. Stir in the reserved pineapple syrup, orange peel, orange juice, water, vinegar, and chili sauce. Micro-cook, uncovered, about 3 minutes or till thickened and bubbly, stirring after each minute. Pour sauce over mixture in casserole. Micro-cook, covered, 12 minutes, stirring every 3 minutes. Makes 8 servings.

Curried Lamb Meatballs

- 1 beaten egg
- 2 tablespoons milk
- 1 cup soft bread crumbs
- ½ teaspoon salt
- 1 pound ground lamb
- ½ cup chopped onion
- 2 tablespoons butter *or* margarine
- 2 tablespoons all-purpose flour
- 4 teaspoons curry powder
- ¼ teaspoon paprika
- ¼ teaspoon dried oregano, crushed
- ¼ teaspoon salt
  Dash pepper
- 1½ cups chicken broth
- 1 medium apple, peeled and chopped
  Hot cooked rice

Combine egg, milk, crumbs, and ½ teaspoon salt. Add lamb; mix well. Shape into 32 meatballs; arrange in a 12x7½x2-inch baking dish. Micro-cook, covered, 6 minutes, rearranging twice; set aside. In a 2-quart casserole micro-cook onion in butter about 2 minutes or till tender. Stir in flour, curry powder, paprika, oregano, ¼ teaspoon salt, and pepper. Stir in broth. Micro-cook, uncovered, 1 minute; stir. Micro-cook about 4 minutes or till thickened and bubbly, stirring every 30 seconds. Stir in meatballs. Micro-cook, covered, 3 minutes. Stir in apple. Micro-cook, covered, 2 minutes longer. Serve with rice. Makes 4 servings.

Barbecued Pork Chops and Rice

- ½ cup Minute Rice
- ¼ teaspoon salt
  Dash chili powder
- 2 pork chops, cut ½ inch thick
- 2 thin onion slices
- 3 tablespoons bottled barbecue sauce

In a 6½x6½x2-inch ceramic baking dish combine rice, salt, chili powder, and ½ cup *water*. Place pork chops atop rice. Season chops with salt. Place one onion slice atop each chop. Combine barbecue sauce and 1 tablespoon *water*; spoon over chops. Micro-cook, covered, 9 to 10 minutes or till chops and rice are done. Give dish a half-turn after 5 minutes. Makes 2 servings.

Lamb Stew

- 1 pound boneless lamb shoulder, cut into 1-inch cubes
- 1 envelope onion gravy mix
- 1 cup water
- 2 tablespoons all-purpose flour
- ½ teaspoon salt
- ⅛ teaspoon garlic powder
- 1 16-ounce can tomatoes, cut up
- 3 medium carrots, sliced
- ½ cup chopped green pepper
- 1 10-ounce package frozen peas

In a 2-quart casserole coat lamb cubes with onion gravy mix. Micro-cook, covered, 5 minutes, stirring twice. In shaker jar combine water, flour, salt, and garlic powder; shake well. Stir into lamb. Stir in *undrained* tomatoes, carrots, and green pepper. Micro-cook, covered, 20 minutes, stirring every 5 minutes. Stir in frozen peas. Micro-cook, covered, 15 minutes, stirring after 8 minutes. Serves 4.

Sausage-Stuffed Acorn Squash

- 1 medium acorn squash (1 pound)
- 6 ounces bulk pork sausage
- 2 tablespoons chopped onion
- 1 tablespoon snipped parsley
- ¼ teaspoon salt
  Dash pepper
- 1 small tomato, peeled and chopped (½ cup)
- ¼ cup sliced fresh mushrooms
- 1 small clove garlic, minced
- ½ teaspoon sugar
- ¼ teaspoon salt
  Dash pepper

Pierce squash with metal skewer in several places. Place on paper plate. Micro-cook, uncovered, 7 to 8 minutes or till done, turning after 4 minutes. Let stand several minutes.

Crumble sausage in a 1-quart casserole; add onion. Micro-cook, covered, about 5 minutes or till meat is cooked and onion is tender, stirring twice. Drain off excess fat. Set aside. Halve squash; remove seeds and string fibers. Scoop out squash; reserve shells. Stir squash, parsley, the ¼ teaspoon salt, and dash pepper into sausage mixture. (If necessary, stir in milk till of desired moistness — 2 to 3 tablespoons.) Fill shells with sausage mixture. Place in a 10x6x2-inch baking dish. Micro-cook, covered, about 4 minutes or till hot. Let stand, covered, while preparing sauce.

In a 1-quart casserole combine tomato, mushrooms, garlic, sugar, the remaining salt, and pepper. Micro-cook, uncovered, 4 to 5 minutes or till of desired consistency, stirring twice. Reheat squash, if necessary, about 1 minute. Serve sauce over squash. Serves 2.

Beef-Stuffed Onions

- 6 large onions
- 2 tablespoons water
- 1 pound ground beef
- ¾ teaspoon salt
- ¾ teaspoon dried basil, crushed
- 1 8-ounce can tomato sauce with mushrooms
- 1 tablespoon all-purpose flour
- 1 cup water
- ½ teaspoon sugar
- 1 tablespoon butter *or* margarine
- ½ cup soft bread crumbs
- 2 tablespoons grated Parmesan cheese

Peel onions. Place in a 2-quart casserole with the 2 tablespoons water. Micro-cook, covered, about 13 minutes or till tender, rearranging onions after 6 minutes. Drain and cool. Remove centers of onions; chop and reserve ½ *cup* of the onion centers.

In the same 2-quart casserole crumble ground beef. Micro-cook, covered, about 5 minutes or till meat is brown, stirring several times to break up meat. Drain off excess fat. Stir in reserved ½ cup onion, salt, and basil. Stuff the onion shells with *half* of the meat.

Stir tomato sauce into flour; stir in the 1 cup water and sugar. Stir into the remaining meat in casserole. Arrange onions in mixture. Spoon a little sauce atop.

In a 1-cup glass measure micro-melt butter or margarine 30 to 40 seconds. Stir in soft bread crumbs and Parmesan cheese; set aside. Micro-cook onions, covered, 8 minutes, turning dish after 4 minutes. Sprinkle onions with crumb mixture. Micro-cook, uncovered, 4 to 6 minutes more or till hot, turning dish once. Makes 6 servings.

Baked Bean Chili

- ½ pound ground beef
- ¼ cup chopped onion
- 1 tablespoon chopped green pepper
- 1 8-ounce can pork and beans in tomato sauce
- 1 8-ounce can tomatoes, cut up
- 2 tablespoons chili sauce
- 2 tablespoons water
- 1 to 1½ teaspoons chili powder

In a 2-quart casserole crumble beef. Add onion and green pepper. Micro-cook, covered, for 3 to 4 minutes or till meat is brown, stirring twice to break up meat. Drain off fat. Stir in *undrained* beans, *undrained* tomatoes, chili sauce, water, chili powder, and ½ teaspoon *salt*. Micro-cook, uncovered, 10 minutes; stir 3 times. Serves 2.

Savory Stuffed Peppers

- 4 large green peppers
- 1 pound ground beef
- 1 12-ounce can whole kernel corn
- 1 8-ounce can tomato sauce
- ¼ cup chopped onion
- ½ teaspoon Worcestershire sauce
- 1 cup shredded American cheese (4 ounces)

Halve peppers lengthwise; remove seeds and membranes. Place peppers in a 12x7½x2-inch baking dish. Sprinkle insides with salt. Micro-cook, covered, 5 minutes. In a bowl crumble ground beef. Drain corn. Add corn to meat with ½ *cup* of the tomato sauce, onion, Worcestershire, and ½ teaspoon *salt*. Micro-cook, covered, 7 to 8 minutes, stirring after 5 minutes. Spoon off fat. Stir in cheese. Spoon into pepper cups. Spoon remaining tomato sauce over peppers. Micro-cook, uncovered, 7 to 8 minutes, turning dish once. Serves 8.

Beef and Bean Cassoulet

A good use for leftover beef —

- 1 8-ounce can tomato sauce with chopped onion
- ⅓ cup dry red wine
- ½ teaspoon salt
- ½ teaspoon dried basil, crushed
- 1 clove garlic, minced
- 1 15-ounce can great northern beans, drained
- 1½ cups cubed cooked beef
- 2 links Polish sausage (6 ounces), cut into ½-inch slices
- ½ cup cold water
- 1 tablespoon all-purpose flour
- 2 tablespoons snipped parsley

In a 3-quart casserole combine the tomato sauce, wine, salt, basil, and garlic. Micro-cook, uncovered, about 5 minutes or till mixture bubbles, stirring once. Stir in the beans, beef, and sausage. Micro-cook, covered, about 5 minutes or till meat and beans are heated through, stirring twice. Stir water into the flour; stir into bean-meat mixture. Micro-cook, uncovered, about 1 minute or till mixture is thickened and bubbly, stirring every 30 seconds. Serve in bowls. Sprinkle with the parsley. Serves 6.

Beef and Bean Patties

1 **beaten egg**
½ **cup Minute Rice**
⅓ **cup water**
1 **teaspoon minced dried onion**
¾ **teaspoon garlic salt**
¼ **teaspoon seasoned pepper**
1 **pound lean ground beef**
1 **16-ounce can barbecue beans**
2 **tablespoons brown sugar**
1 **teaspoon Worcestershire sauce**
  Dash bottled hot pepper sauce
½ **cup shredded American cheese (2 ounces)**

In a bowl combine egg, uncooked rice, water, onion, garlic salt, and seasoned pepper. Add beef; mix well. Shape into six 4-inch patties. Place in a 12x7½x2-inch baking dish. Micro-cook, covered, 6 to 7 minutes or till done, rearranging patties in dish after 4 minutes. Spoon off excess fat. Combine beans, brown sugar, Worcestershire sauce, and hot pepper sauce. Spoon over patties. Micro-cook, covered, about 4 minutes or till heated through, turning dish· after 2 minutes. Top with cheese. Micro-cook, uncovered, about 1 minute or till cheese melts. Serve at once. Makes 6 servings.

Micro-Burgers

¼ **cup milk**
2 **teaspoons minced dried onion**
1 **beaten egg**
¾ **cup soft bread crumbs**
1 **pound lean ground beef**
4 **hamburger or frankfurter buns**

Combine milk and onion; let stand 5 minutes. Add egg, crumbs, ½ teaspoon *salt*, and dash *pepper*. Add ground beef; mix well. Shape into four 3-inch patties. Place in an 8x8x2-inch baking dish. Micro-cook, covered, for 3 minutes, giving dish a half-turn once. Drain. Micro-cook, covered, 2 to 3 minutes more or till meat is done, turning dish once. Brush patties with Kitchen Bouquet, if desired. Serve in buns. Makes 4 servings.

Sweet-Sour Burgers

½ **cup crushed gingersnaps (8)**
1 **8-ounce can tomato sauce**
¼ **cup finely chopped onion**
¼ **cup raisins**
1 **pound ground beef**
2 **tablespoons brown sugar**
2 **tablespoons vinegar**
1 **teaspoon prepared mustard**

Set aside *2 tablespoons* of the crushed gingersnaps. Combine remaining gingersnaps, *2 tablespoons* of the tomato sauce, onion, raisins, and ½ teaspoon *salt*. Add meat; mix well. Shape into four 4-inch patties. Arrange in an 8x8x2-inch baking dish. Micro-cook, covered, 5 minutes, giving dish a half-turn after 3·minutes. Drain. Combine remaining tomato sauce, reserved gingersnaps, brown sugar, vinegar, mustard, 2 tablespoons *water*, and dash *pepper*. Pour over burgers. Micro-cook, covered, about 4 minutes or till done, stirring sauce and turning dish after 2 minutes. Serves 4.

Barbecue Cabbage Rolls

8 **large cabbage leaves**
½ **cup water**
1 **beaten egg**
3 **tablespoons milk**
½ **cup soft bread crumbs**
¼ **cup finely chopped onion**
¾ **teaspoon salt**
¼ **teaspoon dried thyme, crushed**
⅛ **teaspoon pepper**
1 **pound ground beef**
1 **15½-ounce can sandwich sauce**

In a 3-quart casserole combine cabbage and water. Micro-cook, covered, about 8 minutes or till leaves are pliable. Let stand, covered, till cool. Combine egg, milk, crumbs, onion, salt, thyme, and pepper. Add meat; mix well. Place about ¼ *cup* meat in center of *each* cabbage leaf; fold in sides and roll ends over meat mixture. Place rolls, seam side down, in a 12x7½x2-inch baking dish. Pour sandwich sauce over. Micro-cook, covered, about 14 minutes or till meat is done and cabbage is tender, giving dish a quarter-turn every 4 minutes. Remove cabbage rolls to serving plate. Stir sauce in dish; serve with rolls. Serves 4.

Oriental Beef Ring

A favorite dish pictured on page 6 —

- 1 3-ounce can chow mein noodles
- 1 8-ounce can tomato sauce with chopped onion
- 1 beaten egg
- ¼ cup chopped celery
- 2 tablespoons soy sauce
- ⅛ teaspoon ground ginger
- 1 pound ground beef
- 1 tablespoon brown sugar
- 2 teaspoons soy sauce
- 1 6-ounce package frozen pea pods
- 1 tablespoon butter or margarine

Finely crush *1 cup* of the noodles; combine with ⅔ *cup* of the tomato sauce. Let stand 5 minutes to soften. In a large bowl combine egg, celery, the 2 tablespoons soy sauce, ginger, and noodle mixture. Add beef; mix well. Press into an oiled 3-cup ring mold (6½ inches in diameter and 2½ inches deep). Loosen edges. Invert mold into a 9-inch glass pie plate; *remove mold.* Micro-cook, covered with waxed paper, about 10 minutes or till done, turning dish every 3 minutes. Drain off excess fat. Combine remaining tomato sauce, sugar, and 2 teaspoons soy sauce; brush on meat ring. Micro-cook, uncovered, 30 seconds. Cover; keep hot.

In a 1-quart casserole combine pea pods and 2 tablespoons water. Micro-cook, covered, about 4 minutes or till tender, tossing twice with a fork. Drain. Toss with remaining chow mein noodles and butter. Micro-cook, uncovered, 15 seconds. Transfer meat to serving plate. Surround with vegetable mixture. Serves 6.

---

meat loaf toppers

To dress up a meat loaf, try some of these simple suggestions. Spread chili sauce, barbecue sauce, pizza sauce, or enchilada sauce over the top of the meat after removing from the microwave oven. Or, sprinkle with grated Parmesan cheese, top with shredded American cheese, or arrange sliced cheese triangles to melt over the top of the hot meat loaf.

Everyday Meat Loaf

- 2 beaten eggs
- ¾ cup milk
- ½ cup fine dry bread crumbs
- ¼ cup finely chopped onion
- 2 tablespoons snipped parsley
- 1 teaspoon salt
- ¾ teaspoon ground sage
- ⅛ teaspoon pepper
- 1½ pounds ground beef

In a bowl combine beaten eggs, milk, fine dry bread crumbs, onion, parsley, salt, sage, and pepper; mix well. Add ground beef; combine thoroughly. In a 9-inch glass pie plate shape meat mixture into a ring about 1 inch high around a small juice glass having a 2-inch diameter. Micro-cook, covered, for 12 to 13 minutes or till meat is done, giving dish a quarter-turn every 3 minutes. Remove the juice glass. Let meat loaf stand 5 minutes before removing. If desired, garnish with tomato wedges and parsley; or, serve with warmed catsup; or, sprinkle with shredded American cheese before letting loaf stand 5 minutes. Serves 6.

Tangy Meat Loaf

- 1 beaten egg
- 1 cup dairy sour cream
- ½ cup coarsely crushed saltine crackers (11 crackers)
- ½ cup shredded carrot
- 1¼ teaspoons salt
- ⅛ teaspoon pepper
- 1 pound ground beef
- ½ pound ground pork

In a bowl combine beaten egg, dairy sour cream, cracker crumbs, shredded carrot, salt, and pepper; mix well. Add ground beef and pork; combine thoroughly. In a 9-inch glass pie plate shape meat mixture into a ring about 1 inch high around a small juice glass having a 2-inch diameter. Micro-cook, covered, about 13 minutes or till meat is done, giving dish a quarter-turn every 3 minutes. Remove the glass. Let loaf stand 5 minutes before removing to serving plate. If desired, brush meat loaf with Kitchen Bouquet. Makes 6 servings.

Baked Chow Mein

- 1 **pound ground beef**
- ½ **cup chopped onion**
- 1 **16-ounce can chop suey vegetables, drained**
- 1 **10¾-ounce can condensed cream of mushroom soup**
- 1 **3-ounce can sliced mushrooms, drained**
- ½ **cup water**
- 1 **tablespoon soy sauce**
- 1 **3-ounce can chow mein noodles**

In a 10x6x2-inch glass baking dish break up ground beef. Add chopped onion. Micro-cook, covered, 5 minutes, stirring occasionally. Remove from oven; drain off excess fat. Stir together drained chop suey vegetables, mushroom soup, drained mushrooms, water, soy sauce, and *half* of the chow mein noodles. Micro-cook, covered, 6 minutes longer, stirring occasionally. Sprinkle remaining noodles atop beef mixture. Pass additional soy sauce, if desired. Makes 6 servings.

Cheeseburger-Vegetable Casserole

- 1 **pound ground beef**
- ½ **cup chopped onion**
- ¼ **cup butter *or* margarine**
- ¼ **cup all-purpose flour**
- 1 **teaspoon salt**
  Dash pepper
- 1½ **cups milk**
- 1½ **cups shredded American cheese (6 ounces)**
- 1 **teaspoon Worcestershire sauce**
- 1 **10-ounce package frozen mixed vegetables**
- ¼ **cup chopped pimiento**
  Packaged instant mashed potatoes (enough for 4 servings)

In a large bowl crumble the ground beef. Add the chopped onion. Micro-cook, covered, about 5 minutes or till meat is brown, stirring several times to break up meat. Drain off excess fat. In a 4-cup glass measure micro-melt the butter about 45 seconds. Stir in the flour, salt, and pepper. Gradually stir in the milk. Micro-cook, uncovered, 1 minute; stir. Micro-cook about 3 minutes more or till thickened and bubbly, stirring every 30 seconds. Stir in *1 cup* of the cheese and the Worcestershire sauce. Add to meat mixture. Break up frozen vegetables. Stir vegetables and pimiento into meat mixture. Turn mixture into an 8x8x2-inch baking dish. Micro-cook, covered, 10 minutes, turning after 5 minutes.

Prepare the packaged instant mashed potatoes according to package directions *except* decrease water by ¼ cup. Spoon the prepared potatoes around edge of casserole. Sprinkle remaining shredded American cheese over potatoes. Micro-cook, uncovered, about 1 minute or till cheese is melted. Serves 4 to 6.

Beef and Pork Ring

- 1 **beaten egg**
- ½ **cup milk**
- 1½ **cups soft bread crumbs**
- 2 **tablespoons finely chopped onion**
- 2 **tablespoons finely chopped green pepper**
- 1 **teaspoon salt**
  Dash pepper
- 1 **pound ground beef**
- ¼ **pound ground pork**
- 2 **tablespoons catsup**
- 1 **tablespoon brown sugar**
- ¼ **teaspoon dry mustard**

Mix egg, milk, crumbs, onion, green pepper, salt, and pepper. Add meats; mix well. In a 9-inch glass pie plate, shape meat into a ring, 1 inch high, around a small juice glass. Cover with waxed paper. Micro-cook 8 minutes, giving dish a quarter-turn every 2 minutes. Spoon off fat. Mix remaining ingredients; spread over meat. Micro-cook, uncovered, about 2 minutes or till done. Let stand 5 minutes. Serves 4 or 5.

Sour Cream-Chili Bake

When time is short at mealtime, use your microwave oven to prepare this easy-to-make casserole —

- 1 **pound ground beef**
- ¼ **cup chopped onion**
- 1 **10-ounce can hot enchilada sauce**
- 1 **8-ounce can tomato sauce**
- 1 **15-ounce can pinto beans**
- 2⅓ **cups crushed corn chips**
- 1 **cup shredded American cheese (4 ounces)**
- 1 **cup dairy sour cream**

In a 2-quart casserole crumble ground beef. Add onion; micro-cook, covered, about 5 minutes or till meat is brown, stirring several times to break up meat. Drain off excess fat. Stir in enchilada sauce and tomato sauce. Micro-cook, covered, 5 minutes, stirring once. Drain beans; stir beans, *1 cup* of the corn chips, and ¾ *cup* of the cheese into meat. Micro-cook, covered, 6 minutes, stirring once. Stir, then spread the sour cream over top; sprinkle the remaining corn chips and cheese over top. Micro-cook 30 to 45 seconds or just till sour cream is hot. Makes 6 to 8 servings.

Pizza Cubed Steaks

- 1 **8-ounce can pizza sauce**
- ¼ **cup chopped onion**
- ¼ **cup chopped green pepper**
- 1 **teaspoon cornstarch**
- ½ **teaspoon sugar**
- ¼ **teaspoon dried oregano, crushed**
- ¼ **teaspoon dried basil, crushed**
- 4 **beef cubed steaks**
- ¾ **teaspoon salt**
- ⅛ **teaspoon pepper**
- 1 **slice mozzarella cheese**

In a 12x7½x2-inch glass baking dish, combine first 7 ingredients. Cover with waxed paper. Micro-cook 3 minutes; stir. Add meat in single layer; sprinkle with salt and pepper. Cover; micro-cook 5 minutes. Turn meat over; micro-cook, covered, 3 minutes more or till done. Remove from oven. Cut cheese into 4 triangles; place one triangle atop each steak. Let stand 1 minute to melt cheese. Serves 4.

Ravioli Casserole

- ¼ **cup cold water**
- 1 **tablespoon all-purpose flour**
- 1 **cup beef broth**
- 2 **15-ounce cans beef ravioli in sauce**
- 1½ **to 2 cups cubed cooked beef**
- 1 **16-ounce can cut green beans, drained**
- 1 **3-ounce can chopped mushrooms, drained**
- ¼ **cup grated Parmesan cheese**

In a 2-quart casserole stir water into flour; stir in broth. Micro-cook, uncovered, about 5 minutes or till thickened and bubbly, stirring after each minute. Stir in the ravioli in sauce, beef, beans, and mushrooms. Micro-cook, covered, 7 to 8 minutes or till hot, stirring four times. Sprinkle cheese atop. Serves 6.

Mexican-Style Lasagna

- 1 **pound ground beef**
- ½ **cup chopped onion**
- 1 **16-ounce can tomatoes, cut up**
- 1 **10½-ounce can pizza sauce**
- ¼ **cup sliced pitted ripe olives**
- ½ **teaspoon salt**
- ¼ **teaspoon dried oregano, crushed**
  Dash pepper
- 1 **beaten egg**
- 1 **cup shredded American cheese**
- 1 **cup cream-style cottage cheese**
- 4 **cups corn-flavor tortilla chips (4 ounces)**

In a 12x7½x2-inch baking dish crumble ground beef. Add onion; micro-cook, covered, about 5 minutes or till meat is brown, stirring several times to break up meat. Drain off excess fat. Stir in undrained tomatoes, pizza sauce, olives, salt, oregano, and pepper. Micro-cook, covered, 8 minutes, stirring once. Transfer to another dish.

In a bowl combine egg and cheeses. Set aside eight of the tortilla chips; slightly crush remaining chips. Spread one-third of the meat mixture in the 12x7½x2-inch baking dish; top with half of the cheese mixture and half of the crushed tortilla chips. Repeat layers, ending with meat. Micro-cook, uncovered, 10 minutes, turning dish twice. Top with reserved chips. Let stand 5 minutes. Makes 6 servings.

a variety
of vegetables

Oriental Peas

- 1 **6- *or* 7-ounce package frozen pea pods**
- ½ **of an 8-ounce can water chestnuts, drained and sliced**
- 1 **tablespoon chopped pimiento**
- 1 **tablespoon water**
- 1 **tablespoon soy sauce**

In a 1-quart casserole place frozen pea pods, water chestnuts, and pimiento. Pour water and soy sauce over all. Micro-cook, covered, 2 minutes; stir with fork to break apart pea pods. Micro-cook, covered, 2 minutes more; stir well. Micro-cook, covered, about 1 minute more or till vegetables are heated through. Makes 4 servings.

German-Style Spinach

- 1 **slice bacon**
- 1 **tablespoon chopped onion**
- 2 **teaspoons vinegar**
- 1 **teaspoon sugar**
- 1 **7¾-ounce can leaf spinach, drained**

Place bacon in a 1-quart casserole; cover with paper toweling. Micro-cook about 1½ minutes or till crisp. Remove bacon; drain. Reserve drippings in casserole. Crumble bacon; set aside. In reserved drippings cook onion about 1½ minutes or till tender. Stir in vinegar and sugar; stir in spinach. Micro-cook, covered, 2 to 2½ minutes or till heated through. Sprinkle with crumbled bacon. Makes 2 servings.

Easy Baked Beans

- 4 **slices bacon**
- ½ **cup chopped onion**
- 2 **16-ounce cans pork and beans in tomato sauce**
- 2 **tablespoons brown sugar**
- 2 **tablespoons catsup**
- 1 **tablespoon Worcestershire sauce**
- 1 **tablespoon prepared mustard**

Place bacon in a 1½-quart casserole; cover with paper toweling. Micro-cook 3½ to 4 minutes or till crisp. Remove bacon; drain. Reserve about 3 tablespoons drippings in casserole. Crumble bacon and set aside.

Micro-cook onion in reserved drippings 2 minutes or till tender. Stir in pork and beans in tomato sauce, brown sugar, catsup, Worcestershire sauce, and mustard. Micro-cook, uncovered, about 10 minutes or till bubbly; stir twice. Top with bacon. Serves 6.

Orange-Sauced Carrots

- 6 **to 8 carrots, sliced ⅛ inch thick (3 cups)**
- ⅓ **cup water**
- 1 **tablespoon brown sugar**
- 1½ **teaspoons cornstarch**
- ⅔ **cup orange juice**
- 1 **tablespoon butter**
- ¼ **teaspoon salt**
- ⅛ **teaspoon ground ginger**
  Dash ground cloves

In a 1-quart casserole place sliced carrots and water. Micro-cook carrots, covered, 9 to 10 minutes or till tender. Drain well.

Stir together brown sugar and cornstarch; blend in orange juice, butter, salt, ginger, and cloves. Stir mixture into carrots. Micro-cook, uncovered, 2 minutes; stir. Micro-cook, uncovered, 1 to 1½ minutes longer. Serves 4.

Spinach Elegante

- 1 **10-ounce package frozen Welsh rarebit**
- 8 **slices bacon**
- 2 **10-ounce packages frozen chopped spinach**
- ½ **of an 8-ounce can (½ cup) water chestnuts, drained and sliced**
- ½ **of a 3½-ounce can (about ¾ cup) french-fried onions**

Remove frozen rarebit from foil pan; place in a 1-quart casserole. Micro-cook, covered, 5 minutes, stirring once. Set aside. In a 10x6x2-inch baking dish place bacon between layers of paper toweling, layering bacon and toweling if needed. Micro-cook about 7 minutes, rearranging once. Remove bacon and toweling; crumble bacon. Set aside. Drain off excess drippings.

Place spinach in same baking dish. Micro-cook, covered, 6 minutes, stirring once. Drain. Season with salt. Stir in water chestnuts and ⅓ cup of the rarebit. Sprinkle with bacon.

Spread remaining rarebit over all. Top with onion rings. Micro-cook, uncovered, about 5 minutes or till hot, turning dish once. Makes 6 servings.

Corn-Stuffed Onions

Drape this colorful vegetable dish with a creamy cheese sauce —

- 6 medium onions
- 1 12-ounce can whole kernel corn with sweet peppers, drained
- 2 tablespoons butter *or* margarine
- 1 10½-ounce can condensed cream of celery soup
- 1 cup shredded American cheese (4 ounces)

Peel and hollow out onions; chop centers to make 1 cup. Fill onion shells with corn; reserve the remaining corn. Place stuffed onions in an 8x8x2-inch baking dish. Micro-cook, covered, 12 minutes, turning dish once; set aside.

To make the cheese sauce, in a 4-cup glass measure or bowl micro-cook chopped onion in butter 2 to 3 minutes or till tender. Stir in soup, cheese, and remaining corn. Micro-cook, uncovered, 1 minute; stir till the cheese is melted. Spoon the cheese sauce over onions. Micro-cook, uncovered, about 4 minutes or till heated through. Makes 6 servings.

Hominy-Bean Bake

- 1 16-ounce can yellow hominy, drained
- 1 15½-ounce can cut green beans, drained
- 1 cup meatless spaghetti sauce *or* Italian cooking sauce
- 2 tablespoons finely chopped celery
- 1 teaspoon sugar
- ½ teaspoon Worcestershire sauce
- ½ cup coarsely crushed corn chips

In a 1½-quart casserole combine the yellow hominy, green beans, spaghetti sauce or Italian cooking sauce, celery, sugar, and Worcestershire sauce. Micro-cook, covered, 8 to 9 minutes or till heated through, stirring every 3 minutes. Top with corn chips. Makes 6 servings.

Basil Beans

- 8 ounces fresh green beans, cut into pieces (2 cups)
- ¼ cup water
- 2 tablespoons chopped onion
- 2 tablespoons chopped celery
- 2 tablespoons butter *or* margarine
- ½ teaspoon dried basil, crushed
- ¼ teaspoon salt
  Dash pepper

In a 1-quart casserole micro-cook the green beans, water, onion, and celery, covered, about 9 minutes or till beans are almost tender, stirring after 5 minutes. *Do not drain.* Stir in the butter or margarine, basil, salt, and pepper. Micro-cook, covered, about 1 minute or till butter melts. Makes 2 or 3 servings.

Cheese-Sauced Brussels Sprouts

Garnish with chopped egg for a colorful effect —

- 2 8- or 10-ounce packages frozen brussels sprouts
- ¼ cup water
- 2 tablespoons butter *or* margarine
- 2 tablespoons all-purpose flour
- ⅛ teaspoon salt
- ¾ cup milk
- 1 cup shredded American cheese (4 ounces)
- 1 hard-cooked egg, chopped

In a 1½-quart casserole place brussels sprouts and water. Micro-cook, covered, 11 to 12 minutes or till tender, stirring every 4 minutes. Drain; halve sprouts. Return to casserole.

In a 2-cup glass measure micro-melt the butter 30 to 40 seconds. Blend in flour and salt; add milk all at once, stirring well. Micro-cook, uncovered, 1 minute; stir. Micro-cook 2 to 3 minutes or till thickened and bubbly, stirring every 30 seconds. Add cheese; stir till melted. Pour over brussels sprouts. Micro-cook, covered, about 1 minute more or till heated through; stir. Sprinkle chopped egg atop casserole. Makes 6 servings.

Golden Bean Casserole

- 2   **9-ounce packages frozen whole *or* cut green beans**
- 1   **10¾-ounce can condensed cream of mushroom soup**
- ¼   **cup mayonnaise**
- 2   **tablespoons diced pimiento**
- 1   **teaspoon lemon juice**
- ⅓   **cup finely crushed round cheese crackers**

In a 1½-quart casserole micro-cook beans in ⅓ cup *water*, covered, 12 minutes, stirring every 3 minutes. Drain. In same dish mix soup and next 3 ingredients; stir in beans. Micro-cook, covered, 2 minutes. Stir; micro-cook, covered, 2 minutes. Sprinkle with crumbs; micro-cook, uncovered, 1 minute. Serves 6.

Scalloped Succotash

Pictured on page 37 —

- ¼   **cup chopped onion**
- 2   **17-ounce cans whole kernel corn**
- 1   **17-ounce can lima beans**
- 1½ **cups coarsely crushed saltine crackers**
- 1   **10½-ounce can condensed cream of celery soup**
- ½   **cup shredded Swiss cheese**
- ¼   **cup chopped pimiento**
- ¼   **cup milk**
- 1   **tablespoon butter**

In a 2½-quart casserole micro-cook onion in 2 tablespoons *water*, covered, 1½ minutes; drain. Drain corn; reserve ¾ cup liquid. Drain beans. Stir in corn, reserved liquid, beans, 1¼ *cups* crumbs, next 4 ingredients, and dash *pepper*. Micro-cook, uncoverd, 18 minutes, stirring every 5 minutes. Let stand 2 minutes. Meanwhile, micro-melt butter 30 to 40 seconds; toss with remaining crumbs. Sprinkle over vegetables. Serves 12.

how to toast nuts

Spread about ¼ cup nuts on a paper plate or in a glass pie plate. Micro-cook, uncovered, about 3 minutes or till toasted, stirring frequently.

Creamy Vegetable Bake

Pictured on page 37 —

- 1   **pound carrots (about 8 carrots)**
- 2   **cups frozen Southern-style hashed brown potatoes**
- ¾   **cup sliced celery**
- ½   **cup chopped onion**
- 1   **3-ounce can sliced mushrooms, drained**
- 1   **envelope (enough for 1 cup sauce) white sauce mix**
- 2   **cups milk**
- ½   **cup dairy sour cream**
- ½   **of a 3½-ounce can (about 1 cup) french-fried onions**

Peel carrots; quarter lengthwise and cut into 2-inch pieces. In a 2-quart glass bowl or casserole combine carrots, hashed brown potatoes, celery, onion, mushrooms, ¼ cup *water*, and ½ teaspoon *salt*. Micro-cook, covered, about 18 minutes or till tender, stirring every 5 minutes. Do not drain. Sprinkle dry sauce mix over vegetables; stir gently. Gradually stir in milk. Micro-cook, covered, about 5 minutes or till thickened and bubbly, stirring after each minute.

Gently stir in sour cream. Turn into a 1½-quart casserole. Micro-cook, covered, about 3 minutes or till hot. Circle edge of casserole with french-fried onions; micro-cook, uncovered, 30 seconds. Trim with parsley, if desired. Serves 6.

Onions in Cream Sauce

- 2   **pounds small onions**
- 2   **tablespoons water**
- 2   **tablespoons butter *or* margarine**
- 2   **tablespoons all-purpose flour**
- 1   **cup milk**
- 1   **teaspoon instant chicken bouillon granules**
- 1   **teaspoon Worcestershire sauce**
- ¼   **teaspoon dried marjoram, crushed**
   Dash pepper
- ½   **cup dairy sour cream**
- 2   **tablespoons toasted slivered almonds**
   Dash paprika

Peel onions. In a 1½-quart casserole micro-cook onions in water, covered, 10 minutes or till tender. Drain; set onions aside. In same dish micro-melt butter or margarine 30 to 40 seconds. Stir in all-purpose flour. Stir in milk, chicken bouillon granules, Worcestershire sauce, marjoram, and pepper. Micro-cook, uncovered, 1 minute; stir. Micro-cook 3 minutes or till thickened and bubbly, stirring every 30 seconds. Stir in onions. Micro-cook, covered, 3 minutes or till hot, stirring once. Stir ¼ *cup* of the sauce into dairy sour cream; stir into onions. Top with toasted almonds (see tip at left). Sprinkle with paprika. Makes 5 or 6 servings.

Dilled Zucchini

6 cups sliced zucchini (about 1½ pounds)
¼ cup water
½ teaspoon salt
2 tablespoons butter *or* margarine
1 tablespoon all-purpose flour
1 teaspoon lemon juice
½ teaspoon salt
½ teaspoon paprika
½ teaspoon dried dillweed
½ cup milk

In a 1½-quart casserole combine zucchini, water, and the ½ teaspoon salt. Micro-cook, covered, 12 to 13 minutes or till almost done, stirring twice. Keep hot while preparing dill sauce.

For dill sauce, in a 2-cup glass measure micro-melt butter or margarine for 30 to 40 seconds. Stir in flour, lemon juice, the ½ teaspoon salt, paprika, and dillweed. Stir in milk. Micro-cook sauce, uncovered, for 1 minute; stir. Micro-cook about 1½ minutes more or till sauce is thickened and bubbly, stirring every 30 seconds.

Drain cooked zucchini. Pour dill sauce over vegetables and mix thoroughly. If necessary, micro-cook just till hot. Makes 6 servings.

drying herbs

Enjoy fresh herbs all year long by drying them in the microwave oven. Wash fresh herbs; shake off excess water. Arrange herbs in a single layer on a double thickness of paper toweling. Place a single layer of paper toweling on top. Micro-cook for 3 to 4 minutes or till herbs are thoroughly dried and can be crumbled. Store in tightly covered containers.

Scalloped Potatoes

3 medium potatoes, peeled and thinly sliced (1 pound)
½ cup chopped onion
¼ cup chopped green pepper
2 tablespoons butter
1 tablespoon all-purpose flour
1 cup milk
½ teaspoon Worcestershire sauce
3 tablespoons fine dry bread crumbs

In a 1½-quart casserole mix first 3 ingredients and ½ cup *water*. Micro-cook, covered, 9 to 10 minutes, stirring every 3 minutes. Drain. In a 2-cup glass measure micro-melt *1 tablespoon* butter 30 to 40 seconds. Stir in flour, ¾ teaspoon *salt*, and dash *pepper*. Add milk and Worcestershire. Micro-cook, uncovered, 1 minute; stir. Micro-cook 1½ minutes or till bubbly, stirring every 30 seconds. Pour over potatoes. Micro-cook, uncovered, 2 minutes, stirring after 1 minute. Season to taste. In a 1-cup glass measure micro-melt remaining butter 30 to 40 seconds. Stir in crumbs. Sprinkle over potatoes. Serves 6.

Harvard Beets

1 8¼-ounce can sliced beets
1 tablespoon sugar
1 tablespoon cornstarch
2 tablespoons vinegar
1 tablespoon butter *or* margarine

Drain beets; reserve ¼ cup liquid. In a 2-cup glass measure mix sugar, cornstarch, and ⅛ teaspoon *salt*. Stir in reserved liquid, vinegar, and butter. Micro-cook, uncovered, 1 minute or till thickened and bubbly, stirring every 15 seconds. Stir in beets. Micro-cook, covered, about 2 minutes or till hot. Serves 2.

Herbed Potatoes

8 small new potatoes
3 tablespoons butter *or* margarine
2 tablespoons finely snipped parsley
1 tablespoon finely snipped chives
1 teaspoon lemon juice
¼ teaspoon dried dillweed
⅛ teaspoon salt
Dash pepper

Scrub potatoes with a coarse brush; prick several times with a fork. Place paper toweling in bottom of a 10x6x2-inch baking dish. Arrange potatoes atop toweling, about 1 inch apart. Micro-cook potatoes, uncovered, for 8 to 9 minutes or till tender, giving dish a quarter-turn every 3 minutes. Remove toweling; add butter to dish with potatoes. Micro-melt the butter about 30 to 45 seconds. Add parsley and remaining ingredients; stir potatoes to coat. Turn into serving bowl. Makes 4 servings.

cooking frozen vegetables

Unwrap one 9- or 10-ounce package of frozen vegetables *or* measure 1½ cups loose-pack vegetables. Place in a 1-quart casserole. Follow any special instructions below. Cover. Micro-cook, following times suggested and stirring, breaking up, or redistributing vegetables after half of cooking time. Timings are approximate because of the wide variety of appliances available and because vegetables vary in freshness. Be sure to test them for doneness after the shorter cooking time; if necessary, continue cooking till vegetables are almost done. They will finish cooking with stored heat. *Do not overcook vegetables.*

VEGETABLE	SPECIAL INSTRUCTIONS	APPROXIMATE TIME
Asparagus	Add 2 tablespoons water	6 to 8 minutes
Beans, green	Add 2 tablespoons water	6 to 8 minutes
Beans, lima	Add ½ cup water	8 to 10 minutes
Broccoli	Add 2 tablespoons water	6 to 8 minutes
Brussels sprouts	Add 2 tablespoons water	7 to 9 minutes
Carrots	Add 2 tablespoons water	7 to 8 minutes
Cauliflower	Add 2 tablespoons water	6 to 8 minutes
Corn, cut	Add 2 tablespoons water	4 to 6 minutes
Mixed vegetables	Add 2 tablespoons water	5 to 7 minutes
Peas	Add 2 tablespoons water	4 to 6 minutes
Spinach	Add no water	5 to 7 minutes

Baked Potatoes

Select baking potatoes of approximately the same size and shape (about 8 ounces each). Thoroughly wash and scrub potatoes and prick skins with a fork.

In microwave oven arrange potatoes on paper toweling, leaving at least 1 inch between potatoes. Micro-cook, uncovered, till potatoes test done when pricked with a fork. Allow 6 to 8 minutes for two potatoes; 13 to 15 minutes for four potatoes; and 17 to 19 minutes for six potatoes. Halfway through cooking time, rearrange potatoes and turn over.

Corn on the Cob

Husk and silk corn. Wrap each ear in waxed paper; twist ends of paper. Arrange corn on paper toweling; allow at least 1 inch between ears. Micro-cook one ear about 2 minutes; two ears 3 to 4 minutes; four ears 6 to 7 minutes; and six ears 8 to 10 minutes. Halfway through cooking, rearrange corn and turn over.

Or, omit wrapping in waxed paper and place husked and silked corn in a baking dish. Micro-cook, covered, following times given above. Halfway through cooking time, rearrange the ears of corn in the dish.

Parslied Carrots

- 6 to 9 carrots, sliced
     ⅛ inch thick (3 cups)
- 1 tablespoon butter *or*
     margarine
- ½ teaspoon lemon juice
- ¼ teaspoon salt
- ⅛ teaspoon paprika
- 2 tablespoons snipped parsley

In a 1-quart casserole combine carrots and ⅓ cup *water*. Micro-cook, covered, about 9 minutes or till carrots are tender; drain. Stir butter or margarine, lemon juice, salt, and paprika into carrots. Micro-cook, covered, for 1 to 2 minutes or till heated through. Stir in snipped parsley. Makes 6 servings.

Creamy Vegetable Bake, Scalloped Succotash (see recipes, page 34)

Elegant Stuffed Potatoes

 4 medium baking potatoes
 ½ cup cream-style cottage
    cheese with chives
 ¼ cup butter *or* margarine
 1 teaspoon seasoned salt
    Dash pepper
 ¼ cup milk
 1 2-ounce can chopped
    mushrooms, drained
 ½ cup shredded American
    cheese (2 ounces)

Scrub the baking potatoes; prick several times with a fork. In microwave oven arrange the potatoes on paper toweling, leaving at least 1 inch between the potatoes. Micro-cook 13 to 15 minutes or till done; rearrange after 8 minutes. When done, halve the potatoes lengthwise. Scoop out insides; reserve the shells. In a small mixer bowl combine the potatoes, cottage cheese, butter or margarine, seasoned salt, and pepper. Beat at medium speed of electric mixer till potato mixture is of fluffy consistency, adding about ¼ *cup* of the milk. Stir mushrooms into potato mixture. Pile into the reserved shells. Arrange potato shells on a serving plate.

Micro-cook, uncovered, 4 minutes, giving dish a half-turn after 2 minutes. Top with shredded cheese. Micro-cook, uncovered, 30 to 45 seconds or till melted. Makes 8 servings.

Onion-Cauliflower Bake

 1 10-ounce package frozen
    cauliflower
 1 10-ounce package frozen
    onions in cream sauce
 ⅓ cup water
 ½ cup shredded American
    cheese (2 ounces)
 1 tablespoon snipped parsley

In a 1½-quart casserole micro-defrost frozen cauliflower, covered, about 4 minutes, breaking apart cauliflower block with a fork twice. Cut up large cauliflower pieces; return all to casserole. Add frozen onions in cream sauce and water to cauliflower. Micro-cook, covered, 8 to 9 minutes or till done, stirring 3 times. Stir in cheese; micro-cook, covered, 2 to 3 minutes, stirring twice to melt cheese. Garnish with parsley. Makes 6 servings.

savory
soups
and sauces

Seafood-Corn Chowder

- 3 slices bacon, chopped
- 1 7½-ounce can minced clams
- ½ cup chopped onion
- ½ teaspoon salt
  Dash bottled hot pepper sauce
- 1 17-ounce can cream-style corn
- 1 16-ounce can whole white potatoes, drained and diced
- 1 4½-ounce can shrimp, drained
- 2 tablespoons snipped parsley
- 1½ cups milk
- 2 tablespoons all-purpose flour

Place bacon in a 2-quart casserole; cover with paper toweling. Micro-cook about 3 minutes or till crisp. Remove bacon; drain. Reserve 1 tablespoon drippings in casserole. Drain the clams; reserve liquid. To reserved bacon drippings stir in reserved clam liquid, chopped onion, salt, and hot pepper sauce. Micro-cook, covered, about 4 minutes or till onion is tender. Stir in drained clams, corn, potatoes, shrimp, and snipped parsley. Stir ¼ cup of the milk into flour; stir into soup with the remaining milk. Micro-cook, covered, about 10 minutes or till thickened and bubbly, stirring every 4 minutes. Before serving, sprinkle with bacon pieces. Makes 4 to 6 servings.

Cheesy Chicken Soup

- 1 whole small chicken breast, halved lengthwise (8 ounces)
- ½ cup water
- ¼ cup chopped onion
- ¼ cup chopped carrot
- ¼ cup chopped celery
- 1 10½-ounce can condensed cream of chicken soup
- ¾ cup milk
- ½ cup shredded American cheese (2 ounces)

In a 1½-quart casserole combine chicken, water, onion, carrot, and celery. Micro-cook, covered, about 7 minutes or till chicken and vegetables are tender. Remove chicken; cool slightly. Discard skin and bones; cut up meat. Return chicken to casserole. Stir in condensed soup; blend in milk. Micro-cook, uncovered, 4 to 5 minutes or till hot, stirring once. Stir in cheese till melted. Makes 4 servings.

Lemony Ham and Rice Soup

- ¼ cup sliced green onion
- 1 tablespoon butter or margarine
- 2 tablespoons all-purpose flour
- 1 10½-ounce can condensed chicken with rice soup
- 1 soup can water (1¼ cups)
- ½ cup finely chopped fully cooked ham
- 1 tablespoon lemon juice
  Nutmeg

In a 1½-quart casserole combine sliced green onion and butter or margarine; micro-cook about 1½ minutes or till tender. Stir in flour. Add chicken with rice soup, 1 soup can water, ham, and lemon juice. Micro-cook, covered, 8 minutes, stirring every 2 minutes. Sprinkle with freshly grated nutmeg. Makes 3 or 4 servings.

Quick Fish Chowder

- 1 16-ounce package frozen fish fillets
- 2 cups frozen hashed brown potatoes with onion and peppers (8 ounces)
- ½ cup chopped onion
- ½ cup water
- 1 10½-ounce can condensed cream of shrimp soup
- 2¾ cups milk
- ¼ cup snipped parsley
- 1 teaspoon salt
- ½ teaspoon dried thyme, crushed
- 2 tablespoons all-purpose flour
  Paprika
  Butter or margarine

Thaw frozen fish fillets (see tip, page 18). Cut fish into bite-size pieces; set aside.

In a 2-quart casserole combine frozen hashed brown potatoes, chopped onion, and water. Micro-cook, covered, 6 to 7 minutes or till vegetables are tender. Do not drain.

Blend condensed cream of shrimp soup into vegetable mixture; stir in fish pieces, 2 cups of the milk, snipped parsley, salt, and crushed thyme. Micro-cook, covered, 6 to 8 minutes or till fish flakes easily with a fork.

Stir the remaining ¾ cup milk into flour; stir into fish mixture. Micro-cook, uncovered, 6 to 8 minutes or till slightly thickened and bubbly, stirring every 2 minutes. Let stand 2 to 3 minutes before serving.

To serve, sprinkle each serving with a dash of paprika and dot with a little butter or margarine. Makes 6 to 8 servings.

Seafood-Corn Chowder

Cheesy Cauliflower Soup

1 small head cauliflower, broken into flowerets and coarsely chopped (12 ounces)
2 tablespoons sliced green onion
2 tablespoons water
1½ cups chicken broth
1 cup milk
½ teaspoon Worcestershire sauce
2 tablespoons all-purpose flour
½ cup shredded American cheese (2 ounces)
Snipped chives *or* parsley

In a 1½-quart casserole combine the chopped cauliflower, green onion, and water. Micro-cook, covered, about 5 minutes or till tender, stirring once; *do not drain*. Stir in the chicken broth, ¾ cup of the milk, and Worcestershire sauce.

Stir the remaining ¼ cup milk into flour; stir into cauliflower mixture. Micro-cook, uncovered, 5 to 6 minutes or till soup is slightly thickened and bubbly, stirring after each minute. Stir in the shredded cheese till melted. Before serving, sprinkle each serving with a little snipped chives or parsley. Makes 4 servings.

homemade croutons

Plain Croutons: Spread 4 cups ½-inch *bread cubes* (about 5 slices bread) in a 12x7½x2-inch baking dish. Micro-cook, uncovered, about 6 to 7 minutes or till crisp and dry, stirring every 2 minutes. Makes 3 cups.

Cheese Croutons: Micro-melt 2 tablespoons *butter* in a 12x7½x2-inch baking dish 30 to 40 seconds. Add 4 cups ½-inch *bread cubes*, stirring to coat. Micro-cook, uncovered, about 2 minutes or till cubes begin to dry. Sprinkle with 2 tablespoons grated *Parmesan cheese;* mix well. Micro-cook, uncovered, about 6 minutes longer or till croutons are crisp, stirring every 2 minutes. Makes 3 cups.

Vegetable-Cream Soup

½ cup chopped celery
¼ cup chopped onion
1 10¾-ounce can condensed cream of mushroom soup
1 10¾-ounce can condensed vegetable soup
1 soup can milk (1¼ cups)
½ cup dairy sour cream

In a 1½-quart casserole combine celery, onion, and 2 tablespoons *water*. Micro-cook, covered, about 5 minutes or till vegetables are tender. Stir in soups, milk, and ¼ teaspoon *salt*. Micro-cook, covered, 6½ to 7 minutes or just till boiling, stirring every 2 minutes. Blend in sour cream; micro-cook, covered, about 30 seconds. Serves 4.

Creamy Hamburger Chowder

4 ounces ground beef
¼ cup finely chopped celery
2 tablespoons finely chopped onion
4 teaspoons all-purpose flour
¼ teaspoon salt
¼ teaspoon dried basil, crushed
1½ cups milk
½ cup shredded American cheese (2 ounces)
Salt
Pepper
1 tablespoon snipped parsley

In a 1½-quart casserole crumble the ground beef. Stir in chopped celery and onion. Micro-cook, covered, about 4 minutes or till meat is brown and vegetables are almost tender, stirring several times to break up meat. Drain off excess fat.

Stir flour, the ¼ teaspoon salt, and basil into meat. Stir in milk. Micro-cook, uncovered, about 5 minutes or till thickened and bubbly, stirring every 2 minutes. Stir in cheese till melted. Season to taste with additional salt and pepper. Before serving, sprinkle each serving with snipped parsley. Makes 2 servings.

French Onion Sauce

When you need an impressive quick-to-cook sauce, you'll find this recipe is sensational —

- 2 **large onions, thinly sliced and separated into rings (3 cups)**
- 2 **tablespoons butter or margarine**
- 2 **tablespoons cold water**
- 2 **tablespoons cornstarch**
- 1 **10½-ounce can condensed beef broth**
- ¼ **teaspoon Worcestershire sauce**
- 2 **tablespoons grated Parmesan cheese**

In a 1-quart casserole micro-cook onion in butter or margarine, covered, about 5 minutes or till onion is tender, stirring after 3 minutes. Stir the cold water into the cornstarch; stir into the cooked onion mixture. Stir in the beef broth and Worcestershire sauce. Micro-cook, uncovered, about 4½ to 5 minutes or till mixture is thickened and bubbly, stirring after each minute. Stir in the cheese. Micro-cook, uncovered, 1 minute longer. Serve the sauce over meat loaf, ground beef patties, or on sliced roast beef atop French bread. Makes 2½ cups.

Medium White Sauce

- 2 **tablespoons butter**
- 2 **tablespoons all-purpose flour**
- ¼ **teaspoon salt**
- 1 **cup milk**

In a 2-cup glass measure micro-melt the butter 30 to 40 seconds. With a rubber scraper stir in flour, salt, and dash *pepper*; stir in milk till well combined. Micro-cook, uncovered, 1 minute; stir. Micro-cook 2 to 3 minutes or till thickened and bubbly, stirring thoroughly every 30 seconds and scraping bottom and sides of cup to remove all lumps. Makes about 1 cup.

Thick White Sauce: Prepare Medium White Sauce as above, *except* increase butter to 3 tablespoons and flour to ¼ cup. Makes 1 cup sauce.

Cheese Sauce: Prepare Medium White Sauce as above, *except* stir in 1 cup shredded *American cheese* till melted. If necessary, micro-cook 30 seconds to melt cheese. Makes 1½ cups.

Easy Chasseur Sauce

- 2 **tablespoons sliced green onion**
- 2 **tablespoons butter**
- 1 **envelope brown gravy mix**
- 1 **tablespoon tomato paste**
- ½ **cup dry red wine**
- 1 **3-ounce can chopped mushrooms, drained**
- ½ **teaspoon dried fines herbes, crushed**

In a medium glass bowl micro-cook green onion in butter about 1½ minutes or till tender. Stir in dry brown gravy mix and tomato paste. Stir in dry red wine, chopped mushrooms, fines herbes, and ¾ cup *water*. Micro-cook, uncovered, 3 minutes or till thickened and bubbly, stirring every minute. Serve with beef. Makes 1¾ cups.

Cranberry-Orange Sauce

- 1 **pound fresh cranberries (4 cups)**
- 2 **cups sugar**
- ½ **cup water**
- 1 **teaspoon finely shredded orange peel**
- ½ **cup orange juice**
- ½ **cup slivered almonds (optional)**

In a 2-quart casserole combine all ingredients except nuts. Micro-cook, covered, about 12 minutes or till berries pop, stirring every 6 minutes, then every 2 minutes. Stir in nuts. Chill in covered container. Makes 4 cups.

Mustard-Cream Sauce

- 2 **tablespoons butter or margarine**
- 3 **tablespoons all-purpose flour**
- 1 **teaspoon prepared mustard**
- ¼ **teaspoon salt**
  Dash white pepper
- ¾ **cup chicken broth**
- ½ **cup light cream or milk**
- 2 **teaspoons snipped chives**
- 1 **teaspoon prepared horseradish**
- 1 **teaspoon lemon juice**

In a 1-quart casserole micro-melt the butter 30 to 40 seconds. Stir in flour, mustard, salt, and white pepper. Gradually stir in chicken broth and light cream or milk.

Micro-cook, uncovered, 1 minute; stir thoroughly. Micro-cook, uncovered, about 2 minutes longer or till sauce is thickened and bubbly, stirring every 30 seconds. Stir in snipped chives, horseradish, and lemon juice. Micro-cook, uncovered, 45 seconds more. Serve with baked fish, green vegetables, or hard-cooked eggs. Makes 1½ cups.

hearty sandwiches

Pizza Joes

If you use bulk Italian sausage for these popular sandwiches, omit the salt and fennel seed —

1 pound ground beef *or* bulk Italian sausage
¼ cup chopped onion
1 8-ounce can pizza sauce
2 tablespoons grated Parmesan cheese
½ teaspoon salt
¼ teaspoon fennel seed
¼ teaspoon garlic powder
6 hard rolls *or* frankfurter buns
6 slices mozzarella cheese (each about 3 inches square)

In a glass bowl crumble meat; add onion. Micro-cook, covered, 5 to 6 minutes or till meat is brown, stirring several times to break up meat. Drain. Stir in pizza sauce, Parmesan cheese, salt, fennel seed, and garlic powder. Micro-cook, uncovered, about 3 minutes or till hot, stirring once.

Split hard rolls or frankfurter buns; divide and spoon hot filling atop bottom half of rolls. Top each with a cheese slice; cover with roll top. Place sandwich on a paper plate. Micro-cook, uncovered, 20 to 25 seconds for 1 roll or till filling is hot and cheese starts to melt. (*Or,* micro-cook 1 minute for 6 rolls, giving plate a half-turn once.) Makes 6.

Spicy Meatball Sandwiches

1 beaten egg
¼ cup milk
1 cup soft bread crumbs (about 1½ slices)
¼ cup finely chopped onion
¾ teaspoon salt
1 pound ground beef
1 clove garlic, minced
1 tablespoon butter *or* margarine
½ cup catsup
⅓ cup chili sauce
2 tablespoons brown sugar
1 tablespoon prepared mustard
1 teaspoon celery seed
1 teaspoon Worcestershire sauce
¼ teaspoon salt
Few drops bottled hot pepper sauce
6 hard rolls *or* frankfurter buns, split and toasted

In a mixing bowl combine beaten egg, milk, bread crumbs, chopped onion, and ¾ teaspoon salt. Add ground beef; mix well. Shape meat mixture into 18 meatballs; arrange in a 10x6x2-inch baking dish. Micro-cook, covered, 9 minutes, turning and rearranging meatballs twice. Drain off fat.

For the sauce, in a 2-cup glass measure micro-cook garlic in butter or margarine 1 minute. Stir in the catsup, chili sauce, brown sugar, mustard, celery seed, Worcestershire sauce, the remaining ¼ teaspoon salt, and hot pepper sauce. Micro-cook, uncovered, about 2½ minutes or till mixture boils, stirring twice. Pour the sauce over meatballs. Micro-cook about 2½ minutes or till sauce bubbles, stirring twice. Serve meatballs with sauce in toasted hard rolls or frankfurter buns. Makes 6 sandwiches.

Chicken Salad in a Roll

2 cups diced cooked chicken *or* turkey
⅔ cup mayonnaise *or* salad dressing
1 3-ounce can chopped mushrooms, drained
⅓ cup grated Parmesan cheese
¼ cup finely chopped celery
2 tablespoons snipped parsley
1 tablespoon lemon juice
¼ teaspoon dried rosemary, crushed
6 hard rolls *or* frankfurter buns

For chicken salad filling, in a 4-cup glass measure combine cooked chicken or turkey, mayonnaise or salad dressing, mushrooms, Parmesan cheese, chopped celery, snipped parsley, lemon juice, and rosemary. Micro-cook the chicken salad filling, uncovered, for 3 minutes, stirring mixture once.

Split 6 hard rolls or frankfurter buns. Divide and spoon the hot filling atop the bottom half of rolls; cover with tops. Wrap each roll in paper toweling. Micro-cook about 30 seconds for 1 roll or till warm. (*Or,* micro-cook 1 minute for 4 to 6 rolls, giving sandwiches a half-turn once.) Makes 6 sandwiches.

Yankee Codfish Rarebit

8 ounces salted cod
   Water
¼ cup butter *or* margarine
3 tablespoons all-purpose flour
½ teaspoon dry mustard
   Dash cayenne
1¼ cups milk
½ teaspoon Worcestershire sauce
1 cup shredded American cheese (4 ounces)
1 beaten egg
6 English muffins, split and toasted
3 tomatoes, sliced (12 slices)
   Parsley (optional)
   Paprika (optional)

Soak cod in water 12 hours, changing water once; drain and rinse thoroughly. In a 1-quart casserole combine the cod and enough water to cover (about 1 cup). Micro-cook, covered, about 4½ minutes or till fish flakes easily. Drain and dice cod.

For the sauce, in the same casserole micro-melt the butter or margarine about 45 seconds. Stir in flour, dry mustard, and cayenne. Stir in milk and Worcestershire sauce. Micro-cook, uncovered, 1 minute; stir. Micro-cook about 2 minutes or till thickened and bubbly, stirring every 30 seconds. Stir in shredded cheese till melted. Gradually stir ½ *cup* of the hot mixture into egg; return to hot mixture. Micro-cook, uncovered, 30 seconds, stirring after 15 seconds. Stir in cod; micro-cook, covered, about 2 minutes or till hot, stirring once. Top the muffin halves with tomatoes. Cover with the sauce. Trim with parsley and paprika, if desired. Makes 6 servings.

Frank Reubens

8 slices pumpernickel *or* rye bread, toasted
½ cup Thousand Island salad dressing
6 frankfurters, split lengthwise
1 8-ounce can sauerkraut, well drained
4 slices Swiss cheese

Spread one side of toast with the salad dressing. Top *each* of 4 toast slices with 3 frank halves, about *2 tablespoons* of the sauerkraut, and 1 cheese slice. Top with the remaining toast slices. Place on paper toweling. Micro-cook, uncovered, about 1 minute for one sandwich or till cheese melts. *Or* micro-cook 2½ minutes for four sandwiches. Makes 4.

Egg Salad Sandwich Pizzas

2 hard-cooked eggs, chopped
¼ cup chopped pepperoni
2 tablespoons chili sauce
2 tablespoons mayonnaise *or* salad dressing
1 tablespoon finely chopped onion
⅛ teaspoon salt
⅛ teaspoon dried basil, crushed
   Dash garlic powder
2 English muffins, split and toasted
¼ cup shredded mozzarella cheese (1 ounce)

In a glass bowl combine chopped eggs, pepperoni, chili sauce, mayonnaise, onion, salt, basil, garlic powder, and dash *pepper*. Micro-cook, uncovered, 1½ to 2 minutes or till heated through, stirring once. Spread mixture on the 4 muffin halves; sprinkle mozzarella cheese atop. Micro-cook, uncovered, 30 to 60 seconds or till cheese melts. Serves 2.

Ham and Pineapple Ring Sandwiches

Shape the ham patties to fit the pineapple rings —

1 beaten egg
¾ cup soft bread crumbs (1 slice)
2 tablespoons finely chopped onion
½ pound ground fully cooked ham
1 8¼-ounce can sliced pineapple, drained
4 hamburger buns, split and toasted
   Butter *or* margarine
   Prepared mustard
4 lettuce leaves

In a mixing bowl combine beaten egg, soft bread crumbs, and onion. Add ham; mix well. Form into 4 patties slightly larger than pineapple rings. Make a hole in the center of each patty. In a 12x7½x2-inch baking dish place ham patties atop the pineapple rings. Micro-cook, covered, about 6 minutes or till meat is done, giving dish a half-turn and turning patties over once.

Spread the toasted hamburger buns with butter or margarine and mustard. Place a ham patty and pineapple ring on the bottom half of each bun; top with a lettuce leaf, then the bun top. Serve at once. Makes 4 sandwiches.

delectable desserts

Apple-Cranberry Crisp

- ¼ cup granulated sugar
- ½ teaspoon cornstarch
- 3 tablespoons cold water
- ⅓ cup fresh cranberries
- 2 tart apples, peeled, cored, and sliced
- Several drops almond extract
- 2 tablespoons quick-cooking rolled oats
- 2 tablespoons brown sugar
- 1 tablespoon all-purpose flour
- Dash ground cinnamon
- 1 tablespoon butter *or* margarine

In a 1-quart casserole mix granulated sugar and cornstarch; gradually stir in cold water. Stir in cranberries. Micro-cook, covered, about 3 minutes or till berries pop, stirring once. Stir in apples and almond extract. Turn the fruit mixture into two 1-cup glass baking dishes.

In a mixing bowl combine rolled oats, brown sugar, flour, and cinnamon. Cut in butter or margarine till crumbly. Sprinkle crumb mixture atop the fruit in baking dishes. Micro-cook, uncovered, about 3½ minutes or till apples are tender, turning the dishes twice. Serve warm. Makes 2 servings.

Graham Cracker Bars

- 2 cups finely crushed graham crackers (29 squares)
- ⅔ cup sugar
- 3 tablespoons butter *or* margarine
- ½ cup semisweet chocolate pieces
- ¼ cup chopped nuts
- 1 5⅓-ounce can (⅔ cup) evaporated milk
- 1 teaspoon vanilla

In a bowl mix crumbs and sugar; cut in butter till mixture resembles cornmeal. Stir in chocolate and nuts. Add milk and vanilla; mix well. Place a small juice glass in center of a greased 8x8x2-inch baking dish; spread batter around glass. Micro-cook, uncovered, about 7 minutes or till top appears dry, giving dish a quarter-turn every 2 minutes. *Loosen edges; remove glass.* Cool. Cut into bars. Makes 24 cookies.

Strawberry-Banana Cobbler

- 3 firm medium bananas
- 1 21-ounce can strawberry pie filling
- 1 tablespoon lemon juice
- ½ teaspoon vanilla
- 9 coconut bar cookies, crumbled (1 cup)
- ¼ cup chopped pecans
- Vanilla ice cream *or* light cream

Peel and slice bananas; place in a 10x6x2-inch baking dish. Mix pie filling, lemon juice, and vanilla; spoon over bananas. Micro-cook, uncovered, 6 minutes, turning dish every 2 minutes. Mix cookies and pecans; sprinkle over fruit. Micro-cook, uncovered, 1 minute. Serve warm with ice cream or light cream. Makes 6 servings.

Granola Brown Betty

- 7 or 8 tart medium apples, peeled, cored, and sliced
- ⅓ cup apple juice
- ¼ cup raisins
- ¼ cup honey
- 4 teaspoons all-purpose flour
- ½ teaspoon ground cinnamon
- 1 cup granola cereal
- Light cream

Combine apples, apple juice, raisins, honey, flour, and ground cinnamon. Turn mixture into a 10x6x2-inch baking dish. Micro-cook, covered, 12 minutes, turning dish every 2 minutes. Top with granola cereal. Micro-cook, uncovered, 1 minute. Serve with light cream. Serves 4 to 6.

Chocolate-Swirled Pudding

- ¾ cup sugar
- 2 tablespoons cornstarch
- 2 cups milk
- 1 beaten egg
- 2 tablespoons butter
- 1 teaspoon vanilla
- 4 teaspoons fudge topping
- 4 teaspoons peanut butter (optional)
- 2 tablespoons chopped peanuts

In a 4-cup glass measure mix sugar, cornstarch, and ¼ teaspoon *salt;* slowly stir in milk. Micro-cook, uncovered, 3 minutes; stir. Micro-cook for 2 to 2½ minutes or till thickened and bubbly, stirring after each minute. Stir a moderate amount of hot mixture into egg; return to hot mixture. Micro-cook, uncovered, about 1 minute or till bubbly. Stir in butter and vanilla. Spoon into individual dessert dishes. Top *each* with *1 teaspoon* fudge topping and *1 teaspoon* peanut butter, if desired; swirl with knife. Top with nuts. Chill. Serves 4.

Rhubarb Crisp

A springtime favorite topped with ice cream —

- 3 cups rhubarb cut into ½-inch pieces (1 pound)
- ¼ to ⅓ cup packed brown sugar
- 1 tablespoon cornstarch
- ⅔ cup water
- 1 teaspoon vanilla
- ½ teaspoon finely shredded lemon peel
- ⅓ cup all-purpose flour
- ¼ cup packed brown sugar
- ½ teaspoon ground cinnamon
- 2 tablespoons butter *or* margarine
  Vanilla ice cream

Place rhubarb in an 8x1½-inch round baking dish; set aside. In a 2-cup glass measure combine ¼ to ⅓ cup packed brown sugar and cornstarch; stir in water till mixed. Micro-cook, uncovered, 2 to 3 minutes or till mixture is thickened and bubbly, stirring after each minute. Stir in vanilla and lemon peel. Pour sauce over rhubarb in baking dish; stir lightly.

In a small bowl combine all-purpose flour, ¼ cup packed brown sugar, and ground cinnamon. Cut in butter or margarine till crumbly; sprinkle over rhubarb mixture. Micro-cook, uncovered, about 10 minutes or till rhubarb is tender, turning dish once. Serve warm with vanilla ice cream. Makes 4 servings.

Fruity Tapioca

- 1 8¾-ounce can peach slices
  Milk
- 1 3¼-ounce package *regular* orange tapioca pudding mix
- 1 tablespoon lemon juice
- ½ cup tiny marshmallows
- 2 tablespoons sliced maraschino cherries

Drain peaches; reserve syrup; set 4 slices aside for garnish. Dice remaining peaches. Add milk to reserved syrup to equal 2 cups. In a 4-cup glass measure combine the dry pudding mix with the milk mixture. Stir till pudding mix is dissolved. Micro-cook, uncovered, 3 minutes; stir. Micro-cook, uncovered, 3 to 4 minutes more or till thickened and bubbly, stirring every 30 seconds. Stir in lemon juice; cool 45 minutes.

Fold diced peaches, marshmallows, and maraschino cherries into pudding; chill. Spoon pudding into sherbet dishes; garnish with reserved peach slices. Serves 4.

Spicy Fruit Trio

- 1 8¾-ounce can unpeeled apricot halves
- 4 whole cloves
- 4 inches stick cinnamon
- 2 oranges, peeled and sectioned
- 1 cup sliced fresh strawberries

Drain apricot halves, reserving syrup; cut up apricots. In a 1-quart casserole combine reserved apricot syrup, cloves, cinnamon, and ¼ cup *water*. Micro-cook, covered, for 3 minutes; mixture will boil. Stir in apricots; micro-cook, covered, 2 minutes more. Let stand, covered, 20 to 30 minutes, or chill.

Remove spices; discard. Stir in oranges and strawberries. Spoon into sherbet dishes. Serves 4.

Apple-Gingerbread Cobbler

- 4 medium apples, peeled, cored, and sliced (4 cups)
- 1 cup water
- ¼ cup packed brown sugar
- 1 tablespoon lemon juice
- ¼ teaspoon ground cinnamon
- 1 tablespoon cold water
- 2 teaspoons cornstarch
- 1 14-ounce package gingerbread mix
  Whipped cream

In a 1½-quart casserole combine apples, 1 cup water, brown sugar, lemon juice, and cinnamon. Micro-cook, covered, about 6½ to 7 minutes or till apples are tender, stirring once.

Stir 1 tablespoon cold water into cornstarch; stir into apple mixture. Micro-cook, uncovered, 1½ minutes or till thickened and bubbly, stirring twice. Turn into a 12x7½x2-inch baking dish. Prepare gingerbread mix following package directions. Pour 1 cup* of the batter evenly over apple mixture. Micro-cook, uncovered, about 5 minutes or till wooden pick comes out clean, giving dish a half-turn after 2½ minutes. Serve warm with whipped cream. Makes 8 servings.

*Note: To bake remaining batter, half-fill (about 3 tablespoons) 6-ounce custard cups lined with paper bake cups. Micro-cook four at a time, uncovered, 1½ to 2 minutes or till done, rearranging cups once. Makes 8 cupcakes.

Graham Cracker-Prune Pudding

- ½ cup packed brown sugar
- 1 tablespoon cornstarch
  Dash salt
- ½ cup water
- 2 tablespoons light corn syrup
- 2 tablespoons butter *or* margarine
- ½ cup snipped pitted dried prunes
- 3 tablespoons granulated sugar
- 2 tablespoons shortening
- ½ teaspoon vanilla
- 1 egg yolk
- ¼ cup chopped walnuts
- 1 cup finely crushed graham crackers (14 square crackers)
- ½ teaspoon baking powder
- ⅓ cup milk
- 1 stiff-beaten egg white

For sauce, in a 4-cup glass measure combine brown sugar, cornstarch, and salt; mix well. Stir in water and light corn syrup. Micro-cook, uncovered, 3 to 4 minutes or till thickened and bubbly; stir after each minute. Micro-cook 1 minute more. Stir in butter or margarine. Cool 30 minutes without stirring.

Meanwhile, in a 4-cup glass measure micro-cook 1 cup *water* about 3½ minutes or till boiling. Stir in prunes; let stand till cool. Drain.

In small mixing bowl cream granulated sugar with shortening and vanilla. Add yolk; beat well. Stir in prunes and nuts. Mix crumbs with baking powder and ⅛ teaspoon *salt*. Add to creamed mixture alternately with milk. Fold in egg white. Divide among 4 greased 6-ounce custard cups. Arrange cups in oven, leaving space between cups. Micro-cook, uncovered, about 4 minutes or till done, rearranging twice. Serve warm with the sauce. Serves 4.

Apple Spice Cake

- ½ cup packed brown sugar
- ¼ cup butter, softened
- 1 egg
- 1 cup all-purpose flour
- 1 teaspoon baking powder
- ½ teaspoon ground cinnamon
- ¼ teaspoon ground ginger
- ¼ teaspoon ground cloves
- ½ cup milk
- 2 tart medium apples, peeled, cored, and thinly sliced
  Crumb Topping

Thoroughly stir sugar and butter together. Add egg; beat well. Stir together flour, baking powder, spices, and ¼ teaspoon *salt*. Add to creamed mixture alternately with milk; beat after each addition. Spread in a greased and floured 8x1½-inch round baking dish. Arrange apples over batter; sprinkle with Crumb Topping. Micro-cook, uncovered, about 7 minutes, giving dish a quarter-turn every 2 minutes. Serve warm or cool. Cut into wedges; top with whipped cream, if desired.

Crumb Topping: Mix ¼ cup packed *brown sugar*, ¼ cup all-purpose *flour*, and ½ teaspoon *ground cinnamon*. Cut in 2 tablespoons *butter or margarine* till mixture resembles coarse crumbs.

Raisin-Filled Apples

- ⅓ cup raisins
- ¼ cup packed brown sugar
- 2 tablespoons chopped walnuts
- ¼ teaspoon ground cinnamon
- 4 large baking apples, cored

Mix the first 4 ingredients. Peel off a strip around top of apples. Place apples in a 10x6x2-inch baking dish; fill centers with nut mixture. Micro-cook, covered, 5 to 6 minutes or till tender; give dish a half-turn twice. Let stand 15 minutes before serving. Serves 4.

Golden Fruit Compote

- 1 15½-ounce can pineapple chunks
- 3 tablespoons butter *or* margarine
- ¼ cup orange liqueur
- 2 tablespoons brown sugar
- ⅛ teaspoon ground cinnamon
- 1 16-ounce can peach slices
- 1 11-ounce can mandarin orange sections
- 1 medium banana, sliced

Drain pineapple, reserving ⅓ cup syrup. In a 10x6x2-inch baking dish micro-melt butter or margarine 35 to 40 seconds. Stir in reserved syrup, orange liqueur, brown sugar, and cinnamon. Drain peach slices and mandarin orange sections; stir fruits into the butter mixture with pineapple. Micro-cook, uncovered, about 5 minutes, stirring every 2 minutes. Stir in sliced banana; micro-cook 1 minute. Makes 6 servings.

Rice Pudding

- 3 beaten eggs
- 2 cups milk
- ⅓ cup sugar
- 1 teaspoon vanilla
- ½ teaspoon salt
- 2 cups cooked rice
- ⅓ cup raisins
  Ground cinnamon
  Light cream

In a 2-quart casserole combine eggs, milk, sugar, vanilla, and salt. Add rice and raisins; mix well. Micro-cook, uncovered, 8 to 10 minutes or just till thickened, stirring every 1½ to 2 minutes. Sprinkle with cinnamon. Let stand 30 minutes without stirring. Serve warm or chilled with light cream. Makes 6 to 8 servings.

Cherry-Brownie Pudding Cake

- 2 tablespoons butter
- 1 21-ounce can cherry pie filling
- 2 tablespoons lemon juice
- 1 cup sugar
- ¼ cup butter, softened
- 2 egg yolks
- ½ teaspoon vanilla
- 2 1-ounce squares unsweetened chocolate, melted and cooled*
- ¼ cup milk
- 1 cup all-purpose flour
- ½ teaspoon baking powder
- ½ teaspoon salt
- 2 stiff-beaten egg whites
- ⅓ cup chopped walnuts

In a 4-cup glass measure micro-melt 2 tablespoons butter 30 to 40 seconds; stir in pie filling, lemon juice, and ⅓ cup *water*. Spread in a 12x7½x2-inch baking dish; set aside.

Thoroughly beat together sugar and ¼ cup butter. Add yolks and vanilla; beat till fluffy. Stir in chocolate and milk. Mix flour, baking powder, and salt. Add to chocolate mixture; mix well. Fold in whites and nuts. Carefully spoon batter over cherry mixture. Micro-cook, uncovered, about 13 minutes or till wooden pick inserted in center comes out clean, giving dish a half-turn every 3 minutes. Serve warm with vanilla ice cream, if desired. Serves 8 to 10. *See tip at right for melting chocolate.

melting chocolate the easy way

Save messy cleanup by melting chocolate squares in their own paper wrappers. Place unwrapped squares, with folded side of wrapper up, in microwave oven. (Place in dish, if desired.) Micro-melt 2 minutes for 1 square, or 2½ to 3 minutes for 2 squares. Lift wrappers by folded ends.

Nesselrode Custard

- 2 coconut macaroon cookies, crumbled (⅓ cup)
- 2 tablespoons chopped mixed candied fruits and peels
- 2 tablespoons chopped raisins
- 1 beaten egg
- ⅔ cup milk
- 2 tablespoons sugar
- ¼ teaspoon rum flavoring

Pour 2 cups *water* into an 8x8x2-inch baking dish. Micro-cook, uncovered, 4 to 4½ minutes or till hot. Meanwhile, combine first 3 ingredients; divide mixture and press lightly into two 6-ounce custard cups. Mix egg, milk, sugar, flavoring, and dash *salt*; pour into prepared cups. Set cups in hot water in baking dish. Micro-cook, uncovered, about 7 minutes or till almost set, giving dish a quarter-turn after each minute. Remove cups from water; let stand at least 15 minutes before serving. Serves 2.

Citrus Pudding Cake

- 2 tablespoons butter *or* margarine
- ¾ cup sugar
- 1 beaten egg
- 1 cup all-purpose flour
- 1 teaspoon baking powder
- ½ teaspoon salt
- ⅔ cup water
- 1 cup water
- ½ cup orange juice
- ¾ cup sugar
- 3 tablespoons butter *or* margarine
- 1 teaspoon finely shredded lemon peel
- 3 tablespoons lemon juice

In a 2-quart glass mixing bowl micro-melt the 2 tablespoons butter 30 to 40 seconds. Stir in the ¾ cup sugar; add egg. Mix well. Stir together flour, baking powder, and salt. Add to sugar mixture; stir till smooth. Stir in the ⅔ cup water. Pour into an ungreased 8x8x2-inch baking dish, spreading evenly; set aside.

In a 4-cup glass measure micro-cook 1 cup water and orange juice 4 to 4½ minutes or till boiling. Add the remaining ¾ cup sugar and 3 tablespoons butter; stir till butter melts. Stir in lemon peel and lemon juice. Carefully pour over cake batter. Micro-cook, uncovered, about 9 minutes or till wooden pick inserted in center comes out clean, giving dish a quarter-turn every 3 minutes. Serve warm. Serves 6.

Banana-Raspberry Flambé

Cinnamon-Baked Pears

- ¼ cup red cinnamon candies
- 1 cup apple cider *or* apple juice
- 2 ripe large pears Whipped cream cheese
- 1 tablespoon chopped walnuts

In an 8-inch glass pie plate micro-melt candies in cider about 5 minutes. Peel, halve, and core pears; place, cut side down, in syrup. Micro-cook, covered, about 6 minutes or till tender, giving dish a quarter-turn every 2 minutes. Chill. To serve, spoon pears, cut side up, with syrup into dishes. Top *each* with a dollop of cheese and sprinkle with nuts. Serves 4.

Apple-Rice Pudding

- 1 cup apple cider *or* apple juice
- ¾ cup chopped apple (peeled, if desired)
- 1 tablespoon butter *or* margarine
- 1 tablespoon sugar
- ¼ teaspoon salt Dash ground cinnamon
- ⅔ cup Minute Rice
- 1 cup frozen whipped dessert topping, thawed Ground nutmeg

In a 1½-quart casserole combine apple cider or apple juice, chopped apple, butter, sugar, salt, and ground cinnamon. Micro-cook, covered, about 3½ minutes or till mixture bubbles. Stir in rice. Cover and let stand for 5 minutes to absorb liquid; fluff mixture with a fork. Place in the refrigerator to chill.

Just before serving, fold in whipped dessert topping. Spoon into dessert dishes. Sprinkle with ground nutmeg. Makes 4 servings.

Hot Fudge-Rum-Pecan Sundaes

- ½ cup semisweet chocolate pieces
- 2 tablespoons milk
- ½ cup tiny marshmallows
- 2 tablespoons light rum Vanilla ice cream Pecan halves, toasted*

For sauce, in a 2-cup glass measure combine the chocolate pieces and milk. Micro-cook, uncovered, about 2 minutes or till chocolate is melted, stirring once. Stir in the marshmallows and light rum.

To serve, scoop vanilla ice cream into sherbet dishes. Top with some hot fudge sauce, then sprinkle with a few toasted pecan halves (*see tip, page 34, for toasting). Makes ¾ cup sauce.

Banana-Raspberry Flambé

Don't overheat the liqueur — heat just till warm enough to flame —

- 1 **10-ounce package frozen red raspberries, thawed**
- 2 **tablespoons granulated sugar**
- 2 **tablespoons butter *or* margarine**
- 1 **tablespoon brown sugar**
- 4 **medium bananas, sliced (1 to 1¼ pounds)**
- 3 **tablespoons orange liqueur Vanilla ice cream**

In blender container place raspberries and granulated sugar; cover and blend till smooth. Sieve to remove seeds; set aside.

In a 12x7½x2-inch baking dish micro-melt the butter 30 to 40 seconds. Stir in brown sugar till dissolved; stir in raspberry mixture and bananas, stirring to coat all slices. Micro-cook, covered, about 3½ minutes or till heated through and bananas are cooked, stirring twice.

Add liqueur and micro-cook 30 seconds more. (Or, micro-heat liqueur in a 1-cup glass measure 30 seconds, being careful not to overheat. Transfer liqueur to ladle. Carefully flame; pour over fruit.) Serve over ice cream. Makes 2½ cups.

---

jiffy ice cream toppers

Make hot fudge or butterscotch sundaes in a jiffy simply by heating the glass jar of topping, uncovered, in the microwave oven till topping is warm. Serve at once.

Peanut Butter S'Mores

- 2 **graham cracker squares**
- 2 **teaspoons peanut butter**
- 9 **semisweet chocolate pieces**
- 6 **tiny *or* 1 large marshmallow**

For 1 s'more, spread *1* of the graham cracker squares with peanut butter. Top with chocolate pieces and marshmallows. Cover with the remaining graham cracker square; wrap loosely in paper toweling. Micro-cook about 1 minute or till chocolate and marshmallows melt. Makes 1.

Scotch Crunchies

- 1 **6-ounce package butterscotch pieces**
- 1 **6-ounce package semisweet chocolate pieces *or* imitation chocolate-flavored pieces**
- 1 **3-ounce can chow mein noodles**
- 1 **cup tiny marshmallows**

In a large glass bowl place butterscotch and chocolate pieces. Micro-cook, uncovered, about 2½ minutes or till melted, stirring after each minute. Stir in noodles and marshmallows. Drop by a teaspoon onto waxed paper. Chill, if desired. Makes about 36.

Easy Opera Fudge

- ½ **cup butter *or* margarine**
- 2 **3- or 3¼-ounce packages *regular* vanilla pudding mix**
- ½ **cup milk**
- ½ **teaspoon vanilla**
- 1 **16-ounce package sifted powdered sugar (about 4¾ cups)**
- ⅓ **cup nuts *or* candied cherries, chopped**

In a 2-quart glass bowl micro-melt the butter about 1 minute. Stir in dry pudding mix and milk. Micro-cook, uncovered, about 3 minutes or till boiling, stirring occasionally. Micro-cook 1 minute more, stirring every 15 seconds. Add vanilla. Beat in sugar; stir in nuts or cherries. Pour into a buttered 10x6x2-inch baking dish. Top with nut halves, if desired. Chill; cut into 1-inch squares. Store in refrigerator. Makes 2 pounds.

Smoothie Chocolate Fudge

- 1 **6-ounce package semisweet chocolate pieces**
- ½ **cup *sweetened condensed* milk**
- 1 **cup sifted powdered sugar**
- ½ **teaspoon vanilla Dash salt**
- ⅓ **cup chopped walnuts**

In a 1-quart glass bowl combine chocolate and milk. Micro-cook, covered, about 1 minute or till chocolate melts, stirring once. Stir in sugar, vanilla, and salt. Fold in the nuts. Turn into a waxed paper-lined 8½x4½x2½-inch loaf pan. Let stand till set. Turn out; cut into pieces. Makes about 1 pound.

microwave plus the range

Cinnamon-Nut Ring

1 loaf frozen white bread dough (1 pound)
2 tablespoons butter, melted
⅓ cup packed brown sugar
¼ cup chopped walnuts
1 teaspoon ground cinnamon
Confectioners' Icing
Walnut halves

In a 4-cup glass measure micro-cook 3 cups *water* for 7 to 8 minutes or till boiling. Place loaf of frozen bread dough in a greased 9-inch glass pie plate. Place pie plate in oven along with the measuring cup of water. Micro-cook, uncovered, 30 seconds. Let bread and water stand in oven 20 minutes with power off. Repeat cooking and standing step two times or until bread is thawed.

Roll thawed dough on a lightly floured surface into a 13x9-inch rectangle; spread with melted butter. Combine brown sugar, chopped walnuts, and cinnamon; sprinkle over dough. Roll up jelly roll-style, starting at long side; seal seam. Form into ring with seam side down in the greased 9-inch pie plate; seal ends together. Place in microwave oven with measuring cup of hot water. Micro-cook 30 seconds. Let stand in oven 20 minutes with power off. Repeat once more till ring is almost double.

In Conventional Oven: Bake in 375° oven about 20 minutes or till done. Remove from pie plate. Cool. Drizzle Confectioners' Icing over top. Trim with walnut halves. Makes 1 coffee cake.

Confectioners' Icing: Combine ½ cup sifted *powdered sugar*, 1 teaspoon *light corn syrup*, ¼ teaspoon *vanilla*, and enough *milk* to make of drizzling consistency (about 1 tablespoon).

cooking tip

Team the microwave oven with the range — the oven, surface units, or broiler — for a winning cooking combination. Prepare part of the recipe by microwave and use conventional heat for tasks such as baking breads, cooking pasta, frying in fat, preparing crepes, and browning.

Ham Medley

2 cups medium noodles
¾ cup chopped celery
½ cup chopped onion
¼ cup chopped green pepper
3 tablespoons butter
3 tablespoons all-purpose flour
½ teaspoon dried dillweed
1 cup milk
1 cup cream-style cottage cheese
2 cups cubed fully cooked ham
2 tablespoons butter
⅓ cup fine dry bread crumbs

On Range Top: In saucepan cook noodles in boiling salted water following package directions; drain.

In a 2-quart casserole combine celery and next 3 ingredients. Micro-cook, covered, 3 minutes or till tender. Stir in flour, dillweed, ¼ teaspoon *salt*, and ⅛ teaspoon *pepper*. Stir in milk and cheese. Micro-cook, uncovered, 4 to 4½ minutes or till thickened and bubbly, stirring after each minute. Stir in noodles and ham. Micro-cook, uncovered, about 6 minutes or till hot, stirring twice. Let stand 5 minutes.

In a 1-cup glass measure micro-melt 2 tablespoons butter 30 to 40 seconds; stir in crumbs. Sprinkle atop casserole. Serves 6.

Beefy Spaghetti

12 ounces spaghetti
1 pound ground beef
½ cup finely chopped onion
1 clove garlic, minced
1 16-ounce can tomatoes, cut up
1 6-ounce can tomato paste
1 6-ounce can chopped mushrooms
¼ cup snipped parsley
1 tablespoon brown sugar
1 teaspoon dried oregano, crushed
¾ teaspoon salt
Few dashes bottled hot pepper sauce
Grated Parmesan cheese

On Range Top: In large saucepan cook spaghetti in large amount of boiling salted water till tender. Drain and keep hot.

Meanwhile, in a 2-quart casserole crumble ground beef; add onion and garlic. Micro-cook, covered, about 5 minutes or till onion is tender and meat is brown, stirring several times to break up meat. Drain off excess fat. Stir in *undrained* tomatoes, tomato paste, mushrooms with liquid, parsley, brown sugar, and seasonings.

Micro-cook, uncovered, about 10 minutes or till sauce is of desired consistency. Serve over hot spaghetti. Pass cheese. Serves 6.

Enchilada Casserole

Enchilada Casserole

- 12 **corn tortillas**
  Cooking oil
- 3 **tablespoons all-purpose flour**
- ½ **teaspoon salt**
- ¼ **teaspoon paprika**
- 1½ **cups milk**
- 1 **10-ounce can mild enchilada sauce**
- 1 **cup shredded cheddar cheese**
- ½ **cup sliced pitted ripe olives**
- ¾ **pound ground beef**
- ½ **cup chopped onion**
- 1 **10½-ounce can jalapeño bean dip**
- ½ **teaspoon salt**
- ⅛ **teaspoon pepper**
- 1 **large tomato, chopped (¾ cup)**

On Range Top: In medium skillet dip tortillas, one at a time, in small amount of hot cooking oil 5 to 10 seconds for each or just till limp but not crisp. Drain on paper toweling.

In a 4-cup glass measure combine flour, the ½ teaspoon salt, and paprika. Stir in milk and enchilada sauce till blended. Micro-cook, uncovered, 2 minutes; stir. Micro-cook about 4 to 5 minutes or till bubbly, stirring after each minute. Stir in cheese and olives till cheese melts; set sauce aside.

In glass bowl crumble beef; add onion. Micro-cook, covered, about 5 minutes or till meat is brown, stirring several times to break up meat. Drain off fat. Stir in bean dip, the remaining ½ teaspoon salt, and pepper; mix well. On each tortilla place about ⅓ *cup* of the meat mixture and 1 *tablespoon* of the tomato; roll up tightly. Place seam side down in a 12x7½x2-inch baking dish. Pour cheese sauce over; micro-cook, uncovered, 10 minutes or till hot, giving dish a half-turn every 4 minutes. Makes 4 servings.

warm breads in a jiffy

It takes less than a minute to warm dinner rolls. Place rolls in a paper napkin-lined basket or plate. (The napkin absorbs excess moisture.) For one or two rolls, test after 15 seconds of micro-cooking. Do not overcook, since breads become tough when micro-cooked too long. Increase time slightly for additional rolls. Serve the heated rolls at once.

Chinese Beef

1 pound beef round steak
2 tablespoons cooking oil
2 teaspoons instant beef bouillon
   granules
1 small head cauliflower, broken
   into flowerets (3 cups)
¼ cup chopped onion
3 tablespoons soy sauce
1 clove garlic, minced
3 tablespoons cornstarch
1 6-ounce package frozen
   pea pods
   Chow mein noodles

Partially freeze beef; slice thinly across the grain into bite-size strips.

On Range Top: In skillet quickly brown *half* of the meat at a time in hot oil; set aside.

In a 2-quart casserole dissolve bouillon granules in 1½ cups *hot water*. Stir in cauliflower, onion, soy sauce, garlic, and browned beef. Micro-cook, covered, 5 minutes, stirring once. Stir ¼ cup *cold water* into cornstarch; stir into casserole. Micro-cook, covered, 3 minutes, stirring after each minute. Meanwhile, pour hot tap water over pea pods to thaw; drain. Stir pea pods into casserole. Micro-cook, covered, 2½ minutes, stirring once. Serve over chow mein noodles. Serves 6.

Chicken and Broccoli Crepes

   Basic Main-Dish Crepes (see
      recipe, page 204)
1 10-ounce package frozen
   chopped broccoli
2 tablespoons water
2 cups finely chopped cooked
   chicken
¼ cup shredded American
   cheese
2 tablespoons pimiento
2 10¾-ounce cans condensed
   cream of mushroom soup
½ cup shredded American
   cheese
¼ cup milk

On Range Top: Prepare and cook Basic Main-Dish Crepes.

Place frozen broccoli and water in a 12x7½x2-inch baking dish. Micro-cook, covered, 7 to 8 minutes or till done, stirring once. Drain.

In bowl combine cooked broccoli, cooked chicken, the ¼ cup American cheese, and pimiento. Spoon ¾ *cup* of the condensed cream of mushroom soup into the broccoli mixture; mix well. Spoon ¼ *cup* of the filling down the center of unbrowned side of *each* crepe. Roll up jelly roll-style. Place, seam side down, in a 12x7½x2-inch baking dish. (Form two layers to prevent crowding.) Micro-cook, covered, about 12 minutes or till hot, turning dish twice.

In a 4-cup glass measure mix the remaining soup, the remaining ½ cup American cheese, and milk. Micro-cook, uncovered, 5 minutes or till bubbly, stirring 4 times. Pour 1½ cups of the sauce over crepes. Pass remaining. Serves 8.

Cherry Crepes

   Basic Main-Dish Crepes (see
      recipe, page 204)
1 cup yogurt
¾ cup sugar
½ teaspoon ground cinnamon
2 tablespoons cornstarch
2 cups cranberry juice cocktail
1 16-ounce can pitted tart red
   cherries, drained
½ teaspoon finely shredded
   lemon peel
¼ teaspoon vanilla
   Few drops red food coloring

On Range Top: Prepare and cook Basic Main-Dish Crepes.

Combine yogurt, ½ cup of the sugar, and cinnamon; spread on unbrowned sides of crepes. Roll up jelly roll-style. Place in a 12x7½x2-inch baking dish. (Form two layers to prevent crowding.) In a 4-cup glass measure combine remaining sugar and cornstarch. Stir in cranberry juice, cherries, and remaining ingredients. Micro-cook, uncovered, 5 to 7 minutes or till thickened and bubbly, stirring after each minute. Spoon over crepes in dish. Micro-cook, covered, about 4 minutes or till crepes are hot, turning dish once. Serves 6 to 8.

Cherry Crepes

Creole-Style Chicken

- ⅔ **cup long grain rice**
- 2 **slices bacon**
- ¼ **cup chopped onion**
- 1 **small clove garlic, minced**
- 1 **16-ounce can tomatoes, cut up**
- 2 **cups cubed cooked chicken**
- ¼ **cup coarsely chopped green pepper**
- 1 **teaspoon instant beef bouillon granules**
  Few dashes bottled hot pepper sauce
- 1 **tablespoon cornstarch**

On Range Top: In saucepan cook rice following package directions. Drain; keep hot.

In a 1½-quart casserole place bacon; cover with paper toweling. Micro-cook 2 to 2½ minutes or till crisp. Drain bacon, leaving drippings in casserole. Crumble the bacon; set aside.

In reserved drippings micro-cook onion and garlic, uncovered, about 2 minutes or till tender. Stir in *undrained* tomatoes, next 4 ingredients, and ¼ teaspoon *salt*. Micro-cook, covered, 5 to 6 minutes or till bubbly, stirring twice. Stir 1 tablespoon *cold water* into cornstarch; stir into hot mixture. Micro-cook, covered, 3 to 4 minutes or till bubbly, stirring after each minute. Micro-cook 1 minute more. Sprinkle with bacon. Serve over the hot, cooked rice. Serves 4.

Egg and Potato Casserole

- 4 **eggs**
- 4 **medium potatoes, peeled and quartered (1¼ pounds)**
- ¼ **cup chopped onion**
- 2 **tablespoons butter**
- 3 **tablespoons all-purpose flour**
- 1 **8-ounce can imitation sour cream**
- ¾ **cup shredded American cheese**
- ½ **cup milk**
- ⅛ **teaspoon paprika**
- 2 **tomatoes, peeled and thinly sliced**
- ¾ **cup soft bread crumbs**
- ¼ **teaspoon paprika**

On Range Top: In saucepan cover eggs with cold water. Cover; bring to boiling. Reduce heat; simmer 15 to 20 minutes. Cool in cold water. Peel and slice.

In a 1½-quart casserole cover potatoes with water. Micro-cook, covered, 12 to 15 minutes or till potatoes are tender. Drain, slice, and set potatoes aside.

In a glass bowl micro-cook onion in *1 tablespoon* of the butter about 1½ minutes or till tender. Stir in flour; stir in sour cream, shredded cheese, milk, the ⅛ teaspoon paprika, ½ teaspoon *salt*, and ⅛ teaspoon *pepper*. Micro-cook, uncovered, about 1½ minutes or till cheese melts, stirring once. Combine sauce and potatoes.

In same 1½-quart casserole layer *half* of the potato mixture. Top with egg slices and tomato slices. Spoon remaining potato mixture atop. Micro-melt 1 tablespoon butter 30 to 40 seconds; stir in crumbs and the ¼ teaspoon paprika. Sprinkle crumbs atop casserole.

Micro-cook, uncovered, about 7 minutes or till heated through, turning dish twice. Let stand 3 to 5 minutes before serving. Serves 4.

Spanish Chicken and Rice

- 6 **chicken thighs (1½ pounds)**
- 2 **tablespoons cooking oil**
  Paprika
- ¾ **pound ground beef**
- ½ **teaspoon salt**
  Dash pepper
- 1 **10-ounce package frozen peas**
- 1 **16-ounce can tomatoes, cut up**
- 1 **6-ounce package Minute Spanish Rice Mix**
- ¼ **cup sliced pitted ripe olives**

On Range Top: In skillet brown chicken in hot oil. Sprinkle with a little salt, pepper, and paprika; set aside. Meanwhile, combine ground beef, the ½ teaspoon salt, and dash pepper; shape into 18 tiny meatballs. Lightly brown meatballs in same skillet; set aside. Pour boiling water over peas to thaw.

In bowl combine peas, tomatoes, rice mix, olives, and 1 cup *water*. Arrange meatballs in an 8x8x2-inch baking dish. Pour rice mixture over meatballs. Arrange chicken pieces atop rice. Micro-cook, covered, about 20 minutes or till rice and chicken are done, giving dish a quarter-turn every 5 minutes. Makes 6 servings.

Sausage-Sauced Cabbage

1 medium head cabbage, cut into 6 wedges (1 pound)
½ pound bulk Italian pork sausage
½ cup chopped onion
½ cup chopped green pepper
1 8-ounce can tomato sauce
1 8-ounce can tomatoes, cut up
1 tablespoon snipped parsley
2 teaspoons sugar
½ teaspoon salt
½ teaspoon dried oregano, crushed

On Range Top: Cook cabbage, covered, in a 10-inch skillet in a small amount of boiling salted water 10 to 12 minutes or till tender.

Meanwhile, in a glass bowl crumble sausage; add onion and green pepper. Micro-cook, covered, about 5 minutes or till meat is brown, stirring several times to break up meat. Drain off excess fat. Stir in remaining ingredients. Micro-cook, covered, about 3 minutes or till heated through, stirring once. Drain cabbage well. Arrange cabbage wedges on serving plate. Pour some sauce over cabbage. Pass remaining sauce. Makes 6 servings.

Meatball Carbonade

12 ounces noodles
2 slices bacon
1 beaten egg
1 cup beef broth
⅓ cup fine dry bread crumbs
½ teaspoon Worcestershire sauce
1 pound ground beef
2 medium onions, thinly sliced
2 tablespoons butter
2 tablespoons all-purpose flour
½ cup beer
1 teaspoon brown sugar
1 teaspoon vinegar
1 teaspoon beef-flavored gravy base
½ teaspoon dried thyme, crushed

On Range Top: In saucepan cook noodles in boiling salted water following package directions. Drain; keep hot.

Place bacon between layers of paper toweling. Micro-cook 1¾ minutes or till crisp; crumble and set aside. Combine egg, 3 *tablespoons* of the beef broth, bread crumbs, Worcestershire, ¾ teaspoon *salt*, and dash *pepper*. Add beef; mix well. Shape into 34 meatballs. Place in a 12x7½x2-inch glass baking dish. Micro-cook, covered, 5 minutes, rearranging meatballs twice. Discard fat; set aside.

In a 1½-quart casserole combine onion and butter. Micro-cook, covered, about 6 minutes or till onion is tender, stirring every 2 minutes. Stir in flour. Stir in remaining beef broth, beer, brown sugar, vinegar, gravy base, thyme, ¼ teaspoon *salt*, and dash *pepper*. Micro-cook, uncovered, 5 minutes or till mixture thickens and bubbles, stirring 3 times. Stir in meatballs. Micro-cook, covered, 5 to 6 minutes or till meatballs are done, stirring once. Top with bacon and parsley, if desired. Let stand several minutes before serving. Serve with noodles. Serves 4 to 6.

Tuna-Noodle Casserole

Frozen noodles make this casserole extra-fast —

6 cups water
1 8-ounce package frozen noodles
1 cup chopped celery
¼ cup chopped onion
2 tablespoons butter *or* margarine
2 tablespoons all-purpose flour
1 11-ounce can condensed cheddar cheese soup
¾ cup milk
1 9¼-ounce can tuna, drained and flaked
1 2-ounce jar sliced pimiento, drained and chopped
¼ cup grated Parmesan cheese
¼ cup sliced pitted ripe olives

On Range Top: In saucepan bring water to boiling. Add frozen noodles, stirring till separated. Boil rapidly 15 to 20 minutes or till tender. Drain; set aside.

Meanwhile, in a 1½-quart casserole micro-cook chopped celery and onion in butter or margarine, covered, 3½ to 4 minutes or till vegetables are tender, stirring twice. Stir in flour. Stir cheese soup and milk into mixture in casserole.

Micro-cook, uncovered, about 4 minutes or till mixture is thickened and bubbly, stirring after each minute. Fold in tuna, pimiento, and the cooked noodles. Micro-cook, uncovered, 3 to 4 minutes or till heated through, stirring after 2 minutes. Stir mixture, then sprinkle Parmesan cheese and ripe olives over top of noodle mixture. Makes 6 servings.

microwave plus the freezer

Stroganoff Meatballs

Thoroughly blend soup and milk into the softened cream cheese for a smooth sauce —

- 24 **Basic Frozen Meatballs**
- 1 **3-ounce package cream cheese, cut into cubes**
- 1 **10¾-ounce can condensed cream of mushroom soup**
- ¾ **cup milk**
- 2 **tablespoons catsup**
- ¼ **teaspoon dried thyme, crushed**
- ⅛ **teaspoon garlic powder**
- ½ **cup dairy sour cream**
  Hot cooked rice *or* **hot cooked noodles**
  Snipped parsley

Place frozen meatballs in single layer in a 12x7½x2-inch baking dish. Micro-cook, covered, about 4 minutes or till thawed, rearranging meatballs after each minute. Micro-cook, covered, about 6 minutes longer or till done, turning meatballs over and rearranging them twice. Drain off excess fat.

In a 2-quart casserole soften cream cheese in microwave oven about 30 seconds. Thoroughly stir in the soup and milk. Stir in the catsup, thyme, and garlic powder. Micro-cook, covered, about 8 minutes or till cheese is melted and mixture is smooth, stirring every 2 minutes. Add the meatballs. Micro-cook, covered, about 5 minutes or till bubbly, stirring twice.

Stir a moderate amount of the hot sauce into the sour cream; return to casserole. Micro-cook, covered, about 1 minute longer or just till hot. *Do not boil.* Serve over hot cooked rice or noodles. Sprinkle with snipped parsley. Makes 4 to 6 servings.

cooking tip

Use your freezer in conjunction with your microwave oven to simplify menu preparation. Make foods ahead, then freeze them until you're ready for the final preparation steps in the microwave oven.

Basic Frozen Meatballs

- 2 **beaten eggs**
- ⅓ **cup milk**
- 2 **cups soft bread crumbs**
- ⅓ **cup finely chopped onion**
- 1½ **teaspoons salt**
- ⅛ **teaspoon pepper**
- 2 **pounds ground beef**

In large bowl combine beaten eggs, milk, soft bread crumbs, onion, salt, and pepper. Add ground beef; mix well. With wet hands shape meat mixture into forty-eight 1-inch meatballs. Place on baking sheet. Cover; freeze just till frozen.

Using 24 meatballs per package, wrap in 2 moisture-vaporproof bags. Seal, label, and freeze. Makes 48 meatballs. Use in Stroganoff Meatballs or Chili Meatball Supper.

Chili Meatball Supper

- 24 **Basic Frozen Meatballs**
- 1 **16-ounce can tomatoes, cut up**
- 1 **15½-ounce can red kidney beans**
- 1 **12-ounce can whole kernel corn with sweet peppers**
- 1 **8-ounce can tomato sauce with chopped onion**
- 2 **teaspoons chili powder**
- 1 **bay leaf**
- ½ **cup shredded American cheese**
- 1 **cup crushed corn chips**

Place the frozen meatballs in single layer in a 12x7½x2-inch baking dish. Micro-cook, covered, about 4 minutes or till thawed, rearranging the meatballs after each minute. Micro-cook, covered, about 6 minutes more or till done, turning meatballs over and rearranging twice. Drain off excess fat. Add *undrained* tomatoes, red kidney beans, and corn; stir in tomato sauce, chili powder, and bay leaf. Micro-cook, covered, 10 to 12 minutes or till bubbly, stirring every 3 minutes. Remove bay leaf. Serve in individual bowls topped with shredded cheese and chips. Makes 6 servings.

Chili Meatball Supper

Barbecue Sandwiches

- 2 10¾-ounce cans condensed tomato soup
- ½ cup finely chopped onion
- ¼ cup water
- 3 tablespoons vinegar
- 2 tablespoons sugar
- 2 tablespoons Worcestershire sauce
- 1 tablespoon prepared mustard
- ¼ teaspoon bottled hot pepper sauce
- 1 pound cooked pork *or* beef, chilled and sliced very thin (3 cups)
  Hard rolls *or* buns, split

In a 2-quart glass bowl combine tomato soup, onion, water, vinegar, sugar, Worcestershire sauce, prepared mustard, and hot pepper sauce. Micro-cook, covered, about 8 minutes or till bubbly, stirring twice. Stir in sliced pork or beef. Seal, label, and freeze in 3 pint-size freezer containers.

To serve, place contents of 1 container in a 1-quart casserole. Micro-cook, covered, 2 minutes; let stand 2 minutes. Continue cooking 8 to 10 minutes or till thawed and hot, stirring every 2 minutes. (Or, for 2 containers place contents in a 2-quart casserole. Micro-cook, covered, 6 minutes; let stand 2 minutes. Micro-cook 8 minutes more, stirring every 2 minutes.) Serve on hard rolls or buns. Makes 3 or 4 sandwiches per pint container.

Cauliflower-Salmon Bake

- 1 10-ounce package frozen cauliflower
- ½ cup chopped onion
- 1 tablespoon water
- 1 11-ounce can condensed cheddar cheese soup
- 2 tablespoons milk
- 1 3-ounce can chopped mushrooms, drained
- 2 tablespoons snipped parsley
- 1 teaspoon Worcestershire sauce
  Dash cayenne
- 1 7¾-ounce can salmon, drained, bones and skin removed, and broken into chunks
- ¼ cup crisp rice cereal squares, coarsely crushed

Place frozen cauliflower in a 2-quart glass bowl. To thaw, micro-cook, covered, 1 minute. Cut up large pieces. Micro-cook, covered, 1 minute more. Drain cauliflower and set aside.

In same bowl micro-cook chopped onion and water about 2 to 3 minutes or till onion is tender. Stir in cheese soup and milk. Stir in mushrooms, parsley, Worcestershire sauce, and cayenne. Fold in salmon and the cauliflower. Turn mixture into four 1-cup casseroles. Cover, seal, label, and freeze.

To serve, place frozen casseroles on microwave oven glass tray (or set casseroles on waxed paper if oven doesn't have glass tray). Micro-cook 1 casserole, covered, 7 to 8 minutes; 2 casseroles, 11 to 12 minutes; and 4 casseroles, 12 to 13 minutes or till heated through. Rearrange dishes 3 times. Sprinkle rice cereal atop before serving. Makes 4 servings.

Italian-Style Stuffed Peppers

- 6 medium green peppers
- 1 pound ground beef
- ½ cup chopped onion
- 1 8-ounce can tomatoes, cut up
- ¾ cup Minute Rice
- 1 envelope spaghetti sauce mix
- ½ cup shredded mozzarella cheese
  Grated Parmesan cheese

In a 2-quart casserole micro-cook 3 cups *water* about 12 minutes or till boiling. Meanwhile, cut off tops of peppers; remove seeds and membrane. Add 3 peppers at a time to boiling water. Micro-cook, covered, 2 minutes. Remove; drain. Repeat. Discard water. In same casserole crumble meat. Add onion. Micro-cook, covered, about 5 minutes or till meat is brown, stirring several times. Drain. Stir in tomatoes, rice, sauce mix, and ¾ cup *water*. Micro-cook, covered, about 6 minutes or till rice is done, stirring twice. Stir in cheese; fill peppers. Seal, label, and freeze in freezer container.

To serve, place frozen peppers in an 8x8x2-inch baking dish. Micro-cook, covered, 2 minutes. Let stand 2 minutes. Micro-cook 18 to 19 minutes or till filling is hot, rearranging every 5 minutes. Sprinkle tops with Parmesan cheese. Serves 6.

Oriental Beef Casserole

- 1 pound ground beef
- ¼ cup chopped celery
- ¼ cup chopped onion
- ¼ cup chopped green pepper
- 1 cup water
- 2 tablespoons cornstarch
- 1 teaspoon sugar
- ¼ teaspoon ground ginger
- ¼ cup soy sauce
- 2 tablespoons water
- 1 8½-ounce can bamboo shoots, drained
- 1 6-ounce package frozen pea pods, thawed
  Chow mein noodles

In a 1½-quart casserole crumble ground beef. Add celery, onion, and green pepper. Micro-cook, covered, about 5 minutes or till meat is brown and vegetables are tender, stirring several times. Drain off fat. Stir in the 1 cup water. Micro-cook, uncovered, about 3 minutes or till mixture bubbles, stirring once. Combine cornstarch, sugar, and ground ginger; stir in soy sauce and the 2 tablespoons water. Stir into beef mixture.

Micro-cook, uncovered, about 1½ minutes or till thickened and bubbly, stirring twice. Stir in bamboo shoots and pea pods. Turn mixture into four 12-ounce casseroles. Cover, seal, label, and freeze.

To serve, place frozen casseroles, covered with waxed paper, in microwave oven. Micro-cook 2 minutes; let stand 2 minutes. Micro-cook 1 casserole 5 minutes; 2 casseroles 10 minutes; and four casseroles 17 minutes or till heated through. Give dishes half-turns 3 times and rearrange once. Before serving, sprinkle chow mein noodles over tops. Serves 4.

Twice-Baked Potatoes

- 4 medium baking potatoes
- 2 tablespoons butter or margarine
- ½ teaspoon salt
- ⅛ teaspoon pepper
- ½ cup milk
- 1 3-ounce can chopped mushrooms, drained
  Paprika
- 2 slices Swiss cheese, cut in half diagonally

Prepare and micro-cook baking potatoes following directions given for Baked Potatoes on page 36. Cut a lengthwise slice from top of *each* potato; discard skin from slice. Reserving potato shells, scoop out insides and add to potato from slices; mash. Add butter or margarine, salt, and pepper. Beat in enough milk (about ½ cup) to make a stiff consistency. Stir in mushrooms. Pile mixture back into potato shells. Sprinkle with paprika. Wrap, seal, label, and freeze.

To serve, unwrap frozen potatoes and place in a 10x6x2-inch baking dish. Micro-cook, uncovered, about 13 minutes for 4 potatoes or 7 to 9 minutes for 2 potatoes, or till potatoes are heated through, rearranging potatoes 2 or 3 times. Place cheese atop potatoes. Micro-cook 30 seconds more. Serves 4.

Beanless Chili

- 2 pounds ground beef
- 1 cup chopped onion
- ½ cup chopped green pepper
- 1 clove garlic, minced
- 1½ teaspoons salt
- 1 28-ounce can tomatoes, cut up
- 1 10½-ounce can tomato puree
- ½ cup water
- 1 4-ounce can mild green chili peppers, drained, seeded, and chopped
- 1 tablespoon chili powder
- 1 teaspoon sugar
- ½ teaspoon dried basil, crushed
- ½ teaspoon ground cumin
  Hot cooked rice

In a 3-quart casserole crumble ground beef. Add chopped onion, green pepper, garlic, and salt. Micro-cook, covered, about 10 minutes or till meat is brown, stirring several times to break up meat. Drain off fat.

Stir in *undrained* tomatoes, tomato puree, water, chili peppers, chili powder, sugar, basil, and cumin. Micro-cook, covered, 10 minutes, stirring 3 times. Seal, label, and freeze in two 1-quart or four 1-pint freezer containers.

To serve, place 1 quart frozen mixture in a 1½-quart casserole. Micro-cook, covered, 2 minutes; let stand 2 minutes. Micro-cook, covered, about 16 minutes or till hot, stirring 3 times to break up meat. (*Or,* place 1 pint frozen mixture in a 1-quart casserole. Micro-cook, covered, 2 minutes; let stand 2 minutes. Micro-cook, covered, about 9 minutes or till hot, stirring twice.) Serve in bowls over hot cooked rice. Makes 8 servings.

microwave plus the barbecue

Snappy Barbecued Pork Chops

- 1 **8-ounce can tomato sauce**
- ¼ **cup molasses**
- ¼ **cup water**
- 2 **tablespoons vinegar**
- 1 **tablespoon Worcestershire sauce**
- 2 **teaspoons minced dried onion**
- 2 **teaspoons dry mustard**
- 1 **teaspoon salt**
- ¼ **teaspoon chili powder**
  Dash pepper
- 4 **rib *or* loin pork chops, cut 1 inch thick**

For sauce, in a 2-cup glass measure combine tomato sauce, molasses, water, vinegar, Worcestershire sauce, dried onion, dry mustard, salt, chili powder, and pepper. Micro-cook, uncovered, about 3½ minutes or till bubbly. Arrange pork chops in an 8x8x2-inch baking dish. Micro-cook, covered, 12 to 15 minutes, giving dish a quarter-turn every 3 minutes.

Transfer chops to barbecue grill. Grill over *medium* coals about 15 minutes or till done. Brush frequently with sauce and turn chops over occasionally. Micro-heat remaining sauce about 30 seconds; pass with chops. Serves 4.

cooking tip

Speed up the cooking time of some barbecued foods by using your microwave oven. Or, use your microwave to reheat leftover charcoaled foods. By grilling extras over the coals, you can have a spur-of-the-moment barbecued meal without heating up the grill.

Lemon-Marinated Chuck

- 1 **2½- to 3-pound beef chuck roast, cut 1½ inches thick**
- 1 **teaspoon finely shredded lemon peel**
- ½ **cup lemon juice**
- ¼ **cup cooking oil**
- 2 **tablespoons chopped onion**
- 1 **tablespoon sugar**
- 1 **teaspoon Worcestershire sauce**
- 1 **teaspoon Dijon-style mustard**

Score fat edges of meat. Place in a 12x7½x2-inch baking dish, trimming meat to fit dish, if necessary. For marinade, combine remaining ingredients, 1½ teaspoons *salt*, and ⅛ teaspoon *pepper*. Pour marinade over meat. Cover; refrigerate 12 hours or overnight, turning meat several times. Micro-cook meat in marinade, covered, 15 to 20 minutes, turning meat over once. Transfer meat to barbecue grill. Grill over *medium-hot* coals about 5 minutes on each side for rare to medium-rare. Brush often with marinade. To serve, slice thinly across grain. Serves 6 to 8.

Barbecued Hawaiian Chicken

- 1 **3-pound broiler-fryer chicken, cut up**
- ¼ **cup apricot preserves**
- ¼ **cup Russian salad dressing**
- 2 **tablespoons dry onion soup mix**

Arrange chicken, skin side up, in a 10x6x2-inch baking dish. Micro-cook, covered, 15 minutes, giving dish a quarter-turn every 3 minutes. Transfer chicken to barbecue grill and grill over *hot* coals for 5 minutes. Combine the preserves, salad dressing, and soup mix. Brush mixture over chicken. Grill about 10 minutes more or till chicken is done. Brush occasionally with preserves mixture and turn chicken until evenly browned. Makes 4 servings.

Plantation Spareribs

- ½ **cup molasses *or* sorghum**
- ¼ **cup prepared mustard**
- ¼ **cup vinegar**
- 2 **tablespoons Worcestershire sauce**
- ½ **teaspoon salt**
- ½ **teaspoon bottled hot pepper sauce**
- 4 **pounds pork spareribs**

In a 2-cup glass measure stir molasses or sorghum into mustard. Stir in remaining ingredients except spareribs. Micro-cook about 2 minutes or till mixture boils.

Cut spareribs into serving-size pieces. Season with salt. Arrange in a 13x9x2-inch baking dish. Micro-cook, covered, for 20 minutes, rearranging ribs after 10 minutes. Transfer ribs to barbecue grill. Grill over *medium* coals about 15 minutes or till done. Brush often with sauce and turn ribs over occasionally. Pass sauce. Makes 4 or 5 servings.

Peppy Chuck Steak Grill

1 2- to 3-pound beef chuck steak, cut 1 inch thick
½ cup cooking oil
½ cup dry red wine
2 tablespoons catsup
2 tablespoons molasses
2 tablespoons finely snipped candied ginger
1 clove garlic, minced
1 teaspoon salt
¼ teaspoon pepper

Score fat edges of steak, being careful not to cut into meat. Place in a 12x7½x2-inch baking dish. For marinade, combine cooking oil, wine, catsup, molasses, ginger, garlic, salt, and pepper. Pour over steak. Cover; let stand 3 hours at room temperature or 6 hours in refrigerator, turning several times.

Micro-cook meat in marinade, covered, 15 to 20 minutes, turning meat over once. Drain steak, reserving marinade. Pat excess moisture from steak with paper toweling. Transfer meat to barbecue grill.

Grill steak over *medium-hot* coals about 5 minutes on each side for rare to medium-rare. Brush occasionally with reserved marinade.

Remove meat to serving platter. Carve across grain in thin slices. Makes 4 to 6 servings.

Barbecued Marinated Chicken

1 2-pound broiler-fryer chicken
½ cup dry sherry
2 tablespoons honey
1 tablespoon soy sauce
1 teaspoon dry mustard
½ teaspoon ground ginger
¼ teaspoon paprika

Halve chicken lengthwise; place in shallow baking dish. For marinade, combine remaining ingredients; pour over chicken. Cover; refrigerate 4 to 6 hours, occasionally spooning marinade over.

Remove chicken, reserving marinade. Arrange chicken, skin side up, in a 10x6x2-inch baking dish. Micro-cook, covered, 18 minutes, giving dish a quarter-turn every 3 minutes. Transfer chicken to barbecue grill. Grill over *hot* coals about 10 minutes or till done. Brush occasionally with marinade and turn till evenly browned. Serves 2.

Mustard Barbecued Ribs

¼ cup prepared mustard
2 tablespoons molasses
2 tablespoons Worcestershire sauce
   Dash bottled hot pepper sauce
3 pounds pork spareribs
1 12-ounce can (1½ cups) beer
1 small onion, quartered

For sauce, combine first four ingredients; set aside. Cut ribs into serving-size pieces. Arrange in a 12x7½x2-inch baking dish; add beer, onion, 1 teaspoon *salt*, and dash *pepper*. Micro-cook, covered, 20 minutes, rearranging ribs after 10 minutes. Transfer ribs to barbecue grill. Grill over *medium* coals 10 minutes. Brush sauce over ribs. Grill 5 minutes; brush with sauce and turn occasionally. Serves 3 or 4.

Chicken Provençale

4 2½- to 3-pound broiler-fryer chickens, halved lengthwise
   Cooking oil
½ cup butter *or* margarine, softened
2 large tomatoes, peeled, seeded, and finely chopped
¼ cup finely chopped onion
¼ cup snipped parsley
¼ cup dry sherry
1 clove garlic, minced
½ teaspoon sugar

Arrange *1* of the chickens, skin side up, in a 10x6x2-inch baking dish. Micro-cook, covered, 15 minutes, giving dish a quarter-turn every 3 minutes. Remove chicken from dish; set the chicken aside. Repeat micro-cooking with *each* of the remaining chickens. Brush chickens with cooking oil; sprinkle with *salt* and *pepper*. Transfer chicken to barbecue grill; place bone side down. Grill over *hot* coals for 5 minutes. Combine remaining ingredients (will separate slightly). Brush tomato mixture over chicken. Grill about 10 minutes more or till chicken is done. Brush occasionally with tomato mixture and turn chicken till evenly browned. Serves 8.

special microwave features

Vegetable-Stuffed Pork Rolls

½ cup shredded carrot
½ cup finely chopped onion
½ cup finely chopped green pepper
½ cup grated Parmesan cheese
¼ teaspoon dried thyme, crushed
6 pork tenderloin pieces (about 4 ounces each)
1 cup beef broth
4 teaspoons cornstarch
1 2-ounce can chopped mushrooms, drained
¼ teaspoon Kitchen Bouquet

In a 1-quart casserole combine carrot, onion, green pepper, ¼ cup *water*, and ¼ teaspoon *salt*. Micro-cook, covered, on *high* setting about 4 minutes or till crisp-tender. Drain thoroughly. Stir in cheese and thyme; set aside.

Pound each piece of pork into a piece measuring 8x5 inches. Season with *salt* and *pepper*. Spread about ¼ cup of the vegetable mixture on *each* piece. Roll up, beginning with short side; secure with string or wooden picks. Place meat rolls in a 12x7½x2-inch baking dish. Pour beef broth over. Micro-cook, covered, on *simmer* (medium) setting about 30 minutes or till meat is tender, turning rolls over and rear-ranging once. Transfer meat to serving plate. Remove strings or picks. Keep hot.

Strain *1 cup* of the juices into a 2-cup glass measure. Stir 2 table-spoons *cold water* into cornstarch; stir into measuring cup along with mushrooms. Micro-cook, uncov-ered, on *high* setting about 2 min-utes or till thickened and bubbly, stirring every 30 seconds. Stir in the Kitchen Bouquet and season with *salt* and *pepper*. Serve over pork rolls. Makes 6 servings.

Beef-Barley Vegetable Soup
Pictured on page 64 —

8 ounces beef chuck, cut into small pieces
1 16-ounce can tomatoes, cut up
1 cup chopped celery
½ cup chopped onion
2 tablespoons quick-cooking barley
1 tablespoon Worcestershire sauce
¼ teaspoon chili powder
1 8¾-ounce can whole kernel corn

In a 3-quart casserole combine beef, *undrained* tomatoes, and next 5 ingredients. Stir in 4 cups *water*, ¾ teaspoon *salt, and* ⅛ teaspoon *pepper*. Micro-cook, covered, on *high* setting about 15 minutes or till mixture boils. Micro-cook, covered, on *defrost* setting 1 hour, stirring every 20 minutes. Stir in *undrained* corn. Micro-cook, covered, on *high* setting about 1 minute more or till hot. Makes 8 servings.

Burgundy Pot Roast

½ cup chopped onion
½ teaspoon instant beef bouillon granules
¼ cup burgundy
1 tablespoon Worcestershire sauce
1 3-pound beef chuck roast
4 teaspoons cornstarch

In a 2-cup glass measure combine onion and ⅓ cup *water*. Micro-cook, uncovered, on *high* setting about 2 minutes or till tender; do not drain. Stir in bouillon granules. Add burgundy, Worcestershire sauce, ½ teaspoon *salt*, and ⅛ tea-spoon *pepper*. Place meat in a 12x7½x2-inch baking dish. Pour burgundy mixture over.

Micro-cook, covered, on *defrost* setting for 1½ hours, turning meat over in dish and giving dish a half-turn every 30 minutes. Remove meat to platter; keep covered. Pour pan drippings into a 2-cup glass measure; skim off fat. Stir 2 tablespoons *cold water* into cornstarch; stir into meat liquid. Micro-cook, uncovered, on *high* setting 1 minute; stir. Micro-cook 1 to 2 minutes or till thickened and bubbly, stirring every 30 seconds. Serve with meat. Serves 6.

Orange-Baked Cornish Hens

- 2 1-pound Cornish game hens
- ¼ cup chopped onion
- 2 tablespoons butter *or* margarine
- 1½ cups dry bread cubes (2 slices)
- 2 tablespoons chopped walnuts
- 1 teaspoon finely shredded orange peel
- 2 tablespoons orange juice Paprika
- 1 tablespoon orange marmalade
- 1 teaspoon bottled steak sauce

Season inside of hens with *salt and pepper.* In a 4-cup glass measure micro-cook onion in butter, uncovered, on *high* setting about 1½ minutes or till onion is tender. Stir in bread, nuts, peel, and ¼ teaspoon *salt.* Toss with juice. Stuff birds with mixture. Tie legs together. Place, breast side down, in a 10x6x2-inch baking dish. Sprinkle with paprika. Micro-cook, uncovered, on *high* setting 10 minutes. Turn breasts up; sprinkle with paprika. Micro-cook, uncovered, on *roast* (medium-high) setting about 10 minutes or till done. Combine orange marmalade and steak sauce. Brush on birds; micro-cook, uncovered, on *high* setting 1 minute. Let stand 5 minutes. Serves 2.

Lemon Cottage Cheesecake

- 2 tablespoons butter *or* margarine
- ¾ cup finely crushed zwieback
- ¼ cup sifted powdered sugar
- 2 cups cream-style cottage cheese, well drained
- 4 eggs
- 1 cup granulated sugar
- 1 cup whipping cream
- ¼ cup all-purpose flour
- 1 teaspoon finely shredded lemon peel
- 3 tablespoons lemon juice
- ½ teaspoon vanilla
- ¼ teaspoon salt

For crust, in an 8x1½-inch round glass baking dish micro-melt butter on *high* setting 30 to 40 seconds. Stir in crushed zwieback and powdered sugar. Reserve 1 tablespoon for the top; press remainder evenly in bottom of dish. Set aside.

Sieve the drained cream-style cottage cheese into mixing bowl. Add eggs, granulated sugar, whipping cream, flour, lemon peel, lemon juice, vanilla, and salt. Beat just till combined. (*Or,* omit sieving and combine all ingredients in blender container; cover and blend just till smooth.) Pour into crust. Top with the reserved crumbs. Micro-cook, uncovered, on *defrost* setting 21 to 23 minutes or till nearly set in center, giving dish a half-turn after 10 minutes. Chill. Cut into wedges. Serves 8 to 10.

Cake-Style Brownies

- ½ cup butter *or* margarine
- 3 tablespoons unsweetened cocoa powder
- 1 cup all-purpose flour
- 1 cup sugar
- ½ teaspoon baking soda
- ¼ cup buttermilk *or* sour milk
- 1 slightly beaten egg
- 1 teaspoon vanilla
  Fast Fudge Frosting

In a 4-cup glass measure combine butter or margarine, cocoa powder, and ½ cup *water.* Micro-cook, uncovered, on *high* setting about 3 minutes or till boiling, stirring once to blend. Set aside. Stir together the flour, sugar, soda, and ¼ teaspoon *salt;* stir in the buttermilk, egg, and vanilla. Stir in cocoa mixture. Pour into a greased 12x7½x2-inch baking dish. Micro-cook, uncovered, on *roast* (medium-high) setting for 7½ minutes, giving dish a half-turn every 2 minutes. (Top will be slightly moist.) Cool completely. Frost with Fast Fudge Frosting. Makes 28 bars.

Fast Fudge Frosting: Combine 2½ cups sifted *powdered sugar,* ¼ cup *unsweetened cocoa powder,* and ⅛ teaspoon *salt.* Add 3 tablespoons *boiling water,* 3 tablespoons softened *butter,* and 1 teaspoon *vanilla.* Blend well.

Microwave Beef Stew

1 pound beef chuck, cut into
    ¾-inch cubes
2 tablespoons all-purpose flour
1 teaspoon salt
    Dash pepper
1 10¾-ounce can condensed
    tomato soup
1 soup can (1¼ cups) water
1 cup chopped onion
1 teaspoon instant beef bouillon
    granules
1 teaspoon dried savory,
    crushed
¼ teaspoon garlic powder
4 medium carrots, cut into ½-inch
    pieces
3 medium potatoes, peeled and
    cut into 1-inch cubes
½ cup cold water
2 tablespoons cornstarch

Coat beef cubes with a mixture of
flour, salt, and pepper. In a 3-quart
casserole combine tomato soup,
the 1 soup can water, onion, bouillon granules, savory, and garlic
powder. Stir in seasoned cubes of
meat.

Micro-cook, covered, on *simmer*
(medium) setting for 35 minutes,
stirring after 20 minutes. Stir in carrots; micro-cook, covered, on *simmer* setting 5 minutes. Stir in
potatoes; micro-cook, covered, on
simmer setting for 25 to 30 minutes
or till vegetables are tender, stirring
3 times. Stir the ½ cup cold water
into cornstarch; stir into meat mixture. Micro-cook, uncovered, on
high setting about 3 minutes or till
thickened and bubbly, stirring after
each minute. Season to taste.
Serve in bowls. Makes 4 servings.

Microwave Beef Stew, Beef-Barley
Vegetable Soup (see recipe, page 62)

Horseradish-Stuffed Rump Roast

1 5-ounce jar prepared
    horseradish
2 cloves garlic, minced
1 5-pound boned and rolled
    beef rump roast
1 teaspoon beef-flavored gravy
    base
⅓ cup cold water
3 tablespoons all-purpose flour

Combine horseradish and the garlic. Unroll roast; make a lengthwise
cut through thick part of roast,
going to, but not through, other
side. Spread cut sufaces with the
horseradish mixture. Reroll roast
and tie securely with string.

Place roast, fat side down, on inverted saucer in a 12x7½x2-inch
baking dish. Micro-cook, uncovered, on *roast* (medium-high) setting for 30 minutes, giving dish a
half-turn every 10 minutes.

Turn meat, fat side up, and
change setting on microwave
oven to *simmer* (medium) setting.
Micro-cook, uncovered, 25 to 30
minutes or till microwave thermometer registers 140°, giving dish
a half-turn every 10 minutes. Remove roast; cover with foil and let
stand 20 minutes before carving.
(Temperature will increase to 160°
during standing time for medium-
done beef.)

Pour off pan drippings into a
4-cup glass measure. Skim fat. To
drippings add enough water to
make 1½ cups and the beef-
flavored gravy base; set aside.

About 10 minutes before serving,
stir the cold water into the flour.
Add to mixture in glass measure.
Micro-cook, uncovered, on *high*
setting 1 minute; stir. Micro-cook 3½
to 4 minutes or till thickened and
bubbly, stirring after each minute.
Season to taste with *salt* and *pepper*. Serve with meat. Serves 10.

Chicken Divan
Do all cooking on the high setting —

2 8-ounce packages frozen cut
    asparagus
2 tablespoons water
1 10½-ounce can condensed
    cream of chicken soup
1 teaspoon Worcestershire
    sauce
    Dash ground nutmeg
½ cup grated Parmesan cheese
2 cups chopped cooked
    chicken
½ cup whipping cream
½ cup mayonnaise *or* salad
    dressing

Place frozen asparagus side by
side in a 12x7½x2-inch baking dish.
Add water. Micro-cook, covered,
10 to 12 minutes or till tender,
separating pieces with a fork after
6 minutes. Drain well on paper
toweling. Return to same dish.

For sauce, stir together chicken
soup, Worcestershire sauce, and
nutmeg. Pour *half* of the sauce over
asparagus in the 12x7½x2-inch baking dish. Sprinkle ⅓ of the Parmesan cheese over sauce on asparagus. Top with cooked chicken
and the remaining sauce. Sprinkle
with another ⅓ of the Parmesan
cheese. Micro-cook, uncovered, 6
to 8 minutes or till hot. Remove from
oven.

Under Infrared Browning Unit: Preheat unit for 2 minutes. Meanwhile,
whip the whipping cream to soft
peaks; fold in mayonnaise or salad
dressing. Spread over chicken mixture. Sprinkle with the remaining
cheese. Brown on bottom shelf
about 6 inches from infrared unit
about 4 minutes or till top is golden.
Serves 6 to 8.

Chicken Country Captain

- ¼ cup chopped onion
- ¼ cup chopped green pepper
- 1 small clove garlic, minced
- 2 tablespoons butter *or* margarine
- 1 16-ounce can tomatoes, cut up
- 2 tablespoons dried currants
- 2 tablespoons snipped parsley
- 2 teaspoons curry powder
- 1 teaspoon salt
- ½ teaspoon ground mace
- ⅛ teaspoon pepper
- 1 2½- to 3-pound broiler-fryer chicken, cut up
- 2 tablespoons cold water
- 1 tablespoon cornstarch
  Hot cooked rice

For sauce, in a 3-quart casserole combine chopped onion and green pepper, garlic, and butter. Micro-cook, covered, on *high* setting about 2 minutes or till vegetables are tender. Stir in *undrained* tomatoes, dried currants, snipped parsley, curry powder, salt, mace, and pepper. Add chicken, stirring gently to coat with sauce. Micro-cook, covered, on *defrost* setting 35 to 45 minutes or till chicken is done, stirring every 10 minutes. Remove chicken to serving platter; keep hot.

Skim off excess fat. Stir cold water into cornstarch; stir into sauce. Micro-cook, uncovered, on *high* setting about 3 minutes or till mixture thickens and bubbles, stirring after each minute. Serve with chicken and hot rice. Serves 4.

Surprise Cream Pie

- 5 tablespoons butter *or* margarine
- 1¼ cups finely crushed graham crackers
- ¼ cup sugar
- 2 1-ounce milk chocolate candy bars
- 1 4½- or 5-ounce package *regular* vanilla pudding mix
- 3 cups milk
- 2 slightly beaten egg yolks
- 2 egg whites
- ½ teaspoon vanilla
- ¼ teaspoon cream of tartar
- ¼ cup sugar

To prepare crumb crust, in a 9-inch glass pie plate micro-melt butter about 45 seconds. Stir in graham crackers and sugar. Press over bottom and sides of pie plate. Micro-cook, uncovered, 2 minutes, turning dish after 1 minute.

Break up the candy bars and arrange over hot crust; spread till smooth. Set crust aside.

In a 4-cup glass measure combine pudding mix and milk. Micro-cook, uncovered, 3 minutes. Stir. Micro-cook, uncovered, 2 to 3 minutes more or till pudding thickens and bubbles, stirring after each minute. Stir *half* of the hot pudding into egg yolks. Return to hot mixture. Micro-cook 1 minute more. Pour into prepared crust.

In small bowl beat egg whites with vanilla and cream of tartar till soft peaks form. Gradually add sugar, beating till stiff peaks form. Spread atop pie, sealing to edges of crust.

Under Infrared Browning Unit: Do not preheat unit. Brown pie 3 to 4 minutes, turning pie for even browning as necessary. Cool.

Veal Parmesan

- 1 pound boneless veal sirloin steak
- ¼ cup finely crushed saltine crackers
- ¼ cup grated Parmesan cheese
  Dash pepper
- 1 beaten egg
- 1 8-ounce can pizza sauce
- ½ teaspoon sugar
- 1 cup shredded mozzarella cheese
  Parsley

Cut sirloin steak into 4 serving-size pieces. Pound meat till ¼ inch thick. Combine crackers, Parmesan cheese, and pepper. Dip veal into beaten egg, and then into the crumb mixture; set aside.

Heat *browning skillet* or *platter* in microwave oven on *high* setting for 2 minutes. Place 2 *pieces* of meat on dish; micro-cook, uncovered, 1½ minutes or till brown on one side. Turn meat over; micro-cook 1½ minutes longer or till other side of meat is browned. Transfer meat to a 12x7½x2-inch baking dish. Repeat browning with remaining meat.

Combine pizza sauce and sugar; pour over meat in baking dish. Micro-cook, covered, on *high* setting 7 minutes or till meat is done and sauce is heated through, giving dish a quarter-turn every 2 minutes and rearranging meat once. Sprinkle with mozzarella cheese. Micro-cook, uncovered, 1 minute or till cheese melts. Garnish with parsley. Makes 4 servings.

Savory Beef-Vegetable Soup (see recipe, page 85)

CROCKERY COOKER RECIPES

Plug in a crockery cooker and start enjoying meals cooked the easy way. Just place the food into the pot and let it cook for several hours — up to 12, depending on the recipe. In this section, you'll find a winning collection of taste-tempting main dishes, soups, vegetables, desserts, and even steamed breads.

crockery
cooker
know-how

Dinner that cooks by itself is a dream come true for the user of an electric slow crockery cooker. The go-off-and-leave-it feature alone is responsible for much of this appliance's popularity. The big question is, "go off and leave it — for how long?" The answer depends both on the type of cooker you have and on the kind of food you're cooking.

types of crockery cookers

Although individual models have different features, crockery cookers come in three basic types. Cookers with heating wires wrapped entirely around the sides of the cooker, those with heating elements only in the bottom, and those with a separate heating unit, much like a small hot plate.

The recipes in this section were tested only in those cookers with heating elements wrapped around the sides (illustration 1). These are very low wattage units in which the element is on continuously. Foods in liquid can be left unattended 8 or more hours without boiling dry or sticking. This group of cookers can be identified by a heat control with one or two fixed settings, usually low and high.

The second group, with a heating element in the bottom only, usually have thermostatic controls with a wide range of temperatures (illustration 2). The heating unit goes on and off as the thermostat calls for heat. In some models, the settings on the dial range from very low to high enough for deep-fat frying. Slow cooking in crockery cookers heated from the bottom is most successful when you check the food during cooking to be sure it is hot enough but not boiling too hard. An occasional stir also prevents food from sticking to the bottom or sides of this type of cooker.

If you have one of these models, you should not use the recipes in the All-Day Cooking section unless you plan to be at home during the cooking time. These recipes were not tested either in this group of cookers or in those with a separate heating unit (illustration 3). In addition to the example shown in illustration 3, some models are shallow, like a skillet, and their shape also affects the heating pattern.

check your cooker

Just as the design of crockery cookers varies, so does their heating capacity. To check the cooking temperature of your particular cooker, fill it half full with cold tap water. Cover the cooker and set it on the high-heat setting for 2½ hours. If the water is boiling before 2½ hours, reduce the total cooking time for recipes in this section. If the cooker takes longer than 3 hours to boil the water, add to the cooking time.

food safety first

Crockery cookers are designed for long cooking times. Thus, food heats very slowly, particularly on the lowest setting. It follows that the low setting should not be used for meat or egg mixtures that cook in less than 6 hours, since the food won't get hot enough in that amount of time to destroy all bacteria that could cause food poisoning.

Proper handling of foods before and after cooking is another important aspect of crockery cooking. Don't use the cooker to store food at room temperature either before or after cooking. While you'll want to do some advance preparation the night before, you must store the ingredients in the refrigerator and transfer them to the cooker in the morning. Likewise, as soon as the meal is served, remove all food from the cooker and refrigerate it while it's still warm.

To take advantage of the large quantities you can prepare in a crockery cooker, cook more food than you'll need for one meal and freeze the rest. To freeze the food, transfer it to a bowl set in a pan of ice water to quickly cool it to room temperature. Then, immediately package it in moisture-vaporproof containers, allowing a 1-inch headspace for expansion. Store the food in the freezer. To serve, heat the frozen food in a saucepan over low heat, in the top of a double boiler, or in a microwave oven. Or, bake the frozen food in a 400° oven for 1 to 2 hours. *Do not* reheat the food in a crockery cooker.

useful tips

Before using your crockery cooker for the first time, read the instruction booklet to learn about the specific features of your model. You may find that the cooker becomes hot to the touch during long cooking times, so use heavy potholders to move the cooker. Also, remember to place the cord where it will not hang over the counter and be accidentally tangled.

The heat in a coil-wrapped crockery cooker comes from the sides, so a cooker that is at least

1

2

3

half full will cook more efficiently. In some recipes that require thickening a sauce, removing the meat or solids may cause the remaining liquid to fall below the half-full mark. In these recipes, the liquid will be easier to thicken if it is transferred to a saucepan and then heated on the range top.

When the cooking time of a recipe is shorter than the time you'll be away from home, plug the cooker into an automatic timer to start cooking while you're gone. Just before you leave, place *chilled* food in the cooker and cover. Set the timer to turn on the cooker at a specific time, making sure the uncooked food stands *no more than 2 hours* before the cooker comes on.

Sudden temperature changes will damage the ceramic liner of the cooker. Thus, never put cold food or water in a hot cooker. Turn on the cooker only after foods are in the pot. Also, never place the cooker in the refrigerator. Condensation on the electrical parts may interfere with proper performance.

Unless the instructions specify that the cooker is immersible, do not plunge it into water. Also, avoid cleaning the cooker with abrasive cleaners and cleaning pads. Scratches in the liner can trap food particles that never completely come out. For easiest cleanup, add warm water to the cooker just after removing the food, and let the cooker soak before washing it.

all-day cooking
(more than 8 hours)

Mexican Flank Steak

- 2 **1-pound flank steaks**
- ½ **teaspoon salt**
- ⅛ **teaspoon garlic salt**
- ⅛ **teaspoon pepper**
- 1 **15-ounce can tamales in sauce**
- 1 **teaspoon instant beef bouillon granules**
- ¼ **cup hot water**
- 1 **8-ounce can tomato sauce**
  Dash bottled hot pepper sauce
- 2 **tablespoons cold water**
- 4 **teaspoons cornstarch**
  Shredded Monterey Jack cheese

Pound meat on both sides with meat mallet; sprinkle with salt, garlic salt, and pepper. Unwrap tamales; place tamales and sauce in bowl. Break up tamales slightly with fork; spread over steaks. Roll up each steak jelly-roll style, starting with short side; tie or skewer securely. Place in crockery cooker. Dissolve bouillon in the hot water; combine with tomato sauce and hot pepper sauce. Pour over meat. Cover; cook on low-heat setting for 8 to 10 hours. Lift out meat rolls; remove strings or skewers. Pour cooking liquid into saucepan; skim off excess fat. Blend the cold water into cornstarch; stir into liquid. Cook and stir till thickened and bubbly. Spoon over meat; sprinkle cheese atop each roll. Serves 6.

Marinated Flank Fillets
Fancy enough for a company meal —

- 1 **1-pound beef flank steak**
- 1 **cup sliced onion**
- ¾ **cup apple juice *or* cider**
- ½ **teaspoon coarsely ground pepper**
- 8 **slices bacon**
  Cooking oil
- 1 **9-ounce package frozen artichoke hearts**
  Herbed Hollandaise Sauce

Pound meat with meat mallet to even thickness. Cut lengthwise into six 1-inch-wide strips. Cut 2 of the strips in half crosswise. For marinade, in bowl combine onion, juice or cider, and pepper. Add meat; stir to coat. Cover; refrigerate overnight. Turn meat twice.

Drain meat, reserving marinade. Sprinkle strips with salt. For *each* meat roll, roll up *1½ strips* jelly-roll style, starting with short sides; repeat to make 4 meat rolls. Tie or skewer securely. Place meat in crockery cooker; add marinade. Cover; cook on low-heat setting for 10 hours. Remove meat; discard marinade. Remove string or skewers. In skillet cook bacon just till done, but not crisp. Wrap 2 slices around *each* meat roll; secure with picks. Place on broiler pan; brush tops lightly with oil. Broil 3 inches from heat for 2½ to 3 minutes.

Cook artichoke hearts according to package directions; drain. Serve with meat. Spoon Herbed Hollandaise Sauce atop each meat roll; pass remaining. Makes 4 servings.

Herbed Hollandaise Sauce: Prepare 1 envelope *hollandaise sauce mix* according to package directions *except* use 1¼ cups *milk*. Stir in 2 tablespoons chopped *green onion*; ½ teaspoon dried *tarragon*, crushed; and ¼ teaspoon dried *chervil*, crushed.

Vegetable-Topped Rump Roast

- 2 **tablespoons all-purpose flour**
- ½ **teaspoon salt**
- ¼ **teaspoon paprika**
  Dash pepper
- 1 **2-pound boneless beef rump roast, rolled and tied**
- 2 **tablespoons cooking oil**
- 12 **small potatoes, peeled**
- 6 **medium carrots, diced**
- 2 **medium onions, sliced (1 cup)**
- ½ **green pepper, cut into pieces**
- 1 **10½-ounce can condensed vegetable beef soup**
- ¼ **cup water**
- 1 **bay leaf**
- ⅓ **cup cold water (optional)**
- 3 **tablespoons all-purpose flour (optional)**

Combine the 2 tablespoons flour, salt, paprika, and pepper; coat roast with mixture. In heavy skillet brown roast on all sides in hot oil. In crockery cooker place the potatoes, carrots, onions, and green pepper. Place roast atop vegetables. Combine soup, ¼ cup water, and bay leaf; pour over roast. Cover and cook on low-heat setting for 10 to 12 hours. To serve, discard the bay leaf and remove strings from meat. Arrange the meat and vegetables on serving platter. Spoon some of the soup mixture atop. If thicker gravy is desired, in saucepan blend ⅓ cup cold water slowly into 3 tablespoons flour; stir in soup mixture. Cook and stir till thickened and bubbly. Makes 6 servings.

Marinated Flank Fillets

Sour Creamed Pot Roast

```
 2  slices bacon
 1  3-pound beef chuck pot roast
 ¾  cup chopped onion
 ¼  cup water
 1  teaspoon salt
 1  bay leaf
 ¼  teaspoon ground cumin
 ⅛  teaspoon pepper
 ½  cup dairy sour cream
 3  tablespoons all-purpose flour
 2  tablespoons snipped parsley
 ½  teaspoon Kitchen Bouquet
    Hot cooked noodles
```

In skillet cook bacon till crisp; drain, reserving drippings. Crumble bacon; wrap and refrigerate. Trim fat from roast; cut roast in half to fit into crockery cooker. In skillet brown meat in bacon drippings; drain. Place in crockery cooker. Stir together onion, water, salt, bay leaf, cumin, and pepper; pour over meat. Cover; cook on low-heat setting for 8 to 10 hours. Remove roast; discard bay leaf. Skim fat from liquid; pour liquid into saucepan. Return roast to cooker; cover. Blend sour cream and flour; stir into hot liquid. Cook and stir till thickened; *do not boil.* Stir in parsley and Kitchen Bouquet. Season to taste. Serve meat garnished with bacon. Serve gravy over noodles. Makes 6 servings.

Carrot-Pineapple Roast Dinner

```
 1  cup thinly sliced carrots
 1  3-pound beef chuck pot roast
 1  8¼-ounce can crushed
    pineapple
 2  tablespoons brown sugar
 2  tablespoons soy sauce
 1  clove garlic, minced
 ½  teaspoon dried basil, crushed
 ¼  cup cold water
 2  tablespoons all-purpose flour
    Hot cooked noodles
```

Place carrots in crockery cooker. Trim excess fat from pot roast; cut roast in half and fit into cooker atop carrots. Sprinkle with salt and pepper. Combine *undrained* crushed pineapple, brown sugar, soy sauce, garlic, and dried basil. Spoon over roast. Cover; cook on low-heat setting for 8 to 10 hours. Remove roast, drain carrots and pineapple; reserve cooking liquid. Return meat, carrots, and pineapple to cooker; cover to keep warm. Skim fat from reserved liquid. Add enough water to make 1¾ cups liquid; pour into saucepan. Blend the ¼ cup cold water slowly into flour; stir into reserved liquid. Cook and stir till thickened. Place meat on serving platter; top with carrots and pineapple. Pour some of the gravy over meat and hot cooked noodles; pass remaining gravy. Makes 6 servings.

Sauerbraten

```
 1½ cups burgundy
 1½ cups red wine vinegar
 2  medium onions, sliced
 ½  lemon, sliced
 12 whole cloves
 6  bay leaves
 6  whole peppercorns
 1  tablespoon sugar
 1  tablespoon salt
 ¼  teaspoon ground ginger
 1  3- to 4-pound beef rump roast
 2  tablespoons shortening
 ¾  cup water
 ⅔  cup broken gingersnaps
```

For marinade, in a large bowl combine burgundy, red wine vinegar, onions, lemon, whole cloves, bay leaves, whole peppercorns, sugar, salt, and ground ginger. Add beef rump roast; turn to coat. Cover; refrigerate about 36 hours. Turn meat at least twice daily. Remove meat; wipe dry. Strain and reserve marinade. In skillet brown meat on all sides in hot shortening; drain. Place in crockery cooker; add marinade. Cover; cook on low-heat setting for 8 to 10 hours. Remove meat. Measure 1¼ cups cooking liquid into saucepan. Add water and broken gingersnaps. Cook and stir till sauce is thickened. Serve with roast. Makes 8 to 10 servings.

Home-Style Pot Roast

- 1 medium turnip, chopped (½ cup)
- 1 medium onion, chopped (½ cup)
- ¼ cup chopped carrot
- ¼ cup chopped celery
- 1 clove garlic, minced
- 1 3-pound beef chuck pot roast
- 2 tablespoons cooking oil
- 1 teaspoon salt
- ¼ teaspoon pepper
- ½ cup dry red wine *or* water
- 2 tablespoons snipped parsley
- ⅓ cup cold water
- 3 tablespoons all-purpose flour

In crockery cooker place the chopped turnip, onion, carrot, celery, and garlic. Trim excess fat from roast; cut roast in half to fit into crockery cooker. In skillet brown the roast on all sides in hot oil; drain. Place meat atop vegetables. Sprinkle roast with salt and pepper; pour the ½ cup wine or water over roast. Cover and cook on low-heat setting for 8 to 10 hours. Remove roast to a warm serving platter. Strain the vegetables; reserve 2 cups cooking liquid, adding water, if necessary. Spoon the vegetables atop roast; sprinkle with parsley. Cover meat to keep warm while preparing gravy. Skim excess fat from reserved cooking liquid; pour liquid into saucepan. Blend the ⅓ cup cold water slowly into flour; stir into cooking liquid. Cook and stir till thickened and bubbly. Serve with roast and vegetables. Makes 6 to 8 servings.

storing cooked food

Never store leftover cooked food at room temperature in a crockery cooker. Immediately after the meal, remove any remaining food from the cooker. Refrigerate food while still warm, or chill over a bowl of ice water. Do not place crockery cooker in the refrigerator or use it to re-heat cold food.

Cranberry Pot Roast

- 1 3- to 3½-pound beef chuck pot roast
- 2 tablespoons cooking oil
- 1 16-ounce can whole cranberry sauce
- 2 tablespoons water
- 1½ teaspoons salt
- 2 tablespoons cold water
- 2 tablespoons cornstarch
  Hot mashed potatoes

Trim excess fat from pot roast; cut roast in half to fit into crockery cooker. In skillet brown meat in the hot cooking oil; drain. Stir together cranberry sauce, 2 tablespoons water, salt, and ⅛ teaspoon *pepper*; pour into cooker. Place meat on rack in cooker above cranberry mixture. Cover meat loosely with foil. Cover and cook on low-heat setting for 8 to 10 hours. Remove meat. Measure 2 cups cooking liquid; pour into saucepan. Return meat to cooker; cover. Blend the 2 tablespoons cold water slowly into cornstarch; stir into cooking liquid. Cook and stir till thickened and bubbly. Place meat on platter. Serve sauce over potatoes. Serves 6 to 8.

Oriental Sweet-Sour Pot Roast

- 1 3- to 3½-pound beef chuck pot roast
- 2 tablespoons cooking oil
- 1 16-ounce can bean sprouts, rinsed and drained
- 1 8-ounce can water chestnuts, drained and thinly sliced
- 1 medium green pepper, cut into 1-inch squares
- ⅓ cup apricot jam
- ¼ cup vinegar
- 1 tablespoon soy sauce
- 1 clove garlic, minced
- 1 teaspoon salt
- ½ teaspoon ground ginger
- ⅛ teaspoon pepper
- 1 11-ounce can mandarin orange sections
- 3 tablespoons cornstarch
  Hot cooked rice

Trim excess fat from roast; cut roast in half to fit into crockery cooker. In skillet brown meat in hot oil; drain. Place meat in cooker; add bean sprouts, water chestnuts, and green pepper. Stir together jam, vinegar, soy, garlic, salt, ginger, and pepper. Pour over meat and vegetables. Cover; cook on low-heat setting for 8 to 10 hours. Remove meat and vegetables. Skim fat from cooking liquid. Measure 2 cups liquid; reserve. Return meat and vegetables to cooker; cover to keep warm. Drain mandarin oranges, reserving ¼ cup of the syrup. In a saucepan blend reserved syrup slowly into cornstarch; stir in reserved cooking liquid. Cook and stir till thickened and bubbly. Stir in mandarin orange sections; heat through. Season to taste. Place meat and vegetables on platter. Spoon some sauce over; pass remaining. Serve with hot cooked rice. Makes 8 servings.

Pizza Swiss Steak

Serve the meat and sauce on a bed of
hot cooked spaghetti —

- 1 **2-pound beef round steak, cut
  1 inch thick**
- 2 **tablespoons all-purpose flour**
- 2 **teaspoons salt**
- ¼ **teaspoon pepper**
- 2 **tablespoons cooking oil**
- 1 **medium onion, thinly sliced
  and separated into rings**
- 1 **8-ounce can tomato sauce**
- 1 **8-ounce can pizza sauce**
- ½ **cup water**
- ½ **teaspoon sugar**
- ½ **teaspoon dried oregano,
  crushed**
  Hot cooked spaghetti

Trim excess fat from steak; cut
steak into 6 equal pieces. Stir together flour, salt, and pepper; coat
meat pieces with flour mixture.
Pound each piece of steak to
½-inch thickness using meat mallet. In skillet brown meat in hot
cooking oil; drain off fat. Place
onion in crockery cooker. Place
meat atop. Stir together tomato
sauce, pizza sauce, water, sugar,
and oregano; pour over meat.
Cover; cook on low-heat setting for
8 to 10 hours. Serve steak and
sauce over hot cooked spaghetti.
Makes 7 servings.

Steak with Vegetable Gravy

- ¾ **cup finely chopped carrot**
- ¾ **cup finely chopped onion**
- ½ **cup finely chopped celery**
- ¼ **cup finely chopped green
  pepper**
- 1 **2-pound beef round steak, cut
  ¾ inch thick**
- ½ **cup catsup**
- ⅓ **cup water**
- 1 **tablespoon vinegar**
- ½ **cup cold water**
- 2 **tablespoons all-purpose flour**

In crockery cooker place finely
chopped carrot, onion, celery, and
green pepper. Trim excess fat from
round steak; cut steak into 6 equal
pieces. Place meat atop vegetables. Sprinkle with salt and pepper.
Combine catsup, ⅓ cup water,
and vinegar; pour over meat.
Cover and cook on low-heat setting for 8 to 10 hours. Remove meat.
Skim excess fat from cooking liquid; pour cooked vegetable mixture into saucepan. Return meat to
cooker. Blend ½ cup cold water
slowly into flour. Stir into vegetable
mixture. Cook and stir till thickened
and bubbly. Place meat on platter.
Spoon some vegetable mixture
over meat; pass remaining vegetable mixture. Makes 6 to 8
servings.

Deviled Steak Cubes

- 1 **1½-pound beef round steak, cut
  ¾ inch thick**
- 2 **tablespoons cooking oil**
- 1 **cup water**
- ½ **cup tomato sauce**
- ½ **cup chopped onion
  (1 medium)**
- 2 **tablespoons vinegar**
- 1 **tablespoon prepared mustard**
- 2 **teaspoons prepared
  horseradish**
- 1 **clove garlic, minced**
- ¾ **teaspoon salt**
- ¼ **teaspoon pepper**
- ⅔ **cup cold water**
- ⅓ **cup all-purpose flour**
  **Hot cooked noodles or hot
  cooked rice**

Trim excess fat from round steak;
cut steak into cubes. In skillet brown
meat on all sides in hot oil; drain.
Transfer meat to crockery cooker.
Stir in 1 cup water, tomato sauce,
onion, vinegar, mustard, horseradish, garlic, salt, and pepper.
Cover; cook on low-heat setting for
8 to 10 hours. Turn to high-heat setting. Blend cold water slowly into
flour; stir into meat mixture. Cook till
thickened; stir occasionally. Serve
over noodles or rice. Makes 6
servings.

Meat Loaf Dinner

  6 potatoes, peeled and cubed
  4 carrots, thinly sliced
  1 slightly beaten egg
  1 large shredded wheat biscuit, crushed (½ cup)
  ¼ cup chili sauce
  ¼ cup finely chopped onion
  ½ teaspoon salt
  ¼ teaspoon dried marjoram, crushed
  ⅛ teaspoon pepper
  1 pound ground beef

In crockery cooker place potatoes and carrots. Sprinkle lightly with salt. In mixing bowl combine egg, crushed shredded wheat biscuit, chili sauce, finely chopped onion, ½ teaspoon salt, marjoram, and pepper. Add ground beef; mix well. Shape meat mixture into a round loaf slightly smaller in diameter than the cooker; place atop the vegetables, not touching sides of cooker. Cover and cook on low-heat setting for 9 to 10 hours. Remove meat loaf from cooker using two spatulas; drain off fat.

Place meat loaf on warm serving platter; arrange cooked potatoes and carrots around the meat loaf. Makes 4 servings.

meat loaf tip

For easy removal of a crockery-cooked meat loaf, use two spatulas or make foil "handles." Cut two 15x2-inch strips of foil (use heavy-duty foil or a double thickness of regular foil). Crisscross the strips across the bottom and bring them up the sides of the cooker *before* adding the shaped meat loaf. To remove the loaf, grasp the foil "handles" and lift. Be sure to use potholders.

Spicy Cider Corned Beef

  3 medium onions, sliced
  1 small head cabbage, cut into wedges
  1 3- to 4-pound corned beef brisket
  1 cup apple juice *or* cider
  ¼ cup packed brown sugar
  2 teaspoons finely shredded orange peel
  2 teaspoons prepared mustard
  6 whole cloves
  1 14-ounce jar spiced apple rings

In crockery cooker place onions and cabbage. Trim fat from brisket; place meat atop vegetables. Stir together apple juice or cider, brown sugar, orange peel, mustard, and cloves; pour over meat. Cover; cook on low-heat setting for 8 to 10 hours. Garnish platter with apple rings. Pass mustard, if desired. Makes 6 to 8 servings.

Chili Loaf

  2 slightly beaten eggs
  1 10-ounce can mild enchilada sauce
  1 8-ounce can tomatoes, cut up
  1 8-ounce can red kidney beans, drained
  1 cup crushed corn chips
  ¼ cup finely chopped green onion
  2 tablespoons snipped parsley
  1 teaspoon salt
  1 teaspoon chili powder
  1 pound ground beef
  1 pound bulk pork sausage
  ½ cup shredded American cheese (2 ounces)

In a bowl combine eggs, *2 tablespoons* of the enchilada sauce, *undrained* tomatoes, beans, corn chips, green onion, parsley, salt, and chili powder. Add ground beef and sausage; mix well. Shape meat mixture into a round loaf slightly smaller in diameter than the cooker. Place the meat loaf on a rack in cooker, not touching sides of cooker. Cover and cook on low-heat setting for 10 hours. In saucepan heat the remaining enchilada sauce. Pass sauce and cheese to top each serving. Makes 8 servings.

Tangy Meat Loaf

2 beaten eggs
1 8-ounce container sour cream dip with French onion
2¼ cups soft bread crumbs
½ cup finely chopped celery
¼ cup chopped onion
2 tablespoons chopped pimiento
1 teaspoon dried dillweed
¾ teaspoon salt
Dash pepper
1 pound ground beef
1 pound ground pork
Sour Cream-Mushroom Sauce

In large bowl combine the eggs, ½ cup of the sour cream dip, the bread crumbs, celery, onion, pimiento, dillweed, salt, and pepper. Mix in the ground beef and pork. In crockery cooker crisscross two 15x2-inch strips of foil (use heavy-duty foil or a double thickness of regular foil) across the bottom and bring them up the sides. Place the meat mixture atop foil strips, pressing lightly to shape into a round loaf that doesn't touch the side of the cooker. Cover; cook on low-heat setting for 8 to 9 hours. Lift out the meat loaf, using the foil "handles"; drain off excess fat. Serve with Sour Cream-Mushroom Sauce. Makes 8 servings.

Sour Cream-Mushroom Sauce: In saucepan combine remaining ½ cup *sour cream dip with French onion* and one 10¾-ounce can condensed cream of *mushroom soup*. Heat through; stir occasionally.

Dutch-Style Beef and Cabbage

1 1½-pound beef round steak, cut ¾ inch thick
2 tablespoons all-purpose flour
1 teaspoon salt
¼ teaspoon pepper
2 tablespoons cooking oil
3 large onions, sliced (3 cups)
¾ cup hot water
1 tablespoon vinegar
2 teaspoons instant beef bouillon granules
1 small head cabbage

Trim excess fat from meat; cut meat into cubes. Combine flour, salt, and pepper; coat meat with flour mixture. In skillet quickly brown meat on all sides in hot oil. Drain off fat. Transfer meat to crockery cooker; add onions. In same skillet combine water, vinegar, and bouillon granules. Stir together, scraping browned bits from skillet; pour all into cooker. Cover and cook on low-heat setting for 8 hours.

About 15 minutes before serving, cut cabbage into 4 or 5 wedges. Cook in a 3-quart saucepan in a large amount of boiling salted water, 10 to 12 minutes or till tender. Drain well. Serve beef mixture over cooked cabbage wedges. Makes 4 or 5 servings.

Lima-Meatball Casserole

½ pound bulk pork sausage
1 beaten egg
½ cup fine dry bread crumbs
½ cup chopped onion
¼ cup chopped green pepper
½ teaspoon dried marjoram, crushed
½ teaspoon salt
Dash pepper
1 pound ground beef
2 tablespoons all-purpose flour
2 16-ounce cans lima beans
½ teaspoon beef-flavored gravy base
Dash pepper
Chopped green pepper (optional)

In skillet cook sausage till lightly browned; drain. Transfer to crockery cooker. Combine egg, bread crumbs, onion, ¼ cup green pepper, marjoram, salt, and dash pepper. Add ground beef; mix well. Shape mixture into 30 small meatballs. In same skillet brown meatballs on all sides; drain, reserving drippings. Stir flour into drippings. Drain lima beans; reserve liquid. Blend bean liquid slowly into flour mixture; add gravy base and dash pepper. Cook and stir till thickened and bubbly. Combine gravy and beans with sausage in cooker, add meatballs. Cover; cook on low-heat setting for 8 to 9 hours. Sprinkle additional chopped green pepper atop, if desired. Serves 6 to 8.

Dutch-Style Beef and Cabbage

Beef Stew Bourguignonne

Subtly flavored with dry red wine —

- 2 **pounds beef stew meat, cut into 1-inch cubes**
- 2 **tablespoons cooking oil**
- 1 **10¾-ounce can condensed golden mushroom soup**
- ½ **cup chopped onion**
- ½ **cup shredded carrot**
- ⅓ **cup dry red wine**
- 1 **3-ounce can chopped mushrooms, drained**
- ¼ **teaspoon dried oregano, crushed**
- ¼ **teaspoon Worcestershire sauce**
- ½ **cup cold water**
- ¼ **cup all-purpose flour**
  Hot cooked noodles

In skillet brown beef stew meat in hot oil; drain. Transfer meat cubes to crockery cooker. Stir in golden mushroom soup, chopped onion, carrot, dry red wine, mushrooms, oregano, and Worcestershire sauce. Cover; cook on low-heat setting for 10 to 12 hours. Turn cooker to high-heat setting. Blend cold water slowly into flour; stir into beef mixture. Cook and stir till thickened and bubbly. Serve beef mixture over hot cooked noodles. Makes 6 servings.

using a timer

Plug your crockery cooker into an automatic timer to start cooking while you're away from home. Prepare the food for cooking several hours ahead and chill it thoroughly. Just before you leave, place the chilled food in the cooker and cover. Set the timer to start the cooker at a specified time, making sure the uncooked food stands no more than 2 hours before the cooker comes on.

Turkey Chablis

- 1 **28-ounce frozen rolled turkey roast, thawed**
- ¾ **cup dry white wine**
- ½ **cup finely chopped onion**
- 1 **clove garlic, minced**
- 1 **bay leaf**
- ¼ **teaspoon dried rosemary, crushed**
- ⅛ **teaspoon pepper**
- ⅓ **cup light cream or milk**
- 2 **tablespoons cornstarch**
  Snipped parsley (optional)

Place thawed turkey roast in crockery cooker. Combine wine, onion, garlic, bay leaf, rosemary, and pepper; pour over turkey. Cover; cook on low-heat setting for 9 hours. Remove roast; keep warm. Discard bay leaf. For sauce, skim excess fat from cooking liquid; measure 1⅓ cups cooking liquid into saucepan. Blend cream or milk slowly into cornstarch; stir into liquid. Cook and stir till thickened and bubbly. Season to taste. Slice roast. Spoon some sauce over; pass remaining. Garnish with snipped parsley, if desired. Makes 4 to 6 servings.

Simmered Beef Shanks

- 3 **tablespoons all-purpose flour**
- 1 **teaspoon salt**
- ¼ **teaspoon pepper**
- 4 **pounds beef shank crosscuts**
- 2 **tablespoons cooking oil**
- 3 **cups chopped potatoes**
- 1 **cup water**
- 1 **6-ounce can tomato paste**
- 1 **teaspoon dried basil, crushed**
- ½ **teaspoon salt**
- 2 **tablespoons snipped parsley**
- 2 **tablespoons cold water**
- 1 **tablespoon cornstarch**

In plastic bag combine flour, the 1 teaspoon salt, and pepper. Add beef shank crosscuts, one shank at a time; shake to coat. In skillet brown meat in hot cooking oil. Place chopped potatoes in crockery cooker; place meat atop. Stir together the 1 cup water, tomato paste, dried basil, and the ½ teaspoon salt. Pour over meat. Cover; cook on low-heat setting for 9 to 10 hours. Remove meat and potatoes to serving dish. Sprinkle with snipped parsley; cover to keep warm. For gravy, skim fat from cooking liquid; measure 1½ cups cooking liquid into saucepan. Blend the 2 tablespoons cold water slowly into cornstarch; stir into liquid. Cook and stir till thickened and bubbly; season to taste. Serve gravy with meat and potatoes. Makes 4 servings.

Chicken and Spaghetti

Chicken breast pieces cook in a seasoned tomato sauce —

- 4 small chicken breasts, split, skinned, and boned
- 2 tablespoons cooking oil
- 1 8-ounce can tomato sauce
- 1 6-ounce can tomato paste
- ¼ cup water
- 3 cloves garlic, minced
- 2 teaspoons dried oregano, crushed
- 1 teaspoon sugar
- 1 4-ounce package (1 cup) shredded mozzarella cheese
  Hot cooked spaghetti
  Grated Parmesan cheese

In skillet brown the chicken in hot oil; drain. Sprinkle generously with salt and pepper. Transfer to crockery cooker. For sauce, combine tomato sauce, tomato paste, water, garlic, oregano, and sugar. Pour sauce over chicken. Cover and cook on low-heat setting for 8 to 9 hours. Remove chicken and keep warm. Turn cooker to high-heat setting; stir mozzarella cheese into sauce. Cook, uncovered, till cheese melts and sauce is heated through. Serve chicken and sauce over hot cooked spaghetti. Pass Parmesan. Makes 4 servings.

Turkey Rosemary

Ask your meatman to cut the turkey hindquarters into halves or thirds —

- 4 pounds frozen turkey hindquarters, thawed
- 2 tablespoons cooking oil
- 2 medium onions, coarsely chopped (1 cup)
- 2 large stalks celery, coarsely chopped (1 cup)
- 1 cup water
- 2 teaspoons instant chicken bouillon granules
- 1 teaspoon dried rosemary, crushed
- ½ teaspoon salt
  Dash pepper
- ½ cup cold water
- ¼ cup all-purpose flour

In skillet brown turkey pieces in hot oil; drain off excess fat. In crockery cooker combine onion, celery, 1 cup water, bouillon granules, rosemary, salt, and pepper. Place turkey pieces atop. Cover; cook on low-heat setting for 8 hours. Remove turkey pieces. For gravy, skim excess fat from cooking liquid; measure 1½ cups cooking liquid into saucepan. Return turkey pieces to cooker; cover. Blend ½ cup cold water slowly into flour; stir into reserved cooking liquid in saucepan. Cook and stir till gravy is thickened and bubbly; season to taste. Place turkey pieces on serving platter; pass the gravy. Makes 6 servings.

Swiss Onion and Chicken

- 2 cups sliced onions
- 2 tablespoons butter *or* margarine
- 8 slices day-old bread, cubed (8 cups)
- 2 cups chopped cooked chicken
- 1½ cups shredded Swiss cheese (6 ounces)
- 4 eggs
- 2 cups milk
- 1 teaspoon salt
- 2 tablespoons snipped parsley

In skillet cook onion in butter or margarine till tender. Place ⅓ of the bread cubes in a greased 2-pound coffee can *or* 3-pound shortening can. Add *half* the onions, chicken, and cheese. Repeat layers, ending with bread cubes. Press lightly to fit, if necessary. Beat together eggs, milk, and salt; pour over bread. Cover with foil, crimping edges to sides of can; set in crockery cooker. Pour ½ cup water into cooker. Cover; cook on low-heat setting for 8 to 9 hours. Remove from cooker; let stand 5 to 10 minutes. Loosen edges with spatula or knife. Carefully turn into a serving bowl. Garnish with snipped parsley. Makes 6 to 8 servings.

Chicken and Sausage Cassoulet

Crockery-Stewed Chicken

1　**4-pound stewing chicken, cut up**
4　**celery stalks with leaves, cut up**
4　**cups water**
1　**small onion, sliced**
2　**sprigs parsley**
1　**bay leaf**
1　**teaspoon salt**
¼　**teaspoon pepper**
¼　**teaspoon dried thyme, crushed**
¼　**teaspoon dried marjoram, crushed**
¼　**teaspoon celery salt**

In crockery cooker combine all ingredients. Cover and cook on low-heat setting for 8 to 10 hours. Remove chicken from cooker. Strain chicken broth; store in covered container. Chill. As soon as chicken is cool enough to handle, remove meat from bones. Discard bones and skin. Place chicken in covered container; refrigerate. Use within 2 days. Makes 4 cups cooked chicken and 4 cups chicken broth.

Chicken and Sausage Cassoulet
Reminiscent of the French dish —

4　**cups water**
1¼　**cups dry navy beans**
½　**pound bulk pork sausage**
1　**2½- to 3-pound broiler-fryer chicken, cut up**
½　**cup finely chopped carrot**
½　**cup chopped celery**
½　**cup chopped onion**
1½　**cups tomato juice**
1　**tablespoon Worcestershire sauce**
2　**teaspoons instant beef bouillon granules**
1　**teaspoon salt**
½　**teaspoon dried basil, crushed**
½　**teaspoon dried oregano, crushed**
½　**teaspoon paprika**

In large saucepan combine water and beans; bring to boiling. Reduce heat and simmer, covered, for 1½ hours. Pour beans and liquid into bowl. Refrigerate overnight. Shape sausage into 18 meatballs; brown in skillet. Remove meatballs; reserve drippings in skillet. Cover meatballs; refrigerate overnight. Sprinkle chicken with salt and pepper; brown in the reserved drippings. Remove chicken; cover and refrigerate overnight.

In crockery cooker place chicken, meatballs, carrot, celery, and onion. Drain beans. Combine beans, tomato juice, Worcestershire sauce, beef bouillon granules, salt, basil, oregano, and paprika. Pour over meat mixture. Cover; cook on low-heat setting for 8 hours. Remove chicken and meatballs. Mash bean mixture slightly; serve with chicken and meatballs. Makes 6 servings.

Chinese Pork Roast

1 3- to 4-pound pork shoulder
   roast
1 teaspoon salt
2½ teaspoons curry powder
2 tablespoons cooking oil
1 10¾-ounce can condensed
   cream of mushroom soup
1 16-ounce can fancy mixed
   Chinese vegetables, drained
2 cups cooked rice
¼ cup cold water
2 tablespoons all-purpose flour
   Soy sauce

Trim excess fat from roast; cut roast to fit into crockery cooker. Combine salt and ½ *teaspoon* of the curry powder; rub into roast. Brown roast on all sides in hot oil. Place roast on rack in cooker. For sauce, combine mushroom soup and remaining 2 teaspoons curry powder; pour over meat. Cover; cook on low-heat setting for 8 to 10 hours. Turn cooker to high-heat setting; cook 10 minutes or till boiling. Remove roast to platter. Stir Chinese vegetables and rice into sauce. Blend cold water slowly into flour; stir into sauce. Cook and stir till thickened; serve with roast. Pass soy. Makes 8 servings.

Pork Chops in Brew

6 pork chops, cut ¾ inch thick
2 medium onions, thinly sliced
1 teaspoon instant chicken
   bouillon granules
1 12-ounce can (1½ cups) beer
¼ teaspoon dried thyme, crushed
   Hot cooked noodles *or* hot
   mashed potatoes
⅓ cup cold water (optional)
3 tablespoons all-purpose flour
   (optional)
½ teaspoon Kitchen Bouqet
   (optional)

Trim fat from pork chops; cook trimmings in skillet till 1 tablespoon fat accumulates. Discard trimmings. Brown chops on both sides in hot fat; season with salt and pepper. Place onions in crockery cooker. Arrange chops atop. Dissolve chicken bouillon granules in beer. Stir in dried thyme; pour over chops. Cover; cook on low-heat setting for 8 to 10 hours. Arrange chops and onions on warm platter over hot cooked noodles or mashed potatoes. Skim fat from cooking liquid; serve with chops.

If thicker gravy is desired, measure 1½ cups hot cooking liquid into saucepan. Blend cold water slowly into flour; stir into hot liquid. Add Kitchen Bouquet. Cook and stir till thickened and bubbly. Season to taste with salt and pepper. Makes 6 servings.

Cranberry-Wine-Sauced Pork

Serve this flavorful dish next time you have company —

1 2-pound boneless smoked
   pork shoulder
1 8-ounce can whole cranberry
   sauce
⅓ cup sugar
¼ cup dry red wine
1 teaspoon prepared mustard
⅛ teaspoon ground cloves
2 tablespoons cold water
2 tablespoons cornstarch

Cut smoked pork shoulder in half, if necessary, to fit into crockery cooker. Combine whole cranberry sauce, sugar, dry red wine, prepared mustard, and ground cloves; pour over pork. Cover and cook on low-heat setting for 8 to 10 hours. Remove meat to platter; keep warm. Skim excess fat from cranberry mixture; measure 2 cups cranberry mixture, adding water if necessary.

In saucepan blend the 2 tablespoons cold water slowly into cornstarch. Gradually stir in the hot cranberry mixture. Cook and stir about 5 minutes or till thickened and bubbly. Slice pork. Spoon some of the hot cranberry mixture over the slices; pass the remaining. Makes 6 to 8 servings.

Pork Marengo

2 pounds boneless pork, cut into 1-inch cubes
½ cup chopped onion
2 tablespoons cooking oil
1 16-ounce can tomatoes, cut up
1 teaspoon salt
1 teaspoon instant chicken bouillon granules
1 teaspoon dried marjoram, crushed
½ teaspoon dried thyme, crushed
Dash pepper
1 3-ounce can chopped mushrooms, drained
⅓ cup cold water
3 tablespoons all-purpose flour
Hot cooked rice

In skillet brown the pork cubes and chopped onion, half at a time, in hot oil; drain off fat. Transfer meat and onion to crockery cooker. In same skillet combine *undrained* tomatoes, salt, bouillon granules, marjoram, thyme, and pepper. Stir together, scraping browned bits from bottom of skillet; pour over pork. Cover; cook on low-heat setting for 8 to 10 hours. Turn to high-heat setting. Stir in drained mushrooms. Blend cold water slowly into flour; stir into pork mixture. Cook, uncovered, on high-heat setting 15 to 20 minutes or till thickened; stir occasionally. Serve over rice. Makes 6 to 8 servings.

Peachy Pork Steaks

4 pork steaks, cut ½ inch thick (about 1½ pounds)
¾ teaspoon dried basil, crushed
¼ teaspoon salt
Dash pepper
1 16-ounce can peach slices
2 tablespoons vinegar
1 tablespoon instant beef bouillon granules
Hot cooked rice
¼ cup cold water
2 tablespoons cornstarch

Trim fat from steaks. In skillet cook trimmings till about 2 tablespoons fat accumulate; discard trimmings. Brown steaks on both sides in hot fat. Sprinkle with basil, salt, and pepper. Drain peaches, reserving syrup. Place peaches in crockery cooker; place meat atop. Combine reserved peach syrup, vinegar, and bouillon granules; pour over steaks. Cover; cook on low-heat setting for 8 hours. Arrange steaks and peaches atop rice on platter; keep warm. Garnish with snipped parsley, if desired. Skim excess fat from cooking liquid. In saucepan blend cold water slowly into cornstarch; stir in the hot liquid. Cook and stir till thickened and bubbly. Serve with steaks. Makes 4 servings.

Pork Stroganoff

1½ pounds boneless pork shoulder, cut into ¾-inch cubes
1 tablespoon cooking oil
½ cup chopped onion
1 clove garlic, minced
1 cup water
1 3-ounce can chopped mushrooms, drained
1 tablespoon instant beef bouillon granules
1 teaspoon dried dillweed
⅛ teaspoon pepper
½ cup dairy sour cream
¼ cup dry white wine
3 tablespoons all-purpose flour
Hot cooked noodles

In skillet brown the pork cubes on all sides in hot oil; drain. Add the onion and garlic; cook till tender but not brown. Transfer meat mixture to crockery cooker. Combine the water, mushrooms, bouillon granules, dillweed, and pepper; pour over meat. Cover and cook on low-heat setting for 8 to 10 hours. Turn to high-heat setting. Heat 15 to 20 minutes or till bubbly. Blend together the sour cream, wine, and flour. Stir into the hot mixture; heat through, stirring occasionally. *Do not boil.* Serve over noodles. Sprinkle with snipped parsley, if desired. Makes 6 servings.

Spaghetti with Meat Sauce

1 pound ground beef
2 28-ounce cans tomatoes
2 medium onions, quartered
2 medium carrots, cut into chunks
2 cloves garlic, minced
1 6-ounce can tomato paste
2 tablespoons snipped parsley
1 bay leaf
1 tablespoon sugar
1 teaspoon dried basil, crushed
¾ teaspoon salt
½ teaspoon dried oregano, crushed
 Dash pepper
2 tablespoons cold water
2 tablespoons cornstarch
 Hot cooked spaghetti
 Grated Parmesan cheese

In skillet brown the ground beef; drain off excess fat. Transfer meat to crockery cooker. In blender container place *1 can* of *undrained* tomatoes. Add the onion, carrot, and garlic. Cover and blend till chopped; stir into meat in cooker. Cut up tomatoes in remaining can but do not drain; stir into meat mixture with tomato paste, parsley, bay leaf, sugar, basil, salt, oregano, and pepper. Mix well. Cover and cook on low-heat setting for 8 to 10 hours. To serve, turn to high-heat setting. Remove bay leaf. Cover and heat 10 minutes or till bubbly. Blend cold water slowly into cornstarch; stir into tomato mixture. Cover and cook 10 minutes longer. Spoon over the spaghetti. Pass Parmesan cheese to sprinkle atop. Makes 8 servings.

keep your cooker covered

When you lift the cover of your slow crockery cooker to stir, be sure to replace it immediately, especially on the low-heat setting. If you leave the cooker uncovered, it can lose as much as 20 degrees of important cooking heat in only two minutes. A *quick* peek will cool the food only 1 or 2 degrees.

Sausage Chili

1 pound bulk pork sausage
1 pound ground beef
2 15½-ounce cans red kidney beans, drained
1 28-ounce can tomatoes, cut up
1 cup chopped onion
1 cup chopped green pepper
1 cup sliced celery
1 6-ounce can tomato paste
2 cloves garlic, minced
2 teaspoons salt
2 teaspoons chili powder

In skillet cook sausage and ground beef till browned; drain off excess fat. Transfer meat to crockery cooker. Stir in kidney beans, *undrained* tomatoes, onion, green pepper, celery, tomato paste, garlic, salt, and chili powder. Cover and cook on low-heat setting for 8 to 10 hours. Makes 10 to 12 servings.

Mexican Chili

Chili peppers add zip to this chili —

2 15½-ounce cans red kidney beans, drained
1 28-ounce can tomatoes, cut up
1½ cups chopped celery
1 cup chopped onion
1 6-ounce can tomato paste
½ cup chopped green pepper
1 4-ounce can green chili peppers, drained, seeded, and chopped
2 tablespoons sugar
1 bay leaf
1 teaspoon salt
1 teaspoon dried marjoram, crushed
½ teaspoon garlic powder
 Dash pepper
1 pound ground beef

In crockery cooker combine kidney beans, *undrained* tomatoes, celery, onion, tomato paste, green pepper, chili peppers, sugar, bay leaf, salt, marjoram, garlic powder, and pepper. In skillet brown ground beef; drain and stir into tomato mixture. Cover; cook on low-heat setting for 8 to 10 hours. Skim off excess fat. Remove bay leaf; stir before serving. Makes 10 to 12 servings.

Cider Stew

2 pounds beef stew meat, cut into 1-inch cubes
3 tablespoons cooking oil
3 tablespoons all-purpose flour
2 teaspoons salt
¼ teaspoon dried thyme, crushed
¼ teaspoon pepper
4 carrots, chopped
3 potatoes, peeled and chopped (2½ cups)
2 onions, sliced
1 stalk celery, chopped
1 apple, chopped
2 cups apple juice *or* cider
1 tablespoon vinegar
½ cup cold water
¼ cup all-purpose flour

In skillet or large saucepan brown the meat, half at a time, in hot oil. Drain off fat. Combine 3 tablespoons flour, salt, thyme, and pepper. Toss with browned meat to coat. In crockery cooker place carrots, potatoes, onion, celery, and apple. Place meat atop. Combine apple juice or cider and vinegar. Pour over meat. Cover; cook on low-heat setting for 10 to 12 hours. Turn cooker to high-heat setting. Blend cold water slowly into ¼ cup flour; stir into stew. Cover; cook about 15 minutes or till thickened. Season to taste. Serves 8.

Garden Gold Soup

6 medium carrots, cut up (about 1 pound)
3 medium potatoes, peeled and cubed
2 medium onions, quartered
3 stalks celery with leaves, cut up
4 cups water
2 teaspoons instant chicken bouillon granules
1 teaspoon salt
¼ teaspoon dried dillweed
Dash pepper
¼ cup butter *or* margarine
1 cup milk
2 tablespoons all-purpose flour

In blender container, place ¼ of the vegetables and *1 cup* of the water. Cover and blend till vegetables are coarsely chopped. Transfer vegetables and liquid to crockery cooker. Repeat the process 3 times, using remaining vegetables and water. In crockery cooker place chicken bouillon granules, salt, dried dillweed, and pepper. Mix well. Cover and cook on low-heat setting for 10 to 12 hours.

Place ⅓ of the cooked mixture in the blender container; cover and blend about 1 minute or till smooth. Pour into heat-proof bowl. Repeat process twice with the remaining mixture.

(Or, force the hot, cooked mixture through a food mill.) Return pureed vegetable mixture to crockery cooker; add the butter or margarine. Cover cooker and turn to high-heat setting. Blend milk slowly into flour; stir into hot mixture. Cover and cook about 30 minutes or till thickened and bubbly. Ladle into soup bowls and garnish with croutons, if desired. Makes 8 servings.

Savory Beef-Vegetable Soup

All-day cooking develops the flavor of this hearty soup —

1 cup chopped potato
1 cup chopped onion
1 cup chopped carrot
1 cup chopped celery
2 pounds beef shank crosscuts
1 tablespoon salt
Dash pepper
3 cups water
2 teaspoons beef-flavored gravy base
1 15½-ounce can cut green beans
1 16-ounce can whole kernel corn

In crockery cooker combine potato, onion, carrot, and celery. Place beef atop. Sprinkle with salt and pepper. Stir together water and gravy base; pour over beef. Cover and cook on low-heat setting for 10 to 12 hours. Turn to high-heat setting. Remove beef; skim off fat. Stir in the *undrained* green beans and *undrained* corn. Cover and cook 30 minutes longer. Meanwhile, remove meat from bones; chop and return to soup. Season to taste. Cover and cook 5 minutes more. Stir soup before serving. Makes 10 to 12 servings.

Lentil-Pepperoni Soup

Serve this stick-to-the-ribs soup with bulgur wheat, also called cracked wheat —

- 1½ cups dry lentils
- 5 cups water
- 4 ounces pepperoni, thinly sliced and halved
- 1 medium onion, chopped (½ cup)
- 1 6-ounce can tomato paste
- 1½ teaspoons salt
- ¼ teaspoon dried oregano, crushed
- ¼ teaspoon ground sage
- ⅛ teaspoon cayenne
- 2 medium tomatoes, peeled and cut up
- 1 medium carrot, thinly sliced (½ cup)
- 1 stalk celery, sliced (½ cup)
- ½ cup bulgur wheat

Rinse lentils. In large saucepan combine lentils and water; bring to boiling. Reduce heat; cover and simmer for 30 minutes. *Do not drain.* In crockery cooker combine undrained lentils, pepperoni, onion, tomato paste, salt, oregano, sage, cayenne, tomatoes, carrot, and celery. Cover and cook on low-heat setting for 10 hours. Cook bulgur according to package directions. Stir soup. To serve, mound bulgur in soup. Makes 6 to 8 servings.

Meaty Split Pea Soup

- 1 pound ground pork
- 6 cups water
- 1 pound dry split peas (2¼ cups)
- 2 medium potatoes, peeled and diced (2 cups)
- ¾ cup chopped onion
- ½ cup chopped celery
- 2 teaspoons salt
- ½ teaspoon dried marjoram, crushed
- ¼ teaspoon pepper

In skillet brown ground pork; drain off fat. Transfer pork to crockery cooker. Stir in water, peas, potatoes, onion, celery, salt, marjoram, and pepper. Cover and cook on low-heat setting for 10 to 12 hours. Before serving, stir mixture; season to taste with salt and pepper. Makes 8 to 10 servings.

Mulligatawny

- 4 cups chicken broth
- 2 cups chopped cooked chicken
- 1 16-ounce can tomatoes, cut up
- 1 tart apple, peeled and chopped
- ¼ cup finely chopped onion
- ¼ cup chopped carrot
- ¼ cup chopped celery
- ¼ cup chopped green pepper
- 1 tablespoon snipped parsley
- 2 teaspoons lemon juice
- 1 teaspoon sugar
- 1 teaspoon curry powder
- 2 whole cloves
- ¾ teaspoon salt
  Dash pepper

In crockery cooker combine chicken broth, chicken, *undrained* tomatoes, apple, onion, carrot, celery, green pepper, and parsley. Stir in lemon juice, sugar, curry powder, cloves, salt, and pepper. Cover and cook on low-heat setting for 8 to 10 hours. Remove cloves. Makes 6 servings.

Beef Stock

Use in recipes that call for beef broth —

- 4 pounds beef soup bones, cut into pieces
- 5 cups water
- 1 cup sliced onion
- ½ cup chopped celery
- 8 whole black peppercorns
- 4 sprigs parsley
- 2 teaspoons salt
- 1 large bay leaf

Place soup bones in crockery cooker. Add water, onion, celery, peppercorns, parsley, salt, and bay leaf. Cover and cook on low-heat setting for 12 to 14 hours. Remove bones. Strain broth through cheesecloth; clarify,* if desired. Skim off fat. (Or, transfer to a bowl and chill. Lift off fat; leave residue on bottom of bowl for a clearer stock.) Season to taste with salt and pepper. Remove meat from bones; save meat for another use. Cover and store the meat and stock separately in tightly covered containers in the refrigerator. Use within 3 days. Makes about 4 cups beef stock and about 2 cups cooked meat.

*To clarify: Crush 1 *eggshell.* In saucepan mix shell, 1 *egg white,* and ¼ cup *water;* add hot stock. Bring to boiling. Let stand 5 minutes; strain.

Booya

- 1 pound beef short ribs
- ½ pound boneless pork, cut into ½-inch cubes
- ½ pound beef stew meat, cut into ½-inch cubes
- 2 tablespoons cooking oil
- 1 28-ounce can tomatoes, cut up
- 1 large onion, sliced
- 1 cup chopped red cabbage
- 2 medium carrots, chopped (1 cup)
- 1 cup chopped rutabaga
- 2 stalks celery, chopped (1 cup)
- ¼ cup chopped green pepper
- 2 cups water
- 1 cup parsley sprigs
- 1 tablespoon salt
- 1 teaspoon dried oregano, crushed
- 1 teaspoon paprika
- ½ teaspoon dried savory, crushed
- ¼ teaspoon garlic salt
- 1 16-ounce can cut green beans
- 1 8½-ounce can peas
- 1 8-ounce can whole kernel corn

In skillet brown ribs, pork, and beef in hot oil; drain off fat. Place the *undrained* tomatoes, onion, cabbage, carrots, rutabaga, celery, and green pepper in crockery cooker. Place meat atop vegetables. Stir together water, parsley, salt, oregano, paprika, savory, and garlic salt; add to cooker. Cover and cook on low-heat setting for 10 to 12 hours. Remove meat from bones and cube; discard bones. Return meat to cooker; turn to high-heat setting. Add *undrained* beans, *undrained* peas, and *undrained* corn. Cover and cook for 1 hour. Makes 8 to 10 servings.

Beef-Barley Soup

Complete the meal with sandwiches and a dessert —

- 2 pounds beef short ribs
- 2 cups thinly sliced carrot
- 1 cup sliced celery
- ¾ cup chopped green pepper
- 1 large onion, sliced
- 1 16-ounce can tomatoes, cut up
- ⅔ cup barley
- ¼ cup snipped parsley
- 1 tablespoon instant beef bouillon granules
- 2 teaspoons salt
- ¾ teaspoon dried basil, crushed
- 5 cups water
   Croutons (optional)

In skillet slowly brown beef short ribs on all sides; drain well. In crockery cooker place sliced carrot, celery, green pepper, and onion. Place browned short ribs atop. Combine *undrained* tomatoes, barley, snipped parsley, bouillon granules, salt, and basil. Pour over meat. Add water; *do not stir.* Cover; cook on low-heat setting for 10 to 12 hours. Remove bones from soup. Remove meat from bones and chop; discard bones. Skim fat from soup. Return meat to cooker. Season to taste with salt and pepper. Garnish each serving with croutons, if desired. Makes 8 to 10 servings.

Beef Gumbo

- 4 cups beef broth
- 1 teaspoon salt
- 1 teaspoon sugar
- ½ teaspoon paprika
- ½ teaspoon dried thyme, crushed
- ¼ teaspoon chili powder
- 2 cups chopped cooked beef
- 1 16-ounce can tomatoes, cut up
- 1 10-ounce package frozen cut okra
- 1 cup chopped celery
- ½ cup chopped onion
- 2 tablespoons snipped parsley

In crockery cooker combine beef broth, salt, sugar, paprika, thyme, chili powder, and ⅛ teaspoon *pepper.* Stir in cooked beef, *undrained* tomatoes, okra, celery, onion, and snipped parsley. Cover and cook on low-heat setting for 8 hours. Stir soup before serving. Makes 8 to 10 servings.

Vegetable-Bean Soup

- 1¼ cups dry navy beans (½ pound)
- 1 2-pound meaty ham bone *or* 2 pounds smoked pork hocks
- 2 carrots, chopped
- 1 medium potato, peeled and chopped
- 1 medium onion, chopped
- ½ cup chopped celery

In saucepan bring dry navy beans and 4 cups *water* to boiling; reduce heat and simmer, covered, 1½ hours. Pour into a bowl; cover and chill. Drain beans; reserve liquid. Add enough water to liquid to make 3½ cups. Transfer beans and liquid to crockery cooker. Add ham bone or pork hocks, carrots, potato, onion, celery, and ⅛ teaspoon *pepper.* Cover and cook on low-heat setting for 8 to 10 hours. Remove meat from soup. Remove meat from bone; chop and return to soup. Discard bones. Mash beans slightly, if desired. Serves 6.

side dishes and desserts

Swedish Brown Beans

Subtly seasoned with cinnamon —

- 6 cups water
- 1 pound dry Swedish brown beans (2¼ cups)
- ⅓ cup packed brown sugar
- ¼ cup vinegar
- 3 to 5 inches stick cinnamon
- 1½ teaspoons salt
- 2 tablespoons dark corn syrup
  Crisp-cooked bacon, drained and crumbled (optional)

In saucepan bring water and Swedish brown beans to boiling; reduce heat and simmer, covered, for 2 hours. Remove from heat and pour into a large bowl; cover and chill. Drain beans, reserving 1½ cups of the cooking liquid. Transfer beans and reserved bean liquid to crockery cooker; stir in brown sugar, vinegar, stick cinnamon, and salt. Cover and cook on low-heat setting for 12 to 14 hours. *Stir the beans after 10 hours and again after 12 hours* to be sure beans cook evenly. To serve, remove cinnamon stick and stir in dark corn syrup. Mash beans slightly, if desired. Garnish beans with crumbled bacon, if desired. Makes 6 servings.

Bean-Pot Lentils

- 1½ cups water
- 1 cup dry lentils (8 ounces)
- ½ cup chopped onion
- ½ teaspoon salt
- 1 16-ounce can tomatoes, cut up
- 2 tablespoons brown sugar
- 1 tablespoon chili sauce
- ½ teaspoon dry mustard
- 2 slices bacon, crisp-cooked and crumbled

In saucepan bring water, lentils, onion, and salt to boiling. Simmer, covered, 30 minutes. Transfer to crockery cooker; stir in *undrained* tomatoes, brown sugar, chili sauce, and mustard. Cover; cook on low-heat setting for 8 to 10 hours. Uncover; cook on high-heat setting for 30 minutes. Stir; top with bacon. Serves 6.

Maple-Baked Beans

- 8 cups water
- 1 pound dry lima beans (2½ cups)
- 1 cup chopped onion
- 4 slices bacon, diced
- ½ cup maple-flavored syrup
- ½ cup catsup
- 1 tablespoon Worcestershire sauce
- 1 bay leaf
- 1 teaspoon salt
- ⅛ teaspoon pepper

In saucepan bring water and dry lima beans to boiling; reduce heat and simmer, covered, 1½ hours. Pour into bowl; cover and chill. Drain beans, reserving 1 cup liquid. Transfer beans and reserved liquid to crockery cooker. Stir in chopped onion, bacon, maple-flavored syrup, catsup, Worcestershire sauce, bay leaf, salt, and pepper. Cover; cook on low-heat setting for 8 to 10 hours. Remove bay leaf. Makes 6 servings.

Crock-Style Beans

- 8 cups water
- 1 pound dry navy beans (2½ cups)
- 4 ounces salt pork, cut into small pieces (1 cup)
- 1 cup chopped onion
- ½ cup molasses
- ¼ cup packed brown sugar
- 1 teaspoon dry mustard

In saucepan bring water and beans to boiling; reduce heat and simmer, covered, 1½ hours. Remove from heat and pour into bowl; cover and chill. Drain beans; reserve 1 cup liquid. Transfer beans and reserved liquid to crockery cooker. Stir in pork, onion, molasses, brown sugar, and mustard. Cover; cook on low-heat setting for 12 to 14 hours. Stir. Makes 6 servings.

Italian Zucchini

- ½ cup chopped onion
- ½ cup chopped green pepper
- ¼ cup butter *or* margarine
- 1 cup water
- 1 6-ounce can tomato paste
- 1 3-ounce can sliced mushrooms, drained
- 1 envelope spaghetti sauce mix
- 2½ pounds zucchini, cut into ⅜-inch slices (8 cups)
- 1 cup shredded mozzarella cheese (4 ounces)

In a saucepan cook onion and green pepper in butter or margarine till tender but not brown. Transfer to crockery cooker. Stir in water, tomato paste, drained mushrooms, and *dry* spaghetti sauce mix. Add zucchini, stirring gently to coat. Cover and cook on low-heat setting for 8 hours. To serve, spoon into dishes; sprinkle with shredded mozzarella cheese. Makes 8 servings.

Maple-Stewed Apples

1 8-ounce package dried
   apples
1 cup orange juice
1 cup water
½ cup maple-flavored syrup
1 tablespoon lemon juice

Thoroughly rinse dried apples; place in crockery cooker. Stir in the orange juice, water, maple-flavored syrup, and lemon juice. Cover and cook on low-heat setting for 8 hours. Serve warm or chilled. Makes 6 to 8 servings.

Fruit Compote Supreme

1 29-ounce can peach slices
1 cup dried apricots
½ cup packed brown sugar
½ cup water
1 teaspoon finely shredded
   orange peel
⅓ cup orange juice
½ teaspoon grated lemon peel
2 tablespoons lemon juice
1 16-ounce can pitted dark
   sweet cherries, drained

In crockery cooker combine *undrained* peaches, apricots, brown sugar, water, orange peel, orange juice, lemon peel, and lemon juice. Cover; cook on low-heat setting for 9 to 10 hours. To serve, gently stir in drained cherries. Cover; cook on low-heat setting 15 minutes longer. Makes 8 servings.

cookers are not all alike

Remember, these recipes were tested only in 3½- to 4-quart crockery cookers that have the heating element wrapped around a crockery liner. If you have a different type of cooker, you may need to adjust the timing of recipes and stir the food occasionally. See pages 68 and 69 for more information.

Indian-Style Beans and Peppers

4 cups water
1½ cups dry pinto beans
   (10 ounces)
1 teaspoon salt
1 16-ounce can tomatoes, cut up
¾ cup chopped green pepper
½ cup chopped onion
1 tablespoon brown sugar
1 clove garlic, minced
1 teaspoon salt
⅛ teaspoon pepper
3 slices bacon, crisp-cooked,
   drained, and crumbled

In saucepan bring water, beans, and 1 teaspoon salt to boiling; reduce heat and simmer, covered, 1½ hours. Pour into a bowl; cover and chill. Drain beans, reserving 1½ cups liquid. Transfer beans and reserved liquid to crockery cooker. Stir in *undrained* tomatoes, green pepper, onion, brown sugar, garlic, 1 teaspoon salt, and pepper. Cover and cook on low-heat setting for 12 to 14 hours. Stir through beans; top with crumbled bacon. Makes 6 servings.

Breakfast Prunes

2 cups orange juice
1 cup water
¼ cup orange marmalade
1 teaspoon ground cinnamon
¼ teaspoon ground cloves
¼ teaspoon ground nutmeg
1 12-ounce package (1¾ cups)
   pitted, dried prunes
2 thin lemon slices

In crockery cooker combine orange juice, water, orange marmalade, cinnamon, cloves, and nutmeg. Stir in prunes and lemon slices. Cover and cook on low-heat setting for 8 to 10 hours. Serve warm. Makes 6 servings.

Fresh Peach Butter

6 pounds peaches, peeled,
   quartered, and pitted
¼ cup lemon juice
2 teaspoons ground cinnamon
5 cups sugar

Place about *3 cups* of the peaches at a time in blender. Cover; blend till smooth. Repeat process. Measure 11 cups blended peaches; place in crockery cooker. Stir in lemon juice and ground cinnamon. Cook, *uncovered*, on high-heat setting for 7 hours, stirring twice. Stir in sugar. Cook, *uncovered*, 2 hours more, stirring several times. Pour into hot sterilized half-pint jars, leaving ½-inch headspace. Wipe jar rims; adjust lids. Process in boiling water bath 10 minutes (start timing when water returns to boiling). Makes 8 half-pints.

part-day cooking

(less than 6 hours)

Spaghetti Sauce Italiano

- 1 pound ground beef
- ½ pound bulk Italian sausage
- 1 28-ounce can tomatoes, cut up
- 2 6-ounce cans tomato paste
- 1 6-ounce can sliced mushrooms
- 1 cup chopped onion
- ¾ cup chopped green pepper
- ½ cup burgundy
- ½ cup sliced pimiento-stuffed olives
- ⅓ cup water
- 3 bay leaves
- 2 cloves garlic, minced
- 1½ teaspoons Worcestershire sauce
- 1 teaspoon sugar
- 1 teaspoon salt
- ½ teaspoon chili powder
- ⅛ teaspoon pepper
- 2 tablespoons cold water
- 2 tablespoons cornstarch
  Hot cooked spaghetti
  Grated Parmesan cheese

In skillet brown ground beef and sausage; drain off fat. Transfer to crockery cooker. Stir in *undrained* tomatoes, tomato paste, mushrooms, onion, green pepper, burgundy, olives, water, bay leaves, garlic, Worcestershire, sugar, salt, chili powder, and pepper. Cover; cook on high-heat setting for 5 to 6 hours. Blend cold water slowly into cornstarch; stir into tomato mixture. Cover; cook 10 minutes. Remove bay leaves. Serve over hot cooked spaghetti. Pass Parmesan cheese. Makes 8 to 10 servings.

Beef Burgundy

- 1 2-pound beef round steak, cut into ¾-inch cubes
- ¼ cup all-purpose flour
- ½ teaspoon salt
- 3 tablespoons butter *or* margarine
- 1 cup burgundy
- ¾ cup beef broth
- ½ cup chopped onion
- 1 3-ounce can whole mushrooms, drained
- 2 tablespoons snipped parsley
- 2 bay leaves
- 1 clove garlic, minced
- ⅛ teaspoon pepper
  Hot cooked noodles

Coat beef with mixture of flour and salt (use all the flour). In skillet melt butter or margarine; brown meat on all sides. Transfer meat to crockery cooker. Combine burgundy, beef broth, onion, mushrooms, parsley, bay leaves, garlic, and pepper. Stir into meat. Cover; cook on high-heat setting for 3 hours. (Meat may be kept warm another hour by turning to low-heat setting.) Remove bay leaves; discard. Serve beef over hot cooked noodles. If desired, sprinkle with paprika and garnish with parsley. Makes 6 to 8 servings.

Two-Meat Spaghetti Sauce

- 1 28-ounce can tomatoes
- 1 6-ounce can tomato paste
- 1 medium green pepper, cut into pieces
- 1 small onion, cut into pieces
- 1 clove garlic
- 2 teaspoons sugar
- 1 teaspoon salt
- ½ teaspoon dried oregano, crushed
- ½ teaspoon dried basil, crushed
- ½ teaspoon chili powder
- ⅛ teaspoon pepper
- 2 cups cubed cooked beef *or* pork
- 1 4-ounce package (about 1 cup) sliced pepperoni
  Hot cooked spaghetti
  Parmesan cheese

In blender container combine *undrained* tomatoes, tomato paste, green pepper, onion, garlic, sugar, salt, oregano, basil, chili powder, and pepper. Cover; blend till chopped. Pour *half* the mixture into crockery cooker. Add beef or pork and pepperoni to remaining tomato mixture in blender container. Cover; blend till chopped. Add the mixture to cooker. (If blender is not used, finely chop vegetables and meats; stir in tomatoes and spices.) Cover; cook on high-heat setting for 3 to 3½ hours. Serve over hot cooked spaghetti. Pass Parmesan cheese. Makes 4 to 6 servings.

Home-Style Round Steak

For an extra touch, serve the meat and gravy over hot cooked noodles —

- 1 1½-pound beef round steak
- 2 tablespoons all-purpose flour
- 2 tablespoons cooking oil
- 1 teaspoon instant beef bouillon granules
- ½ cup hot water
- 1 cup shredded carrot
- 1 teaspoon sugar
- ½ teaspoon dried thyme, crushed
- ¼ cup cold water
- 2 tablespoons all-purpose flour
- ½ teaspoon salt
- ½ teaspoon Kitchen Bouquet

Cut beef round steak into 6 equal pieces; coat steak pieces with 2 tablespoons flour. In skillet brown steak in hot oil. Season with salt and pepper. Place steak pieces in crockery cooker. Dissolve bouillon granules in the hot water; combine with carrot, sugar, and thyme. Pour over steak. Cover; cook on high-heat setting for 4 hours. Remove meat to platter; keep warm. Measure liquid; add enough water to make ¾ cup liquid. Pour into saucepan. Blend the cold water into 2 tablespoons flour. Stir into liquid; add salt and Kitchen Bouquet. Cook and stir till thickened. Serve over meat. Makes 6 servings.

Smoked Beef-and-Bean Burgers

- 1 8-ounce can red kidney beans
- 1 3½-ounce package sliced smoked beef, finely snipped
- ⅓ cup mayonnaise
- 2 tablespoons sweet pickle relish
- 1 tablespoon prepared mustard Dash bottled hot pepper sauce
- 6 hard rolls, split and toasted
- 6 thin slices onion
- 3 slices American cheese, halved

Drain beans; slightly mash. Combine with beef, mayonnaise, pickle relish, mustard, and hot pepper sauce. Spread about ¼ cup mixture on bottom half of *each* hard roll. Top *each* with *1* onion slice and *½ slice* cheese. Wrap each in foil; place in crockery cooker. Cover; cook on high-heat setting for 1½ hours. Makes 6.

Red Clam Spaghetti Sauce

- 1 medium onion, chopped
- 2 cloves garlic, minced
- 2 tablespoons cooking oil
- 2 7½-ounce cans minced clams
- 1 16-ounce can tomatoes, cut up
- 1 12-ounce can tomato paste
- ¼ cup snipped parsley
- 1 bay leaf
- 1 teaspoon sugar
- 1 teaspoon dried basil, crushed
- ½ teaspoon dried thyme, crushed Hot cooked spaghetti

In skillet cook the onion and garlic in hot oil till onion is tender but not brown. Transfer onion and garlic to crockery cooker. Stir in the *remaining* ingredients and ½ teaspoon *salt*; mix well. Cover and cook on low-heat setting for 4 hours. Serve over hot cooked spaghetti. Remove bay leaf. Serves 4 to 6.

Meat Loaf Florentine

- 1 10-ounce package, frozen chopped spinach, thawed
- 2 slightly beaten eggs
- 1½ cups soft bread crumbs
- ½ cup milk
- 2 tablespoons soy sauce
- 1¼ teaspoons salt
- ¼ teaspoon bottled hot pepper sauce
- 2 pounds ground beef Mushroom Sauce

Drain spinach; combine with eggs, bread crumbs, milk, soy sauce, salt, and hot pepper sauce. Add beef; mix well. Shape into round loaf slightly smaller in diameter than crockery cooker. Lay two 15x2-inch strips of foil (double thickness) crisscross-style across bottom and up sides of cooker. Place loaf atop, not touching sides. Cover; cook on high-heat setting for 4 hours. Use foil strips as lifters to remove loaf from cooker to serving platter. Serve with Mushroom Sauce. Serves 8.

Mushroom Sauce: In saucepan combine one 3-ounce can sliced *mushrooms*, undrained, and 2 tablespoons all-purpose *flour*. Stir in 1 cup dairy *sour cream* and 2 tablespoons snipped *chives*. Cook and stir just till thickened. Do not boil. Makes 1½ cups sauce.

Fondue Italiano

½ pound ground beef
2 8-ounce cans tomato sauce
½ envelope spaghetti sauce mix
  (about 2 tablespoons)
3 cups shredded cheddar
  cheese (12 ounces)
1 cup shredded mozzarella
  cheese (4 ounces)
½ cup chianti
1 tablespoon cornstarch
  Italian bread, cut into bite-
  size cubes, each with crust

In skillet brown ground beef; drain off fat. Transfer meat to crockery cooker. Stir in tomato sauce and *dry* spaghetti sauce mix. Gradually stir in cheddar and mozzarella cheeses. Cover and cook on high-heat setting 40 to 45 minutes or till cheese is melted, stirring occasionally. Blend chianti slowly into cornstarch; stir into cheese mixture. Cook on high-heat setting about 20 minutes longer or till thickened, stirring often. Serve at once. (*Or*, reduce heat and keep warm, covered, on low-heat setting for 1 to 2 hours; stir occasionally.) Spear bread cube with fondue fork; dip in fondue, swirling to coat. Makes 10 to 12 servings.

Tijuana Sandwiches

3 cups chopped cooked beef
1 16-ounce can refried beans
½ cup chopped onion
½ cup chopped green pepper
⅓ cup chopped ripe olives
1 8-ounce can tomato sauce
¾ cup water
2 teaspoons chili powder
1 teaspoon salt
1 teaspoon Worcestershire
  sauce
¼ teaspoon garlic powder
¼ teaspoon pepper
¼ teaspoon paprika
  Dash celery salt
  Dash nutmeg
1 cup crushed corn chips
12 to 15 taco shells, heated
½ medium head lettuce,
  shredded
2 tomatoes, chopped
1 cup shredded American
  cheese (4 ounces)
  Bottled hot pepper sauce

In crockery cooker stir together cooked beef, beans, onion, green pepper, and olives. Stir in tomato sauce, water, chili powder, salt, Worcestershire sauce, garlic powder, pepper, paprika, celery salt, and nutmeg. Cover and cook on high-heat setting for 2 hours. Just before serving, fold in crushed corn chips. Spoon mixture into taco shells; top with lettuce, tomatoes, and cheese. Pass hot pepper sauce. Makes 12 to 15 sandwiches.

Beef-Ham Loaf

1 slightly beaten egg
1 10¾-ounce can condensed
  tomato soup
¾ cup coarsely crushed saltine
  crackers
⅓ cup milk
⅓ cup finely chopped onion
¼ cup snipped parsley
1½ pounds ground beef
½ pound ground fully cooked
  ham
  Mustard Sauce

In a bowl combine egg, *half* of the soup, the crushed crackers, milk, onion, and parsley. Add ground beef and ham; mix well. Shape meat mixture into round loaf slightly smaller in diameter than crockery cooker. Place meat loaf on rack in cooker, not touching sides. Cover; cook on low-heat setting for 6 hours. Remove loaf from cooker using two spatulas; drain off excess fat. Serve with hot Mustard Sauce. Makes 6 servings.

Mustard Sauce: In saucepan stir together the *remaining soup*, 1 beaten *egg*, 2 tablespoons *prepared mustard*, 2 tablespoons *water*, 1 tablespoon *sugar*, 1 tablespoon *vinegar*, and 1 tablespoon *butter or margarine*. Cook and stir till thickened and bubbly. Makes 1 cup.

Barbecued Pork Sandwiches

- ½ cup chopped onion
- ¼ cup chopped celery
- 1 clove garlic, minced
- 2 tablespoons butter *or* margarine
- 1 12-ounce bottle chili sauce
- ½ cup water
- 3 tablespoons brown sugar
- 2 tablespoons Worcestershire sauce
- 2 tablespoons vinegar
- 1 teaspoon chili powder
- ¼ teaspoon salt
  Dash pepper
- 3 cups thinly sliced cooked pork
- 2 tablespoons cold water
- 1 tablespoon all-purpose flour
- 12 hamburger buns, split

In skillet cook onion, celery, and garlic in butter or margarine till tender but not brown. Transfer to crockery cooker. Add chili sauce, ½ cup water, brown sugar, Worcestershire, vinegar, chili powder, salt, and pepper; mix well. Stir in pork, coating all slices. Cover; cook on low-heat setting for 3 to 4 hours. Turn to high-heat setting. Blend 2 tablespoons cold water into flour; stir into pork mixture. Cover; cook 15 to 20 minutes more. Stir occasionally. Toast hamburger buns. Fill *each* with about ⅓ *cup* meat mixture. Makes 12.

Tomato-Sauced Spareribs

- 3 pounds lean pork spareribs
- 1 28-ounce can tomatoes
- 3 stalks celery, chopped
- 1 medium green pepper, chopped
- 1 medium onion, chopped
- 3 tablespoons cold water
- 2 tablespoons cornstarch
  Hot cooked rice

Cut spareribs into serving-size pieces. Brown in skillet. Transfer to crockery cooker; sprinkle with 1 teaspoon *salt* and ¼ teaspoon *pepper*. Stir in *undrained* tomatoes, celery, green pepper, and onion. Cover; cook on high-heat setting for 4 hours. Lift out ribs; spoon fat from sauce. Blend water slowly into cornstarch; stir into cooker. Cook and stir till thickened and bubbly. Serve over rice. Serves 4.

El Paso Ham

- 3 cups chopped fully cooked ham
- 2 cups shredded Monterey Jack cheese (8 ounces)
- 1 8-ounce can tomato sauce
- 1 4-ounce can green chili peppers, rinsed, seeded, and chopped
- ½ cup finely chopped onion
  Few drops bottled hot pepper sauce
  Corn bread, cut into squares

In crockery cooker combine ham, cheese, tomato sauce, green chili peppers, onion, and bottled hot pepper sauce. Cover; cook on low-heat setting for 2 hours.

To serve, split the hot corn bread squares. Spoon ham mixture on the bottom half of each corn bread square. Cover with corn bread tops; spoon more of the ham mixture over. Makes 6 servings.

Curried Ham

- 1 cup chopped apple (1 medium)
- ¾ cup chopped onion
- 3 tablespoons butter *or* margarine
- 2 tablespoons all-purpose flour
- 4 teaspoons curry powder
- 1 10¾-ounce can condensed cream of mushroom soup
- 2½ cups milk
- 6 cups cubed fully cooked ham *or* cooked chicken *or* turkey
- 1 cup dairy sour cream
  Hot cooked rice
  Snipped parsley
  Toasted slivered almonds

In saucepan cook apple and onion in butter or margarine till tender. Stir in flour and curry powder. Add soup; stir in milk. Cook and stir till thickened and bubbly. Transfer to bowl; cool mixture quickly in larger bowl filled with ice water (do not stir). Refrigerate up to 24 hours.

Transfer chilled mixture to crockery cooker; stir in meat. Cover; cook on high-heat setting for 1½ hours. (*Or*, omit chilling step; transfer soup mixture immediately to crockery cooker; stir in meat. Cover; cook on low-heat setting for 1½ hours.) Stir in sour cream. Cover; cook on high-heat setting 30 minutes longer, stirring occasionally. Serve over hot cooked rice; garnish with snipped parsley and toasted slivered almonds. Pass other condiments such as sliced green onion, sliced preserved kumquats, raisins, and flaked coconut, if desired. Makes 12 servings.

South Pacific Pork Roast

1 3-pound boneless pork
　　shoulder roast
½ cup soy sauce
½ cup dry sherry
2 cloves garlic, minced
1 tablespoon dry mustard
1 teaspoon ground ginger.
1 teaspoon dried thyme, crushed
　　Pineapple Sauce

Place the pork shoulder roast in a clear plastic bag; set in a deep bowl. For marinade, thoroughly blend together the soy sauce, dry sherry, minced garlic, dry mustard, ginger, and thyme. Pour marinade over meat in bag; close. Place roast in the refrigerator and marinate for 2 to 3 hours or overnight.

Transfer the pork roast and marinade to crockery cooker. Cover and cook on high-heat setting for 3½ to 4 hours. Lift roast out onto a cutting board; let stand for 10 minutes before slicing. Discard the marinade. Arrange the sliced pork roast on a warm serving platter. Spoon some of the hot Pineapple Sauce over the pork slices; pass the remaining sauce. Makes 8 servings.

Pineapple Sauce: Drain one 8½-ounce can *crushed pineapple;* reserve the syrup. Add enough water to reserved syrup to make ¾ cup. In a small saucepan blend together 2 tablespoons *brown sugar* and 1 tablespoon *cornstarch.* Stir in the reserved syrup, 1 tablespoon *vinegar,* and 1 teaspoon *soy sauce.* Cook, stirring constantly, till sauce is thickened and bubbly. Stir in the drained pineapple; heat through. Makes 1⅔ cups sauce.

Cherry Pork Chops

6 pork chops, cut ¾ inch
　　thick
　　Salt
　　Pepper
½ of a 21-ounce can (1 cup)
　　cherry pie filling
2 teaspoons lemon juice
½ teaspoon instant chicken
　　bouillon granules
⅛ teaspoon ground mace
　　Parsley (optional)

Trim excess fat from pork chops. In a large skillet cook the trimmings till about 1 tablespoon of fat accumulates. Discard the remaining trimmings. Brown the pork chops in the hot fat. Sprinkle each pork chop with salt and pepper.

In crockery cooker stir together the cherry pie filling, lemon juice, chicken bouillon granules, and ground mace; mix well. Place the browned pork chops atop cherry mixture. Cover and cook on low-heat setting for 4 to 5 hours. Place chops on a warm serving platter. Pour some of the cherry sauce over; pass the remaining sauce. Garnish with parlsey, if desired. Makes 6 servings.

Apple- and Raisin-Topped Ham

1 21-ounce can apple pie
　　filling
⅓ cup light raisins
⅓ cup orange juice
2 tablespoons water
1 tablespoon lemon juice
¼ teaspoon ground cinnamon
1 1½-pound fully cooked ham
　　slice (about ¾ inch thick)
　　Hot cooked rice (optional)

Combine pie filling, raisins, orange juice, water, lemon juice, and cinnamon. Cut ham slice into 6 equal pieces. In crockery cooker alternately layer ham with apple mixture, ending with apple mixture. Cover; cook on low-heat setting for 4 to 5 hours. Serve with hot cooked rice, if desired. Makes 6 servings.

Hot Pork-Sauerkraut Salad

1 cup chopped onion
2 tablespoons cooking oil
2 cups cubed cooked pork
1 16-ounce can sauerkraut,
　　drained and rinsed
2 tablespoons water
½ teaspoon salt
½ teaspoon ground sage
½ cup dairy sour cream
1 large apple, cored and
　　chopped

Cook chopped onion in hot cooking oil till tender but not brown. Transfer to crockery cooker. Add pork, sauerkraut, water, salt, and sage. Cover and cook on low-heat setting for 4 to 5 hours. Turn to high-heat setting. Cook 10 minutes. Stir in sour cream and apple. Cover; heat through but *do not boil.* Garnish with apple wedges, if desired. Makes 4 servings.

Lamb-Stuffed Grape Leaves

1   beaten egg
¼   cup long grain rice
¼   cup finely chopped onion
2   tablespoons snipped fresh
     mint leaves *or* 1 tablespoon
     dried mint, crushed
2   tablespoons snipped parsley
3   tablespoons water
¼   teaspoon salt
     Dash pepper
½   pound ground lamb
24   fresh *or* canned grape leaves
2   cups water
2   tablespoons butter *or*
     margarine, melted
¾   teaspoon salt
     Egg-Lemon Sauce

Combine egg, rice, onion, mint, parsley, 3 tablespoons water, ¼ teaspoon salt, and pepper. Add lamb; mix well. Rinse fresh grape leaves; drain and open flat. Spoon *1 tablespoon* filling onto center of each leaf. Fold in sides; roll up. Line crockery cooker with double thickness of cheesecloth. Place stuffed leaves in cooker. Mix 2 cups water, butter or margarine, and ¾ teaspoon salt; pour over grape leaves. Tie corners of cheesecloth together. Cover; cook on high-heat setting for 2½ hours. Remove bag; pour liquid into bowl, reserving ½ cup. Return bag to cooker; cover. Prepare Egg-Lemon Sauce. Place stuffed leaves on platter; garnish with cherry tomatoes and fresh grape leaves, if desired. Serve hot with Egg-Lemon Sauce. Makes 4 servings.

Egg-Lemon Sauce: Beat 1 *egg white* till stiff peaks form. Beat 1 *egg yolk* till light and lemon-colored. Fold egg yolk into white. Slowly stir in 2 tablespoons *lemon juice*. Gradually add ½ cup *reserved cooking liquid*. Cook and stir 5 minutes or till slightly thickened.

Middle Eastern Sandwiches

4   pounds boneless lamb *or* beef,
     cut into ½-inch cubes
¼   cup cooking oil
2   cups chopped onion
2   cloves garlic, minced
1   cup dry red wine
1   6-ounce can tomato paste
2   teaspoons salt
2   teaspoons dried oregano,
     crushed
1   teaspoon dried basil, crushed
½   teaspoon dried rosemary,
     crushed
     Dash pepper
¼   cup cold water
¼   cup cornstarch
     Pita bread
2   cups shredded lettuce
1   large tomato, seeded and
     diced
1   large cucumber, seeded and
     diced
1   8-ounce carton plain yogurt

In skillet brown *1 pound* of the meat in *1 tablespoon* of hot oil; drain. Remove meat. Repeat with remaining meat and oil. Transfer meat to crockery cooker. Add onion and garlic to skillet; cook till onion is tender but not brown. Add to meat with wine, tomato paste, salt, oregano, basil, rosemary, and pepper; mix well. Cover; cook on low-heat setting for 4 hours. To serve, turn cooker to high-heat setting. Blend cold water into cornstarch; stir into meat mixture. Cook till thickened and bubbly, stirring occasionally. Split bread to make a pocket; fill each pocket with meat mixture, lettuce, tomato, cucumber, and yogurt. Makes 10 to 16 sandwiches.

Coq au Vin Blanc

2   2½- to 3-pound broiler-fryer
     chickens, cut up
¼   cup all-purpose flour
1   teaspoon paprika
½   teaspoon salt
⅛   teaspoon pepper
3   tablespoons butter *or*
     margarine, melted
½   cup dry white wine
½   cup chicken broth
2   tablespoons chopped onion
1   tablespoon snipped parsley
¼   teaspoon dried thyme, crushed
¼   teaspoon ground sage
2   egg yolks
¼   cup milk
1   15½-ounce can boiled onions,
     drained
1   3-ounce can sliced
     mushrooms, drained
     Hot cooked noodles

Save chicken backs, necks, and wings for another use. Combine flour, paprika, salt, and pepper; coat chicken pieces thoroughly. Brown chicken on all sides in melted butter or margarine; drain well. Transfer to crockery cooker. Combine wine, chicken broth, onion, parsley, thyme, and sage. Pour over chicken. Cover; cook on low-heat setting for 5 to 6 hours. Remove chicken; pour cooking liquid into saucepan. Return chicken to cooker; cover to keep warm. Skim the excess fat from liquid. Cook the liquid till reduced to 1 cup.

Beat egg yolks and milk together. Stir about *half* of the hot liquid into egg yolk mixture; return all to mixture in saucepan. Cook and stir till mixture thickens slightly. Stir in drained onions and mushrooms. Season to taste. Serve chicken over hot cooked noodles. Pour some sauce over chicken; pass remaining. Makes 6 servings.

Chicken and Cornmeal Dumplings

1 9-ounce package frozen cut green beans
2 cups cubed cooked chicken
2 cups diced potatoes
1 13¾-ounce can chicken broth
1 12-ounce can (1½ cups) vegetable juice cocktail
½ cup sliced celery
½ cup chopped onion
1 teaspoon chili powder
½ teaspoon salt
6 drops bottled hot pepper sauce
1¼ cups packaged biscuit mix
⅓ cup yellow cornmeal
1 cup shredded American cheese (4 ounces)
2 tablespoons snipped parsley
⅔ cup milk

Thaw beans by placing in strainer; run hot water over beans. Transfer to crockery cooker. Add chicken, potatoes, chicken broth, vegetable juice, celery, onion, chili powder, salt, and hot pepper sauce. Cover; cook on low-heat setting for 4 hours. Turn to high-heat setting; heat till bubbly. Combine biscuit mix, cornmeal, ½ cup cheese, and parsley. Add milk; stir just till moistened. Drop dough by tablespoonfuls onto stew. Cover; cook 45 minutes more (do not lift cover). Sprinkle dumplings with remaining cheese. Serves 4 to 6.

Saucy Chicken and Ham

2 2½- to 3-pound broiler-fryer chickens, cut up
2 tablespoons cooking oil
1 cup fully cooked ham cut into strips
1 medium onion, quartered
2 tomatoes
1 11-ounce can condensed cheddar cheese soup
½ teaspoon dried basil, crushed
½ cup cold water
¼ cup all-purpose flour

Save chicken backs, necks, and wings for another use. Season chicken with salt and pepper. In skillet brown chicken on all sides in hot oil; drain. Transfer to crockery cooker. Add ham and onion. Peel and chop 1 tomato; set other aside to cut into wedges for garnish. Combine chopped tomato, soup, and basil; pour over meat. Cover; cook on high-heat setting for 3 to 4 hours. Remove chicken; pour cooking liquid into saucepan. Return chicken to cooker; cover. Skim fat from liquid. Blend cold water into flour; stir into hot liquid. Cook and stir till thickened. Serve sauce with chicken. Garnish with reserved tomato wedges. Makes 6 servings.

Chicken Oahu

2 2½- to 3-pound broiler-fryer chickens, cut up
¼ cup all-purpose flour
½ teaspoon paprika
½ teaspoon salt
   Dash pepper
¼ cup cooking oil
4 cups herb-seasoned stuffing cubes
1 8¼-ounce can crushed pineapple
   Oahu Sauce

Save chicken backs, necks, and wings for another use. Mix flour, paprika, salt, and pepper; coat chicken. Brown chicken in hot oil; drain. In crockery cooker combine stuffing cubes and *undrained* pineapple; place chicken atop. Cover; cook on low-heat setting for 6 hours. Place chicken on platter; spoon Oahu Sauce atop. Spoon stuffing into bowl; pass. Makes 6 servings.

Oahu Sauce: In saucepan combine 1½ cups finely chopped *celery*, ½ cup finely chopped *onion*, ½ cup *water*, and 2 tablespoons finely chopped *green pepper*. Cover; simmer till tender. Add one 10¾-ounce can condensed *cream of mushroom soup*, ½ cup dairy *sour cream*, and 1 tablespoon *soy sauce*; heat through (do not boil). Makes 3 cups sauce.

Lemon Chicken

- 2 2½- to 3-pound broiler-fryer chickens, cut up
- ¼ cup all-purpose flour
- 1¼ teaspoons salt
- 2 tablespoons cooking oil
- 1 6-ounce can frozen lemonade concentrate, thawed
- 3 tablespoons brown sugar
- 3 tablespoons catsup
- 1 tablespoon vinegar
- 2 tablespoons cold water
- 2 tablespoons cornstarch
  Hot cooked rice

Save chicken backs, necks, and wings for another use. Combine the flour and salt; coat chicken thoroughly. Brown chicken pieces on all sides in hot oil; drain. Transfer to crockery cooker. Stir together the lemonade concentrate, brown sugar, catsup, and vinegar; pour over chicken. Cover; cook on high-heat setting 3 to 4 hours. Remove chicken; pour cooking liquid into saucepan. Return chicken to cooker; cover to keep warm. Skim fat from reserved liquid. Blend cold water slowly into cornstarch; stir into hot liquid. Cook and stir till thickened and bubbly. Serve chicken with gravy over hot cooked rice. Makes 6 servings.

Spanish-Style Chicken

- 1 cup chopped onion
- ½ cup chopped celery
- 2 2½- to 3-pound broiler-fryer chickens, cut up
- 1 16-ounce can tomatoes, cut up
- 2 teaspoons instant beef bouillon granules
- 1 clove garlic, minced
- 1 teaspoon paprika
- 1 12-ounce package fully cooked smoked sausage links
- ⅓ cup cold water
- 3 tablespoons all-purpose flour
- ½ teaspoon salt
  Saffron Rice with Peas

In crockery cooker place onion and celery. Save chicken backs, necks, and wings for another use. Sprinkle remaining chicken with salt and pepper; place in cooker. Combine *undrained* tomatoes, bouillon, garlic, and paprika; pour over chicken. Cover; cook on high-heat setting for 2 to 3 hours. Place sausage atop chicken; cover and continue cooking for 1 hour more. Remove meat and vegetables to platter; keep warm. Skim fat from cooking liquid. Slowly blend cold water into flour; add salt. Stir into liquid. Cook and stir on high-heat setting about 15 minutes or till thickened and bubbly. Serve over chicken and Saffron Rice with Peas. Makes 6 servings.

Saffron Rice with Peas: In saucepan combine 2 cups *water*, 1 cup long grain *rice*, ½ teaspoon *salt*, and ¼ teaspoon ground *saffron*; cover. Bring to boiling; reduce heat. Continue cooking till tender. Meanwhile, cook one 10-ounce package *frozen peas* according to package directions; drain. Stir into rice mixture. Makes 3 cups.

Beer-Braised Rabbit

- 1 2- to 2½-pound dressed rabbit, cut up, *or* one 2- to 2½-pound broiler-fryer chicken, cut up
- 2 tablespoons cooking oil
- 3 medium potatoes, peeled and halved
- 3 or 4 carrots, bias-cut into 1-inch pieces
- 1 onion, thinly sliced
- 1 cup beer
- ¼ cup chili sauce
- 1 tablespoon brown sugar
- 1 clove garlic, minced
- ⅓ cup cold water
- 3 tablespoons all-purpose flour
- ½ teaspoon salt

Season meat with salt and pepper. Brown meat on all sides in hot oil; drain. In crockery cooker place potatoes, carrots, and onion; place meat atop. Combine beer, chili sauce, brown sugar, and garlic. Pour over meat. Cover; cook on high-heat setting for 3½ to 4 hours. Remove meat. Drain vegetables; reserve cooking liquid. Return meat and vegetables to cooker; cover. Measure cooking liquid; add additional beer or water if needed to make 1½ cups liquid. In saucepan slowly blend cold water into flour; stir in reserved liquid and the salt. Cook, stirring constantly, till thickened. Place meat and vegetables on platter. If desired, sprinkle with paprika and garnish with parsley. Pass gravy. Makes 4 servings.

Beer-Braised Rabbit

Fish Fillets Florentine

- 4 fresh *or* frozen flounder fillets *or* other fish fillets (1½ pounds)
- 1 10-ounce package frozen chopped spinach
- 1 3-ounce package cream cheese, softened
- 1 tablespoon lemon juice
- 1 tablespoon minced dried onion
- 1 11-ounce can condensed cheddar cheese soup
  Ground nutmeg

Thaw fish, if frozen. Cook spinach according to package directions; drain. Combine spinach, cream cheese, lemon juice, and onion; mix well. Spread about ¼ of the spinach mixture on each fillet. Roll up; secure with wooden pick. Spoon soup into crockery cooker. Place fish on a 12x12-inch piece of cheesecloth. Bring edges over fish; tie securely. Place in cooker. Cover; cook on low-heat setting for 4 hours. Carefully lift cheesecloth bag from cooker. Transfer fish to serving platter; remove picks. Stir sauce; pour some over fish rolls. Sprinkle with nutmeg. Pass remaining sauce. Makes 4 servings.

Salmon Loaf

- 1 16-ounce can salmon
- 2 beaten eggs
- 1½ cups soft bread crumbs
- ¼ cup finely chopped onion
- 2 tablespoons butter *or* margarine, melted
- 1 tablespoon snipped parsley
- 1 tablespoon lemon juice
- ¼ teaspoon salt
  Dash cayenne
- ½ cup shredded American cheese (2 ounces)

Drain salmon; reserve juices. If necessary, add water to juices to make ¼ cup liquid. Combine liquid, eggs, bread crumbs, onion, butter or margarine, parsley, lemon juice, salt, and cayenne. Flake salmon; stir into mixture. Shape into round loaf slightly smaller in diameter than crockery cooker. Line cooker with foil to come up 2 or 3 inches on sides. Place loaf on foil, not touching sides. Cover; cook on low-heat setting for 5 hours. Top with cheese the last 5 minutes. Makes 6 servings.

Bratwurst with Apple Kraut

- 4 tart cooking apples, peeled, cored, and sliced (3 cups)
- 1 27-ounce can sauerkraut, drained and snipped
- 1 pound bratwurst links, halved crosswise
- ¼ cup packed brown sugar
- 1 teaspoon caraway seed
- ¼ cup water

In crockery cooker stir together apples, sauerkraut, bratwurst, brown sugar, and caraway seed. Stir in water. Cover and cook on low-heat setting for 3 to 4 hours. Makes 6 servings.

Sausage-Garbanzo Bake

- 2 15-ounce cans garbanzo beans, drained
- 1 pound Polish sausage, sliced
- 1 15-ounce can tomato sauce
- 1 cup chopped onion
- ¼ cup water
- 2 bay leaves
- 1 clove garlic, minced
- 1 teaspoon dried oregano, crushed
- ½ teaspoon ground cumin
- ⅛ teaspoon pepper

In crockery cooker combine all ingredients. Cover; cook on high-heat setting for 3 to 4 hours. Season to taste; remove bay leaves. Makes 4 to 5 servings.

Hawaiian Sausage Combo

- 1 20-ounce can pineapple chunks (juice pack)
- 1 17-ounce can sweet potatoes, sliced 1 inch thick
- 1 12-ounce package fully cooked smoked sausage links
- 3 tablespoons brown sugar
- 2 tablespoons cornstarch
- 1 tablespoon butter

Drain pineapple, reserving the juice. Add water to juice to make 1 cup; set aside. In crockery cooker place drained pineapple, sweet potatoes, and sausage. In saucepan stir together the brown sugar, cornstarch, and ¼ teaspoon *salt*. Gradually blend in the reserved juice. Cook and stir till thickened and bubbly; cook and stir 1 minute more. Remove from heat; stir in butter. Pour sauce over mixture in cooker. Cover and cook on high-heat setting for 3 hours. Skim off excess fat. Stir carefully before serving. Makes 4 to 6 servings.

Vegetable-Beef Soup

- 3 pounds beef shank crosscuts
- 1 16-ounce can tomatoes, cut up
- 1 10¾-ounce can condensed tomato soup
- ⅓ cup chopped onion
- 3 cups water
- 2 bay leaves
- 1 tablespoon salt
- 2 teaspoons Worcestershire sauce
- ¼ teaspoon chili powder
- 1 16-ounce can lima beans, drained
- 1 8¾-ounce can whole kernel corn
- 1 cup thinly sliced carrots
- 1 cup diced potatoes
- 1 cup diced celery

In crockery cooker place beef shanks. Add *undrained* tomatoes, tomato soup, and onion. Combine water, bay leaves, salt, Worcestershire, and chili powder; pour over beef. Cover; cook on low-heat setting for 4 hours. Turn cooker to high-heat setting. Remove beef; discard bay leaves. Stir the remaining vegetables into soup. Cover cooker and continue cooking. Cut meat from bone; dice and return to cooker. Cover; cook for 2 to 3 hours longer. Serves 12.

---

care of your cooker

Ceramic liners are more delicate than they look, and sudden temperature changes can damage them. So, don't put cold food into a hot cooker, never put your cooker in the refrigerator, and never immerse cooker or cord in water. Clean the liner with a soft cloth and soapy water — avoid abrasive cleaners and cleansing pads. For easiest cleanup, add warm water to the cooker just after removing food. Don't wait until the cooker cools and food has cooked on sides.

Peppy Burger-Vegetable Soup

- ½ pound ground beef
- ½ cup chopped onion
- ½ cup chopped celery
- 1 16-ounce can tomatoes, cut up
- 2 cups diced potatoes
- 1 8-ounce can cut green beans
- 1 teaspoon chili powder
- ½ teaspoon Worcestershire sauce Dash cayenne
- 1 10½-ounce can condensed beef broth

In skillet cook ground beef, onion, and celery till beef is browned; drain off fat. Transfer to crockery cooker. Stir in *undrained* tomatoes, potatoes, green beans, chili powder, ½ teaspoon *salt*, Worcestershire, and cayenne. Add beef broth and 1¼ cups *water*. Cover; cook on high-heat setting for 4 hours. Stir before serving. Serves 6.

Sausage-Lamb Cassoulet

- 3 15-ounce cans great northern beans, drained
- 1 cup dry white wine
- 1 8-ounce can tomato sauce
- 2 bay leaves
- 1 clove garlic, minced
- 1 tablespoon snipped parsley
- ½ teaspoon dried thyme, crushed
- ½ pound boneless lamb, cut into ½-inch pieces
- ¾ cup chopped onion
- 2 tablespoons cooking oil
- ½ pound Polish sausage, sliced ½ inch thick
- ¼ cup cold water
- 2 tablespoons all-purpose flour

In crockery cooker combine beans, wine, tomato sauce, bay leaves, garlic, parsley, and thyme. In saucepan cook lamb and onion in hot oil till lamb is well browned on all sides; drain. Stir lamb, onion, and sliced Polish sausage into bean mixture. Cover; cook on low-heat setting for 5 to 6 hours. Turn to high-heat setting. Heat till bubbly (do not lift cover). Slowly blend the cold water into flour; stir into meat-bean mixture. Cover; cook till slightly thickened. Before serving, remove bay leaves and discard. Makes 6 to 8 servings.

from vegetables to desserts

Corn-Stuffed Onions

- 8 **medium onions**
  Salt
- 1 **16-ounce can whole kernel corn, drained**
- 2 **tablespoons chopped pimiento**
- 2 **tablespoons butter *or* margarine**
- 2 **tablespoons all-purpose flour**
- ½ **teaspoon salt**
  Dash pepper
- 1 **cup milk**
- 1 **cup shredded American cheese (4 ounces)**

Remove centers from onions; chop enough of the centers to make 1 cup (save remaining centers for another use). Salt onion cavities. Combine corn and pimiento; spoon mixture into onion shells. Reserve any remaining corn. Wrap each onion securely in foil. Pour ¼ cup *water* into crockery cooker. Stack onions in cooker. Cover; cook on high-heat setting for 4 to 5 hours.

Just before serving, prepare sauce. In a medium saucepan over moderate heat cook the reserved 1 cup of chopped onion in butter or margarine till tender but not brown. Stir in flour, ½ teaspoon salt, and pepper. Add milk all at once; cook and stir till thickened and bubbly. Add any reserved corn; return sauce to bubbling. Add cheese, stirring till melted. Remove onions from cooker using tongs; unwrap and place on a serving dish. Pour some of the hot cheese sauce over onions; pass remaining sauce. Makes 8 servings.

Ginger-Bean Bake

- 2 **teaspoons minced dried onion**
- ¼ **cup water**
- 2 **16-ounce cans pork and beans in tomato sauce**
- ½ **cup finely crushed gingersnaps (7 cookies)**
- ¼ **cup catsup**
- 2 **tablespoons light molasses**

Place onion and water in crockery cooker; let stand for 5 minute. Add pork and beans, crushed gingersnaps, catsup, and molasses; stir to combine. Cover and cook on low-heat setting for 3 to 4 hours. Makes 6 servings.

Herbed Potatoes

- 1½ **pounds small new potatoes**
- ¼ **cup water**
- ¼ **cup butter *or* margarine, melted**
- 3 **tablespoons snipped parsley**
- 2 **heads fresh dill, snipped**
- 1 **tablespoon lemon juice**
- 1 **tablespoon snipped chives**
  Salt
  Pepper

Wash potatoes, peel strip from around the center of each potato. Place the potatoes in crockery cooker; add the water. Cover and cook on high-heat setting for 2½ to 3 hours. Drain well. In saucepan heat butter or margarine with parsley, dill, lemon juice, and chives. Pour mixture over potatoes; toss till thoroughly coated. Season to taste with salt and pepper. Makes 6 servings.

Ratatouille

Serve this flavorful vegetable dish hot or cold —

- 1¾ **cups coarsely chopped onion**
- 1 **clove garlic, minced**
- 2 **tablespoons cooking oil**
- 4 **medium tomatoes, peeled and coarsely chopped**
- ½ **pound zucchini, cut into ½-inch-wide strips**
- ½ **pound eggplant, peeled and cut into ½-inch-wide strips**
- 2 **medium green peppers, cut into ½-inch-wide strips**
- 1½ **teaspoons salt**
- 2 **or 3 fresh basil leaves, snipped, *or* 1 teaspoon dried basil, crushed**
- 2 **sprigs fresh thyme, snipped, *or* ½ teaspoon dried thyme, crushed**
  Dash pepper

In a large skillet cook onion and garlic in hot oil till onion is tender but not brown. Transfer the mixture to crockery cooker. Add tomatoes, zucchini, eggplant, green peppers, salt, basil, thyme, pepper; stir to combine. Cover and cook on high-heat setting for 3 to 4 hours. Serve as a hot vegetable. (Or, chill and serve as a salad in sauce dishes.) Makes 6 to 8 servings.

Shaker-Style Creamed Onions

2 pounds small onions, peeled
½ cup light raisins
2 tablespoons butter
2 tablespoons all-purpose flour
⅛ teaspoon ground nutmeg
Dash white pepper
1⅔ cups milk

Place onions in crockery cooker. Sprinkle with salt; add 2 cups *water*. Cover and cook on high-heat setting for 3 hours. Drain onions well. Just before serving, cover raisins with very hot water and soak for 5 minutes; drain. In saucepan melt butter; stir in flour, ¾ teaspoon *salt*, nutmeg, and pepper. Add milk and raisins all at once; cook and stir till thickened and bubbly. Stir in onions. Makes 6 to 8 servings.

Fig-Apricot Nut Bread

¼ cup snipped dried apricots
1⅓ cups all-purpose flour
½ cup sugar
1 tablespoon baking powder
1 beaten egg
¾ cup milk
2 tablespoons cooking oil
¼ cup snipped dried figs
¼ cup chopped pecans

Pour boiling water over apricots; cool and drain. Stir together flour, sugar, baking powder, and ½ teaspoon *salt*. Combine egg, milk, and oil; add to dry ingredients, stirring just till smooth. Fold in apricots, figs, and nuts. Turn into 2 well-greased 16-ounce vegetable cans with waxed paper lining the bottoms. Place cans in crockery cooker. Cover; cook on high-heat setting for 3½ hours. Remove cans from cooker; cool 10 minutes in cans. Cool thoroughly. Makes 2.

Cocktail Stewed Tomatoes

6 to 8 medium tomatoes
¼ cup chopped celery
2 tablespoons chopped onion
1 tablespoon lemon juice
¾ teaspoon sugar
½ teaspoon salt
½ teaspoon prepared horseradish
½ teaspoon Worcestershire sauce
1 or 2 drops bottled hot pepper sauce

Wash, peel, and core tomatoes. Place in crockery cooker. Add remaining ingredients; stir to combine. Cover; cook on low-heat setting for 4 to 6 hours. Turn to high-heat setting; bring to boiling. Remove lid; cook 30 minutes longer. Serve hot. Makes 4 cups.

Cream of Celery Soup

2 cups chicken broth
1½ cups finely chopped celery
⅓ cup finely chopped onion
¼ teaspoon salt
2 cups light cream
¼ cup all-purpose flour

In crockery cooker combine chicken broth, celery, onion, and salt. Cover and cook on low-heat setting for 4 to 6 hours.

Turn cooker to high-heat setting; do not remove cover. Heat till bubbly. Blend ½ *cup* of the cream slowly into the flour; stir into broth in cooker along with remaining 1½ cups cream. Cook, covered, about 30 minutes or till heated through and slightly thickened. Season to taste with salt and pepper. If desired, top each serving with a pat of butter or margarine and garnish with a sprinkling of paprika or snipped parsley. Makes 6 servings.

French Onion Soup

6 to 8 onions, thinly sliced (6 to 8 cups)
¼ cup butter or margarine
4 10½-ounce cans consensed beef broth
1 soup can water (1¼ cups)
2 teaspoons Worcestershire sauce
⅛ teaspoon pepper

In large skillet cook onions in butter till tender. Transfer onions and butter to crockery cooker. Add condensed beef broth, water, Worcestershire sauce, and pepper. Cover and cook on low-heat setting for 4 to 6 hours. Ladle soup into bowls; garnish with slices of toasted French bread, if desired. Makes 10 to 12 servings.

Apple-Filled Squash

2 small acorn squash
2 medium baking apples, peeled and chopped
½ cup packed brown sugar
Ground cinnamon or ground nutmeg
Lemon juice
4 tablespoons butter

Cut squash in half lengthwise; remove seeds. Sprinkle cavities with salt. Divide chopped apple evenly among the squash halves. Sprinkle *each half* with about 2 *tablespoons* brown sugar, a dash cinnamon or nutmeg, and a few drops lemon juice. Dot *each* with 1 *tablespoon* butter. Wrap each squash half securely in foil. Pour ¼ cup *water* into crockery cooker. Stack the squash, cut sides up, in cooker. Cover; cook on low-heat setting for 5 hours. Unwrap; place squash on serving platter. Drain any syrup remaining in foil into small pitcher; serve with squash. Makes 4 servings.

Pumpkin Bread

Serve this spicy bread at your next brunch —

- 1 **cup packed brown sugar**
- 1/3 **cup shortening**
- 2 **eggs**
- 1 **cup canned pumpkin**
- 1/4 **cup milk**
- 2 **cups all-purpose flour**
- 2 **teaspoons baking powder**
- 1/2 **teaspoon salt**
- 1/2 **teaspoon ground ginger**
- 1/4 **teaspoon baking soda**
- 1/4 **teaspoon ground nutmeg**
- 1/4 **teaspoon ground cloves**
- 3/4 **cup raisins**

Cream brown sugar and shortening till fluffy. Beat in eggs, one at a time. Stir in pumpkin and milk. Stir together flour, baking powder, salt, ground ginger, baking soda, ground nutmeg, and ground cloves; add to pumpkin mixture. Beat 1 minute with electric mixer or rotary beater. Stir in raisins. Turn into a well-greased 3-pound shortening can. Place can in crockery cooker. Cover; cook on high-heat setting for 3½ hours. Remove can from cooker; cool 10 minutes in can. Remove from can. Cool thoroughly on wire rack. Makes 1.

bread pans

Breads and puddings can be made in a variety of containers — in fact, any heat-proof utensil that fits inside your crockery cooker. Use a 3-pound shortening can, a 2-pound coffee can, a 6-cup mold, or a special pan.

Boston Brown Bread

- 1/2 **cup whole wheat flour**
- 1/4 **cup all-purpose flour**
- 1/4 **cup yellow cornmeal**
- 1/2 **teaspoon baking powder**
- 1/4 **teaspoon baking soda**
- 1/4 **teaspoon salt**
- 1 **beaten egg**
- 1/4 **cup molasses**
- 2 **tablespoons sugar**
- 2 **teaspoons cooking oil**
- 3/4 **cup buttermilk or sour milk**
- 2 **tablespoons raisins**

Stir together flours, cornmeal, baking powder, soda, and salt. Combine egg, molasses, sugar and oil. Add flour mixture and buttermilk or sour milk alternately to molasses mixture; beat well. Stir in raisins. Turn batter into 2 well-greased 16-ounce vegetable cans. Cover cans tightly with foil. Place cans in crockery cooker. Cover and cook on high-heat setting for 3 hours. Remove cans from cooker; cool 10 minutes in cans. Remove from cans. Serve warm. Makes 2 loaves.

Holiday Carrot Pudding

- 1¼ **cups all-purpose flour**
- 1 **teaspoon baking powder**
- 1/2 **teaspoon baking soda**
- 1/2 **teaspoon ground cinnamon**
- 1/2 **teaspoon ground nutmeg**
- 2 **eggs**
- 3/4 **cup packed brown sugar**
- 1/2 **cup shortening**
- 2 **medium carrots, sliced**
- 1 **medium apple, peeled, cored, and cut into eighths**
- 1 **medium potato, peeled and cut into pieces**
- 3/4 **cup raisins**
  Cream Cheese Sauce
  Pecan halves

Stir together flour, baking powder, soda, and spices. Place eggs, brown sugar, and shortening in blender. Cover; blend till smooth. Add carrot to blender mixture; blend till chopped. Add apple; blend till chopped. Add potato; blend till finely chopped. Stir carrot mixture and raisins into dry ingredients; mix well. Turn into greased and floured 6-cup mold; cover tightly with foil. Place in crockery cooker. Cover and cook on high-heat setting for 4 hours. Remove from cooker. Cool 10 minutes; unmold. Drizzle some of the Cream Cheese Sauce over pudding; top with nuts. Pass remaining sauce. Makes 6 to 8 servings.

Cream Cheese Sauce: Beat one 3-ounce package *cream cheese*, softened; ¼ cup *butter*, softened; and 1 teaspoon *vanilla* till fluffy. Slowly beat in 1 cup sifted *powdered sugar*. Stir in 2 tablespoons *milk*; beat till smooth.

Cranberry-Orange Relish

2 cups sugar
1 teaspoon finely shredded orange peel
1 cup orange juice
1 16-ounce package fresh or frozen cranberries (4 cups)

In crockery cooker combine sugar, orange peel, and orange juice; stir till sugar is nearly dissolved. Stir in cranberries. Cover; cook on low-heat setting for 6 hours. Mash berries. Chill thoroughly. Makes 4 cups.

Mincemeat-Stuffed Apples

4 medium baking apples
½ cup prepared mincemeat
2 tablespoons chopped maraschino cherries
2 tablespoons chopped walnuts
2 tablespoons brown sugar
4 teaspoons water
4 teaspoons butter or margarine

Core apples; enlarge openings slightly. Place each apple on a 12-inch square of foil. Combine mincemeat, cherries, nuts, and brown sugar. Divide filling among apples. Sprinkle each apple with 1 teaspoon water and dot with 1 teaspoon butter. Bring foil up around apples; twist ends together to seal. Place in crockery cooker. Cover; cook on low-heat setting for 5 to 6 hours. Makes 4 servings.

Saucy Poached Pears

5 medium pears (about 2 pounds)
½ cup burgundy
¼ cup sugar
1 tablespoon lemon juice
⅛ teaspoon ground cinnamon
⅛ teaspoon ground nutmeg
Dash salt
2 tablespoons orange marmalade

Peel pears; core from bottom, leaving stems on. Place pears upright in crockery cooker. Stir together burgundy, sugar, lemon juice, cinnamon, nutmeg, and salt. Blend in marmalade; carefully pour over pears. Cover and cook on low-heat setting for 3½ to 4 hours. Serve pears warm or chilled with syrup. Pass dairy sour cream or whipped cream cheese, if desired. Makes 5 servings.

Applesauce Bread Pudding

3 beaten eggs
2 cups milk
1 16-ounce can applesauce
¾ cup sugar
2 tablespoons butter, melted
2 teaspoons vanilla
¾ teaspoon ground cinnamon
½ teaspoon salt
9 slices day-old white bread, cubed (about 7 cups)

In a large bowl combine eggs, milk, applesauce, sugar, butter, vanilla, cinnamon, and salt. Gently stir in bread cubes. Turn into a lightly greased 2-pound coffee can; cover tightly with foil. Place can in crockery cooker. Add ½ cup warm water to cooker. Cover; cook on high-heat setting for 3 hours. Remove can from cooker; spoon pudding into serving dishes. Top with whipped cream, if desired. Makes 8 servings.

Devil's Food Pudding

⅓ cup sugar
2 tablespoons shortening
1 egg
1 square (1 ounce) unsweetened chocolate, melted and cooled
1¼ cups all-purpose flour
1 teaspoon baking soda
¼ teaspoon salt
½ cup buttermilk
½ teaspoon vanilla
Satin Sauce or vanilla ice cream

Cream sugar and shortening. Add egg; mix well. Beat in chocolate. Stir together flour, soda, and salt. Add flour mixture and buttermilk alternately to creamed mixture; beat well. Beat in vanilla. Divide into 2 well-greased 16-ounce vegetable cans. Cover tightly with foil. Place in crockery cooker. Pour ½ cup warm water around cans. Cover; cook on high-heat setting 1½ hours. Remove cans from cooker. Cool 10 minutes; unmold. Serve warm with Satin Sauce or ice cream. Makes 8 servings.

Satin Sauce: Combine 2 egg yolks, ½ cup sifted powdered sugar, ½ teaspoon vanilla, and dash salt; beat till fluffy. Whip ½ cup whipping cream; fold in. Chill thoroughly. Stir before serving.

SKILLET RECIPES

For an easy answer to the familiar "what's for dinner?" question, choose a recipe designed for skillets. In this section, you'll find quick-cooking main dishes for those busy days, time-worthy favorites for days when you're not so rushed, and tempting side dishes and desserts for any time.

If the skillets in your kitchen are used only for frying, it's time to take another look at these trusty helpers and match them up with the recipes in this section. You'll find that besides frying pans, they're also griddles, steamers, poachers, panbroilers, and mini-ovens. Any skillet will do all of these jobs, but an electric skillet has the added advantage of a temperature control.

If you own an electric skillet, get the most from this versatile appliance by studying its use-and-care booklet. The temperature control on the electric skillet is keyed to cooking operations similar to those in the tip box at right.

As you cook, you may find that you are choosing a slightly higher or lower setting than the recipes specify. The proper setting depends on the amount of food you're cooking and on the setting at which water boils in your skillet. Since the latter depends in part on the altitude of your region, it's a good idea to run this test. Bring about 2 cups of water to boiling in your electric skillet. In this way you will know more accurately what setting is required to reach a full boil, or to maintain a simmer.

Once you're familiar with your skillet, you can apply the cooking techniques in the glossary on this page to prepare the tasty recipes that follow. Most of these recipes incorporate electric skillet temperatures in the recipe directions. The exceptions are dishes that involve amounts of food too small for such a large appliance. No matter which recipe you choose, you'll be impressed by the versatility of your skillet.

temperature guide

150° to 180° Warm
220° to 250° Simmer
250° to 275° Full Boil
275° to 300° Medium-low (to fry eggs)
300° to 325° Medium (to cook onion, celery, mushrooms, green pepper, etc. in butter or margarine)
350° to 400° High (to brown meat or panbroil or panfry)
400° to 450° Hot (to keep temperature at 365° to 370° for shallow-fat frying)

Skillet Glossary

Bake — To cook in a pan, an oven, or an oven-type appliance, such as an electric skillet with a tight-fitting cover.

Baste — To moisten foods during cooking with pan drippings or a special sauce to add flavor and prevent drying.

Braise — To cook slowly with a small amount of liquid in a covered skillet.

Caramelize — To melt sugar slowly over low heat until it becomes brown.

Dry-heat cook — To cook food, usually meat, in an uncovered pan and without the addition of liquid.

French fry — To cook by immersing food in hot fat at least 1½ inches deep.

Fry — To cook in hot shortening or cooking oil.

Moist-heat cook — To cook food, usually meat, in a tightly covered pan so that the steam held in the pan aids in cooking and tenderizing the meat.

Panbroil — To cook meat, uncovered, in a hot skillet, removing fat as it accumulates in the pan.

Panfry — To cook, uncovered, in a small amount of hot shortening or cooking oil.

Poach — To cook in hot liquid, being careful that food retains its shape.

Pot-roast — To braise a large cut of meat. The roast is usually browned well before the liquid is added.

Sauté — To brown or cook in a small amount of butter or hot shortening.

Shallow-fat fry — To cook by immersing in the minimum depth of hot shortening or cooking oil (see tip on page 131).

Simmer — To cook in liquid over low heat at a temperature where bubbles form at a slow rate and burst before reaching the surface. It is usually achieved by bringing liquid to a rapid boil and then turning down the heat for a long cooking period.

Steam — To cook in steam in a covered pan. A small amount of boiling water is used, and more is added during cooking if necessary.

Stew — To simmer or braise slowly in a small amount of liquid.

Skillet Hamburger Pie
(see recipe, page 110)

quick
and easy
main dishes

Mock Chicken-Fried Steak

- 1 beaten egg
- ¼ cup milk
- 1 cup coarsely crushed saltine crackers (20 crackers)
- 2 tablespoons finely chopped onion
- 1 teaspoon chili powder
- ¼ teaspoon salt
- ¼ teaspoon Worcestershire sauce
- 1 pound ground beef
- 2 tablespoons cooking oil
  Warmed catsup

Combine egg, milk, ½ *cup* crushed crackers, onion, chili powder, salt, and Worcestershire. Add beef; mix well. Shape into 6 patties, each ½ inch thick; coat with remaining crushed crackers. In skillet cook the patties in hot oil over medium-high heat about 3 minutes on each side (325° on electric skillet). Serve with catsup. Makes 6 servings.

Sirloin Especial

- 4 beef top loin steaks, cut ¾ inch thick
- 2 tablespoons butter
- 1 3-ounce can sliced mushrooms, drained
- ¼ cup thinly sliced green onion
- 1 tablespoon lemon juice
- 1 clove garlic, minced
- ¼ teaspoon salt
- ½ teaspoon dried basil, crushed

In skillet cook steaks in butter over medium heat to desired doneness, turning once (350° on electric skillet). (Allow about 9 minutes for rare, about 11 minutes for medium, or about 20 minutes for well-done.) Remove steaks to warm platter. Add mushrooms, onion, lemon juice, garlic, salt, and basil to skillet. Heat till bubbly; serve with steaks. Makes 4 servings.

Cacciatore Sauce with Polenta

You can make the polenta the night before —

- 3¾ cups water
- 1 cup yellow cornmeal
- 1 teaspoon salt
- 1 pound ground beef
- 1 cup chopped onion
- 1 6-ounce can sliced mushrooms, drained
- 1 clove garlic, minced
- 1 15-ounce can tomato sauce
- ½ cup water
- ¼ cup snipped parsley
- 1 teaspoon dried sage, crushed
- 1 teaspoon shredded orange peel
- ½ teaspoon dried thyme, crushed
  Grated Parmesan cheese

For the polenta, in a 10-inch skillet bring 2¾ *cups* of the water to a full rolling boil (250° on electric skillet). Combine remaining 1 cup water, cornmeal, and salt. Slowly stir into boiling water. Cook, stirring frequently, 10 to 15 minutes or till thick. Turn into a 9-inch pie plate. Cover; chill several hours or till firm enough to cut.

For sauce, in a 10-inch skillet cook ground beef, onion, mushrooms, and garlic till meat is browned and onion is tender (350° on electric skillet). Drain off excess fat. Add tomato sauce, water, parsley, sage, orange peel, and thyme. Cover and reduce heat (220°). Simmer 30 minutes. Cut polenta into 8 wedges. Press wedges down into sauce. Cover skillet and continue simmering about 10 minutes or till polenta is heated through. Serve sauce over polenta. Top with grated Parmesan cheese. Pass additional Parmesan, if desired. Makes 8 servings.

Meat Loaf in the Round

- 2 beef bouillon cubes
- 1¼ cups boiling water
- 1 beaten egg
- 1½ cups soft bread crumbs
- ¼ cup chopped onion
- ½ teaspoon ground sage
- ¼ teaspoon salt
  Dash pepper
- 1 pound ground beef
  Kitchen Bouquet
- 1 3-ounce can sliced mushrooms
- 1 tablespoon cornstarch
- ¼ cup dairy sour cream

Dissolve bouillon cubes in the boiling water; combine ¼ cup bouillon with egg, bread crumbs, onion, sage, salt, and pepper. Add ground beef; mix well. In an 8-inch skillet shape mixture into a circle slightly smaller than diameter of skillet. With the handle of a wooden spoon, make indentations in the meat to make 4 wedge-shaped pieces. Rub surface of meat with Kitchen Bouquet. Pour ½ *cup* of remaining bouillon around meat loaf; add mushrooms. Cook, covered, over low heat for 25 to 30 minutes.

Transfer meat loaf to warm serving platter. Combine cornstarch and remaining bouillon; stir into pan juices. Cook and stir over low heat till thickened and bubbly. Stir in sour cream; heat through but do not boil. Serve over meat loaf. Makes 4 servings.

Chinese Beef and Broccoli

1 pound beef sirloin steak, cut ½ inch thick
2 tablespoons soy sauce
4 teaspoons cornstarch
2 teaspoons cooking oil
1 teaspoon salt
1 pound fresh broccoli *or* two 10-ounce packages frozen broccoli spears
1 thin slice fresh gingerroot *or* ½ teaspoon ground ginger
3 tablespoons cooking oil
½ cup water
2 green onions, thinly sliced (2 tablespoons)
  Hot cooked rice

Partially freeze beef; slice diagonally into bite-size strips. Combine soy sauce, cornstarch, the 2 teaspoons oil, and salt in bowl. Add beef; toss to coat well. Slice broccoli lengthwise into thin strips about 3 inches long.

Heat ginger in 3 tablespoons oil in electric wok or skillet at 375°. Add broccoli and stir-fry 3 to 5 minutes. Remove from pan. (Cook *half* the broccoli or beef at a time when using a wok.) Add more oil, if necessary, and stir-fry beef about 5 minutes or till well browned. Return broccoli to pan; add water. Cook and stir till thickened and bubbly. Garnish with green onion slices. Serve with hot cooked rice. Makes 4 servings.

Steak au Poivre

2 to 4 teaspoons whole black peppercorns
4 beef top loin steaks, cut 1 inch thick (2¼ pounds)
¼ cup butter *or* margarine
¼ cup chopped shallots *or* green onions
⅓ cup water
1 beef bouillon cube
3 tablespoons brandy

Coarsely crack peppercorns with mortar and pestle (or crack in a metal mixing bowl with the bottom of a bottle). Place 1 steak on waxed paper. Sprinkle with ¼ *to* ½ *teaspoon* cracked peppercorns; rub over meat and press in with heel of hand. Turn steak and repeat. Continue with remaining steaks. In a 12-inch skillet melt *half* the butter or margarine (325° on electric skillet). Cook steaks over medium-high heat to desired doneness. (Allow 11 to 12 minutes for medium.) Season with salt. Transfer to hot serving plate; keep hot.

Cook shallots or green onions in remaining butter or margarine about 1 minute or till tender but not brown. Add water and bouillon cube; boil rapidly over high heat 1 minute, scraping up browned bits from pan. Add brandy; cook 1 minute more. Pour over steaks. Makes 4 servings.

Skillet Enchiladas

1 pound ground beef
½ cup chopped onion
1 10½-ounce can condensed cream of mushroom soup
1 10-ounce can enchilada sauce
⅓ cup milk
2 tablespoons seeded, chopped, canned green chili peppers
8 frozen *or* canned tortillas Cooking oil
2½ cups shredded American cheese (10 ounces)
½ cup chopped pitted ripe olives

In a 10-inch skillet brown the ground beef and onion; drain off excess fat (350° on electric skillet). Stir in soup, enchilada sauce, milk, and chili peppers. Reduce heat (220°); cover and cook 20 minutes, stirring occasionally.

In a small 6-inch skillet dip the tortillas in a little hot cooking oil just till limp; drain. Reserve ½ cup cheese; place ¼ *cup* remaining cheese on *each* tortilla. Sprinkle *each* with olives. Roll up each tortilla. Place in sauce; cover and cook 5 minutes or till heated through. Sprinkle with reserved cheese; cover and cook about 1 minute or till cheese melts. Makes 4 servings.

Tomato Beef

1½ **pounds boneless beef sirloin steak, cut ½ inch thick**
3 **tablespoons soy sauce**
2 **tablespoons peanut** *or* **cooking oil**
1 **tablespoon cornstarch**
  Dash freshly ground pepper
½ **teaspoon grated fresh gingerroot** *or* ½ **teaspoon ground ginger**
1 **green pepper, sliced**
¼ **pound fresh mushrooms, sliced**
6 **green onions, cut into ½-inch pieces**
2 **small tomatoes, cut into wedges**

Partially freeze beef; slice diagonally into bite-size strips. For marinade, combine soy sauce, *1 tablespoon* oil, cornstarch, and ground pepper in bowl. Add beef; toss to coat well. Cover; let stand several hours in refrigerator. Drain and reserve marinade.

Heat ginger in remaining 1 tablespoon oil in electric wok or skillet at 350°. Add beef and stir-fry 5 to 6 minutes or till browned; push to one side. Add green pepper, mushrooms, and onions. Stir-fry 2 to 3 minutes or till crisp-tender; push to one side. Add tomatoes; cover and cook 2 minutes. Pour reserved marinade over meat; cook and stir till thickened. Makes 4 servings.

Texas Beef Skillet

Garnish with crunchy crushed corn chips —

1 **pound ground beef**
¾ **cup chopped onion**
1 **16-ounce can tomatoes, cut up**
1 **15-ounce can red kidney beans**
¾ **cup quick-cooking rice**
¾ **cup water**
3 **tablespoons chopped green pepper**
1½ **teaspoons chili powder**
½ **teaspoon salt**
½ **teaspoon garlic salt**
¾ **cup shredded American cheese (3 ounces)**
  Corn chips, crushed

In skillet cook the ground beef and onion over medium heat till meat is browned and onion is tender (350° on electric skillet). Stir in tomatoes, kidney beans, quick-cooking rice, water, green pepper, chili powder, salt, and garlic salt. Cover and reduce heat (220°). Simmer, stirring occasionally, 20 minutes. Top with shredded American cheese. Cover and heat about 3 minutes or till cheese melts. Sprinkle crushed corn chips around the edge. Makes 6 servings.

Skillet Hamburger Pie

Pictured on page 106 —

1½ **pounds ground beef**
½ **cup coarsely chopped celery**
½ **cup chopped onion**
1 **16-ounce can cut green beans, drained**
1 **10¾-ounce can beef gravy**
½ **cup water**
1 **teaspoon Worcestershire sauce**
¼ **teaspoon salt**
⅛ **teaspoon pepper**
  Packaged instant mashed potato buds (enough for 6 servings)
2 **cups boiling water**
½ **cup dairy sour cream**
1 **tablespoon snipped chives**
½ **teaspoon salt**
⅓ **cup shredded American cheese**
  Paprika

In skillet cook beef, celery, and onion till meat is browned and vegetables are crisp-tender (350° on electric skillet). Stir in beans, gravy, ½ cup water, Worcestershire sauce, ¼ teaspoon salt, and pepper. Reduce heat (220°); simmer to blend flavors. Whip potatoes and 2 cups boiling water; add sour cream, chives, and ½ teaspoon salt. Spoon in mounds over meat. Top with cheese and paprika. Cover; heat till cheese melts. Makes 6 servings.

Pineapple-Plum Chops

  6 **pork loin chops, cut ½ inch thick (1¾ pounds)**
  1 **20-ounce can pineapple chunks (juice pack)**
  ½ **cup plum jam**
  1 **tablespoon vinegar**
  1 **tablespoon soy sauce**
  ½ **teaspoon ground ginger**
  4 **green onions, sliced (¼ cup)**

Trim fat from chops; cook fat in skillet till 1 tablespoon fat accumulates (350° on electric skillet). Discard trimmings; brown chops in drippings. Reduce heat (220°). Season with salt and pepper. Drain pineapple, reserving juice.

Combine ½ *cup* reserved juice, jam, vinegar, soy, and ginger; pour over chops. Cover and simmer 25 minutes, adding ¼ cup more juice, if needed. Remove cover; add pineapple and onions. Spoon pan juice over. Cover; cook till pineapple is heated through. Makes 6 servings.

Rickshaw Rice

  1 **12-ounce can luncheon meat**
  2 **tablespoons butter**
  1 **20½-ounce can pineapple chunks**
  2 **cups cooked rice**
  1 **10-ounce package frozen peas**
  1 **teaspoon dried dillweed, crushed**
  1 **cup cherry tomatoes, halved**
  ½ **cup dairy sour cream**

Cube meat. In skillet brown the meat in butter (350° on electric skillet). Drain pineapple, reserving ¾ cup syrup. Add pineapple, reserved syrup, rice, peas, and dillweed to skillet. Cover the skillet; reduce heat (220°) and simmer 4 to 5 minutes or till peas are tender. Stir in tomatoes. Top with sour cream. Cover and simmer till tomatoes are hot. Makes 4 to 6 servings.

Veal Paprika

A rich sour cream sauce complements the veal —

  1½ **pounds boneless veal shoulder, cut into 1-inch cubes**
  2 **tablespoons butter *or* margarine**
  1½ **cups chopped onion**
  1¾ **cups water**
  1 **16-ounce can tomatoes, cut up**
  2 **tablespoons paprika**
  1½ **teaspoons salt**
  1 **teaspoon sugar**
  ½ **teaspoon dried marjoram, crushed**
  1½ **tablespoons all-purpose flour**
  1 **cup dairy sour cream**
     Hot cooked noodles

In a 12-inch skillet brown the veal cubes in butter or margarine (350° on electric skillet). Add chopped onion; cook and stir till onion is tender but not brown. Add water, *undrained* tomatoes, paprika, salt, sugar, and marjoram. Cover; simmer, stirring occasionally, 30 to 35 minutes. Stir flour into sour cream. Stir a small amount of the veal mixture into sour cream mixture. Slowly stir sour cream mixture into veal mixture in skillet. Heat through but do not boil. Serve over hot cooked noodles. Make 4 servings.

Curried Eggs

  2 **tablespoons butter *or* margarine**
  2 to 3 **teaspoons curry powder**
  ½ **teaspoon salt**
  1 **cup coarsely chopped apple**
  ½ **cup sliced green onion**
  1 **clove garlic, minced**
  1 **10½-ounce can condensed cream of celery soup**
  ⅔ **cup milk**
  1 **3-ounce can sliced mushrooms, drained**
  4 **hard-cooked eggs, quartered**
     Hot cooked rice
     Raisins
     Shredded coconut
     Chopped peanuts
     Chutney

In medium skillet melt butter or margarine; stir in curry powder and salt (300° on electric skillet). Add apple, onion, and garlic. Cook about 5 minutes or till onion is tender. Add cream of celery soup and milk; bring to boiling, stirring till smooth. Reduce heat (220°); add mushrooms. Gently fold in eggs. Cover and continue cooking till heated through. Serve over hot cooked rice. Pass raisins, shredded coconut, chopped peanuts, and chutney as condiments. Makes 2 servings.

Crab and Avocado

¼ cup butter *or* margarine
¼ cup all-purpose flour
½ teaspoon salt
½ teaspoon prepared mustard
2 cups milk
2 6-ounce packages frozen crab meat, thawed, *or* two 7½-ounce cans crab meat, drained and cartilage removed
1 3-ounce can sliced mushrooms, drained
3 tablespoons dry white wine
   Few drops bottled hot pepper sauce
1 large ripe avocado, peeled and cut into 6 wedges
1 tablespoon lemon *or* lime juice
   Garlic salt
½ cup shredded American cheese (2 ounces)

Melt butter or margarine in blazer pan of chafing dish. Blend in flour, salt, and mustard; add milk all at once. Cook and stir till thickened and bubbly. Stir in crab, mushrooms, wine, and hot pepper sauce; heat through. Brush avocado with some of the lemon or lime juice; sprinkle with garlic salt. Add remaining lemon or lime juice to crab mixture.

Place avocado on crab. Sprinkle with cheese. Cover and continue cooking 4 to 5 minutes or till cheese melts. Makes 6 servings.

coatings for fish

Dress up fried fish with one of the coatings below. To make the coating stick, dip fish in seasoned flour, then in egg mixed with water, then in the coating mixture.

● Try ¼ cup grated Parmesan cheese combined with 1 cup crushed saltine crackers on 6 pan-dressed fish. Fry fish in cooking oil.

● Combine 1 cup packaged instant mashed potatoes with 1 envelope onion salad dressing mix for 4 pan-dressed fish. Fry fish in hot bacon drippings for extra flavor.

● Mix together ⅓ cup all-purpose flour, ½ teaspoon paprika, ¼ teaspoon salt, and dash pepper for 4 pan-dressed fish. Fry fish in butter.

Jambalaya

3 slices bacon
½ cup long grain rice
1 medium onion, chopped (½ cup)
2 cups cubed cooked chicken
1 13¾-ounce can chicken broth
1 8-ounce can tomato sauce
1 cup cubed fully cooked ham
½ teaspoon salt
   Dash freshly ground pepper

In skillet cook bacon (350° on electric skillet). Drain bacon; crumble and set aside. Add rice and onion to drippings and cook till golden, stirring frequently. Reduce heat (220°). Add chicken, chicken broth, tomato sauce, ham, salt, and pepper. Cover and simmer about 25 minutes or till rice is tender; add more water if necessary. Stir in crumbled bacon. Serves 6.

Shrimp Gumbo

Okra contributes to the flavor and texture of this New Orleans dish —

1 pound fresh *or* frozen shelled shrimp
½ cup chopped celery
½ cup chopped onion
2 cloves garlic, minced
2 tablespoons cooking oil
1 16-ounce can tomatoes, cut up
2 cups sliced fresh okra *or* one 10-ounce package frozen cut okra
1 teaspoon salt
¼ teaspoon pepper
2 bay leaves
   Dash bottled hot pepper sauce
½ cup water (optional)
   Hot cooked rice

Thaw shrimp, if frozen. In heavy skillet cook celery, onion, and garlic in hot oil till vegetables are tender (300° on electric skillet). Add tomatoes, okra, salt, pepper, bay leaves, and hot pepper sauce. Reduce heat (220°). Cover; simmer 10 minutes. Add shrimp; cook 10 to 15 minutes more. Remove bay leaves. If thinner consistency is desired, stir in the water; heat through. Serve in soup bowls with hot cooked rice. Makes 6 servings.

New England Fish Chowder

Add a salad and crusty bread for a cold-weather meal —

¼ cup butter *or* margarine
 1 large onion, thinly sliced
 1 pound fresh *or* frozen haddock, skinned, boned, and cubed
 4 cups cubed, peeled potatoes
 2 cups water
 2 tablespoons all-purpose flour
 2 cups milk
¾ teaspoon salt
    Dash freshly ground pepper
    Dash paprika
    Oyster crackers

Melt *half* the butter or margarine in heavy skillet (300° on electric skillet). Add onion and cook till tender. Arrange fish and potatoes in layers in skillet; add water. Cover and cook gently (220°) about 15 minutes or till potatoes are nearly tender. Blend remaining butter or margarine and flour; mix in a little of the hot fish liquid. Stir butter mixture into fish mixture; cook till slightly thickened. Add milk, salt, pepper, and paprika. Simmer 5 minutes. Serve chowder with oyster crackers. Makes 6 servings.

Poached Salmon

 4 fresh *or* frozen salmon steaks, cut 1 inch thick (1 pound)
1¼ cups dry white wine
 2 tablespoons thinly sliced green onion
 2 tablespoons thinly sliced green onion
 2 *or* 3 sprigs parsley
 1 bay leaf
 1 teaspoon salt
    Dash pepper
¼ cup whipping cream
 2 well-beaten egg yolks
½ teaspoon lemon juice
 2 tablespoons snipped parsley

Thaw salmon steaks, if frozen. In skillet combine wine, green onion, parsley sprigs, bay leaf, salt, and pepper (350° on electric skillet). Heat to boiling; add salmon steaks. Cover and reduce heat (220°); simmer about 10 minutes or till fish flakes easily when tested with a fork. Remove fish and bay leaf. Keep salmon steaks warm.

Boil wine mixture down to ¾ cup. Combine whipping cream, egg yolks, and lemon juice; slowly add *part* of wine mixture. Return all to wine mixture in skillet. Cook, stirring constantly, over low heat till thickened and bubbly. Spoon over fish. Garnish with snipped parsley. Makes 4 servings.

Polish Potato Salad

Celery seed flavors the sweet-sour dressing —

 4 slices bacon
¾ cup chopped onion
⅓ cup sugar
 3 tablespoons all-purpose flour
1½ teaspoons salt
¾ teaspoon celery seed
    Dash pepper
¾ cup water
¾ cup vinegar
 3 tablespoons snipped parsley
18 ounces Polish sausage, bias-sliced
 8 medium potatoes, cooked, peeled, and cubed (5 cups)

In skillet cook bacon till crisp (350° on electric skillet). Drain and crumble bacon, reserving 2 tablespoons drippings. Reduce heat. Cook onion in reserved drippings till tender but not brown. Stir in sugar, flour, salt, celery seed, and pepper. Add water and vinegar; cook and stir till thickened and bubbly. Stir in sliced Polish sausage and potatoes. Cover the skillet; reduce heat (220°) and simmer 5 to 10 minutes or till potatoes are heated through, stirring once or twice. Top with crumbled bacon. Sprinkle with snipped parsley. Makes 6 servings.

Chicken-Fried Rice

Pictured on page 117 —

- 3 well-beaten eggs
- 3 tablespoons butter or margarine
- 1 cup long grain rice
- 3 tablespoons cooking oil
- 1 10½-ounce can condensed chicken broth
- 1¼ cups water
- 3 tablespoons soy sauce
- 2 cups finely diced, cooked chicken
- ½ cup sliced fresh or canned mushrooms
- 2 tablespoons thinly sliced green onions

In skillet over medium heat cook eggs in butter or margarine, without stirring, till set (300° on electric skillet). Remove from skillet; cut cooked eggs into thin strips. Keep warm. In same skillet over medium heat brown the rice in hot oil. Add broth, water, and soy sauce. Cover and reduce heat (220°). Simmer 20 to 30 minutes or till rice is tender and liquids are absorbed. Stir in chicken, mushrooms, and green onion. Cook over low heat, stirring occasionally, till fresh mushrooms are cooked or canned mushrooms are heated through. Top with egg strips before serving. Makes 4 servings.

Chicken Livers and Apple Slices

- 3 tablespoons all-purpose flour
- ¾ teaspoon salt
- ¾ teaspoon paprika
- ¾ teaspoon dried sage, crushed
- 1 pound chicken livers (about 12)
- 1 medium onion, sliced (½ cup)
- 3 tablespoons butter or margarine
- 1 apple, cored and sliced ½ inch thick
- 2 tablespoons sugar (optional)
  Toast points

Combine flour, salt, paprika, and sage in paper or plastic bag. Cut large chicken livers in half. Add ⅓ of the livers at a time to flour mixture; shake to coat well. Set aside. In heavy skillet cook onion in 2 tablespoons of the butter or margarine till tender but not brown (300° on electric skillet). Push onion to one side; add livers and cook 5 to 6 minutes or till browned lightly. Push to one side. Add remaining 1 tablespoon butter or margarine and apple slices; cook about 5 minutes or till tender. If desired, sprinkle apples with sugar to glaze. Serve with toast points. Makes 4 servings.

Gingered Ham and Deviled Potatoes

Spoon the potato mixture into individual foil baking pans and heat alongside the ham —

- 1 fully cooked center-cut ham slice, cut 1 inch thick (about 1½ pounds)
  Packaged instant mashed potatoes (enough for 4 servings)
- ½ cup dairy sour cream
- 2 tablespoons chopped green onion
- 1 teaspoon prepared mustard
- ½ teaspoon salt
- ½ teaspoon sugar
  Paprika
- ⅓ cup orange marmalade
- ¼ teaspoon ground ginger
- ⅛ teaspoon ground cloves

Slash fat edge of ham slice. Pan-fry in electric skillet at 300° about 10 minutes. Prepare potatoes according to package directions. Stir in sour cream, green onion, mustard, salt, and sugar. Spoon into 5 small foil baking pans. Sprinkle with paprika. Place in skillet. Turn ham and fry 10 minutes more. Combine marmalade, ginger, and cloves. Spoon over ham. Continue heating 2 to 3 minutes more or till ham is glazed and potatoes are heated through. Makes 5 servings.

Chicken Skillet Pie

  1 **pound ground beef**
  ¾ **cup chopped onion**
  2 **cups diced cooked chicken**
       or **turkey**
  1 **15-ounce can tomato sauce**
  ½ **cup pitted ripe olives, halved**
  ½ **cup shredded American**
       cheese
  ½ **teaspoon dried oregano,**
       crushed
  1 **chicken bouillon cube**
  1 **cup boiling water**
  1 **package (5 biscuits)**
       refrigerated buttermilk
       biscuits
  2 **tablespoons butter** *or*
       margarine, melted
  ¼ **cup cornmeal**

In heavy skillet cook the beef and onion till meat is browned and onion is tender (350° on electric skillet). Add chicken, tomato sauce, olives, cheese, and oregano. Dissolve chicken bouillon cube in boiling water; add to meat mixture. Cover and reduce heat (220°). Simmer 15 minutes, closing vent on electric skillet.

Dip both sides of refrigerated biscuits in melted butter or margarine; coat with cornmeal. Place on top of meat mixture. Cover; cook about 15 minutes or till biscuits are done. Makes 5 servings.

cooking chicken in a skillet

For any recipe calling for 2 cups cubed or diced cooked chicken (or 12 thin slices cooked chicken), buy 2 whole chicken breasts (about 10 ounces each). In a 10-inch skillet combine chicken breasts and 2½ cups salted water or chicken broth. Bring to boiling (350° on electric skillet). Reduce heat, cover, and simmer about 20 minutes or till tender. Do not overcook. Remove chicken from bones.

Hot Chicken Stroganoff Salad

  1 **6-ounce package long grain**
       and wild rice mix
  2 **cups cubed cooked chicken**
  1 **cup sliced celery**
  ¾ **cup dairy sour cream**
  ¼ **cup mayonnaise**
  ½ **cup milk**
  ½ **teaspoon salt**
  ¼ **cup coarsely chopped**
       cashew nuts

In skillet cook rice mix according to package directions (350° on electric skillet); add chicken and celery. Combine sour cream, mayonnaise, milk, and salt. Stir into chicken-rice mixture. Cook and stir over low heat till mixture heats through (220°). Add more milk, if desired; garnish with cashews. Serves 6.

Chicken Breasts Sauté Sec

  3 **whole chicken breasts**
       (2 pounds)
  1 **tablespoon lemon juice**
  ¼ **cup all-purpose flour**
  1 **teaspoon salt**
  1 **teaspoon paprika**
       Dash freshly ground pepper
  3 **tablespoons butter** *or*
       margarine
  1 **clove garlic, halved**
  ½ **cup dry white wine**
       Golden Sauce

Skin and split chicken breasts; rub with lemon juice. Combine flour, salt, paprika, and pepper in paper or plastic bag; add 2 or 3 pieces of chicken at a time and shake to coat well. Heat butter or margarine and garlic in heavy skillet (300° on electric skillet). Discard garlic. Cook chicken till golden on both sides; add wine. Cover and reduce heat (220°). Simmer about 20 minutes or till tender. Uncover; cook till pan liquid is reduced to ½ cup. Remove chicken to platter and keep warm. Prepare Golden Sauce; serve with chicken. Makes 4 servings.

Golden Sauce: In saucepan combine *pan liquid*, 4 beaten *egg yolks*, 1 cup *whipping cream*, 1 tablespoon snipped *parsley*, 1 tablespoon snipped *chives*, and ⅛ teaspoon ground *nutmeg*. Season with *salt* and *white pepper*. Cook and stir over low heat till slightly thickened. Add ½ teaspoon *lemon juice*.

Chicken Breasts Sauté Sec
Chicken-Fried Rice
(see recipe, page 115)

time-worthy favorites

Gypsy Round Steak

1½ pounds beef round steak, cut
    ½ inch thick
2 tablespoons cooking oil
1 large onion, sliced (1 cup)
1 clove garlic, minced
2 teaspoons sesame seed
1 teaspoon salt
¼ teaspoon cayenne
⅛ teaspoon pepper
½ cup water
3 medium potatoes, peeled and
    quartered
1 cup sliced celery (½-inch
    slices)
1 cup sliced carrots (½-inch
    slices)
½ cup water
⅓ cup pimiento-stuffed olives,
    halved
1 teaspoon cornstarch
1 teaspoon cold water

Pound round steak to ¼-inch thickness; cut into 6 serving-size pieces. In skillet brown the steak in hot oil (350° on electric skillet). Remove meat. In same skillet cook onion and garlic till onion is tender. Stir in *1 teaspoon* sesame seed, salt, cayenne, and pepper. Return meat to skillet. Add ½ cup water.

Cover; reduce heat (220°). Simmer 30 minutes. Add potatoes, celery, carrots, and ½ cup water. Cover; simmer 30 minutes or till vegetables are done. Add olives; heat. Combine cornstarch and 1 teaspoon cold water; add to skillet. Cook and stir till bubbly. Top with remaining sesame seed. Makes 6 servings.

Shaker-Style Steak

This steak simmers in a mixture of catsup and vegetables —

2 pounds beef round steak, cut
    ½ inch thick
¼ cup all-purpose flour
    Salt
    Pepper
¾ cup catsup
¾ cup water
¾ cup finely chopped onion
¾ cup finely chopped carrot
½ cup finely chopped celery
¼ cup finely chopped green
    pepper
1 tablespoon vinegar

Trim fat from steak; cook trimmings in skillet till 2 tablespoons drippings accumulate (350° on electric skillet). Pound flour into steak with meat mallet. Brown in hot drippings; spoon off excess fat. Season with salt and pepper. Combine catsup, water, finely chopped onion, carrot, celery, green pepper, and vinegar. Pour over and around round steak. Reduce heat (220°). Cover skillet and simmer about 1 hour or till meat is tender and vegetables are cooked. Serve with the vegetable mixture. Makes 6 to 8 servings.

Beef Roll-Ups with Spinach

2 pounds beef round steak, cut
    ¼ inch thick
1 clove garlic, halved
½ pound fresh spinach, cooked
    and drained (1 cup cooked)
¾ cup soft bread crumbs, toasted
½ cup grated Parmesan cheese
½ teaspoon dried sage, crushed
½ teaspoon dried thyme, crushed
2 tablespoons cooking oil
½ cup dry red wine
¼ cup water
2 tablespoons cold water
1 tablespoon all-purpose flour

Pound steak till very thin; cut into 8 serving-size pieces. Rub steak pieces with cut garlic; season with salt and pepper. Combine spinach, crumbs, cheese, sage, and thyme; mound ¼ cup spinach mixture on each piece of steak. Roll up each steak piece jelly roll-style; tie with string. In heavy skillet brown the steak rolls in hot oil (350° on electric skillet). Reduce heat. Add wine and ¼ cup water.

Cover; simmer about 30 minutes or till meat is tender. Turn occasionally; add water, if needed. Transfer meat to platter; keep warm. Remove strings. Combine the 2 tablespoons cold water and flour; stir into pan juices. Cook, stirring constantly, till thickened and bubbly. Pour over meat. Makes 6 to 8 servings.

Short Ribs with Limas

      3 pounds beef short ribs, cut into
         serving-size pieces
 1½ teaspoons salt
  ⅛ teaspoon pepper
 1½ cups water
  ¾ cup packed brown sugar
  ½ cup chopped onion
  ⅓ cup vinegar
 1½ teaspoons dry mustard
      2 bay leaves
  ¼ cup cold water
      2 teaspoons cornstarch
      2 16-ounce cans cooked dried
         lima beans, drained

Trim excess fat from short ribs; cook trimmings in skillet till 2 tablespoons fat accumulate (350° on electric skillet). Discard trimmings. Brown the ribs on all sides. Drain off excess fat. Reduce heat (220°). Sprinkle ribs with salt and pepper. Add 1½ cups water, brown sugar, onion, vinegar, dry mustard, and bay leaves. Cover; simmer about 2 hours or till ribs are tender. Discard bay leaves. Remove ribs; keep hot. Spoon off fat. Blend ¼ cup cold water and cornstarch. Add to meat juices; cook and stir till thickened and bubbly. Add beans. Cover; simmer 5 to 10 minutes. Serve with short ribs. Makes 6 servings.

Veal Stew

      3 pounds boneless veal, cubed
      3 tablespoons cooking oil
      2 tablespoons all-purpose flour
      1 teaspoon salt
         Dash freshly ground pepper
 1½ cups dry white wine
  ½ cup water
  ½ cup chopped onion
  ¼ teaspoon dried thyme, crushed
      3 or 4 sprigs parsley
      1 bay leaf
      1 clove garlic, halved
      1 cup light cream
      2 beaten egg yolks
      1 tablespoon snipped parsley

In large, heavy skillet lightly brown the cubed veal in hot oil (350° on electric skillet). Reduce heat (220°). Pour off fat. Stir in flour, salt, and pepper. Add wine and water. Tie chopped onion, thyme, parsley sprigs, bay leaf, and garlic together in a cheesecloth bag; add bag to skillet. Cover. Simmer 50 to 60 minutes or till veal is tender. Remove bag; discard. Beat light cream into egg yolks; stir into pan juices. Cook and stir 3 to 5 minutes or till thickened. Sprinkle with snipped parsley. Makes 6 servings.

Porcupine Meatballs

The rice gives the meatballs a "prickly" porcupine look —

  ½ cup day-old bread crumbs
         (¾ slice)
  ½ cup quick-cooking rice
      1 beaten egg
      1 tablespoon milk
  ¾ teaspoon salt
         Dash freshly ground pepper
      1 pound ground beef
      1 tablespoon butter or
         margarine
      1 7½-ounce can tomatoes,
         cut up
      1 cup hot water
      1 sprig fresh basil or ½ teaspoon
         dried basil, crushed

Combine bread crumbs, quick-cooking rice, egg, milk, salt, and pepper; add ground beef and mix well. Shape meat mixture into about 20 small meatballs. In heavy skillet brown meatballs in hot butter or margarine on all sides, turning gently (350° on electric skillet). Drain off excess fat. Add undrained cut-up tomatoes, hot water, and fresh or dried basil. Cover and simmer about 45 minutes or till meatballs are done; turn meatballs once or twice. Makes 4 or 5 servings.

Texas-Style Chili

Corn bread is the perfect accompaniment to this spicy chili —

2¼ **pounds beef round steak, cubed**
1 **clove garlic, minced**
3 **tablespoons cooking oil**
1½ **cups water**
1 **10½-ounce can condensed beef broth**
2 **teaspoons sugar**
2 **teaspoons dried oregano, crushed**
1 **to 2 teaspoons cumin seed, crushed**
2 **bay leaves**
½ **teaspoon salt**
1 **4-ounce can green chili peppers, rinsed, seeded, and mashed**
2 **tablespoons cornmeal**

In large skillet brown the steak cubes and garlic in hot oil; drain off excess fat (350° on electric skillet). Add water, beef broth, sugar, oregano, cumin, bay leaves, and salt. Reduce heat (220°); simmer about 1½ hours or till meat is tender. Stir in chili peppers and cornmeal. Simmer 30 minutes, stirring occasionally. Remove bay leaves. Serve over corn bread, if desired. Makes 4 to 6 servings.

Spicy Orange Pot Roast

1 **3- to 4-pound beef chuck pot roast**
1 **tablespoon all-purpose flour**
1 **teaspoon salt**
¼ **teaspoon pepper**
2 **tablespoons shortening**
1 **teaspoon finely shredded orange peel**
½ **cup orange juice**
¼ **cup packed brown sugar**
½ **teaspoon ground nutmeg**
¼ **teaspoon dried thyme, crushed**
1 **orange, peeled and sliced**
2 **tablespoons cold water**
2 **tablespoons cornstarch**

Coat roast with mixture of flour, salt, and pepper. In large skillet brown the meat on all sides in hot shortening (350° on electric skillet). Pour off excess fat. Combine finely shredded orange peel, orange juice, brown sugar, nutmeg, and thyme; pour over meat. Cover; reduce heat (220°). Simmer 2 to 2½ hours or till meat is tender. Add water during cooking, if needed.

Cut orange slices in half; add to skillet. Cover; cook about 5 minutes or till orange slices are heated through. Remove roast to platter; keep warm. Blend cold water and cornstarch; stir into pan juices. Cook, stirring constantly, till thickened and bubbly. Serve with roast. Makes 6 to 8 servings.

Swedish Pot Roast

1 **3- to 4-pound beef chuck pot roast**
1 **teaspoon salt**
4 **whole cloves**
2 **medium onions, quartered**
1 **cup chopped carrots**
½ **cup chopped celery**
⅓ **cup water**
1 **tablespoon corn syrup**
3 **anchovy fillets**
¼ **cup cold water**
2 **tablespoons all-purpose flour**
   Salt
   Pepper

Trim excess fat from beef chuck roast. Sprinkle the 1 teaspoon salt into skillet. Brown the meat slowly on both sides (350° on electric skillet). Cover skillet; reduce heat (220°). Stick cloves into onions. Add to meat along with carrots, celery, ⅓ cup water, corn syrup, and anchovies. Cover and simmer about 2½ hours or till meat is tender.

Remove meat to heated platter; keep warm. Skim excess fat from pan juices. Blend ¼ cup cold water and flour; stir into pan juices. Mash up the carrot and onion, if desired. Cook and stir till thickened and bubbly. Season with salt and pepper. Serve gravy with roast. Makes 6 to 8 servings.

Swedish Pot Roast

Tomato-Sauced Pork Chops

Whole kernel corn in the sauce adds flavor and color —

- 4 pork chops, cut ¾ inch thick
- 1 medium onion, sliced
- ¼ cup sliced celery
- 1 12-ounce can whole kernel corn
- 1 10½-ounce can condensed tomato soup
- 1 cup water
- ½ teaspoon dried thyme, crushed
- ½ teaspoon dried oregano, crushed
- ½ medium green pepper, cut into strips

Trim excess fat from chops; cook trimmings in skillet till 1 tablespoon fat accumulates (350° on electric skillet). Discard trimmings and brown the chops on both sides in hot fat. Remove chops; cook onion and celery in same skillet till tender but not brown. Drain off excess fat. Stir in corn, soup, water, thyme, and oregano. Add chops to sauce. Cover and reduce heat (220°). Simmer 40 to 50 minutes or till tender. Add green pepper; cook 5 minutes more. Serve sauce with chops. Makes 4 servings.

browning pork chops

Use the fat trimmed from pork chops for browning. Heat the trimmings in a skillet until the desired amount of melted fat accumulates, then discard the trimmings. If there's not enough fat on the meat, add shortening or cooking oil to make up the difference.

Pork Chop-and-Wild Rice Skillet

- 4 pork loin chops, cut ¾ inch thick
- ½ cup chopped onion
- 1 cup wild rice
- 1 10½-ounce can condensed beef broth
- 1⅓ cups water
- 1 medium tomato, sliced

Trim fat from chops; cook trimmings in a 10-inch skillet till 2 tablespoons drippings accumulate (350° on electric skillet). Remove trimmings. Slowly brown the chops on both sides. Remove chops. Cook onion in pan drippings till tender but not brown. Add wild rice, broth, and water. Return chops to skillet; season with salt and pepper. Cover; reduce heat to simmer (225°). Cook 50 to 60 minutes or till chops are tender. Place tomato slices on chops; heat through. Makes 4 servings.

Pork Marengo

- 1¼ cups sliced fresh mushrooms *or* one 3-ounce can sliced mushrooms, drained
- 2 tablespoons butter *or* margarine
- 2 pounds boneless pork *or* veal, cut into ½-inch cubes
- 12 small pearl onions, peeled
- 4 medium tomatoes, quartered
- ½ cup dry white wine *or* chicken broth
- 1 teaspoon salt
- 1 teaspoon dried marjoram, crushed
- 1 teaspoon dried thyme, crushed Dash pepper

In heavy skillet cook mushrooms in butter or margarine for 2 minutes (250° on electric skillet). Remove from skillet. Increase heat (300°). Add pork or veal and onions; brown well. Add tomatoes, wine or chicken broth, salt, marjoram, thyme, and pepper. Cover; reduce heat (220°). Simmer about 1 hour or till pork is tender. (Tomato sauce should be thick. If it isn't, remove meat and onions to platter and keep warm; turn up heat and cook sauce to desired consistency.) Add mushrooms; heat through. Pour sauce over meat. Makes 6 to 8 servings.

Ham with Vegetable Garland

- 1 5- to 7-pound fully cooked boneless ham
- 1 small head cauliflower, broken into flowerets (4 cups)
- 6 carrots, peeled and bias sliced
- 1 cup water
- 1 teaspoon salt
- ½ teaspoon dillweed
- ⅛ teaspoon pepper
- ¼ cup butter *or* margarine
- 2 9-ounce packages frozen Italian green beans
- ¼ cup orange marmalade

Place ham, fat side up, on rack in electric skillet with a high-dome cover. Score top of ham. Insert meat thermometer. Cover; cook at 350° for 1½ to 2 hours or till thermometer registers 130°. Place cauliflower and carrots around ham. Combine water, salt, dillweed, and pepper; pour over vegetables. Dot with butter or margarine. Cover and cook about 35 minutes or till vegetables are tender. Arrange frozen Italian green beans around ham; brush ham with orange marmalade. Cook 10 minutes more. Makes 8 to 10 servings.

Ham Loaves

- 2 beaten eggs
- 1 cup crushed saltine crackers
- ⅔ cup milk
  Dash freshly ground pepper
- 1 pound ground fully cooked ham
- 1 pound ground pork
- 1 8¼-ounce can pineapple slices, drained
- 2 maraschino cherries, halved
- ½ cup packed brown sugar
- 1 teaspoon dry mustard
- 2 tablespoons vinegar

Combine eggs, crushed crackers, milk, and pepper. Add ham and pork; mix well. In bottom of a 7½x3½x2-inch loaf pan arrange *2 slices* pineapple and *2* cherry halves. Firmly press *half* the meat mixture into pan. Loosen sides with spatula. Unmold into a 9x9x2-inch baking pan. For second loaf, repeat with remaining pineapple, cherries, and meat mixture; unmold into same pan. Cover and preheat electric skillet to 375°. Place pan of meat loaves on low rack in skillet. Cover; cook with vent closed for 1 hour and 10 minutes. Drain off fat. Combine brown sugar and mustard; stir in vinegar. Spoon over meat. Cover; cook 10 minutes more. Makes 8 servings.

Scalloped Potatoes and Ham

- 6 medium potatoes, peeled and sliced
- 3 tablespoons butter *or* margarine
- ¾ cup soft bread crumbs (1 slice)
- ½ teaspoon paprika
- ⅛ teaspoon dried thyme, crushed
- 2 tablespoons all-purpose flour
- 1 teaspoon salt
- 1 teaspoon dry mustard
- ⅛ teaspoon pepper
- 1 cup milk *or* light cream
- 2 cups cubed fully cooked ham
- 4 slices American cheese, cut up (4 ounces)

Cook potatoes in boiling salted water 10 to 15 minutes or till tender. Drain, reserving 1 cup cooking liquid. Place potatoes in an 8x8x2-inch baking dish. Melt butter or margarine in skillet (300° on electric skillet). Remove 1 tablespoon butter; toss with soft bread crumbs, paprika, and thyme. Set buttered crumbs aside.

Into remaining butter in skillet, blend flour, salt, mustard, and pepper. Add milk or light cream and reserved liquid from potatoes; cook and stir till thickened and bubbly. Stir in ham and cheese; cook till cheese is melted. Pour over potatoes. Sprinkle with the buttered crumbs. Place on low rack in clean electric skillet. Cover and cook with vent open at 350° for 1 hour. Makes 6 to 8 servings.

Lamb-Lentil Stew

- 1 **pound boneless lamb, cut into 1-inch cubes**
- 2 **tablespoons cooking oil**
- 3 **cups water**
- 1½ **cups chopped onion**
- 1 **cup sliced celery**
- 3 **chicken bouillon cubes**
- 3 **cloves garlic, minced**
- 2 **bay leaves**
- ½ **teaspoon dried oregano, crushed**
- ½ **teaspoon salt**
  Dash pepper
- 1 **cup dried lentils**
- 2½ **cups water**
- 4 **medium carrots, cut up**

In large skillet brown the lamb cubes in hot oil (350° on electric skillet). Pour off excess fat. Add 3 cups water, chopped onion, celery, chicken bouillon cubes, garlic, bay leaves, oregano, salt, and pepper. Reduce heat (220°). Cover and simmer 1 hour. Rinse lentils in cold water; drain. Add lentils, 2½ cups water, and cut-up carrots to lamb. Cover; simmer about 1 hour or till lamb is tender, stirring once or twice. Add additional water, if needed. Remove bay leaves. Makes 4 servings.

Scrapple

Serve with scrambled eggs and applesauce —

- 1 **pound bulk pork sausage**
- 3 **chicken bouillon cubes**
- 3½ **cups boiling water**
- 1 **cup yellow cornmeal**
- ¼ **teaspoon salt**
- ⅛ **teaspoon dried thyme, crushed**
  Dash ground cloves
  All-purpose flour
- 1 **beaten egg**
- 2 **tablespoons milk**
  Shortening
  Warm maple syrup
  Butter or margarine

In skillet brown the sausage slowly, stirring to break into small pieces (350° on electric skillet); drain off fat. Dissolve bouillon cubes in boiling water; add to sausage. Bring to boiling. Slowly stir in cornmeal, salt, thyme, and cloves. Cook 5 minutes, stirring constantly. Pour into a greased 8x4x2-inch loaf dish. Chill till firm. Unmold and cut into ½-inch-thick slices. Dip in flour, then in a mixture of egg and milk, and again in flour. In skillet slowly brown in hot shortening 8 to 10 minutes on each side. Serve with syrup and butter or margarine. Makes 6 servings.

Deviled Chicken

The chicken cooks in a flavorful sauce mixture —

- ⅓ **cup all-purpose flour**
- ½ **teaspoon salt**
- ½ **teaspoon garlic salt**
- ½ **teaspoon pepper**
- ½ **teaspoon dry mustard**
- ½ **teaspoon paprika**
- ¼ **teaspoon cayenne**
- 1 **2½- to 3-pound broiler-fryer chicken, cut up**
- 3 **tablespoons shortening**
- 1 **chicken bouillon cube**
- 1 **cup boiling water**
- ½ **cup chili sauce**
- 2 **tablespoons lemon juice**
  Hot cooked rice (optional)

Combine flour, salt, garlic salt, pepper, dry mustard, paprika, and cayenne in paper or plastic bag; add 2 or 3 pieces of chicken at a time to bag and shake well to coat. In a 12-inch skillet brown the chicken slowly in hot shortening (350° on electric skillet). Reduce heat (220°). Dissolve bouillon cube in boiling water. Stir in chili sauce and lemon juice; add bouillon mixture to skillet. Cover and simmer about 40 minutes or till chicken is tender. Serve with rice, if desired. Makes 4 servings.

Chicken-and-Potato Paprika

1 2½- to 3-pound broiler-fryer chicken, cut up
2 tablespoons butter *or* margarine
1 tablespoon paprika
1 chicken bouillon cube
¾ cup boiling water
½ cup dry white wine
½ cup chopped onion
½ teaspoon salt
Dash pepper
4 medium potatoes, peeled and quartered
1 medium green pepper, finely chopped
½ teaspoon salt
1 tablespoon all-purpose flour
1 cup dairy sour cream

In a 12-inch skillet brown the chicken pieces in butter or margarine (350° on electric skillet). Sprinkle with paprika. Dissolve bouillon cube in boiling water; pour over chicken. Add wine, onion, ½ teaspoon salt, and pepper. Cover and reduce heat (220°); simmer 15 minutes. Add potatoes and green pepper to skillet. Sprinkle ½ teaspoon salt over all. Cover; simmer about 30 minutes or till chicken and potatoes are tender.

Place chicken and potatoes on platter; keep warm. Stir flour into sour cream; stir in ¼ *cup* pan liquid. Slowly add sour cream mixture to liquid in skillet. Cook and stir over low heat till heated through. Spoon over chicken and potatoes. Makes 4 servings.

Lemon Chicken

⅓ cup all-purpose flour
1 teaspoon salt
1 teaspoon paprika
1 2½- to 3-pound broiler-fryer chicken, cut up
1½ teaspoons finely shredded lemon peel (set aside)
3 tablespoons lemon juice
3 tablespoons shortening
1 chicken bouillon cube
¾ cup boiling water
½ cup thinly sliced green onion
2 tablespoons brown sugar
2 tablespoons snipped parsley

Combine flour, salt, and paprika in paper or plastic bag. Brush chicken with lemon juice. Add 2 or 3 pieces of chicken at a time to bag and shake well. In a 12-inch skillet brown the chicken slowly in hot shortening (350° on electric skillet). Dissolve bouillon cube in boiling water; pour over chicken. Stir in thinly sliced green onion, brown sugar, lemon peel, and any remaining lemon juice. Cover; reduce heat (220°). Cook over low heat 40 to 45 minutes or till chicken is tender. Sprinkle with snipped parsley. Makes 4 servings.

Five-Spice Chicken

Makes enough "five-spice" mixture for three chicken recipes —

1 teaspoon ground cinnamon
1 teaspoon aniseed, crushed
½ teaspoon salt
¼ teaspoon ground allspice
⅛ teaspoon ground cloves
⅛ teaspoon freshly ground pepper
4 whole chicken breasts
2 tablespoons peanut *or* cooking oil
1 clove garlic, minced
¾ cup unsweetened pineapple juice
Parsley sprigs

Combine cinnamon, aniseed, salt, allspice, cloves, and freshly ground pepper. Rub chicken breasts with *1 teaspoon* of the spice mixture (save remainder of mixture for another use). Heat peanut or cooking oil and garlic in skillet (350° on electric skillet). Add chicken; brown on both sides. Reduce heat (220°). Add unsweetened pineapple juice; simmer, covered, about 35 minutes or till chicken is tender. Transfer chicken to platter; spoon sauce over chicken. Garnish with parsley. Makes 4 servings.

Batter-Fried Chicken

Batter-Fried Chicken

- 1 2½- to 3-pound broiler-fryer chicken, cut up
- 1 cup packaged pancake mix
- ½ teaspoon salt
- ¾ cup water
  Cooking oil

Simmer chicken in salted water for 20 minutes; drain. Combine pancake mix and salt; stir in water. Beat 2 minutes. Dip chicken in batter; drain well on rack over waxed paper. In a heavy skillet at least 3 inches deep, heat 1¼ inches of oil to 350°. (For electric skillet, see tip on page 131.) Regulate heat so chicken fries at about 325°. Fry a few pieces at a time about 5 minutes or till golden. Drain. Makes 4 servings.

Favorite Fried Chicken

- ⅓ cup all-purpose flour
- 1 teaspoon salt
- 1 teaspoon paprika
- ¼ teaspoon pepper
- 1 2½- to 3-pound broiler-fryer chicken, cut up
  Cooking oil

Combine flour, salt, paprika, and pepper in paper or plastic bag. Add 2 or 3 pieces of chicken at a time; shake well. Dry on rack. Heat ¼ inch of oil in a 12-inch skillet (350° on electric skillet). Brown the chicken slowly, turning with tongs. Reduce heat (220°); cover tightly and cook 30 to 40 minutes or till tender. Uncover last 10 minutes. Serves 4.

Swedish Pancakes

An electric skillet is ideal for baking these pancakes because of its even, controlled heat —

- 2 eggs
- 1 cup milk
- ½ cup all-purpose flour
- 2 teaspoons sugar
- ½ teaspoon salt

Combine eggs, milk, flour, sugar, and salt; beat with rotary beater till smooth. Bake in moderately hot, lightly greased electric skillet (375°), using 2 tablespoons batter for each pancake. Spread batter quickly and evenly to make thin cakes, 6 inches in diameter. When underside is light brown (about 1½ minutes), remove from skillet. Fill with Shrimp in Hollandaise Sauce (see recipe, page 127); bake as directed. Makes twelve pancakes.

Maryland Fried Chicken

1 beaten egg
1¼ cups milk
⅔ cup finely crushed saltine
crackers
½ teaspoon salt
Dash pepper
1 2½- to 3-pound broiler-fryer
chicken, cut up
3 to 4 tablespoons shortening

Combine egg and ¼ *cup* of the milk. Mix crushed crackers, salt, and pepper. Dip chicken pieces into egg mixture; roll in crackers. Heat shortening in a heavy 12-inch skillet (350° on electric skillet). Brown the chicken pieces slowly, turning with tongs. Add remaining 1 cup milk. Reduce heat (220°); cover tightly and simmer 35 minutes. Uncover; cook about 10 minutes more or till tender. From pan drippings, make Cream Gravy (see recipe below), if desired. Makes 4 servings.

Cream Gravy

1½ cups milk
3 tablespoons all-purpose flour
1 teaspoon salt
Dash pepper
3 tablespoons pan drippings
from Maryland Fried Chicken
(see recipe above)

In a screw-top jar shake ¾ *cup* of the milk with flour, salt, and pepper till blended; stir into pan drippings. Add remaining ¾ cup milk. Cook, stirring constantly, till thickened and bubbly. Cook 2 to 3 minutes longer. Makes 1½ cups.

Chicken-Papaya Dish
Subtly seasoned with curry powder —

2 tablespoons all-purpose flour
1 teaspoon curry powder
½ teaspoon salt
⅛ teaspoon pepper
4 small whole *or* 2 large halved
chicken breasts
2 tablespoons shortening
½ cup chopped onion
1 cup light cream
2 teaspoons curry powder
1 chicken bouillon cube
1 small papaya

Combine flour, 1 teaspoon curry powder, salt, and pepper in paper or plastic bag. Add chicken; shake to coat. In medium skillet brown chicken in hot shortening (350° on electric skillet). Remove chicken to platter and keep warm; reserve pan drippings.

Cook chopped onion in reserved pan drippings till tender but not brown. Stir in the light cream, the 2 teaspoons curry powder, and bouillon cube. Return chicken to skillet; cover and cook about 40 minutes or till done. Peel and slice papaya into 8 wedges; discard seeds. Add papaya wedges to skillet; cover and heat through. Makes 4 servings.

Shrimp in Hollandaise Sauce

4 egg yolks
6 tablespoons butter *or*
margarine, softened
⅓ cup boiling water
1 tablespoon lemon juice
1 teaspoon dried dillweed
¾ teaspoon salt
1½ cups chopped, cleaned,
cooked shrimp
12 Swedish Pancakes
(see recipe, page 126)
2 tablespoons grated Parmesan
cheese
1 teaspoon paprika
2 tablespoons butter *or*
margarine

Cream egg yolks and 6 tablespoons butter or margarine in top of double boiler; stir in boiling water. Cook over gently boiling water till thick and smooth; stir constantly. Remove from heat; stir in lemon juice, dillweed, and salt. Stir in shrimp. Put 1 rounded tablespoon shrimp filling on the unbrowned side of each Swedish Pancake; roll up and place in a 9x9x2-inch baking pan. Sprinkle with Parmesan and paprika; dot with the 2 tablespoons butter.

Cover and preheat electric skillet to 350° with vent closed. Place baking pan on rack in skillet; cover skillet and bake pancakes about 30 minutes or till heated through. Makes 4 servings.

Chicken Molé

1 2½- to 3-pound broiler-fryer chicken, cut up
¼ cup butter *or* margarine
    Salt
    Pepper
¼ cup finely chopped onion
¼ cup finely chopped green pepper
1 small clove garlic, minced
1 7½-ounce can tomatoes, cut up
½ cup beef broth
2 teaspoons sugar
½ teaspoon chili powder
⅛ teaspoon ground cinnamon
⅛ teaspoon ground nutmeg
    Dash ground cloves
    Dash bottled hot pepper sauce
¼ of a 1-ounce square unsweetened chocolate
2 tablespoons cold water
1 tablespoon cornstarch

In large heavy skillet brown the chicken slowly in butter or margarine (350° on electric skillet). Season lightly with salt and pepper. Set chicken aside; cover. For sauce, in same skillet cook onion, green pepper, and garlic in butter remaining in pan. Add tomatoes, beef broth, sugar, chili powder, cinnamon, nutmeg, cloves, and hot pepper sauce. Stir in unsweetened chocolate. Return chicken to skillet. Cover and reduce heat (220°); cook about 45 minutes or till tender. Remove chicken to platter; keep warm. Combine cold water and cornstarch; stir into sauce in skillet. Cook and stir till thickened and bubbly. Pour sauce over chicken. Serves 4.

Chicken with Rice

¼ cup all-purpose flour
½ teaspoon salt
⅛ teaspoon pepper
1 2½- to 3-pound broiler-fryer chicken, cut up
2 tablespoons cooking oil
½ cup chopped onion
1 clove garlic, minced
2 cups chicken broth
2 tomatoes, chopped (1½ cups)
1 cup long grain rice
2 tablespoons snipped parsley
1 teaspoon salt
½ teaspoon paprika
¼ teaspoon thread saffron, crushed
⅛ teaspoon pepper
1 bay leaf

Combine flour, ½ teaspoon salt, and ⅛ teaspoon pepper in paper or plastic bag. Add chicken, a few pieces at a time; shake well. In large heavy skillet brown the chicken slowly in hot oil (350° on electric skillet). Remove chicken. Cook onion and garlic in pan drippings till onion is tender but not brown. Add chicken broth, tomatoes, uncooked rice, parsley, 1 teaspoon salt, paprika, saffron, ⅛ teaspoon pepper, and bay leaf. Return chicken to skillet. Cover and cook over low heat 40 to 50 minutes or till chicken is tender. Remove bay leaf. Makes 4 servings.

Pheasant Fricassee

½ cup all-purpose flour
2 teaspoons salt
½ teaspoon pepper
2 1½- to 2½-pound ready-to-cook pheasants, cut up
6 tablespoons butter *or* margarine
1 large onion, finely chopped
1 large carrot, finely chopped
1 13¾-ounce can chicken broth
    Dash ground cloves
1 cup light cream
3 tablespoons all-purpose flour
2 tablespoons snipped parsley
1 tablespoon lemon juice

Combine the ½ cup flour, salt, and pepper in paper or plastic bag. Add pheasant, 2 or 3 pieces at a time; shake to coat well. In large heavy skillet brown the pheasant in butter or margarine (350° on electric skillet). Add onion and carrot; cook 2 minutes. Add broth and cloves. Reduce heat (200°). Cover and simmer 45 to 55 minutes or till tender. Remove to warm platter. Measure 1 cup broth; discard remaining broth. Return broth to skillet. In a screw-top jar, shake light cream and 3 tablespoons flour till blended. Stir into broth in skillet; cook and stir till thickened and bubbly. Stir in parsley and lemon juice. Serve over pheasant. Makes 6 servings.

skillet
side dishes
& desserts

Skillet-Style French Fries

3 medium baking potatoes
    (1½ pounds)
  Cooking oil
  Salt

Peel potatoes and cut lengthwise into ⅜- or ½-inch-wide strips. In a skillet that is at least 3 inches deep, heat 1 inch of oil to 360°. (For electric skillet, see tip on page 131.) Fry a few potatoes at a time in hot oil for 6 to 7 minutes or till crisp and golden*. Drain on paper toweling. Sprinkle with salt. Serve at once. Makes 4 servings.

*For crisper french fries: Fry potatoes at 360° about 5 minutes or till lightly browned. Drain on paper toweling and cool. Just before serving, return french fries to oil at 360° for 2 minutes more. Drain, season, and serve at once.

Peach-Glazed Sweet Potatoes

½ cup peach preserves
¼ cup packed brown sugar
1 tablespoon lemon juice
¼ teaspoon ground cinnamon
4 medium sweet potatoes,
    cooked, peeled, and cut into
    2-inch slices (2 pounds)

In skillet combine preserves, brown sugar, lemon juice, and cinnamon; heat till bubbly (350° on electric skillet). Add sweet potatoes; cook and stir over low heat (220°) 10 to 15 minutes or till heated through and glazed. Serves 4 to 6.

Squash and Apples

3 small acorn squash
1 cup water
  Salt
2 large apples, peeled, cored,
    and chopped
⅓ cup packed brown sugar
¼ cup raisins
2 tablespoons butter or
    margarine

Cut squash in half lengthwise; remove seeds and stringy portions. Place in electric skillet (350°), cut side down; add water. Cover and bring to boiling. Reduce heat (220°); simmer 20 to 25 minutes with vent open. Turn squash cut side up; sprinkle with salt. Combine apples, brown sugar, and raisins; spoon into squash. Dot with butter or margarine. Cover; cook 15 to 20 minutes or till tender. Makes 6 servings.

Skillet Fruit Relish

2 cups cubed, peeled pumpkin
    or winter squash
1½ cups chopped peeled apple
½ cup raisins
½ cup water
¼ cup shelled sunflower seed
3 tablespoons sugar
2 tablespoons vinegar
¼ teaspoon salt
⅛ teaspoon ground cinnamon
⅛ teaspoon ground cloves

In medium skillet combine pumpkin or squash, apple, raisins, water, sunflower seed, sugar, vinegar, salt, cinnamon, and cloves. Bring to boiling (350° on electric skillet). Reduce heat (220°); simmer, covered, 20 to 30 minutes or till pumpkin or squash is tender. Stir carefully to keep pieces whole. Chill. Serve with meats. Makes 3 cups.

Funnel Cakes

2 beaten eggs
1½ cups milk
2 cups all-purpose flour
1 teaspoon baking powder
½ teaspoon salt
2 cups cooking oil
  Sifted powdered sugar

In mixing bowl combine eggs and milk. Stir together flour, baking powder, and salt. Add to egg mixture; beat till smooth. In a deep skillet heat oil to 360°. (For electric skillet, see tip on page 131.) Covering funnel spout with finger, pour ¼ cup batter into funnel. Remove finger and release batter into hot oil in a spiral, starting in center and winding out. Fry about 3 minutes or till golden. Turn carefully; cook 1 minute more. Drain on paper toweling; dust with powdered sugar. Makes 6 to 8 funnel cakes.

Hush Puppies

2 cups cornmeal
½ cup all-purpose flour
1 tablespoon sugar
2 teaspoons baking powder
½ teaspoon baking soda
1 well-beaten egg
1 cup buttermilk
⅓ cup finely chopped onion
  Cooking oil

Combine cornmeal, flour, sugar, baking powder, soda, and ½ teaspoon salt. Combine egg, buttermilk, onion, and ¼ cup water; stir into cornmeal mixture just till moistened. In a skillet that is at least 3 inches deep, heat 1½ inches of oil to 375°. (For electric skillet, see tip on page 131.) Drop batter by tablespoonfuls into hot oil. Fry about 2 minutes or till golden brown, turning once. Drain on paper toweling. Serve hot. Makes about 2 dozen hush puppies.

Sweet and Sour Asparagus Salad

When fresh asparagus isn't available, use frozen asparagus cooked according to package directions —

- 1 pound fresh asparagus spears
- 6 slices bacon
- 2 green onions, finely chopped
- ¼ cup red wine vinegar
- ¼ cup water
- 4 teaspoons sugar
- ⅛ teaspoon salt
  Dash pepper
- 6 cups torn lettuce, well drained
- 2 hard-cooked eggs, sliced

In skillet spread out asparagus; cook in small amount of boiling salted water 8 minutes or till tender (275° on electric skillet). Drain asparagus and set aside. In skillet cook bacon till crisp. Drain, reserving 2 tablespoons drippings; crumble bacon. To reserved drippings in skillet add green onions, vinegar, water, sugar, salt, pepper, and asparagus; heat through. Remove asparagus; toss lettuce with hot dressing 1 minute. Arrange lettuce mixture on plates with asparagus, egg slices, and bacon. Makes 6 servings.

Garbanzo Hot Pot

- 1 cup chopped onion
- ¼ cup chopped green pepper
- 2 tablespoons butter *or* margarine
- 2 15-ounce cans garbanzo beans, drained
- 1 13¾-ounce can chicken broth
- 1 cup chopped peeled tomato
- ½ teaspoon salt
- ¼ teaspoon dried marjoram, crushed
- ⅛ teaspoon pepper
- 1 bay leaf

In large skillet cook chopped onion and green pepper in butter or margarine till tender but not brown (300° on electric skillet). Stir in garbanzo beans, chicken broth, tomato, salt, marjoram, pepper, and bay leaf. Reduce heat (220°); simmer, uncovered, for 20 minutes. Remove bay leaf. Makes 5 servings.

French-Fried Onion Rings

- 1 large onion, cut into ¼-inch-thick slices
- 1 cup packaged pancake mix
- ⅔ cup cold water
- ¼ teaspoon salt
  Cooking oil

Separate onion into rings. In mixing bowl combine pancake mix, cold water, and salt. Beat with electric mixer about 2 minutes. Dip onion rings in batter; drain off excess. In skillet that is at least 3 inches deep, heat 1½ inches of oil to 375°. (For electric skillet, see tip on page 131.) Fry onion rings 2 to 3 minutes or till brown. Drain thoroughly on paper toweling. Makes 3 servings.

Cheese Biscuits

- 2 to 3 tablespoons butter *or* margarine
- 1 package (10 biscuits) refrigerated biscuits
  Cheese spread *or* crumbled blue cheese

In an electric skillet set at 250° to 260°, melt the butter or margarine. Place biscuits in skillet so sides do not touch. Bake, covered, with vent open for 5 minutes. Turn biscuits and bake 5 minutes more. Top each biscuit with a spoonful of cheese spread or crumbled blue cheese. Continue baking about ½ minute or till cheese melts. Makes 10.

New Orleans French Toast

- ⅔ cup milk
- 2 beaten eggs
- 2 tablespoons sifted powdered sugar
- 1 teaspoon finely shredded lemon peel
  Dash salt
- 8 slices day-old French bread, 1 inch thick
  Butter *or* margarine
  Powdered sugar
  Maple syrup *or* honey

Combine milk, eggs, 2 tablespoons powdered sugar, lemon peel, and salt; mix well. Dip bread in egg mixture, coating both sides. In skillet over low heat, brown the bread in butter on both sides (275° on electric skillet). Sprinkle with powdered sugar. Serve hot with additional butter or margarine and syrup or honey. Makes 4 servings.

Skillet Scones

Scones boast a Scottish heritage —

- 1 cup all-purpose flour
- 3 tablespoons sugar
- 2 teaspoons baking powder
- ½ teaspoon salt
- 6 tablespoons butter *or* margarine
- 1 cup quick-cooking rolled oats
- ½ cup currants
- 2 beaten eggs
   Cooking oil
   Butter *or* margarine

In mixing bowl stir together flour, sugar, baking powder, and salt. Using pastry blender, cut in the 6 tablespoons butter or margarine till crumbly. Stir in rolled oats and currants. Stir in beaten eggs till moistened.

On waxed paper pat dough into a 8x7½-inch rectangle, ½ inch thick. Cut into 12 rectangles, each about 2½x2 inches. Brush a 12-inch skillet lightly with cooking oil. In skillet bake scones, covered, over medium-low heat about 10 minutes or till golden brown on bottom (275° on electric skillet). Turn and brown other side in covered skillet 5 minutes more. Serve warm with butter or margarine. Makes 12.

shallow-fat frying in a skillet

Use a skillet at least 3 inches deep to allow for 1½ inches of cooking oil. This means you'll need about 3 quarts of oil for a 12-inch electric skillet.

Set the heat control of an electric skillet at 400° to 450° to maintain an oil temperature of 360° to 375°. Check the oil temperature with a deep-fat thermometer or a 1-inch cube of bread. (If the bread browns in 1 minute, the oil is hot enough to fry most foods.)

Add a few pieces of food at a time so oil doesn't cool down too much. Food fried at too low a temperature tastes greasy.

Use cottonseed or corn oil, or hydrogenated vegetable shortening, all of which can be heated to a higher temperature without smoking than can lard, bacon fat, or butter.

If you follow these simple steps, you'll be able to reuse your oil. Allow the oil to cool, then strain it to remove any crumbs. Refrigerate it in a covered jar. When reusing the oil, add some fresh cooking oil or shortening to it.

Country-Style Doughnut Puffs

For an extra-special treat, serve these warm —

- 2 beaten eggs
- ½ teaspoon vanilla
- ½ cup sugar
- ½ cup light cream
- 2 cups all-purpose flour
- 1½ teaspoons baking powder
- ½ teaspoon salt
- 2 tablespoons butter *or* margarine, melted
   Cooking oil
- 1 cup sifted powdered sugar
- ¼ teaspoon ground nutmeg

Beat eggs, vanilla, and sugar well. Stir in light cream. Stir together flour, baking powder, and salt; gradually stir into egg mixture. Fold in melted butter or margarine. In skillet that is at least 3 inches deep, heat 1½ inches of oil to 375°. (For electric skillet, see tip at left.) Drop dough by teaspoonfuls into hot oil. Balls should be no more than ¾ inch in diameter to cook through. Fry 2 to 3 minutes or till brown, turning once. Drain on paper toweling; cool. Combine powdered sugar and nutmeg in paper or plastic bag. Shake a few puffs at a time to coat well. Makes 3 to 3½ dozen.

Coconut Cake Doughnuts

2 **eggs**
½ **cup sugar**
¼ **cup milk**
2 **tablespoons shortening, melted and cooled**
2⅓ **cups all-purpose flour**
2 **teaspoons baking powder**
½ **teaspoon salt**
¾ **cup flaked coconut**
   Cooking oil
   Sugar (optional)

With electric mixer beat eggs with the ½ cup sugar till light; beat in milk and cooled shortening. Stir together flour, baking powder, and salt; add flour mixture and coconut to egg mixture, stirring just till combined. Cover and chill several hours. Roll dough to ½-inch thickness on lightly floured surface. Cut with a 2½-inch doughnut cutter.

In a skillet that is at least 3 inches deep, heat 1½ inches of cooking oil to 375°. (For electric skillet, see tip on page 131.) Fry doughnuts in hot oil about 1 minute per side or till golden brown. Drain on paper toweling. If desired, shake warm doughnuts with sugar in a paper or plastic bag till coated. Makes 1 dozen doughnuts.

Maine Blueberry Pancakes

1½ **cups fresh blueberries**
1½ **cups all-purpose flour**
3 **tablespoons sugar**
2 **tablespoons baking powder**
½ **teaspoon salt**
2 **beaten eggs**
1¼ **cups milk**
3 **tablespoons cooking oil**

Wash blueberries; drain very thoroughly. Stir together flour, sugar, baking powder, and salt. Combine eggs, milk, and cooking oil; add dry ingredients. Beat till smooth. Gently fold in drained berries. Bake pancakes in hot, lightly greased skillet (375° on electric skillet). Cook till tops are covered with tiny bubbles; turn and brown on other side. Makes 14 (4-inch) pancakes.

Skillet Cobbler

2 **cups packaged biscuit mix**
¼ **cup butter *or* margarine**
⅓ **cup water**
¼ **teaspoon ground cinnamon**
1 **21-ounce can cherry pie filling**
½ **cup shredded cheddar cheese**
   Light cream or milk

Prepare biscuit mix according to package directions for biscuits. Roll ½ inch thick, and cut into six 3-inch circles. Melt butter or margarine in electric skillet at 250°; add biscuits, turning once to coat both sides. Cover; close vent. Bake about 15 minutes or till browned. Turn and bake, covered, 2 or 3 minutes more. Stir water and cinnamon into pie filling; spoon around biscuits. Sprinkle with cheese. Cover and cook 4 or 5 minutes or till heated through. Serve with cream or milk. Makes 6 servings.

Fruited Brown Bread

1 **cup all-purpose flour**
1 **teaspoon baking powder**
1 **teaspoon baking soda**
1 **teaspoon salt**
1 **cup yellow cornmeal**
1 **cup whole wheat flour**
2 **cups buttermilk**
1 **cup raisins**
¾ **cup dark molasses**
½ **cup diced mixed candied fruits and peels**

Thoroughly grease four 16-ounce fruit or vegetable cans. Stir together flour, baking powder, soda, and salt; stir in cornmeal and whole wheat flour. Add buttermilk, raisins, molasses, and candied fruits; beat well. Divide batter equally among the 4 cans. Cover tops of cans tightly with foil. Place in electric skillet with dome lid.

Add water to skillet to 1-inch depth. Cover skillet, close vent, and set temperature at simmer (250°). Steam about 2¼ hours or till done, adding more hot water as needed. Remove bread from cans. Cool on rack. Wrap in foil and store overnight before serving. Makes 4 cylindrical loaves.

Caramel Floating Island

5 eggs
⅓ cup sugar
3 cups milk
¾ cup sugar
Dash salt
1½ teaspoons vanilla

Separate 3 of the eggs; beat whites till soft peaks form. Gradually add the ⅓ cup sugar, beating till stiff peaks form. In a 10-inch skillet heat milk to simmering. Drop egg white mixture in 8 portions into milk; simmer, uncovered, about 5 minutes or till firm. Lift from milk (reserve milk for custard); drain on paper toweling. Chill.

Slightly beat egg yolks with remaining 2 eggs; add ½ cup sugar and salt. Stir into reserved, slightly cooled milk. Cook and stir over low heat till mixture coats a metal spoon. Remove from heat; cool quickly in ice water. Add vanilla. Turn into serving bowl; chill. Top with meringues. Melt the remaining ¼ cup sugar in a small heavy skillet over low heat, stirring constantly, till golden brown. Remove from heat. Immediately drizzle melted sugar over meringues in a thin, threadlike pattern. Makes 8 servings.

Spicy Sugared Pecans

¾ cup sugar
¼ cup water
¾ teaspoon pumpkin pie spice
2 cups pecan or walnut halves

In skillet combine sugar, water, and pumpkin pie spice. Bring mixture to a full rolling boil (250° on electric skillet); boil 3 to 6 minutes or till sugar crystals form on sides of skillet. Add pecan or walnut halves; stir till nuts are sugar-coated. Turn out onto waxed paper or foil. Quickly separate nuts, using two forks. Cool. Makes 2 cups.

Toasted Almond Sponge

1 envelope unflavored gelatin
½ cup cold water
¾ cup sugar
1¼ cups milk, scalded
¼ cup sugar
½ teaspoon salt
1 teaspoon vanilla
1 cup whipping cream
½ cup slivered almonds, toasted

Soften gelatin in cold water. In a heavy skillet caramelize ¾ cup sugar, stirring constantly so it doesn't burn. Remove from heat when a deep golden color. Slowly add milk. Cook and stir till all caramel dissolves. Remove from heat. Add softened gelatin, the ¼ cup sugar, and salt; stir till dissolved. Add vanilla. Pour into bowl and chill till thick and syrupy. Whip cream; fold into gelatin mixture. Fold in almonds, reserving a few for garnish. Chill 2 to 3 hours or till firm. Spoon into sherbet dishes. Top with reserved almonds. Makes 8 to 10 servings.

Norwegian Fattigmann

2 beaten eggs
¼ cup whipping cream
2 tablespoons sugar
1 tablespoon butter or margarine, melted
1 teaspoon lemon juice
1½ cups all-purpose flour
½ teaspoon ground cardamom
¼ teaspoon salt
Cooking oil
Powdered sugar

Mix together eggs, whipping cream, and sugar. Stir in butter or margarine and lemon juice. Add flour, cardamom, and salt; mix well. Cover and chill 2 or 3 hours. Divide dough in half; keep 1 portion refrigerated. Roll the other portion to ⅛-inch thickness on lightly floured surface. Cut into 2-inch diamonds. Cut a slit in the center of each and pull one corner through. Repeat with remaining dough.

In skillet that is at least 3 inches deep, heat 1½ inches of oil to 375°. (For electric skillet, see tip on page 131.) Fry a few at a time about 2 minutes or till light brown, turning once. Drain on paper toweling. Sprinkle with powdered sugar while warm. Makes 3½ dozen.

Mocha Brownie Pudding

1½ cups all-purpose flour
1¼ cups granulated sugar
3 tablespoons unsweetened cocoa powder
1 tablespoon baking powder
1 tablespoon instant coffee powder
¾ teaspoon salt
¾ teaspoon ground ginger
¾ cup milk
3 tablespoons cooking oil
1½ teaspoons vanilla
1 cup chopped walnuts
1 cup packed brown sugar
⅓ cup unsweetened cocoa powder
2½ cups hot water
   Vanilla ice cream
   Shredded orange peel
   (optional)

Sift together flour, granulated sugar, 3 tablespoons cocoa powder, baking powder, coffee powder, salt, and ginger. Add milk, oil, and vanilla; mix till smooth. Stir in nuts. Spread evenly in a greased 12-inch electric skillet. Combine the brown sugar and ⅓ cup cocoa powder; stir in hot water. Pour over batter. Set temperature control at 325°. Cover and bake, with vent closed, 12 to 15 minutes or till cake springs back when touched gently. Spoon into serving dishes immediately. Top with ice cream and orange peel. Makes 8 servings.

Steamed Chocolate Custard

Delicious served warm or chilled —

½ cup semisweet chocolate pieces
2 cups milk, scalded
3 beaten eggs
⅓ cup sugar
1 teaspoon vanilla
⅛ teaspoon salt
   Whipped cream or frozen whipped dessert topping, thawed
   Ground Cinnamon

In small skillet melt chocolate pieces over low heat; gradually stir into milk. Cool slightly. In mixing bowl combine beaten eggs, sugar, vanilla, and salt. Gradually stir into chocolate mixture. Pour into six 6-ounce custard cups. Set custard cups on wire rack in electric skillet; set temperature control at 250°. Pour hot water into skillet to depth of ¾ inch. Cover, leaving vent open; steam custards 12 to 15 minutes or till knife inserted just off-center comes out clean. Serve warm or chilled in sherbet dishes; garnish each serving with a dollop of whipped cream or dessert topping and a dash of ground cinnamon. Makes 6 servings.

Swedish Toasted Almond Cake

3 tablespoons butter *or* margarine, melted
¼ cup finely crushed graham crackers
¾ cup milk, scalded
1½ cups all-purpose flour
2 teaspoons baking powder
1 teaspoon salt
3 eggs
1½ cups sugar
1 teaspoon vanilla
   Almond Topping

Preheat electric skillet at 425°. Combine *1 tablespoon* butter or margarine and crushed graham crackers; coat bottom and sides of a 9x9x2-inch baking pan with cracker mixture. Pour remaining melted butter or margarine into milk. Stir together flour, baking powder, and salt. Beat eggs till thick and foamy. Gradually add sugar; continue beating till thick and lemon colored. (Do not underbeat.) Add vanilla. Fold in flour mixture; stir in milk mixture. Pour into prepared pan. Place on low rack in skillet. Bake, covered, for 65 to 70 minutes. Gently spread Almond Topping around the outer edges of cake; bake, covered, 10 minutes more. Serve warm or cooled. Serves 10 to 12.

Almond Topping: In a small skillet melt ⅓ cup *butter or margarine*. Add ¾ cup sliced *almonds*. Cook over low heat till lightly browned. Combine ⅓ cup *sugar* and 3 tablespoons all-purpose *flour;* add 2 tablespoons *light cream*. Stir into almond mixture; cook and stir till bubbly.

Beef Fondue (see recipe, page 141)

FONDUE RECIPES

Tired of working in the kitchen? Then bring a fondue to the table. That way, everyone participates in the cooking and nobody misses out on the fun. Don't save fondue for a party or for special dinner guests. Any time is the right time to cook at the table with fondue.

the abc's of fondue

Learning the hows, whys, and whats of fondue cooking will help you serve an exquisite fondue meal the first time and every time. Refer to the following pages for facts, hints, and ideas on using your fondue cooker efficiently and safely. With this information at hand, you can confidently dazzle your family and friends with unique and delicious fondue dishes.

types of fondue pots

Many kinds of fondue units are available. Each includes a fondue pot, a stand on which the pot rests, and a burner for cooking or keeping the fondue mixture hot. Of the many shapes, sizes, and colors available, there are three basic types: metal cookers, ceramic pots, and dessert pots.

If you're looking for an all-purpose fondue unit, the metal cooker is the most versatile choice because of the variety of foods you can cook in it. Metal cookers usually are made of stainless steel, plain or colored aluminum, copper, or sterling silver. Since metal can withstand very high temperatures, metal containers are best suited for fondues that must be cooked in hot oil — meat fondue, for example. But by turning the heat down, they're also appropriate for cheese or dessert fondues. Provide one fondue cooker for every four persons when serving a hot-oil fondue. The oil won't stay hot enough for cooking when more than four cook in the same container.

Shape, metal gauge, and added features are important points to consider when selecting a metal container. A bowl-shaped cooker that's larger at the bottom than at the top does a good job of containing possible oil spatters. (Add 1 teaspoon salt to the hot oil to reduce spatters.) A heavy-gauge metal ensures even heat distribution. And interior non-stick coatings, available on some cookers, can make for easier cooking and cleaning.

Ceramic, pottery, or earthenware pots — some with decorations — most closely resemble the original Swiss caquelons used for cheese fondue. Shaped like a shallow casserole dish with a handle, the pot's large surface area provides plenty of room for swirling a cheese or sauce-type dessert fondue. However, never use a ceramic pot for a hot-oil fondue; the intense heat will crack it. A ceramic fondue pot can efficiently serve six to eight at sit-down dinners, and more at buffets since no actual tabletop cooking is involved.

Smallest of the containers, the dessert fondue pot is specially designed to hold rich, saucy mixtures. For this reason, the container is considerably smaller than other metal or ceramic pots. A candle warmer adequately keeps the dessert mixture hot whether the container is metal or ceramic. Like the large ceramic container, one dessert pot will adequately serve six to eight people.

Whichever kind of fondue unit you own, be certain to read its use-and-care booklet thoroughly, and learn the dos and don'ts of that particular pot. Set the unit on a heat-resistant tray (some units include a tray) or mat to protect the table from spattering oil, food spills, or heat from the burner. After the meal, allow the fondue pot to come to room temperature before cleaning.

types of burners

Alcohol, canned heat, and candles are the most common heat sources used in fondue units. However, thermostatically controlled electric burners are increasingly popular. Candle warmers are suitable only for sauce-type dessert fondues since they don't produce enough heat to cook meat or cheese. Most burners provide some means of regulating amount of heat released.

Alcohol burners, with a wick or a compressed-fiber pad, use denatured (wood) alcohol as fuel. This type of alcohol, which can be purchased at drug- or hardware stores, is poisonous, so label it as such and store it out of children's reach. Since wood alcohol can ruin wood finishes, always fill the burner over a newspaper-covered area. Fill it only half full and never refill the burner while it's burning or still hot. After filling, wipe outside surfaces with a dry cloth to catch all spills.

Raise or lower the wick to regulate the flame of wick-type burners. You can regulate burners with a compressed-fiber pad by opening or closing the damper. To extinguish an alcohol burner, just replace the cover or snuffer. Because of the hazard of fire, always empty and thoroughly dry an alcohol burner before storing the fondue unit.

Canned-heat units consist of a stand with a holder for the container of canned heat (solidified alcohol). These holders usually have a movable cover for regulating the heat, but the can lid also may be used. Close the cover or set the can lid in place to extinguish the flame.

fondue accessories

Besides the fondue unit, fondue forks or sturdy bamboo skewers are the only accessories you'll need. Fondue plates are convenient but not essential.

The fondue fork consists of a long metal shaft with two or three tines for spearing food. Since metal readily conducts heat, fondue forks should have handles made of an insulating material such as plastic or wood. The different-colored handle tips on some fondue forks help diners identify and keep one fork throughout the meal.

1 This metal fondue cooker is designed with burner and heat-resistant tray.

2 A small dessert pot keeps sauce-type mixtures warm over a candle flame.

3 The ceramic pot is designed for swirling foods in cheese or saucy dessert mixtures.

Fondue plates take the mess out of sampling several different sauces by providing separate compartments for different foods. Available in china, pottery, or plastic, and in an assortment of colors, fondue plates can add a finishing touch to a table setting.

safety tips

The same safety precautions you take when cooking in the kitchen apply to cooking at the table. Although the possibility of flare-ups or burns is remote, it's always better to be safe than sorry.

Your most important responsibility in tabletop cooking is to stay in complete control of the procedure. Use a sturdy fondue stand and level table to reduce the chances of accidental tipping. And set the fondue unit beyond reach of young children and their quick, unpredictable movements. In fact, fondue is easiest to serve at an all-adult party. You can serve the kids a precooked fondue or other menu ahead of time.

Keep safety equipment handy at all times. If a flare-up develops during dinner, quickly smother the flames by sliding the cover of the fondue pot over the burning area or by tossing handfuls of baking soda at the base of the flames. A fire extinguisher should be as easily accessible to the dining area as it is to other parts of the house.

Occasionally someone may burn a finger from contacting the hot equipment or food. Treat minor burns by running cold water over the burn for 5 minutes, then drying and dressing it with dry gauze. Needless to say, more extensive burns should receive prompt medical attention.

appetizer
fondues

Fondue appetizers make great party foods, snacks, or meal starters. You may want to set up a buffet fondue featuring several hot dips served in fondue pots, or begin a dinner with cook-at-the-table nibbles. With plenty of food available, guests will feel free to help themselves to a tidbit whenever they like.

Reuben Appetizers

An unusual version of the popular sandwich —

- 1 3-ounce package cream cheese, softened
- 1 teaspoon instant minced onion
- 1 16-ounce can sauerkraut, well drained and chopped
- 1 12-ounce can corned beef
- ¼ cup fine dry bread crumbs
- ½ cup all-purpose flour
- ½ cup evaporated milk
- ¾ cup fine dry bread crumbs
    Cooking oil
- 1 teaspoon salt

Combine cream cheese and dried onion. Add sauerkraut, corned beef, and the ¼ cup bread crumbs; mix well. Shape into 1-inch balls. Roll in flour; dip in milk, then in the remaining ¾ cup bread crumbs.

Pour cooking oil into fondue cooker to no more than ½ capacity or to depth of 2 inches. Heat over range to 375°. Add salt. Transfer cooker to fondue burner. Have appetizers at room temperature in serving bowl. Spear with fondue fork; fry in hot oil for 1 to 2 minutes. Transfer to dinner fork before eating. Makes about 100 appetizers.

Crab-Potato Nibblers

Packaged instant mashed potatoes (enough for 2 servings)
- 1 teaspoon instant minced onion
- 1¼ teaspoons Worcestershire sauce
- ⅛ teaspoon garlic powder
    Dash white pepper
- 1 7½-ounce can crab meat, drained, flaked, and cartilage removed
- 1 slightly beaten egg
- ½ cup fine dry bread crumbs
    Cooking oil
- 1 teaspoon salt

Prepare mashed potatoes according to package directions, using 2 *tablespoons less milk* than called for, and adding the instant minced onion to the water before boiling. Stir in Worcestershire sauce, garlic powder, and white pepper. Add crab meat; mix well. Shape into bite-size balls; dip into beaten egg, then roll in bread crumbs.

Pour cooking oil into fondue cooker to no more than ½ capacity or to depth of 2 inches. Heat over range to 375°. Add salt. Transfer cooker to fondue burner. Have appetizers at room temperature in serving bowl. Spear with fondue fork; fry in hot cooking oil for 2 to 3 minutes. Transfer to dinner fork before eating. Makes 36 appetizers.

Tiny Pronto Pups

- 2 beaten eggs
- 1 cup milk
- 2 tablespoons cooking oil
- ½ teaspoon prepared mustard
- 1½ cups pancake mix
    Cooking oil
- 1 teaspoon salt
- 1 5½-ounce package cocktail frankfurters (16), halved crosswise*

For batter, combine eggs, milk, 2 tablespoons cooking oil, and mustard; add pancake mix. Beat with rotary beater till smooth.

Pour cooking oil into fondue cooker to no more than ½ capacity or to depth of 2 inches. Heat over range to 375°. Add salt. Transfer cooker to fondue burner. Have meat at room temperature in serving bowl. Spear a frank with fondue fork; dip into batter, letting excess drip off. (If batter becomes too thick, add a little more milk.) Fry in hot oil about 1 minute. Transfer to dinner fork; dip in sauce. Makes 32 appetizers.

*Or, substitute regular frankfurters cut into 1-inch pieces.

Suggested sauces: Mustard Sauce, Horseradish Sauce, Marmalade Sauce, warmed extra-hot catsup.

Bacon-Wrapped Chicken

- 3 **medium chicken breasts, split**
- 1 **cup water**
- ¼ **cup soy sauce**
- 2 **tablespoons dry sherry**
- 1 **tablespoon sugar**
- 1 **tablespoon vinegar**
- ¼ **teaspoon ground ginger**
- 6 **slices bacon**
  Cooking oil
- 1 **teaspoon salt**

In saucepan combine chicken breasts and water; bring to boiling. Reduce heat; cover and simmer for 15 to 20 minutes or till chicken is tender. Remove chicken; cool slightly. Discard skin and bones. Cut meat into ¾-inch cubes.

In bowl combine soy sauce, sherry, sugar, vinegar, and ginger; mix well. Add cubed chicken; let stand 30 minutes at room temperature, turning occasionally. Drain well.

Cut each bacon slice into thirds crosswise, then in half lengthwise (36 pieces). Wrap one piece around each chicken cube, securing with end of bamboo skewer. Chill well, for at least 1 hour before cooking.

Pour cooking oil into fondue cooker to no more than ½ capacity or to depth of 2 inches. Heat over range to 375°. Add salt. Transfer cooker to fondue burner. Have chicken cubes at room temperature on serving plate. Fry chicken in hot oil about 1 minute or till bacon is cooked. Makes 36 appetizers.

French-Fried Cheese

Assorted *natural* cheeses, cut into ½-inch cubes*
Beaten egg
Fine dry bread crumbs
Cooking oil

For soft cheeses, shape cheese crust around soft center as much as possible. Dip in egg, then crumbs; repeat for second layer. (A thick coating prevents cheese from leaking through.)

Pour oil into fondue cooker to no more than ½ capacity. Heat on range to 375°. Add 1 teaspoon *salt*. Transfer to fondue burner. Spear cheese with fondue fork; fry in hot oil ½ minute. Cool slightly

*Use soft cheeses with a crust (Camembert or Brie), semihard (Bel Paese or brick), or hard (cheddar, Edam, and Gouda) cheeses.

Shrimp Toast

- 1 **pound fresh *or* frozen shelled shrimp**
- 1 **beaten egg**
- 3 **tablespoons chopped onion**
- 2 **teaspoons lemon juice**
- 1 **teaspoon all-purpose flour**
- 6 **slices bread**
  Cooking oil

Thaw shrimp, if frozen. Finely chop or grind *uncooked* shrimp. Stir in egg, onion, lemon juice, flour, ¾ teaspoon *salt*, and dash *pepper*. Trim crusts from bread; cut each slice into 4 pieces. Spread shrimp mixture on *both sides* of bread.

Pour cooking oil into fondue cooker to no more than ½ capacity or to depth of 2 inches. Heat over range to 375°. Add 1 teaspoon *salt*. Transfer cooker to fondue burner. Have shrimp bread at room temperature on serving plate. Spear with fondue fork; fry in hot oil for 1 to 2 minutes. Transfer to dinner fork before eating. Makes 24 appetizers.

Indian Curry Dip

- 1 **tablespoon butter *or* margarine**
- 1 **teaspoon curry powder**
- ¼ **teaspoon salt**
- ¼ **teaspoon garlic powder**
- 1 **13¾-ounce can chicken broth (1¾ cups)**
- 3 **tablespoons cornstarch**
- ¼ **cup catsup**
- ½ **cup dairy sour cream**
  Cooked turkey *or* chicken cubes, cooked shrimp, *or* assorted crackers

In medium saucepan melt butter or margarine. Add curry powder, salt, and garlic powder; mix well. Combine chicken broth and cornstarch; stir into butter-curry mixture. Cook, stirring constantly, till thickened and bubbly. Pour into a fondue pot; place over fondue burner.

Stir catsup into curry mixture; blend in dairy sour cream. Heat through. Serve hot as a dip with turkey or chicken, shrimp, or assorted crackers. Makes 2 cups.

Cheese-and-Bean Dunk

- 1 **6-ounce roll garlic cheese food**
- 1 **11½-ounce can condensed bean with bacon soup**
- 1 **cup dairy sour cream**
- 2 **tablespoons sliced green onion**

Cut garlic cheese roll into chunks. In saucepan combine cheese chunks and bean with bacon soup. Heat slowly, stirring constantly, till blended. Stir in sour cream and green onion. Heat through.

Transfer to fondue pot; place over fondue burner. Garnish with additional sliced green onion, if desired. Makes 2⅔ cups.

meat,
fish,
and seafood

Dinner is easy on the cook when the main dish is a meat, fish, or seafood fondue. Simply set the table and let the guests serve themselves. It's instant fun for everyone.

The traditional fondue recipe in this section is Beef Fondue. Also called Fondue Bourguignonne (Fondue Burgundian), this recipe's connection with the Burgundy region of France or Burgundy wine is obscure. Beef Fondue consists of beef cubes cooked in hot oil and then dipped in a zesty sauce. Similar fondues substitute other meat, fish, or seafood for the beef.

When planning a fondue meal, allow ⅜ pound trimmed, uncooked meat per person and a fondue cooker for every four people. Provide each person with a fondue fork, plate, dinner fork, napkin, and any other appointments needed for the rest of the meal.

Simple accompaniments are all the cook needs to prepare. For a minimum menu, serve a tossed salad to nibble on while the meat is cooking, a light dessert, and a beverage. For a heartier meal, add bread and butter or a cooked vegetable.

One to two hours before the meal, cut the meat into bite-size pieces and allow it to come to room temperature. At serving time, heat the oil-filled pot over the range, add salt to reduce spattering, and transfer it to the fondue burner.

At the table, each person spears a meat cube with a fondue fork or bamboo skewer and cooks it to desired doneness — rare (15 seconds) to 'well-done' (about 1 minute). If the cooking oil cools during the meal, reheat it over the range.

Fish and Seafood Fondue

hot-oil fondues

When heating oil for fondue, use a thermometer to assure that the specified temperature has been reached. Do not allow the oil to smoke. If the oil cools over the fondue burner, reheat it on the range.

Cooking oil is usually used for meat fondue. It's easy to use for cooking, and doesn't flavor the food. Though less popular, peanut oil, a blend of about 3 parts oil to 1 part clarified butter*, or olive oil are sometimes chosen. Like cooking oil, peanut oil doesn't add flavor to the food. However, the butter-oil mixture does have a buttery aroma and gives the meat a slight richness. Olive oil smokes more readily than the other oils, and its characteristic flavor carries over to the meat.

*To clarify butter, melt over low heat; cool. Pour off the oily top layer; discard the bottom layer.

Beef Fondue

    Cooking oil
1   teaspoon salt
1½ pounds trimmed beef
    tenderloin, cut into ¾-inch
    cubes

Pour cooking oil into fondue cooker to no more than ½ capacity or to depth of 2 inches. Heat over range to 425°. Add salt. Transfer cooker to fondue burner. Have beef cubes at room temperature in serving bowl. Spear meat with fondue fork; fry in hot oil to desired doneness. Transfer to dinner fork and dip in sauce. Makes 4 servings.

Suggested sauces: Green Goddess Sauce, Olive Sauce, Dill Sauce, Onion Sauce, Mushroom Sauce, Horseradish Sauce, Bordelaise Sauce, Garlic Butter.

Fish and Seafood Fondue

½   pound *each* fish fillets,
    shelled lobster, and peeled
    and cleaned shrimp, cut into
    bite-size pieces*
    Cooking oil
1   teaspoon salt

Drain *uncooked* fish and seafood thoroughly; pat dry with paper toweling. Pour cooking oil into fondue cooker to no more than ½ capacity or to depth of 2 inches. Heat over range to 375°. Add salt. Transfer cooker to fondue burner. Have fish and seafood at room temperature in serving bowl.

Spear fish or seafood with fondue fork; fry in hot oil till lightly browned. Transfer to dinner fork; dip in sauce. Makes 4 servings.

*Some fish and seafood such as crabs, oysters, and scallops are not well-suited for fondue.

Suggested sauces: Dill Sauce, Sauce a la Relish, Tartar Sauce, Sweet-Sour Sauce, Cocktail Sauce.

Chicken Fondue

Cooking oil
1 teaspoon salt
2 pounds chicken breasts, skinned, boned, and cut into ¾-inch cubes

Pour cooking oil into fondue cooker to no more than ½ capacity or to depth of 2 inches. Heat over range to 425°. Add salt. Transfer cooker to fondue burner. Have chicken cubes at room temperature in serving bowl. Spear cube with fondue fork; fry in hot oil for 2 to 3 minutes. Transfer to dinner fork; dip in sauce. Makes 4 servings.

Suggested sauces: Béarnaise Sauce, Tangy Cranberry Sauce, 1-2-3 Sauce, Curry Sauce.

Veal Strips

1½ pounds veal cutlet
¼ cup all-purpose flour
¼ teaspoon salt
2 beaten eggs
½ cup fine dry bread crumbs
Cooking oil
1 teaspoon salt

Pound veal to about ⅛-inch thickness. Cut into 3x1-inch strips. Combine flour and ¼ teaspoon salt. Coat veal strips with flour mixture; dip in beaten eggs, then in bread crumbs. Loosely thread each strip on bamboo skewer, accordion style.

Pour oil into fondue cooker to no more than ½ capacity or to depth of 2 inches. Heat over range to 425°. Add 1 teaspoon salt. Transfer cooker to fondue burner. Have skewered veal at room temperature on serving plate. Fry in hot oil about 1 minute. Dip in sauce. Makes 4 servings.

Suggested sauces: Garlic Butter, Bordelaise Sauce, Anchovy Butter, Spicy Tomato Sauce.

Pork or Ham Fondue

Cooking oil
2 pounds pork tenderloin, trimmed and cut into 1-inch cubes, *or* 1½ pounds fully cooked ham, cut into ¾-inch cubes

Pour oil into fondue cooker to no more than ½ capacity or to depth of 2 inches. Heat over range to 425°. Add 1 teaspoon *salt*. Transfer cooker to fondue burner. Have meat at room temperature. Spear meat with fondue fork; fry in hot oil for 2 to 3 minutes. Transfer to dinner fork; dip in sauce. Makes 4 servings.

Suggested sauces: Marmalade Sauce, Basil Butter, Mustard Sauce.

Fondued Flank Steak
The marinade acts as a built-in sauce —

1 pound beef flank steak
½ cup cooking oil
½ cup dry red wine
2 tablespoons catsup
2 tablespoons molasses
2 tablespoons finely snipped candied ginger
1 clove garlic, minced
½ teaspoon curry powder
Cooking oil

Bias-slice steak into very thin 3x1-inch strips. For marinade, combine ½ cup oil, red wine, catsup, molasses, ginger, garlic, curry, ½ teaspoon *salt*, and ½ teaspoon *pepper*. Pour over meat. Cover; marinate 2 hours at room temperature. Drain well; pat dry with paper toweling. Thread on bamboo skewers, accordion style.

Pour oil into fondue cooker to no more than ½ capacity or to depth of 2 inches. Heat over range to 425°. Add 1 teaspoon *salt*. Transfer cooker to fondue burner. Have meat at room temperature. Fry in hot oil for 1 to 2 minutes or to desired doneness. Makes 4 servings.

Sausage Meatballs

½ pound bulk pork sausage
¼ cup finely chopped onion
1 14-ounce can sauerkraut, well drained and snipped
2 tablespoons fine dry bread crumbs
1 3-ounce package cream cheese, softened
2 tablespoons snipped parsley
1 teaspoon prepared mustard
¼ teaspoon garlic salt
⅛ teaspoon pepper
¼ cup all-purpose flour
2 well-beaten eggs
¼ cup milk
¾ cup fine dry bread crumbs
Cooking oil
1 teaspoon salt

Cook sausage and onion till meat is browned, finely breaking up meat. Drain off fat. Stir in sauerkraut and 2 tablespoons bread crumbs.

Combine softened cream cheese, parsley, mustard, garlic salt, and pepper. Stir into meat mixture; chill. Shape meat mixture into ¾-inch meatballs; coat with flour. Combine eggs and milk. Roll meatballs in egg mixture, then in ¾ cup bread crumbs.

Pour cooking oil into fondue cooker to no more than ½ capacity or to depth of 2 inches. Heat over range to 375°. Add salt. Transfer cooker to fondue burner. Have meatballs at room temperature. Spear meatball with fondue fork; fry in hot oil for ½ to 1 minute or till golden. Transfer meatball to dinner fork; dip in desired sauce. Makes 60 meatballs.

Suggested sauces: Sweet-Sour Sauce, Mustard Sauce, Curry Sauce, Creamy Catsup Sauce.

Sweet-Sour Sauce

- 1 **cup sugar**
- ½ **cup white vinegar**
- ½ **cup water**
- 1 **tablespoon chopped green pepper**
- 1 **tablespoon chopped pimiento**
- ½ **teaspoon salt**
- 1 **tablespoon cold water**
- 2 **teaspoons cornstarch**
- 1 **teaspoon paprika**

In saucepan combine sugar, vinegar, ½ cup water, green pepper, pimiento, and salt. Bring to boiling; simmer for 5 minutes. Combine 1 tablespoon cold water and cornstarch; add to hot mixture. Cook and stir till thickened and bubbly. Cool. Stir in paprika. Makes 1½ cups.

Bordelaise Sauce

- ½ **cup chopped fresh mushrooms *or* one 2-ounce can chopped mushrooms**
- 2 **teaspoons butter *or* margarine**
- 1 **cup beef broth**
- 4 **teaspoons cornstarch**
- 1 **tablespoon lemon juice**
- 1 **tablespoon dry red wine**
- ¾ **teaspoon dried tarragon, crushed**
- **Dash pepper**

Cook fresh mushrooms in butter or margarine till tender (if canned, combine with melted butter). Combine cool beef broth and cornstarch; add to mushrooms. Cook and stir till boiling. Stir in lemon juice, red wine, tarragon, and pepper; simmer mixture for 5 to 10 minutes. Makes 1 cup sauce.

Mushroom Sauces

- In small skillet cook 1 cup sliced fresh *mushrooms* and ¼ cup finely chopped *green onion* in ¼ cup *butter or margarine* just till tender. Blend in 4 teaspoons *cornstarch.* Add ¾ cup *red burgundy*, ¾ cup *water*, 2 tablespoons snipped *parsley*, ¾ teaspoon *salt*, and dash *pepper*; mix well. Cook and stir till thickened and bubbly. Makes 1½ cups.
- Drain one 3-ounce can chopped *mushrooms;* chop mushrooms more finely. Dissolve 1 *beef bouillon cube* in ⅔ cup *boiling water.* In small saucepan melt 2 tablespoons *butter or margarine* over low heat. Blend in 2 tablespoons all-purpose *flour.* Add bouillon all at once; mix well. Cook quickly, stirring constantly, till mixture is thickened and bubbly. Stir in ½ cup dairy *sour cream*, 2 teaspoons *Worcestershire sauce*, and the finely chopped mushrooms; heat through. Serve hot. Makes about 1⅓ cups.
- In saucepan combine one 10½-ounce can condensed *cream of mushroom soup* and ½ cup dairy *sour cream;* heat through. Makes about 2¼ cups.

Curry Sauce

- 3 **tablespoons butter *or* margarine**
- 1 **teaspoon curry powder**
- 2 **tablespoons all-purpose flour**
- ½ **teaspoon salt**
- **Dash pepper**
- 1 **cup milk**

In saucepan melt butter or margarine. Stir in curry powder; cook for 1 to 2 minutes. Blend in flour, salt, and pepper. Add milk all at once. Cook and stir till thickened and bubbly. Serve hot. Makes 1 cup.

Tomato Sauces

1-2-3 Sauce: Combine one 12-ounce bottle *extra-hot catsup*, 3 tablespoons *vinegar*, 2 teaspoons *celery seed*, and 1 clove *garlic*, halved. Cover and chill mixture; remove garlic. Makes 1¼ cups.

Creamy Catsup Sauce: In small mixer bowl beat one 3-ounce package softened *cream cheese* till fluffy. Gradually blend in ¼ cup dairy *sour cream*, 2 tablespoons *catsup*, ¼ teaspoon *salt*, ¼ teaspoon *Worcestershire sauce*, and dash bottled *hot pepper sauce.* Stir in 2 tablespoons finely chopped *green pepper.* Makes about 1 cup.

Red Sauce: Combine 3 tablespoons *catsup*, 3 tablespoons *chili sauce*, 1½ tablespoons prepared *horseradish*, 1 teaspoon *lemon juice*, and dash bottled *hot pepper sauce;* mix well. Cover and chill. Makes about ½ cup.

Spicy Tomato Sauce: Combine ½ cup dairy *sour cream*, 2 tablespoons *chili sauce*, ½ teaspoon prepared *horseradish*, ¼ teaspoon *salt*, and dash *pepper.* Cover and chill. Makes ⅔ cup.

Cocktail Sauce: Combine ¾ cup *chili sauce*, 2 to 4 tablespoons *lemon juice*, 1 to 2 tablespoons prepared *horseradish*, 2 teaspoons *Worcestershire sauce*, ½ teaspoon *grated onion*, and dash bottled *hot pepper sauce;* mix well. Add salt to taste. Cover and chill. Makes 1¼ cups.

Mexican Hot Sauce: In saucepan combine 1 cup *chili sauce;* ¼ cup chopped *onion;* 3 tablespoons *vinegar;* 1 tablespoon *cooking oil;* 1 teaspoon *brown sugar;* 1 clove *garlic*, minced; ¼ teaspoon *salt;* ¼ teaspoon *dry mustard;* and ¼ teaspoon bottled *hot pepper sauce.* Bring to boiling. Simmer for 10 minutes, stirring occasionally. Serve warm or cool. Makes 1¼ cups.

Green Goddess Sauce

- 2 **3-ounce packages cream cheese, softened**
- 3 **tablespoons milk**
- 2 **tablespoons finely snipped chives**
- 1 **tablespoon snipped parsley**
- 2 **teaspoons anchovy paste**
- 1 **teaspoon finely chopped onion**

Blend softened cream cheese and milk. Add snipped chives, snipped parsley, anchovy paste, and chopped onion; mix well. Makes 1 cup.

Olive Sauce

- ½ **cup dairy sour cream**
- 1 **3-ounce package cream cheese, softened**
- 2 **tablespoons chopped pimiento-stuffed olives**
- 1 **tablespoon finely chopped onion**
- 1 **teaspoon snipped parsley**

Blend together sour cream and softened cream cheese. Fold in pimiento-stuffed olives, onion, and snipped parsley. Makes 1 cup.

Tartar Sauce

- 1 **cup mayonnaise** *or* **salad dressing**
- 3 **tablespoons finely chopped dill pickle**
- 1 **tablespoon snipped parsley**
- 2 **teaspoons chopped pimiento**
- 1 **teaspoon grated onion**

Combine mayonnaise or salad dressing, dill pickle, snipped parsley, chopped pimiento, and grated onion; cover and chill. Makes 1¼ cups.

Horseradish Sauces

- Fold 3 tablespoons drained prepared *horseradish* into ½ cup *whipping cream*, whipped. Add ½ teaspoon *salt*. Makes about 1 cup.
- In mixing bowl combine 1 cup dairy *sour cream*, 3 tablespoons drained prepared *horseradish*, ¼ teaspoon *salt*, and dash *paprika*. Cover and chill. Makes 1 cup.
- Whip one 8-ounce package softened *cream cheese* and 2 to 3 tablespoons drained prepared *horseradish* till fluffy. Blend in 2 tablespoons *milk*. Cover and chill. Makes 1⅓ cups.
- In saucepan melt 3 tablespoons *butter or margarine*; blend in 1 teaspoon all-purpose *flour*. Stir in ¼ cup *vinegar*, ¼ cup *beef broth*, ¼ cup *horseradish mustard*, and 3 tablespoons *brown sugar*. Cook slowly, stirring constantly, till thickened. Gradually add a little hot mixture to 1 slightly beaten *egg yolk*; return to hot mixture. Bring to boiling, stirring constantly. Makes 1 cup.

Onion Sauces

- In saucepan melt 2 tablespoons *butter or margarine* with 1 tablespoon *sugar* over low heat, stirring till sugar turns golden. Add ½ cup chopped *onion*; cook for 2 minutes more. Blend in 3 tablespoons all-purpose *flour*; add 1 cup *condensed beef broth*. Cook and stir till thickened. Stir in 1 tablespoon *vinegar*. Reduce heat; cover and simmer 10 minutes. Makes 1 cup.
- Combine ½ cup dairy *sour cream*, 1 envelope *green onion dip mix*, ½ teaspoon *Worcestershire sauce*, and 2 drops bottled *hot pepper sauce*. Cover and chill thoroughly. Makes ½ cup.
- Combine 1½ cups dairy *sour cream* and 2 tablespoons dry *onion soup mix*. Stir in ½ cup crumbled *blue cheese* and ⅓ cup chopped *walnuts*. Cover; chill. Makes 2 cups.

Marmalade Sauce

- ½ **cup orange marmalade**
- 1 **tablespoon soy sauce**
- ⅛ **teaspoon garlic powder Dash ground ginger**
- ⅓ **cup cold water**
- 2 **tablespoons cornstarch**
- 2 **tablespoons lemon juice**

In small saucepan combine marmalade, soy sauce, garlic powder, and ginger; bring to boiling. Combine cold water and cornstarch; stir into hot mixture. Cook and stir till thickened and bubbly. Stir in lemon juice. Makes 1 cup.

Dill Sauce

- 1 **cup dairy sour cream**
- 1 **tablespoon snipped chives**
- 1 **teaspoon vinegar**
- ½ **teaspoon grated onion**
- ½ **teaspoon dried dillweed**
- ¼ **teaspoon salt**

Combine sour cream, snipped chives, vinegar, grated onion, dillweed, and salt; mix well. Makes 1 cup.

Sauce a la Relish

- 1 **8-ounce can tomato sauce**
- ¼ **cup chili sauce**
- 2 **tablespoons finely chopped onion**
- 2 **tablespoons drained sweet pickle relish**
- 1 **tablespoon vinegar**
- 1 **teaspoon Worcestershire sauce**
- ½ **teaspoon prepared horseradish**
- ⅛ **teaspoon pepper**

In saucepan combine all ingredients. Cook, uncovered, over low heat about 20 minutes, stirring frequently. Makes 1¼ cups.

Béarnaise Sauce

- 3 **tablespoons white wine vinegar**
- 1 **teaspoon finely chopped shallot** *or* **green onion**
- 4 **whole peppercorns, crushed**
  Dash dried tarragon, crushed
  Dash dried chervil, crushed
- 1 **tablespoon cold water**
- 4 **egg yolks**
- ½ **cup butter, softened**
- 1 **teaspoon snipped fresh tarragon** *or* **¼ teaspoon dried tarragon, crushed**

In saucepan combine wine vinegar, shallot or green onion, peppercorns, dash tarragon, and chervil. Simmer till liquid is reduced to half. Strain, discarding solids. Add cold water to herb liquid.

Beat egg yolks in top of double boiler (not over water). Slowly add herb liquid. Add *2 tablespoons* of the butter to egg yolks; place over *hot, not boiling* water. Cook and stir till butter melts and sauce begins to thicken. Continue adding remaining butter, 2 tablespoons at a time, while stirring constantly. Cook and stir till sauce is the consistency of thick cream. Remove from heat. Stir in 1 teaspoon fresh tarragon or ¼ teaspoon dried tarragon; salt to taste. Makes about ¾ cup.

Garlic Butter

- ½ **cup butter** *or* **margarine, softened**
- 1 **small clove garlic, minced**

Cream butter or margarine till fluffy. Beat in garlic. Let mixture mellow at room temperature at least 1 hour before serving. Makes ½ cup.

Basil Butter

- ½ **cup butter** *or* **margarine, softened**
- 1 **teaspoon lemon juice**
- ¾ **teaspoon dried basil, crushed**

Cream softened butter or margarine till fluffy. Beat in lemon juice and basil. Let mixture mellow at room temperature at least 1 hour before serving. Makes ½ cup.

Anchovy Butter

- 2 **cups butter, softened**
- 1 **2-ounce can anchovy fillets**
- 2 **tablespoons snipped parsley**

With electric mixer beat together softened butter or margarine, anchovy fillets, and parsley till well blended. Let mixture mellow at room temperature at least 1 hour before serving. Makes about 2 cups.

Tangy Cranberry Sauce

- ½ **cup orange juice**
- 1 **tablespoon cornstarch**
- 1 **16-ounce can whole cranberry sauce**
- 1 **tablespoon brown sugar**
- ¼ **teaspoon ground cinnamon**

In saucepan blend orange juice and cornstarch. Stir in cranberry sauce, brown sugar, and cinnamon. Cook, stirring constantly, till thickened and bubbly. Makes 2 cups.

Mustard Sauces

- In small saucepan melt 2 tablespoons *butter or margarine* over low heat. Blend in 2 tablespoons all-purpose *flour*, ¼ teaspoon *salt*, and dash *white pepper*. Add 1 cup *milk* all at once. Cook quickly, stirring constantly, till thickened and bubbly. Remove from heat. Add 1½ to 2 tablespoons *prepared mustard*; mix well. Serve hot. Makes about 1 cup.
- In top of double boiler combine 2 beaten *egg yolks*, 3 tablespoons *prepared mustard*, 2 tablespoons *vinegar*, 1 tablespoon *sugar*, 1 tablespoon *water*, 1 tablespoon *butter*, 1 tablespoon drained prepared *horseradish*, and ½ teaspoon *salt*; mix well. Place over boiling water; cook and stir about 2 minutes or till thickened. Remove from heat. Stir vigorously, if necessary, till sauce is smooth. Cool. Fold in ½ cup *whipping cream*, whipped; cover and refrigerate. Makes 1 cup.
- In small saucepan blend ½ cup *milk* into 3 tablespoons dry *onion soup mix*; let stand 5 to 10 minutes. Stir in 1 cup dairy *sour cream* and 2 tablespoons *prepared mustard*. Heat through, stirring occasionally. Makes 1⅓ cups.
- In a jar mix together ½ cup *dry mustard* and ½ cup *vinegar*. Cover and let stand overnight. In saucepan beat 1 *egg*; stir in ¼ cup *sugar*, dash *salt*, and mustard mixture. Cook and stir over low heat till mixture thickens slightly and coats a spoon; cool. Stir in 1 cup *mayonnaise or salad dressing*. Makes about 2 cups.

cheese fondues

Originally a natural Swiss cheese melted in dry white wine, cheese fondue is an ingenious Swiss concoction. This elegant dish has many uses. Serve it to introduce a multi-course meal of meat, vegetable, bread, salad, and dessert. Or, let it stand alone as a main dish by adding simple accompaniments such as relishes or a salad, a beverage, and a light dessert.

Cheese fondue is prepared right before serving, using the easily mastered techniques of simmering and continual stirring. Warm the wine and lemon juice in a heavy saucepan to just below boiling. Start the vigorous and constant stirring when the shredded cheeses, coated with cornstarch, are added, a handful at a time. Apply enough heat to melt the cheeses, but not enough to boil them. All is not lost if the mixture separates, though. To restore a separated mixture, combine 1 tablespoon cornstarch with 2 tablespoons wine and stir into the fondue.

Quickly transfer the cheese-wine mixture to a fondue pot. Metal cookers or ceramic pots, similar to traditional Swiss caquelons, make equally suitable containers. Keep the cheese bubbly over the fondue burner — not hot enough to become stringy or cool enough to become tough. If the fondue thickens during the meal, preheat a little more wine and add it to the fondue, stirring briskly.

cheese fondue dippers

All dippers should be bite-size. Cut bread cubes so that each has one crust. To estimate how many dippers you'll need, consider appetites and accompanying dishes. Generally, 1 large loaf of French bread serves 6 to 8. Serve cooked-meat and vegetable dippers warm, and raw vegetables at room temperature.

Bread dippers: French bread, hard rolls, melba toast, Italian bread, breadsticks, toasted rye or whole wheat bread, English muffins.

Cooked meat or fish dippers: Cooked shrimp, chicken or turkey, ham.

Vegetable dippers: Cherry tomatoes, cooked whole green beans, artichokes, carrot sticks, cooked mushrooms, celery or green pepper pieces, fried potato nuggets, french-fried potatoes, boiled potatoes.

Each person spears a bread cube, piercing the crust last, then swirls the dipper through the cheese in a figure-eight motion. This dipping and swirling helps keep the fondue stirred.

Oops — who dropped a bread cube into the fondue? Tradition has it that they must give a kiss to the friend of their choice. For those who never lose their bread cubes, there's another reward, the crusty cheese in the bottom of the pot.

Classic Cheese Fondue

- 12 ounces *natural* Swiss cheese, shredded (3 cups)
- 4 ounces Gruyère cheese, shredded (1 cup)
- 1½ teaspoons cornstarch
- 1 clove garlic, halved
- 1 cup sauterne
- 1 tablespoon lemon juice
  Dash ground nutmeg
  Dash pepper

Combine Swiss cheese, Gruyère cheese, and cornstarch. Rub inside of heavy saucepan with garlic; discard garlic. Pour in sauterne and lemon juice. Warm till air bubbles rise and cover surface. (Do not cover or allow to boil.)

Remember to stir vigorously and constantly from now on. Add a handful of cheeses, keeping heat medium (*do not boil*). When cheese melts, toss in another handful. After cheese is blended and bubbling and while still stirring, add nutmeg and pepper.

Quickly transfer to fondue pot; keep warm over fondue burner. (If fondue becomes too thick, add a little more *warmed* sauterne.) Spear bread cube with fondue fork, piercing crust last. Dip bread in fondue and swirl to coat. The swirling is important to keep the fondue in motion. Serves 4 to 6.

Suggested dippers: French bread, hard rolls, Italian bread.

Classic Cheese Fondue

Caraway-Cheese Fondue

- 1½ cups tomato juice
- 2 teaspoons caraway seed
- 1 pound cheddar cheese, shredded (4 cups)
- 2 tablespoons all-purpose flour
- ¼ cup milk
- ¼ teaspoon Worcestershire sauce

In saucepan heat tomato juice and caraway seed but *do not boil.* Combine cheddar cheese and flour. Slowly add cheese mixture to tomato juice, stirring constantly till cheese melts and mixture is smooth. Stir in milk and Worcestershire sauce.

Transfer to fondue pot; place over fondue burner. Spear dipper with fondue fork; dip in fondue, swirling to coat. Serves 6 to 8.

Suggested dippers: French bread, rye bread, hard rolls.

Buttermilk Fondue

- 2 tablespoons cornstarch
- ½ teaspoon salt
  Dash ground nutmeg
  Dash pepper
- 1 pound *natural* Swiss cheese, shredded (4 cups)
- 2 cups buttermilk

In mixing bowl combine cornstarch, salt, nutmeg, and pepper. Toss Swiss cheese with cornstarch mixture.

In saucepan carefully heat buttermilk. When buttermilk is warm, gradually add cheese mixture; stir constantly till cheese melts and mixture thickens. Transfer to fondue pot; place over fondue burner. Spear dipper with fondue fork; dip in fondue, swirling to coat. Makes 6 to 8 servings.

Suggested dippers: French bread, English muffins, hard rolls.

Rarebit-Style Fondue

Good with toasted breads —

- 1½ cups sauterne
- ½ cup water
- 2 tablespoons snipped chives
- 1 pound American cheese, shredded (4 cups)
- 2 tablespoons all-purpose flour
- 4 beaten egg yolks
- ¼ teaspoon ground nutmeg

In saucepan heat wine, water, and chives. Coat cheese with flour. Add slowly to hot wine, stirring constantly till cheese melts and mixture thickens.

Stir a moderate amount of hot cheese mixture into egg yolks. Return to saucepan; cook and stir over low heat 2 minutes more. Stir in nutmeg. Pour into fondue pot; place over fondue burner. Spear dipper with fondue fork; dip in fondue, swirling to coat. Makes 6 to 8 servings.

Suggested dippers: French bread, celery, cherry tomatoes, mushrooms.

Crab-Cheese Fondue

- 8 ounces American cheese, shredded (2 cups)
- 8 ounces cheddar cheese, shredded (2 cups)
- ¾ cup milk
- 2 teaspoons lemon juice
- 1 7½-ounce can crab meat, drained, flaked, and cartilage removed

In saucepan slowly heat and stir cheeses and milk till cheeses are melted. Stir in lemon juice. Add crab; heat. Transfer to fondue pot; place over fondue burner. Spear dipper with fondue fork; dip in fondue, swirling to coat. Makes 8 to 10 servings.

Suggested dippers: French bread, cherry tomatoes, cooked artichokes.

Cottage Swiss Fondue

Mustard adds zesty background flavor —

- 2 tablespoons butter *or* margarine
- 2 tablespoons all-purpose flour
  Dash garlic powder
- 1 teaspoon prepared mustard
- 1¼ cups milk
- 1 cup cream-style cottage cheese (8 ounces)
- 8 ounces *natural* Swiss cheese, shredded (2 cups)

In medium saucepan melt butter or margarine; blend in flour and garlic powder, then mustard. Add milk all at once. Cook quickly, stirring constantly, till mixture is thickened and bubbly. Add cream-style cottage cheese. Beat till smooth with electric mixer (or blend in blender).

Over medium heat gradually add shredded Swiss cheese, stirring till cheese is melted. Pour into fondue pot; place over fondue burner. Spear dipper with fondue fork; dip in fondue, swirling to coat. (If mixture becomes too thick, add a little more milk.) Makes 4 to 6 servings.

Suggested dippers: French bread, fried potato nuggets, french-fried potatoes.

Fondue Italiano

Start the fondue ahead of time by browning the meat and mixing in the tomato sauce and spaghetti sauce mix, then chill the mixture. When it's time to eat, the final recipe steps will take only a few minutes to complete —

- ½ pound ground beef
- 1 15-ounce can tomato sauce
- ½ envelope spaghetti sauce mix
- 12 ounces cheddar cheese, shredded (3 cups)
- 4 ounces *natural* mozzarella cheese, shredded (1 cup)
- ½ cup Chianti
- 1 tablespoon cornstarch Italian bread, cut into bite-size pieces, each with one crust

In saucepan brown ground beef; drain off excess fat. Stir in tomato sauce and spaghetti sauce mix. Add cheeses gradually; stir over low heat till cheese is melted. Blend together wine and cornstarch; add to cheese mixture. Cook and stir till thickened and bubbly.

Transer to fondue pot; place over fondue burner. Spear bread cube with fondue fork; dip in fondue, swirling to coat. (If mixture becomes too thick, add a little *warmed* Chianti.) Makes 4 to 6 servings.

Beer-Cheese Fondue

- 1 small clove garlic, halved
- ¾ cup beer
- 8 ounces *process* Swiss cheese, shredded (2 cups)
- 4 ounces sharp cheddar cheese, shredded (1 cup)
- 1 tablespoon all-purpose flour Dash bottled hot pepper sauce

Rub inside of heavy saucepan with cut surface of garlic; discard garlic. Add beer and heat slowly. Coat cheeses with flour. Gradually add to beer, stirring constantly till mixture is thickened and bubbly. (Do not allow mixture to become too hot.) Stir in pepper sauce.

Transfer to fondue pot; place over fondue burner. Spear dipper with fondue fork; dip in fondue, swirling to coat. (If mixture becomes too thick, stir in a little more *warmed* beer.) Serves 4 to 6.

Suggested dippers: French bread, warm boiled potatoes.

Creamy Parmesan Fondue

- 1½ cups milk
- 2 8-ounce packages cream cheese, softened
- ½ teaspoon salt
- ½ teaspoon garlic salt
- 1 2½-ounce container grated Parmesan cheese (¾ cup)

With electric mixer beat milk into cream cheese, mixing till well blended. Heat slowly in saucepan; add salt and garlic salt. Slowly add Parmesan, stirring till smooth.

Pour into fondue pot; place over fondue burner. Spear dipper with fondue fork; dip in fondue, swirling to coat. (If mixture becomes too thick, stir in a little more milk.) Makes 8 to 10 servings.

Suggested dippers: Breadsticks, warm cooked turkey or chicken.

Cheese-Sour-Cream Fondue

- 6 slices bacon
- ¼ cup minced onion
- 2 teaspoons all-purpose flour
- 1 pound American cheese, shredded (4 cups)
- 2 cups dairy sour cream
- 1 teaspoon Worcestershire sauce

In saucepan cook bacon till crisp; drain, reserving 1 tablespoon drippings. Crumble bacon; set aside. Cook onion in reserved drippings till tender but not brown. Stir in flour. Stir in shredded cheese, sour cream, and Worcestershire sauce. Cook over low heat, stirring constantly, till cheese is melted.

Pour into fondue pot. Top with crumbled bacon. Place over fondue burner. Spear dipper with fondue fork; dip in fondue. Makes 6 to 8 servings.

Suggested dippers: Hard rolls, rye bread, mushrooms.

Quick Fondue

- 2 10½-ounce cans condensed cheddar cheese soup
- ⅓ cup dry white wine Few drops Worcestershire sauce

In saucepan combine cheddar cheese soup, white wine, and Worcestershire sauce; heat through. Pour into fondue pot; place over fondue burner. Spear dipper with fondue fork; dip in fondue, swirling to coat. Makes 4 to 6 servings.

Suggested dippers: French bread, warm cooked shrimp, celery.

Wine Guide

Wines can be classified in five groups by their common characteristics. This chart lists some wines in each group and tells how to serve them with cooked-at-the-table dishes. Although food-and-wine combinations ultimately should be based on personal preference, foods most suited to each group are indicated. Selection of the appropriate wine should be coupled with proper serving techniques. Here are some general guidelines to follow. Sweet wines should not be served with main dishes; robust red wines usually are not served with fish. Uncork red wines an hour before serving to develop full flavor.

Wine Group	Foods Served with Group	Wine Types to Serve
Appetizer Wines (Serve at room temperature, 60° to 70°, or chilled, 40° to 45°.)	Alone as an appetizer or with all appetizer foods	Sherry, especially dry varieties Vermouth, both dry and sweet Flavored Wines
Red Table Wines (Serve at room temperature, 60° to 70°, *except* for Rosé.) (Served chilled, 45° to 50°.)	All red meats including steaks, veal; game, goose, duck, turkey; cheese	Burgundy (Pinot Noir) Beaujolais (Gamay) Red Chianti (Barbera) Claret (Cabernet Sauvignon) Rosé
White Table Wines (Served chilled, 45° to 50°.)	All poultry, chicken, turkey; fish, shellfish; veal; cheese dishes The traditional Swiss wines served with cheese fondue	Rhine (Riesling) Sauterne, drier varieties (Semillon, Sauvignon Blanc) Chablis Moselle White Burgundy (Pinot Chardonnay) Neuchatel, Dézaley, Fendant de Sion
Dessert Wines (Serve at room temperature, 60° to 70°.)	Alone as after-dinner wine or with fruit, nuts, cakes, some dessert cheeses	Port, Ruby or Tawny Muscatel White Tokay Sherry, Sweet or Cream Sweet Madeira Sauterne, sweeter varieties
Sparkling Wines (Serve chilled, 40° to 45°.)	Most types of foods	Champagne — very dry (brut) semi-dry (sec), less dry (demi-sec), or sweet (doux) Sparkling Burgundy Sparkling Rosé

Wines To Use In Cheese Fondue

Cheese fondue recipes using wine as an ingredient usually specify a dry white wine, the most traditional being the Swiss wine, Neuchatel. Those listed below may be used interchangeably in Classic Cheese Fondue (see page 166). Several types listed include wines with colors and flavors other than those described here. Wines with the characteristics indicated, however, are best suited for cheese fondue.

For This Type of Cheese Fondue	Use This Type of Wine	With These Characteristics
Appetizer	Sherry	Very dry to dry, pale amber, nutty flavor
Appetizer or Main Dish	Champagne	Dry (brut, sec, or demi-sec), pale gold, fruit flavor
	Neuchatel	Dry, pale gold, light-bodied, lively, crisp
	Fendant de Sion	Dry, pale gold, lively, crisp
Main Dish	Rhine	Dry, pale gold to slightly green-gold, light-bodied, tart
	Moselle	Dry, pale, light-bodied
	Chablis	Very dry, pale gold, fruit flavor
	Sauterne	Dry, golden, full-bodied, fragrant

Classic Cheese Fondue Variations

Cheeses vary considerably in appearance, texture, and flavor. In this respect, they are very individualistic. Therefore, one cheese cannot be substituted at random for another in a cooked cheese dish.

Traditionally, cheese fondue recipes use a well-aged natural Swiss (Emmentaler) cheese or a blend of Swiss cheese and Gruyère. Nevertheless, processed forms of these cheeses also are suitable. To give interesting flavor variation to your cheese fondue, the other natural cheeses listed below (most are not available in a processed form) can be substituted for the Swiss cheese in Classic Cheese Fondue (see page 166). Use *12 ounces (3 cups shredded)* of one of these cheeses. Adjust wine and lemon juice levels as indicated in the columns adjacent to each cheese, then continue preparing the fondue following the Classic Cheese Fondue method.

Note: Several other cheeses tested produced mixtures that separated into two layers of wine and cheese, or were too runny in the proportions established in the Classic Cheese Fondue recipe. These include Gouda, mozzarella, provolone, and Stilton. This is not to say they cannot be used for cheese fondue, but proportions must be carefully adjusted. Several of the tested variations with the necessary adjustments will be found elsewhere in this section.

Natural Cheese	Wine	Lemon Juice	Flavor of Cheese
Brick	1 cup	1 tablespoon	Mild to moderately sharp; midway between cheddar and Limburger
Colby	¾ cup	2 teaspoons	Mild to mellow; similar to cheddar
Fontina	1 cup	1 tablespoon	Delicate; nutty flavor
Monterey Jack	¾ cup	2 teaspoons	Mild
Muenster	1 cup	1 tablespoon	Mild to mellow

fondue
meal
cappers

A rich, warm chocolate sauce, with tender cake cubes or fresh fruit dippers, Chocolate Fondue is the classic dessert fondue. Originally developed to promote Swiss chocolate, Chocolate Fondue soon sparked ideas for a variety of dessert fondues, including other warm dessert sauces and deep-fat-fried desserts.

Dessert fondue sets usually include a stand with candle warmer and a small ceramic or metal fondue pot. However, you can use any metal pot for this type of fondue, or even ceramic containers for fondues that don't require hot oil.

A dessert fondue makes a welcome final course or between-meals refreshment. Since most dessert fondues are rich, they're best enjoyed with a beverage after a light meal. Serve one or two fondues, an assortment of dippers, and a beverage to complement an afternoon bridge club, a small party with friends, or an after-theater get-together.

You can prepare most of the dessert fondues before serving time. For fondues that involve deep-fat frying, cut dippers into bite-size pieces and store them properly to maintain freshness. Then, just before serving time, heat cooking oil over the range. Or, prepare a sauce-type fondue in a saucepan and then transfer it to the fondue pot. Keep sauces over low heat so they're warm but not too hot. At the table, each person can fry their choice of dippers in hot oil or dip them in a warm sauce.

dessert fondue dippers

Cut your dippers into bite-size pieces and serve them at room temperature. Drain canned or frozen fruits thoroughly. Allow 8 to 12 dippers per serving. *To keep fresh fruit dippers bright, dip them in ascorbic acid color keeper or lemon juice mixed with a little water.

Fruit dippers: Cherries, strawberries, bananas*, apples*, seedless grapes, pears*, pineapple, oranges, mandarin oranges, melons, peaches*, maraschino cherries, dates.

Baked dippers: Angel, sponge, chiffon, or pound cake; doughnuts; cookies.

Other dippers: Marshmallows, large salted nuts, large puffy popcorn kernels, pretzels.

Chocolate Fondue

- 6 **1-ounce squares unsweetened chocolate**
- 1½ **cups sugar**
- 1 **cup light cream**
- ½ **cup butter *or* margarine**
- ⅛ **teaspoon salt**
- 3 **tablespoons crème de cacao *or* orange liqueur**

In saucepan melt chocolate over low heat. Add sugar, cream, butter, and salt. Cook, stirring constantly, about 5 minutes or till thickened. Stir in liqueur. Pour into fondue pot; place over fondue burner. Spear dipper with fondue fork; dip in sauce. Makes 6 to 8 servings.

Suggested dippers: Angel cake, pound cake, apples, maraschino cherries, marshmallows.

Chocolate-Nut Fondue

- 1 **6-ounce package semisweet chocolate pieces**
- ½ **cup sugar**
- ½ **cup milk**
- ½ **cup chunk-style peanut butter**

In saucepan combine chocolate pieces, sugar, and milk. Cook, stirring constantly, till chocolate is melted. Add peanut butter; mix well. Pour into fondue pot; place over fondue burner. Spear dipper with fondue fork; dip in sauce. Makes 6 to 8 servings.

Suggested dippers: Bananas, apples, pound cake, angel cake, marshmallows.

French-Toasted Fondue

Served with a light maple-butter sauce —

- 2 **well-beaten eggs**
- ½ **cup milk**
- ¼ **teaspoon salt**
  Cooking oil
- 1 **teaspoon salt**
  French bread, cut into about 50 bite-size pieces, each with one crust
  Fluffy Maple Sauce

In bowl combine eggs, milk, and ¼ teaspoon salt. Set aside. Pour cooking oil into fondue cooker to no more than ½ capacity or to depth of 2 inches. Heat over range to 375°. Add 1 teaspoon salt. Transfer cooker to fondue burner.

Spear French bread cube through crust with fondue fork; dip bread in egg mixture, letting excess drip off. Fry in hot cooking oil till golden brown. Transfer to dinner fork; dip in Fluffy Maple Sauce. Makes 6 to 8 servings.

Fluffy Maple Sauce: In bowl thoroughly cream together 1½ cups sifted *powdered sugar,* ½ cup *butter or margarine,* ½ cup *maple-flavored syrup,* and 1 *egg yolk.* Fold in 1 stiffly beaten *egg white.* Cover and refrigerate sauce. Makes 2 cups.

Fruit Fritters

- ½ **teaspoon grated orange peel (set aside)**
- 2 **tablespoons orange juice**
- 1 **tablespoon sugar**
- 2 *firm* **bananas**
- 1 **medium apple**
- 1 **small fresh pineapple**
- 1 **cup all-purpose flour**
- ½ **teaspoon baking powder**
- 1 **slightly beaten egg**
- ⅔ **cup milk**
- 2 **tablespoons butter, melted**
- ¼ **teaspoon lemon extract**
- ½ **cup sugar**
- 2 **tablespoons cornstarch**
- ¼ **cup orange juice**
- 2 **tablespoons butter**
- ¼ **teaspoon grated lemon peel**
- 1 **tablespoon lemon juice**
  Cooking oil
- 1 **4-ounce jar maraschino cherries, well drained**

Combine 2 tablespoons orange juice and 1 tablespoon sugar. Cut fruits into bite-size pieces. Let stand in orange juice mixture till needed.

Combine flour, baking powder, and ½ teaspoon *salt.* Combine egg, milk, melted butter, and extract; add to flour mixture. Beat smooth.

For sauce, combine ½ cup sugar, cornstarch, and dash *salt.* Stir in ¾ cup *water.* Cook and stir till bubbly; cook and stir 3 minutes more Remove from heat; stir in orange peel, ¼ cup orange juice, remaining butter, lemon peel, and lemon juice. Keep warm.

Pour cooking oil into fondue cooker to no more than ½ capacity or to depth of 2 inches. Heat over range to 375°. Add 1 teaspoon *salt.* Transfer cooker to fondue burner. Have *well-drained* bananas, apple, pineapple, and maraschino cherries at room temperature in serving bowls. Spear with fondue fork; dip in batter. Fry in hot oil 2 to 3 minutes or till golden. Transfer to dinner fork; dip in sauce. Serves 6 to 8.

Butterscotch Fondue

- ½ **cup butter *or* margarine**
- 2 **cups packed brown sugar**
- 1 **cup light corn syrup**
- 2 **tablespoons water**
- 1 **15-ounce can *sweetened condensed* milk (1⅓ cups)**
- 1 **teaspoon vanilla**

In saucepan melt butter; stir in brown sugar, corn syrup, and water. Bring to boiling. Stir in milk; simmer, stirring constantly, till mixture reaches thread stage (230°). Stir in vanilla.

Pour into fondue pot; place over fondue burner. Spear dipper with fondue fork; dip in fondue, swirling to coat. (If mixture becomes too thick, stir in a little more milk or water.) Makes 8 servings.

Suggested dippers: Pound cake, vanilla wafers, apples, popcorn.

Caramel Fondue

- 1 **14-ounce package vanilla caramels**
- ⅓ **cup water**
  Dash salt

In top of double boiler combine caramels and water; melt over hot water, stirring frequently. Add salt. Pour sauce into fondue pot; place over fondue burner. (If mixture becomes too thick, stir in a little more water.) Spear dipper with fondue fork; dip in fondue, swirling to coat. Makes 4 servings.

Suggested dippers: Apples, bananas, peaches, marshmallows.

Skillet Pork Chops and Hot Slaw (see recipe, page 175)

FOOD PROCESSOR RECIPES

From appetizer to dessert, let your food processor simplify recipe preparation. Use the following primer to become more familiar with your machine and to learn which tasks it performs best. Then refer to it when making the easy-to-fix salads, main dishes, and other food processor specialties that follow.

food processor primer

A food processor can be a time-saver when you know how to make the best use of it. But be prepared to spend a little time getting to know your machine and discovering what it can do.

First and foremost, read the owner's manual that came with your processor. It should tell you how to assemble the processor and what specific procedures are recommended.

parts of the machine

Food processors differ from one another in many respects, but they all have certain basic parts in common.

The *motor base* supplies power and is either direct-driven or belt-driven, as explained on page 157.

The *work bowl* holds the food for processing. The *cover* for the work bowl has a vertical chute, called the *feed tube*. A *pusher* fits inside the feed tube and is used to guide food into the rotating disks and to reduce spattering when the steel or plastic blade is used.

The work bowl and cover are made of either clear or tinted plastic. Because dark-tinted plastic is hard to see through, you may need to remove the cover in order to judge when the food has been processed to the desired degree.

The sizes and shapes of feed tubes vary. Most, however, are longer than your fingers and are wider at the bottom than at the top. Thus, it is sometimes easier to load foods from the bottom, especially when trying to wedge for a tight fit or when inserting a single food, such as a potato.

processing tips

The food processor is a speedy machine that can quickly turn whole foods into slices, shreds, chopped pieces, or pureed mixtures. A major factor in the successful use of the machine is realizing just how fast it works and learning to stop before food is overprocessed.

For the most even slices, fit the food into the feed tube as tightly as possible. This prevents pieces from leaning to one side, producing diagonal slices. For the tightest fit, you may want to fill the feed tube from the bottom, since the bottom opening is usually slightly larger than the top. When placing the cover over the slicing disk, be careful not to scrape your hand.

When slicing foods with peels, such as apples and green peppers, some machines may tend to skin off the peel rather than cut through it. If you have trouble with this, place the piece of food into the feed tube so that the peel faces the center of the work bowl. The blade of the slicing disk will hit the peel side first and be more likely to cut through it.

For both slicing and shredding, you should cut the food to be processed into lengths 1 inch shorter than the feed tube. With room at the top of the feed tube for the pusher to be partially inserted, all of the food will be forced into the disk with the same amount of pressure, producing a more uniform product.

When first used, your processor's bowl cover may not turn easily on the bowl. Rub a little cooking oil on the lip of the cover and on the rim of the bowl, then place the cover on the bowl and turn back and forth several times till it moves smoothly.

When processing, try to keep the rim of the work bowl as clean as possible so the cover will always be easy to turn on the bowl.

All processors come with at least three interchangeable cutting tools: the *steel blade* (above, left), which is used for chopping, pureeing, mixing, and kneading; the *slicing disk* (above, second from left); and the *shredding disk* (above, second from right). A *plastic blade* (above, right) comes with some processors; it is used to mix foods when no chopping is required. These symbols appear at the beginning of each recipe to indicate which blades or disks are to be used.

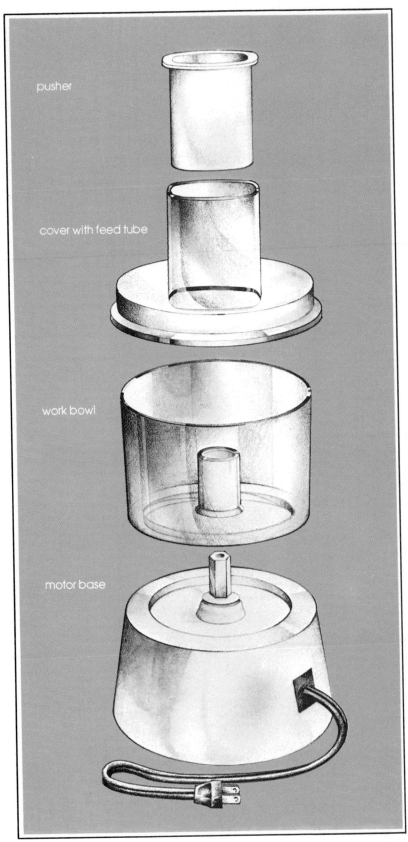

pusher

cover with feed tube

work bowl

motor base

In food processors with a direct-driven motor, the work bowl sits directly atop the motor base, as shown at left. In belt-driven units, the motor base is either behind or beside the work bowl, as shown below. In most cases, belt-driven processors require a little more counter space than direct-driven machines, which are higher rather than wider.

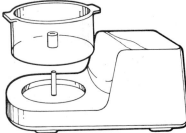

how much to process

Check the owner's manual for the suggested amount of food to process at one time. If it isn't given, use a liquid measure to determine how much liquid your work bowl will hold before overflowing at the top or center. Some bowls are marked with a fill line.

The thickness of a food mixture also affects the amount that can be processed at one time. Thin mixtures, such as thin soups or beverages, are easily spattered, and must be processed in smaller amounts. Usually 2 cups of liquid is the maximum suggested.

Thick mixtures, such as thick soups or batters, can be processed in larger amounts. Usually 4 cups total mixture is the maximum suggested. This means recipes calling for more than 3 cups of flour must be processed half at a time.

Most processors will handle small amounts of food as easily as they handle large amounts. This is an important feature when processing leftovers or small quantities of food for use in special diets or as baby food.

The actual minimum amount that can be processed varies with each processor. In some models, the blade sits closer to the bottom of the bowl, which allows the processing of smaller amounts.

When you are processing larger amounts of food, it is usually necessary to process in several batches to prevent the work bowl from overflowing.

emptying the work bowl

Some work bowls have a handle that makes them easy to hold while emptying. Most bowls also can be held from the bottom by inserting a finger in the center shaft.

When processing liquids, remove the work bowl from the base but keep the steel or plastic blade in place. This permits the blade to slip down to the bottom of the work bowl and seal the shaft opening.

Hold the blade in place with either a spatula or a finger, and tip the bowl to empty the contents, as shown above. This prevents any of the liquid from running down the center shaft. Some processors have blades with a finger hole in the stem that allows you to hold the blade in the work bowl from the underside.

To remove chopped foods, it is usually easiest to remove the blade first. Then you can hold the work bowl with one hand while using a spatula in the other hand to scrape.

When using the slicing or shredding disk, carefully remove the disk before emptying the work bowl.

product uniformity

Like all appliances, the processor has its shortcomings. It does not *perfectly* chop, slice, or shred a food into pieces exactly the same size. If you demand complete uniformity in a certain food task, then you must do it by hand with a knife. However, most processors perform most of these tasks with near uniformity, and in a fraction of the time they would take to do by hand.

If the processed food is used in cooked dishes or mixtures, more than likely it will be next to impossible to tell how uniformly the food was chopped, shredded, or sliced.

The following pages offer specific tips for helping to make chopped or sliced food as uniform as possible.

processing hot foods

Hot foods can be processed in almost all processors, but be sure to check your owner's manual first. Do not process more than the recommended amount, as described previously. Processed soups, cooked vegetables, and sauces usually can be served immediately after processing. Or, a quick reheating may be necessary.

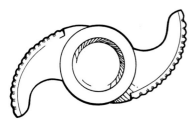

steel blade

The steel blade is the most often used of all the cutting tools. It performs many tasks: chopping, pureeing, mixing, and kneading. Its razor-sharp edges will reduce a bowl of mushrooms to a finely minced mixture in a matter of seconds. The cutting action of the steel blade is amazingly fast, so extreme caution is required to avoid overprocessing food.

To use the steel blade, first lock the work bowl on the motor base. Place the steel blade on the motor shaft, making certain the blade is all the way down on the shaft. Cover and process.

chopping basics

A fairly dry work bowl is needed for most chopping tasks. Some foods, such as parsley, nuts, breads, and crackers, require a thoroughly dry bowl. If you think there may be moisture in the work bowl, insert the steel blade in the empty work bowl and cover the bowl. Then start and stop the machine. Use a paper towel to carefully wipe away any moisture that appears on the sides of the bowl. Repeat till the bowl stays dry after the machine has been run empty for a few seconds.

When chopping, never attempt to process more than 2 cups of food at one time. For meat, chop only ½ pound or 1 cup of meat cubes at a time before emptying the work bowl. By limiting the amount of food chopped at once, you will get a more uniform chop.

Another way to help achieve a uniform chop is to start with food pieces of approximately the same size. If you start with a combination of large and small pieces, the final chop will be a mixture of coarsely and finely chopped food. The pieces of food also should be distributed evenly in the work bowl, as shown below.

A commonly used method for chopping is to place the food in the work bowl, and then quickly start and stop the processor by turning it on and off.

This on/off method usually is used to process soft or medium-firm foods, such as apples, onions, and mushrooms. The quick starting-and-stopping action gives you better control over the coarseness or fineness of the chop because you can easily check the food each time you stop the processor. Also, this method permits the larger pieces to fall away from the sides of the work bowl and into the path of the blade, resulting in a more uniform chop. If necessary, use a spatula to scrape down the sides of the work bowl when the machine is stopped.

The on/off method involves very quick action. To better understand just how fast this method is, place the cover on the empty work bowl and practice starting and stopping your machine several times in quick succession. The trick is to turn off the machine immediately after you have turned it on.

Some processors are equipped with a pulse-action button that quickly turns the machine on and off as you touch and release the button.

As you become more experienced with the quick cutting action of the blade, you may not need to start and stop the machine quite as frequently as in the beginning.

A second, less commonly used method of chopping involves adding food to the work bowl through the feed tube while the machine is running. It usually is used with firm foods, such as root vegetables and hard cheeses. One disadvantage of this method is that food added first may become overprocessed.

This method is designed to prevent a piece of food from becoming wedged between the bowl and steel blade, thus stalling the processor. Should a piece of food become wedged, simply disconnect the machine, remove the cover, and carefully remove the trapped food. If it is necessary to remove the steel blade in order to free the food, make certain the blade is properly reinserted in the work bowl before resuming processing.

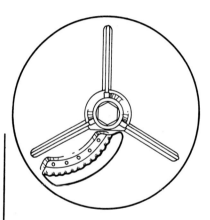

pureeing basics

To puree in the processor, place the steel blade in the work bowl, then add the food. Place the cover on the work bowl; turn the machine on and process till the food is smooth. Stop the machine occasionally to scrape the bowl's sides.

When pureeing foods cooked in liquids, such as soups, puree the strained solids first, then return to the cooking broth. It is not necessary to add liquid to the work bowl when pureeing; in fact, smoother puree results when cooked foods are processed alone. Remember not to process more than 2 cups at a time.

mixing basics

Although the processor is not an electric mixer, it can perform some of the same functions in preparing recipes.

For some recipes, all ingredients are added to the work bowl at once and are processed together. In other recipes, as for cookies and quick breads, the sugar and butter are creamed before the flour and seasonings are added.

Remember, there's no need to bring butter, shortening, or cream cheese to room temperature before processing, as the processor will easily cream them when they're cold. Simply quarter or cube them before adding to the work bowl.

kneading doughs

The steel blade is also efficient in kneading bread and pastry doughs. If you've been hesitant to attempt homemade bread, the processor offers a quick method for making a handsome loaf. However, some processors will not handle heavy doughs, so be sure to follow the manufacturer's recommendations for your machine.

When working with any dough in the processor, never use more than 3 cups of flour. Also, to avoid a tough product, never process the dough more than 60 seconds. If the motor begins to slow down, immediately stop the machine and add a little more flour to the work bowl (1 to 2 tablespoons is usually enough). This should free the dough from the blades and allow the motor to return to normal speed.

beating and whipping

The food processor is not designed to incorporate air into the food it processes; instead, it breaks the air bubbles as they form. Thus it can't replace your rotary beater or electric mixer for beating egg whites or whipping cream. When processing these foods, the final volume is considerably less than when they are beaten or whipped in the conventional way.

It is possible, however, to process whipping cream when volume is not so important, such as for dessert toppings. Watch carefully, because the processing can quickly turn the cream into butter.

slicing disk

The slicing disk is an efficient tool for slicing soft foods as well as firm ones. Your satisfaction with the sliced product will depend on the particular processor you use. Some slice strawberries as well as they do carrots; others work satisfactorily only on the firmer foods. Also, most machines offer only one thickness of slice, which may be thinner than that usually obtained when slicing by hand.

The slicing disk on some processors successfully slices raw and cooked meat as well as hard sausages (remove casing before slicing). However, be sure to check the manufacturer's recommendations for your machine before slicing meat; you could do serious damage to a processor not designed for this purpose.

To slice, lock the work bowl on the motor base, then place the slicing disk on the motor shaft in the bowl. Make certain the disk is all the way down on the shaft. Place the cover on the work bowl; note that the cutting edge of the disk is resting directly below the cover of the bowl. Place the food in the feed tube, trimming the food if necessary to fit. Leave at least an inch of space at the top of the feed tube when filling. Slice, using the pusher to guide the food through the blade. The space left at the top of the feed tube gives the pusher more leverage, making it more useful as a guiding tool.

The thickness of the slices varies with the pressure exerted by the pusher. Heavy pressure produces thicker slices, and light pressure gives thinner slices. In general, use light-to-medium pressure for soft-textured foods; medium-to-firm pressure for firm-textured foods. Never use your fingers or any utensil except the pusher to guide the food into the cutting disk.

Foods often require trimming or halving before they will fit into the feed tube. However, before trimming food that appears too large for the feed tube, try to insert it from the bottom of the tube. The feed tube is designed so that it is slightly larger at the base than at the top.

When uniform slices are not important, merely drop the food into the feed tube, as shown below. If this method is used for slicing small foods, such as mushrooms, olives, and strawberries, the slices will be uniform in thickness. However, the slices will be angled as well as straight. Food is sliced very quickly in this manner, and the slices, although not perfect in appearance, are quite acceptable for use in casseroles, sauces, cooked dishes, and frozen desserts.

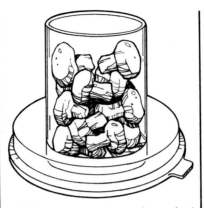

When you need nearly perfect slices, arrange the food in the feed tube in layers, as shown above. It is sometimes helpful to cut a flat edge on the side of the food that rests on the slicing disk. Fit the food snugly in the tube to prevent the force of the whirling disk from flipping the pieces of food crosswise before slicing.

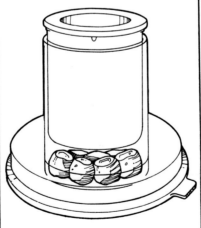

When slicing foods for garnishes, you will usually have better results if you slice only one layer of food at a time, as shown above. This is much more time-consuming but produces more nearly perfect slices. Because the feed tube is longer than your fingers, use small tongs, long-handled tweezers, or the tip of a knife to arrange the food in the tube so it rests on the disk.

When slicing longer foods, such as carrots, bananas, or pickles, cut the food into equal lengths about 1 inch shorter than the feed tube. Wedge food vertically in the tube, making a snug fit as shown below. Wedging prevents the food from falling over in the feed tube, which would result in angled slices.

Medium- to large-size foods, such as onions and cucumbers, must be halved vertically before being placed in the feed tube. However, you often can wedge together two small halves in the tube by placing the two cut surfaces face to face with edges overlapping, as shown below.

When slicing a fruit or vegetable that has peel on one side only, such as a halved green pepper or apple, position the food in the tube so the peel faces the center of the work bowl. This way the cutting edge of the disk will come in contact with the peel first. If the food is placed with the peel facing out, some machines may tend to skin off the peel rather than cut through it.

It is not uncommon for a small amount of food to remain atop the slicing disk after having been sliced. However, the waste is minimal because the succeeding food placed in the tube usually forces the food that remained atop the disk through the blade.

If the work bowl is marked with a fill line, empty the bowl when the processed food reaches this level. For work bowls without such markings, empty the bowl when it is almost full.

julienne basics

Julienne or matchstick cuts are ideal for salads, soups, and shoestring potatoes. They are made by slicing slices. First slice the food as just described. Empty the bowl and reinsert the slicing disk. Reassemble the cut food slices and place them in the feed tube.

Some foods such as sliced beets are wet enough to stick together when reassembled and can be carefully dropped into the feed tube from the top.

Other foods, however, may need to be inserted from the bottom. Turn the cover of the work bowl on its side and pull the pusher out of the feed tube about 2 inches. Insert the cut slices parallel to the sides of the feed tube, as shown below. Wedge in the last slice for a snug fit. Carefully replace the cover on the work bowl and slice.

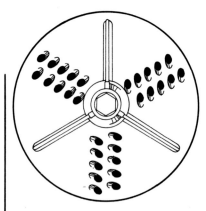

shredding disk

Shredding in the processor not only is fast and easy but eliminates the nicks and cuts on fingers you may get from hand shredders. It often is more convenient to shred some foods in quantity, then wrap in small amounts and refrigerate or freeze for later use.

Metal shavings sometimes remain on the cutting edges of the shredding disk as it comes from the manufacturer. To remove these stray particles, shred a firm food, such as a carrot, turnip, or potato, and then discard it. Thoroughly wash the disk and work bowl, and they will be ready to use.

The shred produced in the processor can be very fine. In some recipes you may prefer to chop the food with the steel blade rather than to shred it. Preparing cabbage for coleslaw is an example of this.

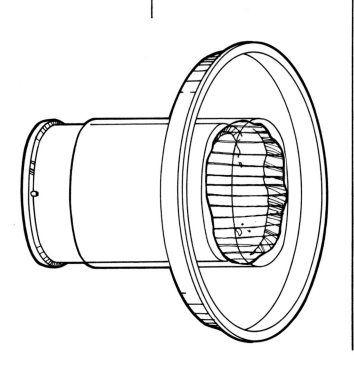

To shred, lock the work bowl on the motor base. Place the shredding disk on the motor shaft in the bowl. Make certain the disk is all the way down on the shaft. Place the cover on the work bowl; note that the cutting edge of the disk is directly below the cover. Halve or trim the food to fit in the feed tube, if necessary. Remember, it's sometimes easier to insert food from the bottom, but wedge it tightly so it won't fall out when placed over the disk. Remember, also, to leave at least an inch of space at the top of the feed tube to allow for the pusher.

Place the food in the feed tube and shred, using the pusher to guide the food through the disk. As with slicing use light-to-medium pressure for soft-textured foods and medium-to-firm pressure for firm-textured foods. Always follow your owner's manual when shredding. Some foods may become mushy. Or, as in the case of soft cheese, the heat generated by the rapid turning of the disk may warm the food to the extent that it forms little balls atop the disk or becomes gummy.

Depending on how food is placed in the feed tube, the shreds may be either short or long. For short shreds, wedge the food upright in the feed tube. For longer shreds, drop the food horizontally into the feed tube.

If the work bowl is marked with a fill line, empty the bowl when the food reaches this level. For bowls without such markings, empty the bowl when it is almost full.

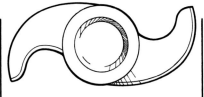

plastic blade

The plastic blade is a standard tool with some processors. Its use is limited to mixing or blending ingredients since it does not have a cutting edge.

Use the plastic blade for mixing foods that require no chopping, such as dips, sauces, and salad dressings. You also can use it for mixing thin batters, such as for crepes. However, the steel blade works equally well in performing all of the tasks assigned to the plastic blade, so use the plastic blade according to personal preference.

To use the plastic blade, lock the work bowl on the motor base. Place the plastic blade on the motor shaft, making certain it is all the way down on the shaft. Add the ingredients to the bowl and process till well blended, stopping as needed to scrape down the sides of the bowl. Leave the blade in place and remove the work bowl to empty the processed food.

recipe & meal preparation

Use the processor to short-cut preparation tasks in individual recipes as well as in total meal preparation. Learn to think through the total menu, looking for ways to consolidate preparations before starting to work. For example, if you need chopped onion for a meat loaf and for a vegetable casserole, process enough onion for both foods at the same time.

To eliminate excess bowl washing, process dry foods before wet ones, even though the dry ones may not be needed till last.

If several foods for a recipe require chopping, it is often possible to process similar-textured foods together, such as apples and pears. Just remember not to process more than the recommended amount at one time.

Foods that are not similar in texture must be processed separately. You will not get a satisfactory chop if you attempt to chop green peppers, which are watery, with carrots, which are firm. If you have any doubt as to whether you can satisfactorily chop two foods together, it is better to chop them separately.

One way to short-cut recipe preparation is to process foods in quantity and store them in the refrigerator or freezer for later use. A few examples are shredded cheese, shredded coconut, chopped onion, chopped nuts, chopped parsley, and soft and dry bread crumbs. These commonly used foods are convenient to have already prepared and ready to use.

With a little practice, you will quickly learn how to mentally rearrange the ingredients in your favorite recipes to make the most efficient use of your food processor.

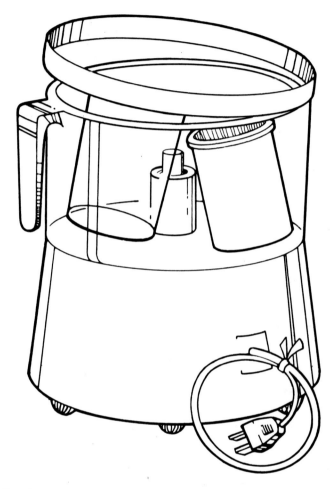
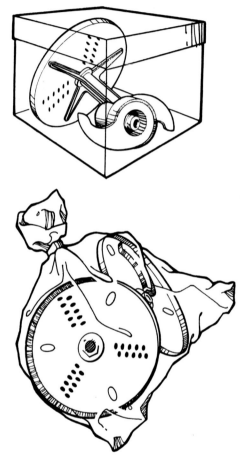

storing your processor

A food processor can be an important aid to meal preparation once you master the basic techniques of its use and learn to look for tasks it can simplify in the kitchen. But, it is useful only if it's easily accessible. Try to store it in a convenient location where it's easy to get at every day.

When storing your processor, never leave the work bowl atop the motor base with the cover turned to the "on" position. Instead, store the cover in the "off" position atop the work bowl, or invert the cover and place it in the open bowl, as shown above. Leaving the cover in the "on" position may eventually damage the spring mechanism in the motor start switch on some processors.

It is also a good idea to store the processor with the pusher out of the feed tube; this allows air to circulate through the work bowl, not only drying it, but also eliminating odors.

Store cutting tools either in specially designed racks for processor blades or in a separate location away from other often used kitchen utensils. Cut fingers are inevitable if you store processor tools in frequently opened drawers. It is important also to store processor blades out of the reach of small children. It may be easiest to keep all the blades and disks in a heavy plastic bag or box.

cleaning your processor

The key to an easy cleanup is to rinse the parts immediately after using them. There's no need to thoroughly dry the work bowl and its parts unless further processing requires a dry bowl. Promptly wipe up any spills on the motor base or cord using a clean, damp cloth.

Never soak the steel blade or cutting disks in a dishpan of soapy water. You might forget they are there, reach into the water, and cut your fingers on them.

A vegetable brush or other dishwashing brush with a long handle makes cleaning the blades and disks not only easier but safer. It eliminates the possibility of cut fingers and ensures that minute food particles are removed from the sharp cutting tools.

A pipe cleaner or small round brush, such as the kind you use to clean coffeepot stems, is ideal for removing any food that might become trapped on the underside of cutting-tool stems.

Parts of some processors are dishwasher-proof. Be certain to follow manufacturer's recommendations before placing any parts in the dishwasher.

safety precautions

1. All family members who will be using the processor should carefully read and follow all instructions that accompany the machine before operating it.

2. The cutting edges of the disks and the steel blade are very sharp and must be handled carefully.

3. Disconnect the processor before changing blades or disks, before cleaning, and when not using it.

4. Always lock the work bowl on the motor base before inserting the blade or disk.

5. Make certain the cutting tool is all the way down on the motor shaft before starting to process. Serious damage to the processor could result if the cutting tool is not properly in place.

6. Always use the pusher for feeding food through the feed tube; never use other utensils or your fingers.

7. Make certain the blade or disk has come to a complete stop before removing the cover of the work bowl.

8. Store blades and disks in a safe place out of the reach of small children.

9. Keep hands, utensils, and spatulas away from moving blades or disks to prevent personal injury or damage to the processor.

10. Do not let the cord of the processor hang over the countertop or touch hot surfaces.

11. Never immerse the processor base in water or other liquid.

12. Most processors have an automatic circuit breaker that shuts off the motor when it overheats. Follow manufacturer's directions for restarting.

13. If your processor doesn't have an automatic circuit breaker, be alert for signs of overheating, especially when processing thick or heavy batters, or when using the processor for long periods of time. Stop immediately if the motor sounds overworked or if the motor base feels warm.

appetizers, snacks, & spreads

Chicken Liver Pâté

- 1 **pound chicken livers**
- ¼ **cup chopped onion**
- 2 **tablespoons butter *or* margarine**
- 3 **tablespoons mayonnaise *or* salad dressing**
- 2 **tablespoons butter *or* margarine**
- 2 **tablespoons lemon juice**
- 8 to 10 **drops bottled hot pepper sauce**
- ½ **teaspoon salt**
- ½ **teaspoon dry mustard**
  Dash pepper
  Chopped hard-cooked egg *or* egg yolk, snipped chives, *or* parsley sprigs (optional)
  Assorted crackers

In heavy skillet cook livers and onion in 2 tablespoons butter or margarine, covered, over medium-high heat about 5 minutes or till livers are no longer pink; stir occasionally. Drain, reserving 3 tablespoons liquid.

Place steel blade in work bowl. Add livers and reserved liquid. Process till finely chopped. Add mayonnaise or salad dressing, 2 tablespoons butter or margarine, lemon juice, hot pepper sauce, salt, mustard, and pepper. Process till smooth.

Turn mixture into well-oiled 2-cup mold or bowl. Cover; chill 6 hours or overnight. Carefully unmold. If desired, garnish pâté with chopped hard-cooked egg or yolk, snipped chives, or parsley sprigs. Serve with assorted crackers. Makes about 1⅔ cups.

Ham and Kraut Snacks

If desired, serve hot with your favorite sauce for dipping —

- 2 **slices dry bread, broken**
- ½ **medium onion, cut into 1-inch pieces**
- 1 **small clove garlic, cut up**
- 1 **tablespoon butter *or* margarine**
- 5 **ounces fully cooked ham, cut into 1-inch pieces (1 cup)**
- ¼ **cup lightly packed parsley (stems removed)**
- 1 **14-ounce can sauerkraut**
- ½ **cup packaged pancake mix**
  Cooking oil *or* shortening for deep-fat frying

Place steel blade in work bowl; add dry bread pieces. Process till very finely crushed; empty bowl and set bread crumbs aside. Reinsert steel blade in work bowl; add onion and garlic. Process with on/off turns till finely chopped. Cook onion and garlic in butter or margarine till tender but not brown.

Meanwhile, reinsert steel blade in work bowl; add ham and parsley. Process with on/off turns till finely chopped. Remove to a mixing bowl. Drain sauerkraut, reserving ⅓ cup liquid. Reinsert steel blade in work bowl; add sauerkraut. Process with on/off turns till chopped. Add to ham in mixing bowl; add onion-garlic mixture and the reserved sauerkraut liquid. Mix well. Add the pancake mix; stir till combined. Cover and chill.

With a tablespoon measure, form mixture into balls; roll in reserved bread crumbs. Fry 4 to 6 at a time in deep hot oil or shortening (365°) for 1½ to 2 minutes or till crisp and golden brown. Serve hot. Makes about 3 dozen.

Dessert Cheese Ball

Shaping in cheesecloth gives this cheese ball a textured surface —

- 2 **cups cream-style cottage cheese (16 ounces)**
- 1 **3-ounce package cream cheese, quartered**
- 2 **ounces blue cheese, cut into 1-inch pieces**
- 1 **cup whipping cream**
  Assorted crackers
  Sliced apples *and* pears
  Lemon juice *or* ascorbic acid color keeper

Place steel blade in work bowl; add cottage cheese, cream cheese, and blue cheese. Process till mixture is smooth and creamy, stopping as needed to scrape down sides of work bowl.

With machine running, gradually pour whipping cream through feed tube. Process about 25 seconds or just till mixture is thickened.

Line a sieve or colander with several thicknesses of cheesecloth; set in a bowl. Pour in cheese mixture. Tie cheesecloth at top. Let drain overnight in refrigerator.

Untie cloth; turn cheese ball out onto serving platter. Remove cheesecloth. Decorate top of cheese with lemon or mint leaves, if desired. Surround cheese with assorted crackers and with apples and pears brushed lightly with lemon juice or ascorbic acid color keeper. Makes 6 to 8 servings.

Clockwise from top left: Chicken Liver Pâté, Ham and Kraut Snacks, Salmon Dip (see recipe, page 168), Sunflower-Nut Spread (see recipe, page 169), and Dessert Cheese Ball.

Chilled Chicken Loaf

   5 **slices bacon**
1½ **cups fresh mushrooms**
   4 **green onions, cut into 1-inch pieces**
   8 **ounces chicken livers**
   3 **tablespoons butter**
   ½ **teaspoon salt**
   ¼ **teaspoon dried thyme, crushed**
   8 **ounces boneless veal**
   8 **ounces skinned and boned uncooked chicken breasts**
   8 **ounces bulk pork sausage**
   ⅓ **cup dry white wine**
   1 **egg**

Cook bacon till brown but not crisp; drain. Arrange slices crosswise across bottom and up sides of an 8x4x2-inch loaf pan.

Place steel blade in work bowl; add mushrooms and green onions. Process with on/off turns till finely chopped. In skillet cook chopped vegetables and livers in butter over medium-high heat about 5 minutes or till livers are no longer pink; stir occasionally. Stir in salt, thyme, and ⅛ teaspoon *pepper;* cool.

Cut veal and chicken into 1-inch pieces. Reinsert steel blade; add veal. Process with on/off turns till finely chopped; transfer to mixing bowl. Reinsert steel blade; add chicken. Process till finely chopped. Add to veal; add sausage and wine. Mix well.

Reinsert steel blade; add liver mixture. Process till nearly smooth. With machine running, add egg through feed tube. Process till smooth. Spread *half* of the liver mixture into bacon-lined pan. Top with veal mixture, then remaining liver mixture, spreading evenly. Bake in 350° oven for 1½ hours. Drain off fat and juices; cover surface with foil. Place another loaf pan containing a weight atop hot meat. Let cool; chill at least 8 hours. Remove from pan; cut into slices. Makes 16 appetizer servings.

Shrimp-Cheese Balls

   ½ **cup toasted pecans *or* mixed salted nuts**
   2 **3-ounce packages cream cheese, quartered**
   1 **thin slice of small onion**
1½ **teaspoons prepared mustard**
   1 **teaspoon lemon juice**
     Dash salt
     Dash cayenne
   1 **4½-ounce can shrimp, drained**

Place steel blade in work bowl; add nuts. Process till finely chopped; remove and set aside. Reinsert steel blade; add cream cheese, onion, mustard, lemon juice, salt, and cayenne. Process till smooth. Add drained shrimp; process with 2 or 3 on/off turns just till mixed. Transfer cheese mixture to covered container; chill about 2 hours. Shape chilled mixture into ½-inch balls; roll in chopped nuts. Makes 40.

Tuna-Cheese Ball

   ½ **cup lightly packed parsley (stems removed)**
   ½ **stalk celery, cut up**
   1 **7-ounce can tuna (water pack), drained**
   1 **3-ounce package Neufchatel cheese, quartered**
   2 **teaspoons Worcestershire sauce**
   1 **teaspoon lemon juice** •
   ¼ **teaspoon salt**

Place steel blade in work bowl; add parsley. Process till finely chopped; remove and set aside. Reinsert steel blade; add celery. Process till coarsely chopped. Add the tuna, cheese, Worcestershire, lemon juice, and salt. Process till well mixed; chill. Shape chilled mixture into a ball; roll in chopped parsley. Chill several hours before serving. Makes 1 cheese ball.

Guacamole

   2 **ripe medium avocados, quartered, seeded, and peeled**
   1 **tablespoon lemon juice**
   1 **thin slice of small onion**
   1 **clove garlic, quartered**
   ½ **teaspoon salt**
     Bottled hot pepper sauce (optional)
     Vegetable dippers

Place steel blade in work bowl. Add avocados, lemon juice, onion, garlic, and salt. Process till smooth, scraping bowl as necessary. If desired, add pepper sauce to taste. Serve immediately with vegetables. Makes 1¼ cups.

Salmon Dip

Pictured on page 166 —

   1 **8-ounce can water chestnuts, drained**
   ½ **cup lightly packed parsley (stems removed)**
   1 **16-ounce can salmon, drained and flaked with skin and bones removed**
   1 **8-ounce package cream cheese, quartered**
   2 **green onions, cut up**
   ¼ **cup milk**
   1 **tablespoon lemon juice**
   1 **teaspoon prepared horseradish**
   ¼ **teaspoon salt**
     Assorted crackers

Place steel blade in work bowl. Add water chestnuts and parsley; process with on/off turns till coarsely chopped. Remove from bowl. Reinsert steel blade; add salmon, cream cheese, green onions, milk, lemon juice, horseradish, and salt. Process till blended, stopping to scrape bowl. Add water chestnuts and parsley; process just till mixed. Cover; chill. Serve with crackers. Makes about 3 cups.

Classic Steak Tartare

Serve immediately after making, or chill
no longer than 1 hour —

- 1 cup lightly packed parsley
  (stems removed)
- 1 medium onion, cut into 1-inch
  pieces
- 1 pound boneless lean beef
  sirloin *or* round steak
- 6 egg yolks
  Prepared horseradish
  Condiments (choose any or all
  of the following: anchovy
  fillets, lemon wedges,
  drained capers, freshly
  ground pepper, salt, paprika,
  bottled hot pepper sauce,
  and Worcestershire sauce)
  Buttered toast, cut into quarters

Place steel blade in work
bowl; add parsley. Process
with on/off turns till finely chopped.
Remove from bowl; set aside. Rinse
work bowl; reinsert steel blade. Add
onion; process with on/off turns till
chopped. Remove onion from
bowl; set aside.

Trim all gristle and fat from meat;
cut meat into 1-inch pieces. Place
steel blade in work bowl. Add *half* of
the meat; process with on/off turns
till finely chopped. Remove
chopped meat from work bowl; repeat steps with remaining meat.

Divide uncooked meat into six
portions; shape into mounded patties on chilled plates. Make an indentation in center of each patty;
place an uncooked egg yolk
in each indentation. Pass the
chopped parsley, chopped onion,
horseradish, and condiments to
sprinkle atop and mix into meat
and yolk before eating, if desired.
Serve with buttered toast. Makes 6
servings.

Chinese Egg Rolls

Homemade Egg Roll Skins
(see recipe at right)
- 1 medium carrot
- 2 stalks bok choy, cut up
- 1 cup fresh mushrooms
- 2 stalks celery, cut up
- 1 small onion, cut up
- 8 canned water chestnuts
- 1 ½-inch piece gingerroot,
  peeled
- 8 ounces lean pork, cubed
- 4 ounces fresh *or* frozen shrimp,
  shelled and deveined
- 1 tablespoon cooking oil
- 1 egg
- 2 tablespoons soy sauce
- 1 tablespoon dry sherry
- ½ teaspoon sugar
- ½ teaspoon salt
- 1 beaten egg
  Cooking oil *or* shortening for
  deep-fat frying

Prepare Homemade Egg
Roll Skins. Layer between
waxed paper. Cover; chill. Insert
shredding disk; shred carrot. Transfer to mixing bowl.

Place steel blade in work bowl.
Add bok choy and mushrooms;
process till finely chopped. Add to
carrots. Reinsert steel blade. Add
next 4 ingredients; process till finely
chopped. Add to carrots.

Reinsert steel blade in work bowl.
Add pork and shrimp; process till
coarsely chopped. Preheat wok or
skillet; add 1 tablespoon oil. Stir-fry
pork and shrimp till browned. Add
vegetables; stir-fry 2 to 3 minutes.
Combine 1 egg, soy, sherry, sugar,
and salt. Stir in pork mixture; cool.

, Spoon 1½ tablespoons pork mixture onto each Homemade Egg
Roll Skin; fold bottom edge up and
sides in. Brush top of skin with beaten
egg; overlap. Seal. Place, seam
down, on waxed paper. Cover with
damp cloth. Fry, 2 or 3 at a time, in
deep hot oil (365°) for 2 to 3 minutes.
Drain. Makes 24 egg rolls.

Homemade Egg Roll Skins

- 6 eggs
- 2 cups all-purpose flour
- 2 cups water
- 1 teaspoon salt

Place steel blade in work bowl.
Add 3 of the eggs, *1 cup* flour, *1
cup* water, and *½ teaspoon* salt.
Process till smooth; pour into mixing
bowl. Repeat. Heat a lightly
greased 6-inch skillet. Remove from
heat; add 2 tablespoons batter. Lift
and tilt skillet to spread batter
evenly. Return to heat; cook 1 minute on one side only (skins will not
brown). Invert onto paper toweling.
Repeat with remaining batter,
greasing skillet occasionally.
Makes 24 egg roll skins.

Sunflower-Nut Spread

Pictured on page 166 —

- ¼ cup shelled sunflower seed
- 1 cup cocktail peanuts
- 2 tablespoons butter *or*
  margarine, cut into chunks
- 1 tablespoon light molasses

Place steel blade in work
bowl. Add sunflower seed;
process with on/off turns till coarsely
chopped. Remove from bowl; set
aside. Reinsert steel blade in work
bowl; add cocktail peanuts. Process with on/off turns till coarsely
chopped. Continue processing till a
paste forms.

Add butter and molasses; process till of desired thickness. Add
chopped sunflower seed; process
just till blended. Cover and store in
refrigerator. Bring to room temperature for easier spreading. Serve on
crackers or as sandwich filling.
Makes about 1 cup.

salads
& vegetables

Sweet Fruit Slaw

1 small head cabbage, cored
  (about 1 pound)
1 medium apple, cored and cut
  into 1-inch pieces
1 11-ounce can mandarin orange
  sections, drained
½ cup grapes, halved and
  seeded
¼ cup raisins *or* chopped nuts
⅓ cup honey
3 tablespoons lemon juice
1 teaspoon celery seed, poppy
  seed, *or* toasted sesame seed
½ teaspoon dry mustard
½ teaspoon paprika
¼ teaspoon salt
½ cup salad oil

Insert slicing disk in work bowl. Cut cabbage into wedges to fit into feed tube; slice. As work bowl fills, transfer sliced cabbage to a large bowl (should have about 5 cups).

Place steel blade in work bowl; add apple. Process with on/off turns till chopped. Stir apple, oranges, grapes, and raisins or nuts into cabbage. Cover and chill.

For dressing, reinsert steel blade in work bowl; add honey, lemon juice, desired seed, dry mustard, paprika, and salt. Process just till ingredients are mixed. With machine running, gradually pour oil through feed tube in a steady stream (should take about 1 minute). Process about 15 seconds more or till slightly thickened. Transfer to small bowl. Cover and chill.

Just before serving, pour dressing over fruit mixture; toss gently to coat cabbage and fruit. Serve immediately. Makes 10 servings.

24-Hour Cabbage Salad

1 medium head cabbage,
  cored
1 medium onion
1 small green pepper
1½ cups sugar
1 cup vinegar
½ cup water
2 teaspoons salt
2 teaspoons mustard seed *or*
  celery seed
¼ cup chopped pimiento

Place steel blade in work bowl. Cut cabbage, onion, and pepper into 1-inch pieces; add 2 *cups* to work bowl. Process with on/off turns till chopped; transfer to large bowl. Reinsert steel blade and repeat with remaining vegetables, processing 2 cups at a time.

Stir together remaining ingredients till sugar dissolves. Pour over cabbage mixture; toss. Cover; chill at least 24 hours. Drain. Serves 12.

Frozen Cranberry Squares

3 cups fresh *or* frozen cranberries
  (12 ounces)
3 large apples, cored and cut
  into 1-inch pieces
1 cup sugar
1 7-ounce jar marshmallow
  creme
1 cup whipping cream, whipped

Place steel blade in work bowl. Add 1 *cup* of the cranberries; process with on/off turns till very finely chopped. Remove. Reinsert steel blade; repeat with rest of cranberries and apples; process 1 cup at a time. Stir sugar and marshmallow creme into cranberry mixture. Cover; let stand 3 to 4 hours. Fold whipped cream into cranberry mixture. Turn into a 9x9x2-inch pan. Cover; freeze overnight. Serves 12.

Chicken Stack-Up Salad

2 cups cubed cooked chicken
¾ teaspoon curry powder
¼ teaspoon salt
¼ teaspoon paprika
⅛ teaspoon pepper
1 large green pepper, cut into
  1-inch pieces
4 ounces cheddar cheese
1 medium head lettuce, cored
2 small cucumbers
1 cup macaroni, cooked and
  drained
1½ cups Homemade Mayonnaise
  (see recipe, page 171) *or*
  salad dressing
2 tablespoons milk
2 tablespoons lemon juice
½ teaspoon salt
  Dash pepper
1 small tomato, cut into wedges

Place steel blade in work bowl; add chicken. Process with on/off turns till chopped. Transfer chicken to mixing bowl; add curry powder, the ¼ teaspoon salt, paprika, and the ⅛ teaspoon pepper. Toss to coat well; set aside.

Reinsert steel blade; add green pepper. Process with on/off turns till chopped. Remove; set aside.

Insert shredding disk; shred cheese. Remove and set aside. Reinsert shredding disk. Cut lettuce into wedges to fit into feed tube; shred lettuce. Transfer to large clear salad bowl. Insert slicing disk; slice cucumbers. In salad bowl layer chicken, cucumber, macaroni, and green pepper atop lettuce.

Stir together Homemade Mayonnaise or salad dressing, milk, lemon juice, ½ teaspoon salt, and dash pepper. Spread over salad mixture. Sprinkle with shredded cheese. Cover; chill several hours or overnight. Garnish with tomato wedges. Makes 8 servings.

Cranberry Relish Salad

1   6-ounce package raspberry-
    flavored gelatin
½   cup sugar
3   cups boiling water
1   8¼-ounce can crushed
    pineapple
1   tablespoon lemon juice
2   stalks celery, cut into 1-inch
    pieces
1   medium apple, cored and cut
    into 1-inch pieces
2   cups fresh or frozen cranberries
1   small orange, seeded and cut
    into 1-inch pieces
    Lettuce

Dissolve gelatin and sugar in boiling water. Stir in *undrained* crushed pineapple and lemon juice. Chill till partially set.

Meanwhile, place steel blade in work bowl. Add celery and apple; process with on/off turns till finely chopped. Transfer to mixing bowl. Reinsert steel blade. Add *1 cup* cranberries; process with on/off turns till finely chopped. Add to apple mixture; repeat with remaining 1 cup cranberries.

Reinsert steel blade in work bowl; add unpeeled orange. Process with on/off turns till finely chopped. Add to apple mixture; mix well. Fold the fruit mixture into partially set gelatin.

Pour into 10 to 12 individual molds or into a 6½-cup mold. Chill till firm. Unmold onto lettuce-lined plate. Makes 10 to 12 servings.

Garden Pasta Salad

6   ounces elbow or shell
    macaroni (about 2 cups)
½   cup lightly packed parsley
    (stems removed)
1   small green pepper, cut into
    1-inch pieces
½   small onion, halved
1   medium cucumber
2   medium tomatoes, peeled and
    quartered
    Fresh Herb Dressing
4   ounces feta cheese, crumbled

Cook macaroni in a large amount of boiling salted water for 10 to 12 minutes or just till tender; drain. Rinse and set aside.

Place steel blade in work bowl; add parsley. Process with on/off turns till finely chopped. Remove to mixing bowl. Reinsert steel blade; add green pepper and onion. Process with on/off turns till finely chopped; add to parsley.

Reinsert steel blade. Halve cucumber lengthwise; remove seeds. Cut cucumber into 1-inch pieces; add to work bowl. Process with on/off turns till finely chopped; add to parsley. Reinsert steel blade in work bowl; add tomatoes. Process with on/off turns till finely chopped; add to parsley.

Pour Fresh Herb Dressing over vegetables. Toss to combine. Turn drained macaroni into serving bowl. Spoon vegetables with dressing over macaroni. Sprinkle with cheese. Cover; chill thoroughly. Toss to serve. Makes 6 servings.

Fresh Herb Dressing: Place steel blade in work bowl. Add ¼ cup *salad oil*, 3 tablespoons *dry white wine*, 2 tablespoons *lemon juice*, 1 tablespoon *sugar*, 1 tablespoon lightly packed *fresh basil*, (stems removed) or 1 teaspoon *dried basil*, 1 teaspoon *salt*, ¼ teaspoon freshly ground *pepper*, and several dashes bottled *hot pepper sauce*. Process till well blended. Makes about ½ cup.

Homemade Mayonnaise

Do not try to halve this recipe or the volume will be too small in most processor bowls to ensure formation of the necessary emulsion —

2   egg yolks
2   tablespoons vinegar
2   tablespoons lemon juice
1   tablespoon salt
½   teaspoon dry mustard
¼   teaspoon paprika
    Dash cayenne
2   cups salad oil

Place steel blade in work bowl; add first 7 ingredients. Process just till blended. With machine running, quickly add oil through feed tube in a steady stream. Process till of desired consistency. Transfer to covered container; chill and use within 1 month. Makes 2 cups.

Peanut Fruit Dressing

Using dry roasted peanuts usually results in a grainy texture —

1   cup cocktail peanuts
1   7-ounce jar marshmallow
    creme
½   cup unsweetened pineapple
    juice
2   tablespoons lemon juice

Place steel blade in work bowl; add peanuts. Process with on/off turns till coarsely chopped. Continue processing for 1 to 1½ minutes or till a butter forms, scraping bowl as needed. Add marshmallow creme. With machine running, pour pineapple juice and lemon juice through feed tube. Process till of desired consistency. Transfer to covered container; chill thoroughly (mixture thickens on chilling). Serve on fruit salads. Makes 1⅔ cups.

Stir-Fried Vegetables

- 2 **tablespoons cold water**
- 2 **teaspoons cornstarch**
- 2 **tablespoons soy sauce**
- 1 **tablespoon dry sherry**
- 2 **teaspoons sugar**
- ¼ **teaspoon salt**
  Dash pepper
- 4 **stalks celery**
- 2 **medium zucchini**
- 1 **medium onion, halved**
- 1 **large sweet red** or **green pepper, halved**
- 8 **ounces fresh mushrooms**
- 2 **tablespoons cooking oil**

In small bowl combine water and cornstarch; stir in soy sauce, dry sherry, sugar, salt, and pepper. Set aside.

Insert slicing disk in work bowl; cut celery into equal lengths about 1 inch shorter than feed tube. Place vertically in feed tube, wedging in last piece of celery; slice. Slice zucchini and onion; transfer vegetables to another bowl. Reinsert slicing disk in work bowl; slice the pepper and mushrooms.

Preheat a wok or large skillet over high heat; add cooking oil. Stir-fry the celery, zucchini, and onion in hot oil for 1 minute. Add the pepper and mushrooms; stir-fry for 3 to 4 minutes or till vegetables are crisp-tender.

Stir the soy mixture; stir into vegetables. Cook and stir about 2 minutes or till thickened and bubbly. Serve at once. Makes 6 servings.

Stir-Fried Vegetables

Green Noodles

Pictured on page 176 —

- 2½ **cups tightly packed torn spinach leaves**
- 2 **eggs**
- 2½ **cups all-purpose flour**

In covered pan cook spinach in ¼ cup *water* till tender (it cooks down to about ½ cup); cool. Place steel blade in work bowl; add *undrained* spinach, eggs, and 1 teaspoon *salt*. Process till smooth. Add flour; process till ball forms.

On floured surface, roll *half* of the dough at a time into an 18x15-inch rectangle. Let stand 20 minutes. Roll up loosely. Slice ¼ inch wide; unroll. Cut into desired lengths. Spread out on racks; dry 2 hours. Store, covered, in the refrigerator. Cook, uncovered, in boiling salted water or soup for 10 to 12 minutes. Makes 7 cups (1 pound).

Pesto

- 1 **ounce Romano cheese, cubed**
- 2 **tablespoons pine nuts, walnuts, or almonds**
- 1 **small clove garlic, quartered**
- 1 **cup lightly packed fresh basil (stems removed)**
- ½ **cup lightly packed fresh parsley (stems removed)**
- 3 **tablespoons olive oil** or **cooking oil**

Place steel blade in work bowl; add cheese, nuts, garlic, and ⅛ teaspoon *salt*. Process with on/off turns till very finely chopped. Add basil and parsley. Process till a paste forms; scrape bowl as needed. With machine running, slowly add oil through feed tube; process till consistency of soft butter.

Refrigerate or freeze till used. Toss with hot buttered noodles (use about ⅓ cup pesto to about 8 ounces noodles). Makes ⅔ cup.

Potato Pancakes

- 4 **slices bacon**
- 1 **small onion, quartered**
- ¼ **cup lightly packed parsley (stems removed)**
- 1 **egg**
- 2 **tablespoons all-purpose flour**
- 1 **teaspoon salt**
- ¼ **teaspoon pepper**
- ⅛ **teaspoon ground nutmeg**
- 4 **medium potatoes (1¼ pounds)**
  Shortening

Cook bacon in 10-inch skillet till crisp; drain, reserving drippings. Crumble bacon and place in medium mixing bowl.

Place steel blade in work bowl; add onion and parsley. Process with on/off turns till very finely chopped. Add egg, flour, salt, pepper, and nutmeg; process with on/off turns till well mixed. Pour egg mixture into mixing bowl with crumbled bacon.

Insert shredding disk in work bowl. Peel potatoes; cut to fit into feed tube; shred. Stir into egg mixture. Heat 2 *tablespoons* of the reserved bacon drippings in skillet.

For each pancake, spoon ¼ *cup* of the potato mixture into hot drippings; spread slightly to flatten. Cook over medium heat for 2 to 3 minutes on each side or till browned. Drain on paper toweling. Serve immediately. Add additional bacon drippings or shortening as necessary to keep pancakes from sticking. Makes 10 pancakes.

main
dishes

Veal and Zucchini

1 pound veal leg round steak *or* beef round steak, cut ¼ inch thick
2 tablespoons all-purpose flour
1 tablespoon cooking oil
3 to 4 tablespoons water
8 ounces unpeeled zucchini (1 or 2)
4 ounces fresh mushrooms (1½ cups)
1 clove garlic, halved
4 sprigs parsley (stems removed)
1 cup dairy sour cream
⅓ cup milk
1 tablespoon all-purpose flour
1 tablespoon Dijon-style mustard
1 tablespoon dry sherry
¼ teaspoon salt

Cut meat into four portions; pound with meat mallet to flatten slightly. Coat with 2 tablespoons flour. In 10-inch skillet brown meat, 2 pieces at a time, in hot oil. Return all meat to skillet; add water. Reduce heat; cover and simmer for 15 minutes.

Meanwhile, place slicing disk in work bowl; slice zucchini and mushrooms. Add to meat; simmer, covered, about 15 minutes longer or till meat is tender. Transfer to platter; keep warm. Place steel blade in work bowl; add garlic and parsley. Process with on/off turns till finely chopped. Add sour cream, milk, the 1 tablespoon flour, mustard, sherry, and salt. Process just till mixed. Pour into skillet; cook and stir over low heat till mixture starts to bubble. *Do not boil.* Spoon over meat and vegetables. Makes 4 servings.

Glazed Ham Balls

⅓ cup lightly packed parsley (stems removed)
1 pound fully cooked ham, cut into 1-inch cubes
½ pound boneless lean beef, cut into 1-inch cubes
1 slice bread, torn
½ cup milk
½ teaspoon dry mustard
¾ cup unsweetened pineapple juice
½ cup maple *or* maple-flavored syrup
2 tablespoons cornstarch
1 teaspoon lemon juice
4 cups hot cooked rice

Place steel blade in work bowl; add parsley. Process with on/off turns till finely chopped. Remove parsley; set aside.

Wipe bowl; reinsert steel blade. Add *half* of the ham; process with on/off turns till chopped. Remove and set aside. Repeat with remaining ham. Reinsert steel blade in work bowl; add beef cubes and torn bread. Process with on/off turns till meat is chopped.

To meat in work bowl add chopped ham, milk, dry mustard, and *half* the parsley. Process till well blended. Shape mixture into twenty 1½-inch meatballs. Place in an 8x8x2-inch baking dish. Bake, uncovered, in 350° oven for 20 minutes.

Meanwhile, in small saucepan combine pineapple juice, maple syrup, cornstarch, and lemon juice. Cook and stir till thickened and bubbly; pour over meatballs and bake 20 minutes longer. Toss hot cooked rice with remaining parsley. Arrange meatballs and sauce atop parslied rice on platter. Makes 4 or 5 servings.

Leek Quiche

The white portion of the leek is more tender than the green portion —

1 unbaked 9-inch pastry shell
8 slices bacon
2 large leeks
8 ounces Swiss cheese
3 eggs
1½ cups milk
1 tablespoon all-purpose flour
½ teaspoon salt
Dash ground nutmeg

Bake the unpricked pastry shell in 425° oven about 6 minutes or just till lightly browned. (Pastry may puff but will settle.) Remove from oven; reduce temperature to 325°.

In skillet cook bacon till crisp; drain, reserving 2 tablespoons drippings in skillet. Crumble bacon; set aside 2 tablespoons. Sprinkle remaining in pastry shell.

Insert slicing disk in work bowl; slice leeks (should have about 2 cups). Cook leeks in reserved drippings about 5 minutes or till tender but not brown; drain.

Meanwhile, insert shredding disk in work bowl; shred cheese. Sprinkle cheese and leeks atop bacon in pastry shell. Place steel blade in work bowl; add eggs, milk, flour, salt, and nutmeg. Process till blended. Pour mixture into pastry shell. Sprinkle with reserved bacon.

Bake in 325° oven about 45 minutes or till nearly set in center. Let stand 10 to 15 minutes before serving. Makes 6 servings.

Stuffed Steak

If you don't have an oven-proof skillet, transfer the browned steaks to a 12x7½x2-inch baking dish —

- 2 **tablespoons all-purpose flour**
- ½ **teaspoon salt**
- ¼ **teaspoon garlic salt**
- ⅛ **teaspoon pepper**
- 2 **pounds beef round steak, cut ½ inch thick**
- 8 **canned water chestnuts**
- 3 **green onions, cut into 1-inch pieces**
- 1 **cup fresh mushrooms**
- 2 **medium carrots**
- 2 **tablespoons shortening**
- ⅔ **cup dry red wine**

Combine flour, salt, garlic salt, and pepper; sprinkle on meat. Pound with meat mallet till meat is about ¼ inch thick. Cut meat into 6 pieces.

Place steel blade in work bowl; add water chestnuts and green onions. Process with on/off turns till coarsely chopped; spoon vegetables over each piece of meat. Reinsert steel blade. Add mushrooms to work bowl; process with on/off turns till coarsely chopped; spoon over meat.

Insert shredding disk in work bowl; shred carrots. Spoon some shredded carrot over each piece of meat. Sprinkle generously with salt. Roll up each piece of meat, starting from shortest side. Tie or skewer to secure.

In 10-inch oven-proof skillet brown meat slowly on all sides in hot shortening. Pour wine over meat. Cover and bake in 350° oven for 45 minutes. Uncover; bake about 15 minutes more or till tender. Pass juices with meat. Makes 6 servings.

Skillet Pork Chops and Hot Slaw

Pictured on page 155 —

- 4 **pork chops, cut ½ inch thick (1½ to 2 pounds)**
- 2 **tablespoons cooking oil**
- 2 **tablespoons water**
- ½ **medium head cabbage, cored**
- 2 **medium carrots**
- 1 **medium onion, cut into 1-inch pieces**
- 1 **medium green pepper, cut into 1-inch pieces**
- ¼ **cup vinegar**
- ¼ **cup water**
- 1 **tablespoon all-purpose flour**
- 1 **tablespoon sugar**
- 1 **tablespoon prepared mustard**
- 2 **teaspoons Worcestershire sauce**
- 1 **teaspoon salt**
- ½ **teaspoon celery seed**

In a 10-inch skillet slowly brown chops on both sides in hot oil, allowing about 10 minutes total time. Season with a little salt and pepper. Add 2 tablespoons water; cover. Simmer 20 to 25 minutes.

Meanwhile, insert slicing disk in work bowl. Cut cabbage into wedges to fit into feed tube; slice. Transfer to mixing bowl. Insert shredding disk; shred carrots. Add to cabbage. Place steel blade in work bowl. Add onion and green pepper; process with on/off turns till chopped. Add to cabbage mixture. Reinsert steel blade in work bowl. Add vinegar, ¼ cup water, flour, sugar, mustard, Worcestershire sauce, salt, and celery seed; process till smooth.

When chops are tender, remove from skillet; keep warm. Stir vinegar mixture into pan drippings; cook and stir till thickened. Add vegetables, stirring to coat with vinegar mixture; top with chops. Simmer, covered, 5 minutes more. Serves 4.

Beef Tacos

Heat taco shells while preparing meat mixture, if desired. Arrange shells on baking sheet lined with paper toweling; warm in 250° oven —

- 4 **ounces sharp cheddar cheese**
- 1 **small head lettuce, cored**
- 2 **medium tomatoes, quartered**
- 1 **medium onion, quartered**
- 1 **clove garlic**
- 1 **pound boneless beef chuck, gristle and excess fat removed**
- 1 **to 2 teaspoons chili powder**
- ¾ **teaspoon salt**
- 12 **packaged taco shells Bottled taco sauce**

Insert shredding disk in work bowl; shred cheddar cheese. Remove and set aside. Insert slicing disk in work bowl. Cut lettuce into wedges to fit into feed tube; slice lettuce. Remove and set aside.

Place steel blade in work bowl; add tomatoes. Process with 1 or 2 on/off turns just till chopped. Remove and set aside. Reinsert steel blade in work bowl; add onion and garlic. Process till chopped; remove to skillet.

Reinsert steel blade in work bowl. Cut the meat into 1-inch pieces. Place *half* of the meat in work bowl; process till chopped. Add to onion mixture in skillet. Repeat with remaining meat.

Cook meat, onion, and garlic till meat is brown and onion is tender; drain off fat. Season with chili powder and salt. Fill each taco shell with some of the meat mixture, tomatoes, lettuce, and cheese. Pass bottled taco sauce to drizzle atop. Makes 6 servings.

Tomato Sauce with Pepperoni

1   large onion, cut into 1-inch pieces
¼   cup lightly packed parsley (stems removed)
¼   cup lightly packed fresh basil (stems removed) *or* 2 teaspoons dried basil
2   cloves garlic, halved
6   large tomatoes, peeled and quartered (6 cups)
1   cup water
1   8-ounce can tomato sauce
2   teaspoons instant beef bouillon granules
1   teaspoon sugar
½   teaspoon salt
6   ounces pepperoni, casing removed
1   tablespoon cornstarch
    Hot cooked pasta

Place steel blade in work bowl; add onion, parsley, basil, and garlic. Process with on/off turns till finely chopped. Transfer to 3-quart saucepan. Reinsert steel blade in work bowl. Add *2 cups* of the tomatoes; process till smooth. Add to saucepan. Repeat with remaining tomatoes, processing 2 cups at a time. Add the water, tomato sauce, bouillon granules, sugar, and salt to saucepan. Bring to boiling; reduce heat and simmer for 45 minutes, stirring occasionally.

Rinse work bowl; insert slicing disk. Slice pepperoni; add to sauce. Blend cornstarch and 1 tablespoon *cold water;* add to sauce. Cook and stir about 5 minutes or till thickened and bubbly. Serve over pasta. Makes 6 servings.

Tomato Sauce with Pepperoni served on Green Noodles (see recipe, page 173)

Moussaka

1   slice bread
2   ounces American cheese
2   medium eggplants, peeled (2 pounds)
2   medium onions, quartered
8   sprigs parsley (stems removed)
1   pound boneless beef chuck, gristle and excess fat removed
¼   cup dry red wine
¼   cup water
1   tablespoon tomato paste
1   teaspoon salt
    Dash pepper
2   eggs
¼   teaspoon ground cinnamon
3   tablespoons butter *or* margarine
3   tablespoons all-purpose flour
½   teaspoon salt
⅛   teaspoon ground nutmeg
    Dash pepper
1½ cups milk
1   beaten egg
    Cooking oil

Insert shredding disk in work bowl. Fold the slice of bread in half; shred. Remove and set aside. Shred cheese; remove and set aside. Insert the slicing disk in work bowl. Cut eggplants into pieces to fit into feed tube; slice. Transfer sliced eggplant to another dish; sprinkle with a little salt and set aside.

Place steel blade in work bowl. Add onions and parsley; process till coarsely chopped. Remove and set aside. Reinsert steel blade in work bowl. Cut meat into 1-inch pieces; add *half* of the meat to work bowl. Process with on/off turns till chopped; transfer to large skillet. Repeat with remaining meat; add to skillet. Add onion mixture. Cook till browned; drain off excess fat.

Stir in wine, water, tomato paste, 1 teaspoon salt, and dash pepper.

Simmer about 4 minutes or till liquid is nearly evaporated; cool slightly. Stir in *half* of the bread, *half* of the cheese, 2 eggs, and the cinnamon; set aside.

For sauce, in saucepan melt the butter or margarine; stir in flour, ½ teaspoon salt, nutmeg, and dash pepper. Add milk all at once; cook and stir till thickened and bubbly. Stir *half* of the hot mixture into the 1 beaten egg; return all to saucepan. Cook and stir over low heat for 2 minutes; set aside.

Brown eggplant slices in a little hot oil. Sprinkle bottom of a 12x7½x2-inch baking dish with remaining bread. Cover with half the eggplant; spoon on the meat mixture. Arrange remaining eggplant slices atop; pour sauce over all. Bake, uncovered, in 350° oven about 45 minutes or till set. Sprinkle with remaining cheese. Bake 2 to 3 minutes longer to melt cheese. Makes 6 to 8 servings.

Parmesan Chicken

3   ounces Parmesan cheese, cut up
2   slices dry bread, broken up
¼   cup lightly packed parsley (stems removed)
1   2½- to 3-pound broiler-fryer chicken, cut up
¼   cup butter *or* margarine, melted

Place steel blade in work bowl. Add cut-up Parmesan; process till coarsely chopped. Add dry bread and parsley; process till all are finely chopped. Transfer to shallow dish.

Brush chicken pieces with melted butter; roll in cheese mixture. Place chicken, skin side up, in shallow baking pan. Drizzle remaining butter atop; sprinkle on remaining cheese mixture. Bake in 375° oven for 45 to 60 minutes or till tender; do not turn. Makes 4 servings.

desserts

Cheesecake Supreme

- ¾ **cup all-purpose flour**
- 6 **tablespoons cold butter, cut into pieces**
- 3 **tablespoons sugar**
- 4 **1-inch strips lemon peel (cut with vegetable peeler)**
- 1 **egg yolk**
- ¼ **teaspoon vanilla**

🌀 For crust, place steel blade in work bowl; add ¾ cup flour, butter, 3 tablespoons sugar, and 4 strips lemon peel. Process till peel is finely chopped and mixture is crumbly. Add 1 egg yolk and ¼ teaspoon vanilla; process just till mixture forms a ball. Pat ⅓ of the dough on bottom of an 8-inch springform pan (sides removed).

Bake in 400° oven about 7 minutes or till golden; cool. Butter sides of pan; attach to bottom. Pat remaining dough on sides of pan to height of 1¾ inches; set aside.

- 3 **8-ounce packages cream cheese, quartered**
- 1 **cup sugar**
- ¼ **cup milk**
- 2 **tablespoons all-purpose flour**
- 2 **1-inch strips lemon peel (cut with vegetable peeler)**
- ¼ **teaspoon salt**
- ¼ **teaspoon vanilla**
- 2 **eggs**
- 1 **egg yolk**

For filling, place steel blade in work bowl (no need to wash work bowl after preparing crust). Add cream cheese, 1 cup sugar, milk, 2 tablespoons flour, 2 strips lemon peel, salt, and ¼ teaspoon vanilla. Process till mixture is creamy, scraping bowl as needed. With machine running add eggs and 1 egg yolk through feed tube. Process till smooth, scraping bowl occasionally. Turn into crust-lined pan.

Bake in 350° oven for 50 to 60 minutes or till center appears set. Remove from oven; cool 15 minutes in pan. Loosen sides of cheesecake from pan with spatula. Cool 30 minutes more. Remove sides of pan. Cool 2 hours more before adding glaze.

- 1 **cup fresh pineapple cut into chunks (½ of 1 medium) or ¾ cup canned crushed pineapple**
- ¼ **cup water**
- 3 **to 4 tablespoons sugar**
- 1 **tablespoon cornstarch**

For glaze, place steel blade in work bowl; add fresh pineapple chunks. Process with on/off turns till chopped. Transfer to 1-quart saucepan; add water. (Or, combine canned crushed pineapple and water.) Bring to boiling over medium-high heat. Boil gently, uncovered, for 2 minutes.

Thoroughly stir together 3 to 4 tablespoons sugar (taste pineapple for sweetness) and cornstarch; stir into the boiling fruit. Cook and stir about 1 minute or till thickened. Cool to room temperature. Spoon over cooled cheesecake; chill at least 2 hours before serving. Makes 12 servings.

Cranberry-Cheese Pie

- 1 **14-ounce can *sweetened condensed* milk**
- 2 **3-ounce packages cream cheese, quartered**
- ⅓ **cup lemon juice**
- ½ **teaspoon vanilla**
  Graham Cracker Crust
- 1 **16-ounce can whole cranberry sauce**
  Unsweetened whipped cream

🌀 Place steel blade in work bowl. Add the sweetened condensed milk, cream cheese, lemon juice, and vanilla. Process till smooth; turn into chilled Graham Cracker Crust. Carefully spoon cranberry sauce atop cheese mixture in pie shell; stir gently to marble.

Freeze several hours or overnight till firm. Let pie stand about 10 minutes at room temperature before serving. Garnish with unsweetened whipped cream. Slice pie and serve immediately.

Graham Cracker Crust

- 18 **graham cracker squares**
- ¼ **cup sugar**
- 6 **tablespoons butter, melted**

🌀 Place steel blade in work bowl; break crackers into bowl. Add sugar. Process till very finely crushed. With machine running add melted butter through feed tube; process till well mixed. Press mixture firmly and evenly onto bottom and sides of a 9-inch pie plate. Chill 45 minutes or till firm. (Or, bake in 375° oven for 6 to 9 minutes or till edges are just brown; cool.) Makes one 9-inch crust.

Almond Bars

2 cups all-purpose flour
1 cup cold butter *or* margarine,
    cut into 8 chunks
¼ cup ice-cold water
1 cup Homemade Almond Paste
    or 1 8-ounce can almond
    paste
1 cup sugar
2 eggs
½ teaspoon vanilla

Place steel blade in work bowl; add flour and butter. Process with on/off turns till mixture resembles cornmeal. Have ice-cold water in cup. With machine running pour ice-cold water all at once through feed tube. Process about 20 seconds or till most of mixture is crumbly (some dry areas may still be visible).

Remove dough and use hands to form it into a ball; divide in half. Wrap in waxed paper; chill several hours or overnight.

To make filling, reinsert steel blade in work bowl; crumble Homemade Almond Paste or canned almond paste into work bowl. Add sugar, eggs, and vanilla; process till smooth.

To prepare bars, let chilled dough stand at room temperature about 30 minutes or till just soft enough to handle. On lightly floured surface roll *half* the dough into a 14x10-inch rectangle. Place in bottom and ½ inch up the sides of a 13x9x2-inch baking dish. Spread filling over dough to within ½ inch of pastry edge. Roll out remaining dough into a 14x10-inch rectangle; place atop filling. Press edges to seal. Bake in 400° oven 30 to 35 minutes. Cool; cut into bars. Makes 4 dozen.

homemade almond paste

If you can't find whole blanched almonds, follow the directions below for blanching —

1 cup whole blanched
    almonds (6 ounces) *or*
    1⅓ cups slivered
    almonds
1⅓ cups sifted powdered
    sugar
2 tablespoons water
½ teaspoon almond extract
    (optional)

Place almonds in a single layer on baking sheet. Heat in 300° oven for 10 minutes; do not brown. Remove; cool 5 minutes.

Place steel blade in work bowl; add almonds. Process about 1 minute or till ground. Add powdered sugar, water, and extract (if desired for a stronger almond flavor). Process about 15 seconds or till mixture forms a ball. Use immediately or wrap and store in refrigerator or freezer. Makes about 1 cup.

How to blanch almonds:
Place almonds in saucepan; cover with water. Bring to boiling; drain. Skins should slip off easily when almond is pressed between thumb and forefinger.

Letterbanket

Pictured on page 181 —

½ cup Homemade Almond Paste
    or ½ of an 8-ounce can
    almond paste
1 egg yolk
2 tablespoons sugar
1½ cups all-purpose flour
¼ teaspoon salt
¾ cup butter *or* margarine,
    chilled and cut into pieces
¼ cup ice-cold water
1 egg white
2 teaspoons water

Place steel blade in work bowl; crumble Homemade Almond Paste into work bowl. Add egg yolk and sugar; process till thoroughly mixed. Remove; cover and chill.

Return steel blade to work bowl; add flour and salt. Process with 3 on/off turns just to mix. Add butter; process with on/off turns till mixture resembles coarse crumbs. With machine running add ice water quickly through feed tube; process just till dough is moistened (overprocessing will make dough tough).

Remove dough and use hands to shape it into a ball. Cover; let stand 30 minutes. Divide dough in half. On lightly floured surface roll one half into an 8-inch square; cut into four 8x2-inch strips. Repeat to make four more strips.

Roll about 1½ tablespoons of the chilled almond paste mixture into a rope about 7½ inches long; repeat to make 8 ropes. Place one rope in center of each strip of dough. Fold dough over rope, completely sealing sides and ends (moisten edges of dough, if necessary, to ensure a complete seal).

Shape into desired letters on ungreased cookie sheets. Combine the egg white and 2 teaspoons water; brush on letters. Bake in 375° oven about 25 minutes or till golden brown. Cool. Makes 8 letters.

Carrot-Pineapple Cake

2 **or** 3 carrots
¾ cup fresh pineapple cut into 1-inch pieces **or** ½ cup canned crushed pineapple
1½ cups all-purpose flour
1 cup sugar
1 teaspoon baking powder
1 teaspoon baking soda
1 teaspoon ground cinnamon
½ teaspoon salt
⅔ cup cooking oil
2 eggs
1 teaspoon vanilla
Cream Cheese Frosting

Insert shredding disk in work bowl; shred carrots to make 1 cup. Set aside. Place steel blade in work bowl; add fresh pineapple. Process with on/off turns till finely chopped; measure ½ cup pineapple. Set aside.

Rinse work bowl; dry. Reinsert steel blade. Add flour, sugar, baking powder, soda, cinnamon, and salt; process with 3 or 4 on/off turns. Add the 1 cup shredded carrot, ½ cup fresh or canned pineapple, oil, eggs, and vanilla. Process with on/off turns just till all is moistened, scraping bowl as needed; let machine run 20 seconds more. Pour batter into greased and lightly floured 9x9x2-inch baking pan. Bake in 350° oven 35 minutes. Cool. Frost with Cream Cheese Frosting.

Cream Cheese Frosting: Place steel blade in work bowl. Add 2½ cups *powdered sugar;* one 3-ounce package *cream cheese,* quartered; ¼ cup *butter or margarine,* cut into pieces; 1 teaspoon *vanilla;* and dash *salt.* Process till smooth and creamy, scraping bowl as needed. (If mixture is too stiff, add 1 teaspoon *milk;* process till smooth.) Add ½ cup *pecans;* process with on/off turns just till nuts are coarsely chopped. Spread over cooled cake.

Deluxe Fruit Ice Cream

2 cups fresh **or** frozen unsweetened raspberries
1 pound fresh peaches, pitted and peeled, **or** 2 cups frozen unsweetened peaches
1 ripe banana, cut up
2 cups sugar
1 cup orange juice
½ cup lemon juice
3 cups milk
2 cups whipping cream

Thaw frozen fruits. Place steel blade in work bowl; add fruits. Process till smooth, scraping bowl as necessary; transfer to large bowl. Reinsert steel blade; add sugar, orange juice, lemon juice, and ¼ teaspoon *salt.* Process till sugar is dissolved. Add to fruit mixture; pour into 4-quart ice cream freezer container. Add milk and whipping cream; stir well. Freeze according to manufacturer's directions. Makes 3½ quarts.

Frozen Cherry Macaroon Dessert

6 coconut macaroon cookies, broken
¼ cup maraschino cherries, drained
1 quart chocolate ice cream

Place steel blade in work bowl; add cookies. Process till finely crushed; remove. Reinsert steel blade; add cherries. Process with on/off turns till finely chopped; add to crumbs. Reinsert steel blade; add *one-fourth* of the ice cream. Process till softened. Continue processing ice cream, adding one-fourth at a time. Add crumb mixture. Process just till blended.

Spoon into muffin pans lined with paper bake cups **or** into one 8x4x2-inch loaf pan. Cover; freeze 4 hours or overnight. Makes 8 or 9 servings.

Watermelon Ice

½ medium watermelon
1½ cups sugar
⅓ cup lemon juice
Dash salt
1 envelope unflavored gelatin
⅓ cup water

Scoop out watermelon pulp, discarding seeds. Place steel blade in work bowl; add about 2 *cups* of the watermelon pulp. Process till smooth; measure and remove to large bowl.

Repeat with enough of the remaining watermelon to make a total of 6 cups puree. Stir in the sugar, lemon juice, and salt, mixing well.

In small saucepan soften gelatin in water; stir over low heat till gelatin is dissolved. Add gelatin to melon mixture; blend thoroughly. Pour mixture into a 13x9x2-inch pan; cover and freeze till partially frozen.

Place steel blade in work bowl; add *half* of the partially frozen mixture. Process with on/off turns till machine runs smoothly, then let machine run till ice is smooth, fluffy, and lighter in color. Return to pan. Repeat with remaining partially frozen mixture. Cover and freeze till firm. Makes about 8 cups ice.

Cantaloupe Ice: Halve 2 medium *cantaloupes* and discard seeds. Scoop out pulp. Process 2 *cups* cantaloupe pulp as directed above for watermelon. Repeat, processing 2 cups at a time, to make a total of 6 cups puree. Continue as directed above.

Deluxe Fruit Ice Cream
Letterbanket (see recipe, page 179)

BLENDER RECIPES

It's time to take full advantage of the many time-saving features of what may be your most under-used kitchen appliance — your blender. There's more to blender cooking than making malts and frozen daiquiris. In this section you'll discover frothy beverages as well as blender-fast salads, main dishes, breads, and desserts.

what your blender will do for you

Meal preparation is easier and more fun once you "think blender." At the push of a button, this versatile kitchen helper trims minutes from cooking jobs while it blends, chops, crumbs, emulsifies, or purees foods to suit your recipe needs. Keep your blender handy so you'll use it whenever there's a time-saving job it can do.

You'll find something the blender can do to save you time at almost every meal. Even traditional dishes that you've always made "the long way around" adapt beautifully to the blender. Mexican favorites are good examples. The Guacamole appetizer dip served with corn or tortilla chips is made velvety smooth in the blender (see recipe, page 187). Likewise, the colorful vegetables and tasty cheese for Mexican Beef Tostadas are blender-chopped one at a time (see recipe, page 191). The layer of Mexican Fried Beans came out of the blender, and so did the peppy Hot Sauce for Tostadas (see recipes, page 191).

Recipes you struggled with for years are suddenly no trouble at all when you put the blender to work. Think of all the vegetables, fruits, and nuts that you no longer need to chop by hand. The blender lets you turn out bread and cracker crumbs by the cupful in just a few seconds. And when you blender-chop vanilla wafers, graham crackers, or gingersnaps, desserts and piecrusts are easier than ever.

Of course, beverages were among the first blender specialties. Beyond milk shakes and cocktails, the blender can make short work of frozen juices for breakfast, as well as quantity party punches.

Blender Gazpacho
(see recipe, page 194)

blender action

The first thing to remember about your blender is that it's fast. Even at the lowest speed, seconds make a tremendous difference in the texture of the final product. Although this is most obvious in chopped foods such as cabbage, or in smooth combinations such as those prepared for baby food, it also applies to sauces, salad dressings, appetizer dips, sandwich fillings, and leftovers.

Also remember that it's the cutting action of the blades that does the work. The blender cuts rather than mixes. When liquids and solids are blended together, whirlpool action draws the solids in and out of the blades to produce uniform-size pieces. The longer the blender runs, the smaller the pieces become.

Blender Mayonnaise is another favorite (see recipe, page 195). The action of the blender readily breaks up the oil droplets and disperses them throughout the dressing for a smooth, creamy mixture with great stability. In other types of dressings, the blender evenly distributes the seasonings for full, uniform flavor.

Certain packaged mixes also are especially easy in the blender. You can create delicious dips from dry mixes and sour cream or cream cheese thinned with milk. And blended instant puddings are ready to serve on a moment's notice.

Be sure to carefully read the manufacturer's instructions for your blender. They may suggest that you start and stop the blender often at first so you don't accidentally overprocess some foods. As you become more familiar with the blender's actions, you'll be able to choose the speed that's best suited to each recipe.

As helpful as the blender is, however, there are some things that it can't do well. The same speed and cutting action that makes the blender so versatile also makes it unsuitable for whipping cream and egg whites. Because the blender cuts through foods without trapping air in them, it can't produce the volume associated with conventional whipping. Also, while the blender readily chops cooked meats for leftovers, its motor is not powerful enough to chop raw meats. Finally, remember that the blender chops rather than whips cooked white potatoes. The texture of blended potatoes will differ from that of mashed potatoes.

special techniques

Making the best use of your blender involves a few basic rules. Although much depends on the specific food involved, here are some techniques you'll use again and again.

- Cut fresh fruits and vegetables, cooked meats, fish, or seafood into ½- to 1-inch pieces before chopping.
- Cut firm cheeses into ½-inch pieces. Cube and soften cream cheese before blending it with liquid ingredients.
- Place liquid ingredients into the blender container first, unless the recipe instructs otherwise. (Many blender containers are marked in cups and ounces for easy measuring directly into the container.)
- Stop the blender and use a rubber spatula to scrape down the sides of the blender container when blending thick mixtures. Guide the mixture toward the blades for better blending.
- Blend large quantities of foods, such as cracker crumbs or raw vegetables, in several small batches. You'll find it easier to control the fineness of the chop, and you won't overtax the blender's motor.

care and cleaning

Keep your blender operating at peak efficiency by following a few simple rules for its use and maintenance. Although each model will have some specific dos and don'ts listed in the manufacturer's instructions, these rules apply to all brands, old and new.

use and care

- Operate the blender on a dry, clean surface. A dry surface is recommended for all electrical appliances, and a clean surface free of crumbs keeps foreign material from getting into the blender mechanism.

- Be sure that the blender container and cutting assembly rest firmly in the base before turning on the motor. If the cutting assembly screws onto the bottom of the blender container, make sure the rubber sealing ring is in place and that the threaded base is screwed on tightly. If the container should turn during processing, switch the blender off and tighten the screw band.
- Always cover the blender container before turning on the motor. Place the cover firmly on the container and rest your hand lightly on the lid when starting the motor. If for some reason the lid is not on securely, your hand will prevent it from coming off the container.
- Do not remove the container from the base until the motor stops. Likewise, don't replace the container while the motor is running.
- When blending is completed, lift the container straight up. If it doesn't lift easily, rock it gently and lift up — do not twist.
- Transfer blended foods to another container for storage. This will keep your blender container free for further use.
- Avoid overtaxing the motor with heavy mixtures. When the motor labors, try switching to a higher speed, or remove part of the contents and blend it in smaller batches.
- If food becomes packed around the blades, switch the blender off and use a rubber spatula to dislodge the food, or add several drops of liquid and continue blending.
- When adding ingredients while the motor is running, use caution to prevent splattering. If the container lid has a removable insert, add ingredients through this smaller opening. If the lid is a single unit, fit a piece of foil over the top of the

blender container and cut an opening in the foil large enough to accommodate the food you're adding.
- Switch the blender off and wait for the blades to stop turning before putting a spatula or other utensil into the blender container. This prevents splattering and any possibility of catching the spatula in the blades. The only exception to this rule is when blending a thick mixture in which a vortex or whirlpool does not form. Then, use a narrow rubber spatula to push down food from the sides of the container while the motor is running. Keep the spatula close to the sides of the container to avoid the blades.
- Check the manufacturer's instructions regarding how to add hot liquids. Some recommend cooling liquids slightly before pouring them into the container.

cleaning guide

- Wash the blender container after each use. Fill it ⅓ full with lukewarm water and add a small amount of detergent. Adjust the lid on the blender container and run the motor for a few seconds until the container is clean. Rinse, dry, and return the container to the motor base.
- If the blender container has a removable cutting assembly, take it apart and wash it separately. Dry each part, reassemble, and return the container to the motor base.
- Check the manufacturer's instructions before putting the blender container in an automatic dishwasher.
- Never immerse the motor base in water. Merely wipe the outside surfaces with a clean, damp cloth and dry well. Since most motors are sealed, don't lubricate them unless the instructions so specify.

blender arithmetic

Ingredients	Measure	Blender Yield	Hints
Cheese			
Natural (cheddar, Swiss)	1 cup	1 cup	Chop process cheeses with
Process	1 cup	1 cup	½ slice white bread.
Crumbs			
Saltine crackers	13-14	½ cup	Blend all at once.
White bread	1 slice	¾ cup	Tear into pieces.
Chocolate wafers	8	½ cup	Break into pieces.
Graham crackers	6-7	½ cup	Break into pieces.
Vanilla wafers	12	½ cup	Blend 6-7 at one time.
Zwieback	6-8	½ cup	Break into pieces.
Fruits			
Apples	1 medium	½ cup	Chop wet or dry.
Cranberries	1 cup	1 cup	Chop fresh or frozen.
Nuts	½ cup	½ cup	Chop dry or with other ingredients.
Meat, cooked			
All kinds	½ cup	¾ cup	Chop dry.
Vegetables			
Cabbage	1 medium head	7 cups	Chop wet (you can fill blender container).
Carrot	1 medium	½ cup	Chop dry.
Celery	1 medium stalk	⅓ cup	Chop wet or dry.
Green pepper	1 medium	½ cup	Chop wet or dry.
Onion	1 small	½ cup	Chop wet or dry.
	1 slice	1 table-spoon	Chop with other ingredients.
Parsley	½ cup	¼ cup	Chop dry.
Miscellaneous			
Eggs, hard-cooked	3	1 cup	Chill before chopping.
Chocolate, baking	2 ounces	⅓ cup	Cut into quarters; add pieces while blender is on.
Peppermint candies	8 pieces	¼ cup	Blend all at once.

appetizers
and
beverages

Three-Cheese Mold

- 2 tablespoons cold water
- 1½ teaspoons unflavored gelatin
- 2 tablespoons boiling water
- 3 ounces sharp cheddar cheese, cut into cubes (¾ cup)
- ½ cup cream-style cottage cheese
- 1 ounce blue cheese, crumbled (¼ cup)
- ¼ cup dairy sour cream
- 1 thin slice onion
- 2 sprigs parsley
- ½ teaspoon Worcestershire sauce
  Parsley
  Assorted crackers

Put cold water and gelatin in blender container; let stand for a few minutes to soften. Add boiling water; blend till gelatin is dissolved.

Add cheddar cheese, cottage cheese, blue cheese, sour cream, onion, 2 sprigs parsley, and Worcestershire sauce to mixture in blender container; blend till smooth. (If necessary, stop blender and use rubber spatula to scrape down sides of container.)

Pack cheese mixture into a 1½-cup mold; cover and chill till serving time. Unmold cheese mixture onto a serving plate; garnish with additional parsley. Serve with assorted crackers.

Quiche Wedges

- Piecrust mix for one 8-inch pie shell
- 3 eggs
- 1 10-ounce package frozen Welsh rarebit, partially thawed
- ⅛ teaspoon pepper
- 5 slices bacon, crisp-cooked and drained
  Pimiento strips (optional)
  Parsley sprigs

Prepare pie shell according to package directions. Bake; cool. Put eggs in blender container; blend till foamy. Break Welsh rarebit into pieces; add to blender container. Add pepper. Blend till combined. Add bacon to blender container; blend till coarsely chopped. Pour into pie shell. Bake in 350° oven about 40 minutes or till knife inserted near center comes out clean.

Let stand at room temperature for 10 to 15 minutes before serving. With knife, cut into small wedges to serve. Top each piece with a pimiento strip, if desired. Garnish with parsley sprigs. Makes 12 appetizers.

Creamy Clam Dip

- 1 7½-ounce can minced clams
- 1 8-ounce package cream cheese, cut into cubes and softened
- 1 green onion, sliced

Drain minced clams; reserve 3 tablespoons of the clam liquid. Set clams aside. Put reserved clam liquid, cream cheese, and green onion in blender container; blend till mixture is smooth. Add drained clams to cheese mixture in blender container; blend till mixed. Makes 1½ cups dip.

Apple-Stuffed Edam

Stuff a red Edam shell with this apple-cheese mixture —

- 8 ounces Edam or Gouda cheese
- 1 medium apple, cut into eighths and cored
- ½ cup milk
- 1 teaspoon lemon juice
  Dash salt
  Assorted crackers

Cut top off cheese. Carefully remove cheese from shell. Cut cheese into cubes; set aside. Put apple, milk, lemon juice, and salt in blender container; blend till finely chopped. Add cheese cubes, a few at a time, to mixture in blender container; blend till nearly smooth. (When necessary, stop blender and use rubber spatula to scrape down sides of container.)

Spoon into cheese shell. Chill. (Chill any extra mixture separately and use to replenish red shell.) Serve with assorted crackers.

Bacon-Blue Dip

- ½ cup dairy sour cream
- 1 3-ounce package cream cheese, cut into cubes and softened
- 2 ounces blue cheese, crumbled (½ cup)
- 1 tablespoon instant minced onion
- 4 slices bacon, crisp-cooked, drained, and crumbled
- 1 large green pepper, top and seeds removed (optional)

Place sour cream, cream cheese, blue cheese, and minced onion in blender container; blend till mixture is smooth. Chill. Before serving, stir in crumbled bacon. Serve mixture in green pepper shell, if desired. Makes about 1 cup.

Guacamole

- 2 tablespoons lemon juice
- ¾ teaspoon salt
- 1 small tomato, peeled and cut into pieces
- ¼ medium onion
- 2 *or* 3 canned green chili peppers, rinsed and seeded
- 2 ripe avocados, seeded, peeled, and cut into cubes
  Corn chips *or* tortilla chips

Put all ingredients in blender container. Blend ingredients till smooth. (When necessary, stop blender and use rubber spatula to scrape down sides of container.) Serve with corn or tortilla chips. Makes 2 cups.

Special cooking tip: For a more colorful dip, reserve half the tomato; add reserved tomato at end and blend only till tomato is coarsely chopped.

Stuffed Mushrooms

- 2 6-ounce cans whole mushrooms
- 3 slices bacon
- 1 thin slice onion
- 1 slice bread, torn into pieces
  Dash Worcestershire sauce
  Salt
- 1 tablespoon grated Parmesan cheese

Hollow out mushrooms; reserve ¼ cup of the pieces. Crisp-cook bacon; drain, reserving drippings. Cook onion in drippings till tender.

Put onion, bacon, reserved mushroom pieces, bread, and Worcestershire in blender container; blend till chopped. Sprinkle mushroom crowns with salt; pile chopped mixture in crowns. Top with Parmesan cheese. Broil 3 to 4 inches from heat till hot and golden. Makes 30 appetizers.

Party Reubens

- ½ of a 12-ounce can corned beef, cut into pieces
- 1 8-ounce can sauerkraut, drained
- ½ cup Thousand Island salad dressing
- 30 slices party rye bread
- 2 ounces Swiss cheese, torn into pieces (½ cup)

Place *half* the corned beef in blender container; blend till chopped. Remove chopped meat to bowl; repeat with remaining corned beef. Put drained sauerkraut and Thousand Island salad dressing in blender container; blend till sauerkraut is chopped and mixture is blended. Combine with corned beef in bowl.

Lightly toast one side of rye bread under broiler, 3 to 4 inches from heat. Spread corned beef mixture on untoasted sides of rye bread. Top each with Swiss cheese. Broil 3 to 4 inches from heat for 1 to 2 minutes or till cheese melts and meat is heated through. Makes 30 appetizer sandwiches.

Peppy Deviled Eggs

- 6 hard-cooked eggs, halved
- ¼ cup mayonnaise *or* salad dressing
- 5 small pimiento-stuffed olives
- 1 small dill pickle
- 1 teaspoon prepared mustard
  Dash pepper
  Paprika

Remove yolks from egg halves; put yolks, mayonnaise, stuffed olives, dill pickle, mustard, and pepper in blender container. Blend till olives and pickle are finely chopped. Fill egg white halves with mixture; sprinkle with paprika. Chill well. Makes 12 appetizers.

Marinated Shrimp

- 1 cup cooking oil
- ¼ cup white vinegar
- 1½ teaspoons salt
- 1 teaspoon paprika
- 1 small clove garlic
  Dash bottled hot pepper sauce
- 1 stalk celery, sliced
- ½ green pepper, cut into pieces
- 2 sprigs parsley
- 2 green onions, sliced
- 1 pound shelled cooked shrimp

Put cooking oil, white vinegar, salt, paprika, garlic, and bottled hot pepper sauce in blender container; blend till mixture is combined. Add celery, green pepper, parsley, and green onion to mixture in blender container; blend till finely chopped.

Pour vinegar mixture over shrimp in bowl. Cover; marinate in refrigerator for 24 hours, spooning mixture over shrimp occasionally. Serve shrimp on cocktail picks.

Shrimp Cocktail Dip

- 1 8-ounce package cream cheese, cut into cubes and softened
- 1 cup chili sauce
- 4 teaspoons lemon juice
- 1 tablespoon prepared horseradish
- 2 teaspoons Worcestershire sauce
- ½ teaspoon salt
  Shelled cooked shrimp, chilled

Put all ingredients, except shrimp, in blender container. Blend till mixed. (When necessary, stop blender and use rubber spatula to scrape down sides of container.) Pour mixture into a small bowl; chill thoroughly. Serve with shrimp. Makes about 2 cups.

Snow-Capped Pâté

½ cup chopped onion
1 small clove garlic, minced
¼ cup butter *or* margarine
1 pound fresh *or* frozen chicken livers, thawed
2 teaspoons all-purpose flour
¼ teaspoon salt
¼ teaspoon dried thyme, crushed
  Dash pepper
2 tablespoons dry sherry
2 3-ounce packages cream cheese, cut into cubes and softened
3 tablespoons milk
½ cup stemmed parsley sprigs, packed
½ cup pecans
  Assorted crackers

Cook onion and garlic in butter or margarine till tender. Add chicken livers; cook, covered, over low heat for 7 to 8 minutes or till no longer pink. Stir in flour, salt, thyme, and pepper. Add sherry; cook and stir for 1 minute. Transfer to blender container; blend till smooth. (When necessary, stop blender and use rubber spatula to scrape down sides of container.) Mold in a small greased bowl; chill. Unmold chicken liver mixture onto serving plate. Add cream cheese and milk to blender container; blend till smooth. Spread cream cheese mixture over chicken liver mixture. Chill till serving time. Put parlsey and pecans in blender container; blend till chopped. Sprinkle atop pâté. Serve with assorted crackers.

Sherried Cheese Balls

8 ounces sharp cheddar cheese, cut into cubes (2 cups)
2 tablespoons butter *or* margarine, softened
½ teaspoon dry mustard
⅓ cup dry sherry
3 tablespoons milk
½ cup stemmed parsley sprigs, packed
2 tablespoons sesame seeds, toasted
  Paprika
  Assorted crackers

Put *half* the cheese in blender container; blend till chopped. Remove and set aside. Repeat with remaining cheese. Put cheese, softened butter or margarine, dry mustard, dry sherry, and milk in blender container; blend till smooth. Chill. Divide into thirds; form each third into a ball.

Put parsley in blender container; blend till chopped. Roll one ball in chopped parsley, another in toasted sesame seed, and the third in paprika. Serve cheese balls with assorted crackers.

Wine-Cheese Dip

¼ cup tawny port *or* sauterne
1 8-ounce package cream cheese, cut into cubes and softened
2 ounces blue cheese, crumbled (½ cup)
  Dash garlic salt
  Assorted crackers

Put tawny port or sauterne, softened cream cheese, blue cheese, and garlic salt in blender container; blend till mixture is smooth. Serve with assorted crackers. Makes 1⅓ cups dip.

Fresh Strawberry Malt

¾ to 1 cup cold milk
2 tablespoons malted milk powder
1 cup fresh strawberries
1 tablespoon sugar
1 pint vanilla ice cream
  Fresh strawberries (optional)

Put cold milk, malted milk powder, 1 cup fresh strawberries, and sugar in blender container; spoon in vanilla ice cream. Blend till mixture is smooth. Garnish with additional fresh strawberries, if desired. Makes 3 servings.

Malted Milk

1 cup cold milk
¼ cup chocolate syrup *or* other flavored syrup
2 tablespoons malted milk powder
1 pint vanilla ice cream

Put cold milk, syrup, and malted milk powder in blender container; spoon in ice cream. Blend till mixture is smooth. Makes 3 servings.

Raspberry Froth
Use flavored gelatin to make this easy drink —

1 3-ounce package raspberry-flavored gelatin
½ cup boiling water
1 10-ounce package frozen red raspberries, partially thawed
1½ cups cold milk
1 cup crushed ice

Put gelatin and boiling water in blender container; blend till gelatin is dissolved. Add partially thawed raspberries, cold milk, and crushed ice; blend till ice dissolves. Serve immediately. Serves 4 or 5.

Peachy-Cream Milk Shake

¼ cup milk
1 cup sliced peaches
1 pint peach ice cream
¾ cup milk
  Sugar (optional)
  Peach slices (optional)

Put the ¼ cup milk and 1 cup sliced peaches in blender container; blend till smooth. Spoon in peach ice cream. Blend till ice cream is softened.

Add ¾ cup milk; blend till mixture is combined. Sweeten with sugar, if desired. Pour into tall glasses. Garnish each serving with additional peach slices, if desired. Makes 3 or 4 servings.

Golden Slush

1 12-ounce can peach nectar, chilled
1 6-ounce can frozen orange juice concentrate
1 tablespoon lemon juice
3 cups crushed ice

Put chilled peach nectar, frozen orange juice concentrate, lemon juice, and crushed ice in blender container. Blend till ingredients are combined. Makes 3 or 4 servings.

Strawberry-Lemon Slush

Spruce up favorite old-time lemonade by combining it with fresh pureed strawberries —

3 cups water
1 cup lemon juice
1 cup sugar
2 cups fresh strawberries
  Few drops food coloring (optional)
  Crushed ice
  Sliced fresh strawberries
  Lemon slices

Put *1 cup* of the water, lemon juice, sugar, and 2 cups fresh strawberries in blender container. Blend till the strawberries are pureed and the sugar is completely dissolved.

In a pitcher combine blended strawberry mixture, the remaining 2 cups water, and red food coloring; mix well. Add crushed ice, sliced fresh strawberries, and lemon slices to strawberry mixture in pitcher. Makes 6 servings.

Frosty Lime Fizz

1 12-ounce can pineapple juice, chilled (1½ cups)
½ cup lime juice
½ cup sugar
1 quart lime sherbet
1 28-ounce bottle lemon-lime carbonated beverage, chilled

Put pineapple juice, lime juice, and sugar in blender container; spoon *half* of the lime sherbet into blender container. Blend till mixture is smooth.

Pour ½ cup of the pineapple-lime mixture into each of six 12-ounce glasses. Add an additional scoop of lime sherbet to each glass. Fill each glass with chilled lemon-lime carbonated beverage. Makes 6 servings.

Lemon-Tea Frosty

3 cups cold water
2 tablespoons instant tea powder
1 6-ounce can frozen lemonade concentrate
1 pint lemon sherbet

Put cold water, instant tea powder, frozen lemonade concentrate, and lemon sherbet in blender container. Blend till ingredients are combined. Makes 5 servings.

Apple Eggnog

3 eggs
2 cups apple juice, chilled
  Dash ground cinnamon
  Dash ground ginger
1 pint vanilla ice cream
  Ground nutmeg

Put eggs, chilled apple juice, cinnamon, and ginger in blender container; blend till mixed. Spoon in ice cream; blend till smooth. Top with nutmeg. Makes 6 to 8 servings.

Tropical Hot Chocolate

4 cups milk
6 tablespoons presweetened instant cocoa powder
1 large banana, cut into pieces
½ teaspoon vanilla
  Marshmallows

Blend *1 cup* of the milk, the instant cocoa powder, and banana in blender till smooth. Heat with vanilla and rest of milk. Top with marshmallows. Makes 4 servings.

main
dishes

Three-Cheese Burger Bake

- 2 ounces American cheese, cut into cubes (½ cup)
- 1 slice bread, torn into pieces
- 2 pounds ground beef
- 1 15-ounce can tomato sauce
- ½ small onion, cut into pieces
- 1 teaspoon sugar
- 1 teaspoon salt
- ⅛ teaspoon garlic salt
- 1 cup quick-cooking rice
- ⅓ cup milk
- 1 cup cream-style cottage cheese
- 1 3-ounce package cream cheese, cubed
- ½ small green pepper, cut into pieces

Put American cheese and bread in blender container. Blend till cheese is chopped; set aside. In skillet brown ground beef; drain off fat. Put tomato sauce, onion, sugar, salt, and garlic salt in blender container; blend till onion is chopped. Add to ground beef. Stir in rice. Put milk, cottage cheese, and cream cheese in blender container; blend till smooth. Add green pepper; blend till green pepper is chopped.

Put *half* of the meat mixture in an 8x8x2-inch baking dish. Pour cottage cheese mixture over. Top with remaining meat mixture. Cover and bake in 350° oven for 35 to 40 minutes. Uncover; top with American cheese mixture. Bake till American cheese is melted. Makes 6 to 8 servings.

Stuffed Beef Rounds
Mellow cheese flavors the stuffing —

- 2 pounds beef round steak, ½ inch thick
- 4 ounces American cheese, cut into cubes (1 cup)
- ½ slice bread
- ½ medium onion, cut into pieces
- 3 stalks celery, sliced
- 3 sprigs parsley
- ¼ cup all-purpose flour
- 1 teaspoon salt
- ⅛ teaspoon pepper
- 2 tablespoons cooking oil
- 1 10½-ounce can condensed beef broth
- ½ teaspoon dry mustard
- ¼ cup water
- 1 tablespoon all-purpose flour

Cut steak into 6 pieces; pound to ¼-inch thickness. For stuffing, place cheese and bread in blender container; blend till cheese is coarsely chopped. Remove from blender to mixing bowl. Place onion, celery, and parsley sprigs in blender; blend till coarsely chopped. Add to cheese.

Divide the stuffing mixture among pieces of steak. Roll up each steak jelly roll-style; secure with wooden picks or tie with string. Combine the ¼ cup flour, the salt, and pepper. Roll meat in flour mixture to coat. In a 10-inch skillet slowly brown meat in hot oil. Drain off excess fat. Combine beef broth and dry mustard; pour over steak rolls. Cover and cook over low heat for 1 to 1¼ hours or till meat is tender. Remove to serving platter.

Skim excess fat from pan juices. Combine water and the 1 tablespoon flour; stir into pan juices. Cook and stir till mixture thickens and bubbles; pour over meat. Makes 6 servings.

Cheese-Sauced Meat Loaf

- ¾ cup milk
- 2 eggs
- 2 slices bread, torn into pieces
- ¼ small onion
- 1 teaspoon salt
- ½ teaspoon ground sage
  Dash pepper
- 2 pounds ground beef
- 1 cup milk
- 2 tablespoons butter *or* margarine
- 2 tablespoons all-purpose flour
- 4 ounces American cheese, cut into cubes (1 cup)
- 1 tablespoon chopped pimiento

Place ¾ cup milk, eggs, bread, onion, salt, sage, and pepper in blender container. Blend till combined; add to ground beef in large mixing bowl. Mix well. Pat mixture into a 9x5x3-inch loaf pan. Bake in 350° oven for 1½ hours.

For cheese sauce, place milk, butter or margarine, flour, American cheese, and pimiento in blender container. Blend till ingredients are combined and cheese is finely chopped. Transfer to saucepan. Cook and stir over low heat till sauce is thick and smooth. Transfer meat loaf to a serving platter. Spoon cheese sauce over loaf. Makes 8 servings.

Mexican Beef Tostadas

  1 **small onion, cut into pieces**
  1 **clove garlic, halved**
  1 **pound ground beef**
  ½ **teaspoon salt**
  ½ **teaspoon chili powder**
  8 **ounces American cheese, cut into cubes (2 cups)**
  ½ **slice bread, torn into pieces**
  1 **small head lettuce, cut into eighths**
  2 **medium tomatoes, quartered**
 12 **canned or frozen tortillas**
    Cooking oil
    Mexican Fried Beans
    Hot Sauce for Tostadas

Put onion and garlic in blender container; blend till coarsely chopped. In skillet cook ground beef, onion, and garlic till meat is browned. Drain off fat. Stir in salt and chili powder.

Place cheese and bread in blender container; blend till coarsely chopped. Transfer to small bowl. Place lettuce in blender; cover with cold water. Blend till coarsely chopped. Drain well. Transfer to small bowl. Place tomatoes in blender container; blend till coarsely chopped. Drain well. Transfer to small bowl.

In skillet fry tortillas in ¼ inch hot cooking oil till crisp. Drain. Spoon about ¼ cup meat mixture onto each· tortilla. Top with Mexican Fried Beans, tomato, lettuce, and cheese. Pass Hot Sauce for Tostadas. Make 12 tostadas.

Mexican Fried Beans: In a 10-inch skillet cook 6 slices *bacon* till crisp. Drain, reserving 2 tablespoons drippings. Put one 15-ounce can *undrained* red *kidney beans* in blender container. Add crisp-cooked bacon, the 2 tablespoons reserved bacon drippings, and ½ teaspoon *salt*. Blend till ingredients are thoroughly combined. (When necessary, stop blender and use rubber spatula to scrape down sides of container.)

Return bean mixture to skillet. Drain one 15-ounce can red *kidney beans;* stir beans into blended mixture in skillet, mashing slightly. Cook, uncovered, over low heat about 10 minutes or till mixture is thickened, stirring frequently.

Special cooking tip: Be sure to refrigerate or freeze any leftover fried beans. When heated another day in hot cooking oil or shortening, this Mexican favorite becomes Refried Beans.

Hot Sauce for Tostadas: Drain one 16-ounce can *tomatoes,* reserving 2 tablespoons juice. Put tomatoes; reserved tomato juice; 1 tablespoon *cooking oil;* 1 small *onion,* cut into pieces; ½ teaspoon dried *oregano,* crushed; 1 tablespoon *wine vinegar;* and 1 canned green *chili pepper,* rinsed and seeded, in blender container. Blend till almost smooth. Add more canned green chili peppers, if desired. Blend till mixture is smooth.

Chicken Croquettes

  ½ **cup chicken broth**
  ¼ **cup milk**
  ¼ **cup all-purpose flour**
  3 **tablespoons butter or margarine**
  1 **thin slice small onion**
  1 **sprig parsley**
  1 **teaspoon lemon juice**
  ¼ **teaspoon salt**
    Dash pepper
    Dash paprika
 1½ **cups cubed cooked chicken**
  2 **or 3 slices dry bread**
  1 **beaten egg**
  2 **tablespoons water**
    Cooking oil or shortening for deep-fat frying

For sauce, put chicken broth, milk, flour, butter or margarine, onion slice, parsley sprig, lemon juice, salt, pepper, and paprika in blender container. Blend till onion and parsley are finely chopped. Transfer mixture to a small saucepan. Cook and stir till thickened and bubbly. Cook and stir 1 minute longer. Cool.

Put *half* the chicken in blender container; blend till finely chopped. Remove. Repeat with remaining chicken. Add to sauce; chill thoroughly.

Break bread in blender container; blend into fine crumbs. With wet hands, shape chicken mixture into 8 balls. Roll in dry bread crumbs. Shape balls into cones. Dip into mixture of egg and water; roll again in crumbs. Fry in deep hot fat (365°) for 2½ to 3 minutes. Drain croquettes on paper toweling. Makes 4 servings.

Ham Fiesta Rolls

1½ **cups cubed fully cooked ham**
6 **to 8 large hard rolls**
4 **ounces American cheese, cut into cubes (1 cup)**
2 **green onions, sliced**
8 **small pimiento-stuffed olives**
1 **hard-cooked egg, quartered**
¼ **cup chili sauce**
¼ **cup mayonnaise or salad dressing**
   Sliced pimiento-stuffed olives

Put ⅓ of the cubed ham in blender container; blend till coarsely chopped. Remove ham to mixing bowl. Repeat with the remaining ham, ⅓ at a time. Slice the tops off hard rolls. Scoop out the centers; place crumbs, American cheese, and green onion in blender container. Blend till ingredients are chopped. Combine with ham. Put the 8 pimiento-stuffed olives and hard-cooked egg in blender container; blend till chopped. Add to ham and cheese. Stir in chili sauce and mayonnaise or salad dressing.

Spoon ham mixture into hard rolls; wrap in foil. Heat in 400° oven for 20 to 25 minutes. Garnish with additional sliced olives. Makes 6 to 8 servings.

Speedy Stroganoff Loaf

4 **ounces sharp cheddar cheese, cut into cubes (1 cup)**
¼ **small onion**
2 **tablespoons butter or margarine**
2 **cups cubed cooked roast beef**
8 **medium pitted ripe olives**
1 **envelope stroganoff seasoning mix**
1 **cup water**
½ **cup dairy sour cream**
1 **unsliced loaf Vienna bread**
   Butter or margarine, softened
   Green pepper rings
   Cherry tomatoes, halved

Put cheese in blender container; blend till chopped. Remove and set aside. Put onion in blender container; blend till chopped. In medium saucepan cook onion in 2 tablespoons butter or margarine till tender but not brown. Meanwhile, place about half of the roast beef at a time in blender container; blend till chopped. Remove.

Put pitted ripe olives in blender container; blend till coarsely chopped. Stir stroganoff seasoning mix into onion in saucepan; gradually blend in water. Add chopped beef and olives to mixture in saucepan. Cover and simmer for 8 to 10 minutes, stirring occasionally. Stir in sour cream. Heat through over low heat; *do not boil.*

Cut Vienna bread in half lengthwise. Toast under broiler till golden brown; spread cut surfaces with softened butter or margarine. Spread *half* of the meat mixture on each half of bread; arrange green pepper rings alternately with tomato halves atop. Sprinkle with cheese. Place on baking sheet. Bake in 375° oven for 7 to 10 minutes. Makes 8 to 10 servings.

Paul Revere Sandwiches

1 **cup cubed cooked roast pork, chicken, or turkey**
1 **slice onion**
⅓ **cup mayonnaise or salad dressing**
1 **teaspoon prepared mustard**
¼ **teaspoon salt**
1 **package refrigerated biscuits (10 biscuits)**
1 **medium dill pickle, cut into 10 slices**
   Parsley

Put cubed cooked meat, onion slice, mayonnaise or salad dressing, prepared mustard, and salt in blender container; blend till meat is chopped. (When necessary, stop blender and use rubber spatula to scrape down sides of container.) On floured surface, roll each refrigerated biscuit into a 4-inch circle.

Place a rounded tablespoon of the meat mixture in center of each biscuit circle; top with pickle slice. Fold up 3 sides of biscuit and pinch edges together to seal (see photo). Place biscuits on lightly greased baking sheet. Bake in 425° oven for 8 to 10 minutes or till golden brown. Garnish with parsley. Serve warm. Makes 10 sandwiches.

Speedy Stroganoff Loaf
Ham Fiesta Rolls
Paul Revere Sandwiches

side dishes and desserts

Blender Gazpacho

Pictured on page 182 —

- 3 cups tomato juice
- 2 tablespoons olive oil *or* cooking oil
- 2 tablespoons wine vinegar
- 1 clove garlic
- 2 medium tomatoes, peeled and quartered
- 1 small cucumber, cut into pieces
- 1 small green pepper, cut into pieces
- 3 medium stalks celery, sliced
- ¼ medium onion, cut into pieces
- 4 sprigs parsley
- 2 slices bread, torn into pieces
- 1 teaspoon salt
- ¼ teaspoon pepper
- 1 cup croutons
  Cucumber slices

Put *1 cup* of the tomato juice, olive oil or cooking oil, wine vinegar, and garlic in blender container. Blend mixture till garlic is finely chopped.

Add *half each* of the tomato, cucumber, green pepper, celery, onion, parsley, bread, salt, and pepper to blender container. Blend till vegetables are pureed. Transfer to a 2-quart container. Repeat with remaining tomato juice, vegetables, bread, and seasonings. Cover and chill thoroughly in the refrigerator. Serve in chilled mugs or bowls topped with croutons and cucumber slices. Makes 6 servings.

Basic Blender Coleslaw

- 3 stalks celery, sliced
- ½ green pepper, cut into pieces
- 2 green onions, sliced
- 1 small head cabbage, cored and cut into small wedges
- 1 cup dairy sour cream
- ¼ cup tarragon vinegar
- 2 tablespoons sugar
- 1 teaspoon salt

Put *half* the vegetables in blender container in order listed; add cold water to cover. Blend till coarsely chopped. Drain. Repeat with remaining vegetables. Chill.

Put dairy sour cream, vinegar, sugar, and salt in container; blend till combined. Chill. Before serving, drain vegetables again and toss lightly with sour cream mixture. Makes 8 servings.

Carrot-Fruit Slaw

- 1 medium apple, unpeeled
- 3 medium carrots, sliced
- 3 medium oranges, peeled and diced
- ½ cup raisins
- ¾ cup mayonnaise *or* salad dressing
  Lettuce cups

Cut apple into quarters; remove core. Put apple and sliced carrots in blender container; cover with cold water. Blend till apple and carrots are coarsely chopped. Drain.

In large bowl combine chopped apple and carrot mixture, oranges, raisins, and mayonaise or salad dressing; toss lightly. Chill before serving. Serve salad mixture in lettuce cups. Makes 10 to 12 servings

Apricot-Orange Mold

- 2 3-ounce packages orange-flavored gelatin
- 2 cups boiling water
- 1 11-ounce can mandarin orange sections
- 1 17-ounce can apricot halves
- ⅓ cup pecans
- 2 tablespoons lemon juice
- ½ teaspoon salt

Put gelatin in blender container; add boiling water. Blend on low speed to dissolve gelatin. Drain oranges, reserving liquid. Set oranges aside. Add reserved liquid, *undrained* apricot halves, pecans, lemon juice, and salt to mixture in blender container; blend just till pecans are chopped. Remove from blender container. Chill till partially set; fold in orange sections.

Turn mixture into a 6½-cup mold or ten to twelve individual ½-cup molds. Chill till firm. Makes 10 to 12 servings.

Green Goddess Dressing

- 1 cup mayonnaise *or* salad dressing
- ½ cup dairy sour cream
- 1 sprig parsley
- 1 2-ounce can anchovy fillets, drained
- 2 tablespoons tarragon vinegar
- 1 tablespoon lemon juice
  Dash pepper

Put all ingredients in blender container; blend till smooth. (When necessary, stop blender and use rubber spatula to scrape down sides of container.) Makes 1¾ cups.

Blender Mayonnaise

1 large egg
1 tablespoon vinegar
½ teaspoon salt
¼ teaspoon dry mustard
⅛ teaspoon paprika
  Dash cayenne
1 cup salad oil
1 tablespoon lemon juice

Put egg, vinegar, salt, dry mustard, paprika, and cayenne in blender container; blend till mixed. With blender running slowly, gradually pour *half* of the oil into blender container. (When necessary, stop blender and scrape down sides.)

Add lemon juice to mixture in blender container. Slowly pour remaining salad oil into blender container with the blender running slowly. Makes about 1¼ cups.

Blender White Sauce

Use thin sauce for soups, medium sauce for sauces and creamed dishes or vegetables, and thick sauce for croquettes and soufflés —

Thin:
1 cup milk
1 tablespoon all-purpose flour
¼ teaspoon salt
1 tablespoon butter
Medium:
1 cup milk
2 tablespoons all-purpose flour
¼ teaspoon salt
2 tablespoons butter
Thick:
1 cup milk
¼ cup all-purpose flour
¼ teaspoon salt
3 tablespoons butter

Put milk, flour, salt, and butter in blender container; blend till smooth. Pour into saucepan. Cook quickly, stirring constantly, till thickened and bubbly. Makes 1 cup.

Cottage-Herb Dressing

1 tablespoon milk
1 12-ounce carton cream-style cottage cheese
1 teaspoon lemon juice
1 thin slice onion
3 radishes, halved
1 teaspoon mixed salad herbs
1 sprig parsley

Put milk, cottage cheese, and lemon juice in blender container; blend till smooth. Add remaining ingredients and ¼ teaspoon *salt* to cottage cheese mixture in blender container; blend till vegetables are chopped. Chill. Makes 1½ cups.

Stuffed Zucchini

3 medium zucchini (1½ pounds)
24 saltine crackers
1 egg
2 ounces sharp cheddar cheese, cut into cubes (½ cup)
1 thin slice onion
1 tablespoon chopped pimiento
2 sprigs parsley
½ teaspoon salt
1 tablespoon butter, melted

Wash zucchini; cut off ends. Cook zucchini in boiling salted water for 5 minutes. Halve zucchini lengthwise; scoop out pulp and reserve. Put *half* of the crackers in blender container; blend to make coarse crumbs. Repeat with remaining crackers. Pour into bowl, reserving ¼ cup.

Place zucchini pulp, egg, cheese, onion, pimiento, parsley, salt, and dash *pepper* in blender container; blend till zucchini is coarsely chopped. Stir into crumbs in bowl. Fill zucchini shells with cheese mixture. Toss reserved ¼ cup crumbs with butter; sprinkle over top. Bake in 350° oven for 30 to 35 minutes. Makes 6 servings.

Cheesy Broccoli Fritters

1 cup milk
1 egg
2 cups all-purpose flour
2 teaspoons baking powder
¾ teaspoon salt
1½ cups fresh broccoli, cut into 1-inch pieces
  Cooking oil *or* shortening for deep-fat frying
1 cup milk
2 ounces American cheese, cut into cubes (½ cup)
2 ounces *process* Swiss cheese, cut into cubes (½ cup)
2 tablespoons all-purpose flour
2 tablespoons butter, softened

Put 1 cup milk, egg, 2 cups flour, baking powder, salt, and broccoli in blender container. Blend till broccoli is finely chopped. (When necessary, stop blender and use rubber spatula to scrape down sides of container.) Drop mixture from tablespoon into deep hot fat (375°). Fry, a few at a time, for 3 to 4 minutes or till golden brown. Drain on paper toweling.

Put 1 cup milk, American cheese, Swiss cheese, 2 tablespoons flour, and softened butter in blender container; blend till ingredients are combined. In saucepan cook and stir mixture over low heat till thickened and bubbly. Serve cheese sauce over fritters. Makes 24.

Blender White Bread

3¼ to 3½ cups all-purpose flour
1 package active dry yeast
1 cup milk
¼ cup shortening
2 tablespoons sugar
1 teaspoon salt
1 egg

Place *1½ cups* of the flour and the yeast in blender container. Switch blender on and off to combine. In saucepan heat together milk, shortening, sugar, and salt just till warm, stirring till shortening is melted. Add to dry ingredients in blender container. Add egg. Blend at low speed until combined. Blend at high speed only 4 to 5 seconds or till smooth. (When necessary, stop blender and use rubber spatula to scrape down sides of container.)

Pour the blended mixture into a large mixing bowl. By hand, stir in enough of the remaining flour to make a moderately stiff dough. Cover and let rise in warm place till double (about 45 minutes). Punch down. Turn onto lightly floured surface. Cover; let rest 10 minutes. Shape into loaf. Place in greased 9x5x3-inch loaf pan. Cover; let rise till double. Bake in 375° oven for 40 to 45 minutes. Remove from pan; cool on rack. Makes 1 loaf.

Cranberry-Pecan Bread

3 cups all-purpose flour
1 cup sugar
4 teaspoons baking powder
1 teaspoon salt
1½ cups milk
1 egg
2 tablespoons cooking oil
1 cup fresh *or* frozen cranberries
½ cup pecans

In mixing bowl stir together flour, sugar, baking powder, and salt; set aside. Place milk, egg, and oil in blender container; blend to combine. Add cranberries and nuts. Blend till cranberries are coarsely chopped. Pour blended mixture over dry ingredients; stir just to moisten. Turn batter into a greased 9x5x3-inch loaf pan. Bake in 350° oven about 1¼ hours. Remove from pan; cool on rack. Makes 1 loaf.

Carrot Muffins

The delicate carrot flavor and golden hue give these muffins special appeal —

1¾ cups all-purpose flour
2½ teaspoons baking powder
1 teaspoon salt
⅔ cup milk
⅓ cup cooking oil
1 egg
¼ cup sugar
2 medium carrots, sliced

In mixing bowl stir together flour, baking powder, and salt; set aside. Place milk, oil, egg, sugar, and carrots in blender container; blend till carrots are very finely chopped. Pour carrot mixture over dry ingredients. Mix just enough to moisten dry ingredients. Spoon mixture into greased muffin pans, filling ⅔ full. Bake in 425° oven about 25 minutes. Makes 8 to 10 muffins.

Onion Bread

2½ cups all-purpose flour
1 package onion dip mix
1 package active dry yeast
¼ teaspoon baking soda
1 cup cream-style cottage cheese
⅓ cup water
1 tablespoon butter *or* margarine
1 egg
Butter *or* margarine
Coarse salt (optional)

In blender container place *1 cup* of the flour, the dip mix, yeast, and baking soda. Switch blender on and off to combine. In saucepan heat together cottage cheese, water, and 1 tablespoon butter, stirring just till butter melts. Add to mixture in blender container; add egg. Blend at medium speed till thoroughly blended. (When necessary, stop blender and use rubber spatula to scrape down sides of container.)

Pour the blended mixture into a large mixing bowl. By hand, gradually stir in the remaining flour. Cover dough; let rise in warm place till double (about 1½ hours). Stir down. Shape into loaf and place in well-greased 8x4x2-inch loaf pan. Cover; let rise till nearly double (about 40 minutes). Bake in 350° oven for 50 to 55 minutes. Cover loaf loosely with foil during last 15 minutes to prevent over-browning of the loaf. Remove from pan; brush with additional butter. Sprinkle with coarse salt, if desired. Makes 1 loaf.

Frozen Pineapple Dessert

36 vanilla wafers
¼ cup butter *or* margarine, melted
3 egg yolks
1 15-ounce can *sweetened condensed* milk
1 6-ounce can frozen pineapple juice concentrate, thawed
2 tablespoons lemon juice
3 egg whites
2 tablespoons cold water
1 tablespoon cornstarch
1 10-ounce package frozen red raspberries, thawed
3 tablespoons sugar

Break 6 or 7 vanilla wafers into blender container; blend into fine crumbs. Transfer to mixing bowl. Repeat with remaining wafers. Toss crumbs with butter. Reserve ⅓ cup buttered crumbs; pat remainder into an 8x8x2-inch dish. Chill.

Put egg yolks, sweetened condensed milk, pineapple juice concentrate, and lemon juice in blender container; blend till mixture is smooth.

In mixing bowl beat egg whites till stiff peaks form. Fold condensed milk mixture into egg whites. Pour over crumbs in pan. Top with reserved crumbs. Cover and freeze for 8 hours.

In saucepan combine water and cornstarch. Add undrained raspberries. Cook and stir till thickened and bubbly. Remove from heat. Strain, discarding seeds. Stir in sugar; cool. Cut dessert into squares just before serving. Top with sauce. Makes 9 servings.

Orange-Pecan Pie

Piecrust mix for one 9-inch pie shell
1 medium orange
3 eggs
1 cup dark corn syrup
⅔ cup sugar
¼ cup butter, melted
1 cup whole pecans

Prepare pie shell according to package directions. Do not bake. Peel orange, reserving a 1-inch square of peel. Quarter orange; remove seeds. Put orange pieces, reserved peel, eggs, corn syrup, sugar, butter, and dash *salt* in blender container. Blend till mixture is smooth and light colored and peel is finely chopped.

Sprinkle pecans evenly in pie shell; pour egg mixture over pecans. Bake in 350° oven about 1 hour or till knife inserted near center comes out clean. Cool.

Lemon Bars Deluxe

2 cups all-purpose flour
½ cup sifted powdered sugar
1 cup butter *or* margarine
4 eggs
2 cups granulated sugar
⅓ cup lemon juice
¼ cup all-purpose flour
½ teaspoon baking powder

Stir together the 2 cups flour and the powdered sugar. Cut in butter till mixture clings together. Press in a 13x9x2-inch baking pan. Bake in 350° oven for 20 to 25 minutes or till lightly browned.

Put eggs, 2 cups granulated sugar, and lemon juice in blender; blend till thick and smooth. Stir together ¼ cup flour and baking powder. Add to blender; blend to combine. Pour over crust. Bake in 350° oven about 25 minutes. Sift additional powdered sugar atop, if desired. Cool. Makes 30 bars.

Holiday Carrot Pudding

1¼ cups all-purpose flour
1 teaspoon baking powder
½ teaspoon baking soda
½ teaspoon ground cinnamon
½ teaspoon ground nutmeg
2 eggs
¾ cup packed brown sugar
½ cup shortening
1 medium apple, peeled, cut into eighths, and cored
2 medium carrots, sliced
1 potato, peeled and cut into pieces
¾ cup raisins
Brandy Hard Sauce

In mixing bowl stir together flour, baking powder, baking soda, and spices. Place eggs, brown sugar, and shortening in blender container; blend till smooth. Add apple; blend till finely chopped. Add carrot slices; blend till coarsely chopped. Add potato pieces; blend till finely chopped. Add apple mixture and raisins to dry ingredients; mix well.

Spoon into a greased and floured 4-cup mold. Cover tightly. Place on rack in deep kettle; pour water into kettle to depth of 1 inch. Cover kettle; steam for 2½ hours. Cool pudding for 10 to 15 minutes. Unmold. Serve with Brandy Hard Sauce. Serves 8 to 10.

Brandy Hard Sauce: Place 2 tablespoons *brandy or rum* and ⅓ cup very soft *butter* in blender container; blend to combine. Add 1 cup sifted *powdered sugar*; blend till smooth. Spoon mixture into mold or small bowl; cover and chill. At serving time, unmold and sprinkle surface lightly with ground *nutmeg*.

Special cooking hint: If you prefer to use light cream instead of the brandy or rum, add vanilla or rum flavoring to taste.

Trifle

Serve this famous British specialty in your prettiest glass bowl, or use individual dessert dishes —

- 1 **frozen loaf pound cake**
- ½ **cup raspberry preserves**
- 1 **17-ounce can apricot halves, drained**
- ½ **cup dry sherry**
   Vanilla Dessert Sauce
- ¼ **cup walnuts**
- ½ **cup whipping cream**

Thaw cake. Slice pound cake horizontally into 4 layers; spread 2 layers with preserves. Top each with one of the remaining layers. Cut into 16 finger sandwiches. Put apricots in blender container; blend till coarsely chopped.

Assemble dessert using either of the following methods. *To assemble in serving bowl:* Place *half* of the sandwiches spoke-fashion in bottom of a 2-quart bowl. Sprinkle with *half* of the sherry. Place remaining sandwiches on top; sprinkle with remaining sherry. Spoon apricots over cake. Pour Vanilla Dessert Sauce over dessert. *To assemble as individual desserts:* Trim sandwiches to fit dishes. Sprinkle each dessert with about *1 tablespoon* of the sherry. Spoon apricots over cake. Spoon Vanilla Dessert Sauce over desserts. Chill Trifle for 8 hours or overnight.

Before serving, put walnuts in blender container; blend till coarsely chopped. In mixing bowl whip cream. Top Trifle with whipped cream and nuts. Makes 8 to 10 servings.

Vanilla Dessert Sauce: Place 2¾ cups *milk*, one 3⅝- or 3¾-ounce package *instant vanilla pudding mix*, and ½ teaspoon *vanilla* in blender container. Blend at high speed about 30 seconds. Chill sauce, if desired.

Anise Sugar Cookies

Spinning aniseed and sugar in the blender crushes the seed and distributes the delicate licorice flavor in one easy operation —

- 6 **vanilla wafers**
- 1 **tablespoon sugar**
- 3½ **cups all-purpose flour**
- 1 **teaspoon baking soda**
- ½ **teaspoon baking powder**
- 1 **cup sugar**
- 2 **teaspoons whole aniseed**
- ½ **cup shortening**
- 2 **eggs**
- 1 **cup dairy sour cream**
- 2 **tablespoons butter** *or* **margarine, melted**

Break the vanilla wafers into blender container. Blend till wafers are finely crushed. Transfer to small mixing bowl. Stir in the 1 tablespoon sugar; set aside.

In large mixing bowl stir together flour, baking soda, and baking powder. Place the 1 cup sugar and aniseed in blender container; blend at high speed till aniseed is crushed. Add the shortening and eggs to blender container; blend till thick and smooth. Add sour cream; blend just till combined. Stir sour cream mixture into dry ingredients; mix well. Chill dough thoroughly.

Using ½ of the dough at a time, roll out on floured pastry cloth into a 16x12-inch rectangle. Brush rolled-out dough with *half* of the melted butter. Sprinkle with *half* of the crumb mixture. Cut into 3x2-inch rectangles. Place on ungreased cookie sheet. Bake in 375° oven for 8 to 10 minutes or till lightly browned. Cool. Repeat with remaining dough, butter, and crumbs. Makes 64 cookies.

Mocha Roll

- 4 **eggs**
- ½ **teaspoon salt**
- ¾ **cup sugar**
- 1 **teaspoon vanilla**
- ¾ **cup packaged pancake mix**
   Powdered sugar
- 1½ **cups milk**
- 1 **4½-ounce package** *instant* **chocolate pudding mix**
- 1 **tablespoon instant coffee crystals**
   Powdered sugar
   Shaved chocolate

Place eggs and salt in blender container; blend till frothy. Add sugar and vanilla; blend till smooth and thick. Add pancake mix; blend to combine. Spread in greased and floured 15x10x1-inch baking pan. Bake in 400° oven for 8 to 10 minutes. Loosen sides; turn out onto towel dusted with powdered sugar. Starting at narrow end, roll cake and towel; cool.

Place milk, instant chocolate pudding mix, and coffee crystals in blender container; blend till ingredients are well combined.

Unroll cooled cake; spread with chocolate pudding mixture. Reroll cake and chill. At serving time, sift powdered sugar over cake roll. Top with shaved chocolate. Makes 10 servings.

CREPE PAN RECIPES

The next time you need a meal idea with a touch of class, serve tempting main-dish or dessert crepes. Choose Beef Stroganoff Crepes, Garden Salad Ham Crepes, Rich Cannoli Crepes, or any of the crepe pan specialties you'll find in this section — compliments are guaranteed.

crepe
basics

Elegant restaurants have long had a monopoly on crepes, but not any more. Now it's your turn to discover just how easy it is to make these tender, thin pancakes with delicious fillings and savory sauces. In no time at all you'll be duplicating the crepe masterpieces of famous chefs, and maybe even creating a few of your own.

The delicate pancake batter used for crepes is a smooth mixture of flour, eggs, milk, salt, and cooking oil or melted butter. Batter for dessert crepes usually contains a small amount of sugar, too. You also can concoct intriguing variations with ingredients such as buttermilk or cornmeal that will complement special fillings. These versions, together with basic crepe recipes, begin on page 224.

is it crêpes or crepes?

Fortunately, it's no more difficult to pronounce crepes than it is to make them. The word crêpes (rhymes with preps) is French and sounds just right with Crêpes Suzette. But thin pancakes are wraparounds for meats and sweets in a good many other countries, too, so you can call them crepes (rhymes with drapes), if you prefer.

what equipment is needed?

For hundreds of years crepes have been made in six-inch skillets, and this is still the utensil many people prefer. However, the inverted crepe pan, such as the one illustrated on page 222, deserves credit for generating much of the current popularity of crepes.

Both pans make thin, tender crepes. To make crepes in a skillet,

Crêpe Suzettes (see recipe, page 208)

simply pour and cook the batter on the inside of the pan. To make crepes with an inverted pan, dip the bottom of the pan in the batter and cook it on the outside surface.

when should you serve crepes?

Anytime! Crepe creations fit a multitude of serving situations. One time, make them small for party appetizers. Another time, serve two regular-size crepes as a satisfying entrée. Choose a flaming dessert crepe as the grand finale for a special dinner, or simply layer sliced fruit between a stack of crepes for a quick snack. You also can serve crepes wrapped around ice cream or layered with cream cheese. And you can even make crepes ahead of time to reheat later in your oven, chafing dish, or microwave oven.

how to make crepes

Each little pancake is made from about two tablespoons of batter cooked in a small skillet (see how-to drawings on page 223) or on an inverted crepe pan (see how-to drawings on page 222). A little practice with either piece of equipment will make you an expert. And, don't worry if there's an occasional break or if a bubble leaves a tiny hole while the crepe is cooking. Simply patch it with a little more batter and continue cooking a few seconds until the patch is set.

You'll notice that there's no need to flip a crepe if you make a point of spooning the filling on the unbrowned side. Then when you roll up the crepe, only the golden brown exterior will show. Likewise, when you stack several crepes, be sure to layer all but the bottom one

with unbrowned side down.

Some crepe connoisseurs insist that the secret to tender, no-stick crepes is to let the batter stand one or two hours before use. *Better Homes and Gardens* Test Kitchen experience shows that you can skip this step when preparing all of the crepe batters in this section. Granted, the batter is important, but success really depends on a seasoned skillet (or a pan with a nonstick surface) that is heated to the right temperature. Seasoning directions come with most pans that require it, but if you need more information about seasoning, refer to the tip box on page 224.

Unfilled crepes freeze well, so make up an extra batch and store them in your freezer. Just make a stack, alternating each crepe with two layers of waxed paper so they'll be easy to separate. Then seal the entire stack in a moisture-vaporproof bag. Before freezing, protect the crepes from breaking by placing the bag in a glass or plastic container. Keep crepes frozen for two to four months. To use, remove as many crepes as you need, then reseal the bag and return to the freezer. Let frozen crepes thaw about one hour before filling.

fillings and toppings

Crepe combinations come in an unbelievable variety. In fact, you can chop or slice almost any cooked meat, cooked vegetable, or fruit and roll it inside a crepe — leftovers, too.

Recipes in this section specify the type of crepe, tell how to make the filling and sauce, and then give easy-to-follow directions for assembling and serving the finished dish. Once you've mastered these recipes, experiment with new combinations of your own.

crepes
on an
inverted pan

Crepes on an inverted pan: Prepare cooking surface according to manufacturer's directions. Pour batter into a shallow bowl or pie plate. Dip heated crepe pan, rounded side down, into the batter. Hold a few seconds to be sure surface is covered with batter. Quickly turn right side up.

Set electric model on the counter top and cook crepes according to manufacturer's directions. Return the non-electric model to the range top and cook crepes 45 to 60 seconds.

When crepe is lightly browned, hold the pan over a paper towel and loosen crepe with a spatula. (If the crepe pan has a nonstick coating, be sure to use a nylon or other nonmetal utensil.) Let each crepe cool competely before stacking with two layers of waxed paper in between.

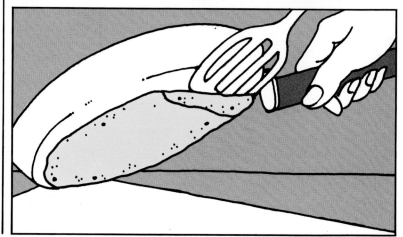

crepes
in a
skillet

Crepes in a skillet: Holding a heated skillet with one hand, pour 2 tablespoons of crepe batter into the pan. Quickly tilt and rotate the pan so that batter covers the bottom in a thin, even layer. Return skillet to heat and cook 45 to 60 seconds.

When crepe is lightly browned on the bottom, invert the pan and let the crepe drop out onto a paper towel. You may need to loosen it with a small spatula. Let each crepe cool completely before stacking with two layers of waxed paper in between.

Electric skillet crepe pan: This appliance has a heat regulator to maintain an even cooking temperature. Refer to the owner's manual for settings and timings. Follow the same quick tilting and rotating motion when pouring batter into this type of pan.

Basic Main-Dish Crepes

1½ cups milk
1 cup all-purpose flour
2 eggs
1 tablespoon cooking oil
¼ teaspoon salt

In a bowl combine milk, flour, eggs, oil, and salt; beat with a rotary beater until blended. Heat a lightly greased 6-inch skillet. Remove from heat; spoon in about 2 table-spoons batter. Lift and tilt skillet to spread batter evenly. Return to heat; brown on one side only. (Or, to cook on an inverted crepe pan, see page 202.) To remove, invert pan over a paper towel; remove crepe. Repeat with remaining bat-ter to make 16 to 18 crepes, greas-ing skillet occasionally.

Tangy Buttermilk Crepes

1 cup buttermilk
¾ cup all-purpose flour
½ cup milk
2 eggs
1 tablespoon cooking oil
1 teaspoon sugar
¼ teaspoon salt

In a bowl combine buttermilk, flour, milk, eggs, oil, sugar, and salt; beat with rotary beater till blended. Heat a lightly greased 6-inch skillet. Re-move from heat; spoon in 2 table-spoons batter. Lift and tilt skillet to spread batter. Return to heat; brown on one side only. (Or, to cook on an inverted crepe pan, see page 202.) Invert pan over a paper towel; remove crepe. Repeat to make 16 to 18 crepes, greasing skil-let occasionally.

cooking tips for crepes

Before cooking in your crepe maker or skillet for the first time, season it by rubbing it generously with cooking oil. Then, heat it over medium heat for 5 minutes. Remove from heat and allow to cool.

Use the water-drop test to determine when the crepe pan is at the right cooking temperature. As the pan is preheating over medium heat, sprinkle a few drops of water in the pan. If the drops sizzle and bounce, the pan is at the right temperature.

When cooking crepes, brown them on one side only. When done, the tops will look dry and the edges will curl; this takes 45 to 60 seconds.

Basic Dessert Crepes

1½ cups milk
1 cup all-purpose flour
2 eggs
2 tablespoons sugar
1 tablespoon cooking oil
⅛ teaspoon salt

In a bowl combine milk, flour, eggs, sugar, oil, and salt; beat with a ro-tary beater till blended. Heat a lightly greased 6-inch skillet. Re-move from heat. Spoon in 2 table-spoons batter; lift and tilt skillet to spread batter. Return to heat; brown on one side only. (Or, to cook on an inverted crepe pan, see page 202.) Invert pan over a paper towel; remove crepe. Repeat to make 16 to 18 crepes, greasing skil-let occasionally.

Fluffy All-Purpose Crepes

3 eggs, separated
1 cup milk
¾ cup all-purpose flour
2 tablespoons cooking oil
1 teaspoon sugar
⅛ teaspoon salt

Beat egg whites till stiff peaks form; set aside. In a bowl combine egg yolks, milk, flour, oil, sugar, and salt; beat with rotary beater till blended. Fold in stiff-beaten egg whites. Heat a lightly greased 6-inch skillet. Remove from heat. Spoon in 2 tablespoons batter; lift and tilt skil-let to spread batter. Return to heat; brown on one side only. (Or, to cook on an inverted crepe pan, see page 202.) Invert over a paper towel; remove crepe. Repeat with remaining batter to make 20 crepes, greasing skillet often.

Yellow Cornmeal Crepes

1½ cups milk
⅓ cup all-purpose flour
⅔ cup yellow cornmeal
2 eggs
1 tablespoon cooking oil
¼ teaspoon salt

In a bowl combine milk, flour, cornmeal, eggs, oil, and salt; beat with rotary beater till blended. Heat a lightly greased 6-inch skillet (don't use an inverted crepe pan). Remove from heat. Spoon in about 2 table-spoons batter; lift and tilt skillet to spread batter evenly. Return to heat; brown on one side only. Invert pan over a paper towel; remove crepe. Repeat to make 16 to 18 crepes, greasing pan occasion-ally. Stir batter frequently to keep cornmeal from settling. Don't freeze these crepes.

main-dish
crepes

Chicken Crepes with Rum Sauce

- 4 whole medium chicken breasts, skinned, boned, halved lengthwise, and cut into strips
- 2 tablespoons cooking oil
- 1 cup chopped onion
- 1 clove garlic, minced
- 1 16-ounce can tomatoes, cut up
- 2 tablespoons lime juice
- 1 teaspoon salt
- ½ teaspoon dried oregano, crushed
- ⅛ teaspoon pepper
- ¼ cup raisins
- 1 8¼-ounce can pineapple chunks
- ⅓ cup rum
- ¼ cup cold water
- 2 tablespoons all-purpose flour
- 10 to 12 Basic Main-Dish Crepes (see recipe, page 204)

For Sauce: In a skillet brown the chicken lightly in oil. Add onion and garlic; cook until onion is tender. Drain tomatoes; reserve liquid. Set tomatoes aside. Add reserved liquid, lime juice, salt, oregano, and pepper to chicken. Cover and simmer for 10 minutes. Add tomatoes and raisins. Simmer, covered, for 15 minutes. Remove chicken; set aside. Cut up pineapple; add to sauce with rum. Blend cold water into flour; stir into sauce. Cook and stir till thickened and bubbly.

To assemble: Divide chicken among crepes, placing strips along center of the unbrowned side of each crepe. Fold two opposite edges of each crepe to overlap atop filling. Place in skillet with sauce. Spoon sauce over. Cover and heat through. Makes 5 or 6 servings.

Elegant Crepes Divan

- 1 10¾-ounce can condensed cream of chicken soup
- 1 teaspoon Worcestershire sauce
  Dash ground nutmeg
- 1 8-ounce package frozen cut asparagus
- 2 cups chopped cooked turkey *or* chicken
- 12 Tangy Buttermilk Crepes (see recipe, page 204)
- ½ cup grated Parmesan cheese
- ½ cup whipping cream
- ½ cup mayonnaise *or* salad dressing

For sauce: Blend together soup, Worcestershire, and nutmeg.

For filling: Cook asparagus according to package directions; drain. Combine asparagus and turkey or chicken. Blend in ¼ *cup* of the sauce.

To assemble: Spoon about ¼ cup filling along center of the unbrowned side of each crepe. Fold crepes in half. Place crepes in a 13x9x2-inch baking dish. Spoon remaining sauce over crepes. Top with *half* of the cheese. Bake, covered, in 375° oven 25 to 30 minutes or till heated through. Whip cream till soft peaks form; fold in mayonnaise or salad dressing. Spread over crepes. Top with remaining cheese. Broil 3 to 4 inches from heat 2 to 3 minutes or till golden. Makes 6 servings.

Curried Turkey Stack-Ups

  Yellow Cornmeal Crepes batter (see recipe, page 204)
- ¼ cup chopped onion
- ¼ cup chopped green pepper
- 1 small clove garlic, minced
- 2 tablespoons butter
- 2 cups chopped cooked turkey
- 1 16-ounce can tomatoes, cut up
- 2 tablespoons dried currants
- 2 tablespoons snipped parsley
- 1 to 2 teaspoons curry powder
- 1 teaspoon salt
- ⅛ teaspoon pepper
  Dash ground mace
- 2 tablespoons cold water
- 1 tablespoon cornstarch
- ½ cup shredded American cheese

For crepes: Using 1 tablespoon batter for each, prepare 24 crepes by spooning batter into a hot lightly greased 6-inch skillet, spreading batter with the back of a spoon to make a *4-inch circle.* Brown on one side only.

For sauce: In a saucepan cook onion, green pepper, and garlic in butter till tender but not brown. Stir in turkey, *undrained* tomatoes, currants, parsley, curry powder, salt, pepper, and mace. Cook, stirring occasionally, till heated through. Blend cold water into cornstarch; stir into turkey mixture. Cook, stirring constantly, till mixture is bubbly.

To assemble: Arrange 4 crepes in a single layer, browned side down, in a 13x9x2-inch baking dish. Spread 2 tablespoons sauce over each crepe. Repeat layering crepes *(browned side up)* and sauce four more times, ending with sauce. Add another crepe to each stack, making four stacks of 6 crepes each. Sprinkle *each* stack with *2 tablespoons* of the cheese. Bake, uncovered, in 350° oven for 15 to 20 minutes or till heated through. Makes 4 servings.

Garden Salad Ham Crepes

- 2 cups sliced cauliflower flowerets (½ medium head)
- 2 tablespoons chopped onion
- 2 tablespoons cooking oil
- 2 tablespoons cornstarch
- 1 tablespoon sugar
- 1 teaspoon prepared mustard
- ½ teaspoon garlic salt
  Dash pepper
- ¾ cup water
- ⅓ cup vinegar
- 2 cups diced fully cooked ham
- 3 cups shredded lettuce
- 12 Basic Main-Dish Crepes (see recipe, page 204)
  Grated Parmesan cheese
- 1 cup halved cherry tomatoes

For sauce: Cook cauliflower in boiling salted water 6 to 7 minutes or till crisp-tender. Drain; set aside. In a 2-quart saucepan cook onion in hot oil till tender. Blend in cornstarch, sugar, mustard, garlic salt, and pepper. Stir in water and vinegar. Cook and stir till thickened and bubbly. Stir in ham and cauliflower; heat through.

To assemble: Place about ¼ cup lettuce along center of the unbrowned side of crepe. Roll up crepe. Place seam side down on serving platter. Repeat with remaining crepes and lettuce. Spoon sauce over crepes. Sprinkle with Parmesan; garnish with tomatoes. Makes 6 servings.

Shrimp Chow Mein Dinner

- 6 to 8 Basic Main-Dish Crepes (see recipe, page 204)
- 1½ pounds fresh **or** frozen shelled shrimp
- ¼ cup cooking oil
- 1 16-ounce can bean sprouts, drained
- 2 cups sliced fresh mushrooms
- 1 cup shredded cabbage **or** bok choy
- 1 6-ounce package frozen pea pods, thawed and halved crosswise
- 1 medium onion, sliced and halved
- ½ cup sliced water chestnuts
- 1 clove garlic, minced
- 1 13¾-ounce can chicken broth
- ¼ cup soy sauce
- ¼ teaspoon salt
- 3 tablespoons cornstarch
- ½ cup slivered almonds, toasted
  Soy sauce

For baked crepe cups: Invert a custard cup on a baking sheet. Generously grease outside of custard cup. Place a crepe, brown side up, atop cup. Press crepe lightly to fit cup. Repeat with remaining crepes. Bake in 375° oven 20 to 22 minutes or till crisp.

For sauce: Thaw shrimp, if frozen; halve lengthwise, if desired. Cook and stir shrimp in hot oil for 1 to 2 minutes; remove. Add bean sprouts, mushrooms, cabbage or bok choy, pea pods, onion, water chestnuts, and garlic to oil. Cook and stir 2 to 3 minutes. Add *1¼ cups* of the chicken broth, ¼ cup soy, and salt. Cover; simmer 6 to 8 minutes. Add shrimp to vegetables. Blend remaining broth into cornstarch; stir into mixture in skillet. Cook and stir till mixture is bubbly.

To assemble: Serve shrimp mixture in baked crepe cups; garnish with almonds. Pass additional soy sauce. Makes 6 to 8 servings.

Avocado-Sauced Tuna Crepes

- 1 cup dairy sour cream
- 1 tablespoon snipped parsley
- ¼ teaspoon onion powder
- 1 9¼-ounce can tuna, drained and flaked
- ¼ cup finely chopped celery
- 8 Yellow Cornmeal Crepes (see recipe, page 204)
- 1 6-ounce carton frozen avocado dip, thawed
  Dash bottled hot pepper sauce
  Avocado slices (optional)
  Watercress (optional)

For filling: Combine ¾ *cup* of the sour cream, the snipped parsley, and onion powder. Fold in the tuna and chopped celery.

To assemble: Spread about 3 tablespoons tuna filling over the unbrowned side of crepe, leaving a ¼-inch rim around edge. Roll up crepe jelly-roll style. Place seam side down in a 10x6x2-inch baking dish. Repeat with remaining crepes and filling. Cover with foil. Bake in 350° oven for 20 to 25 minutes.

For sauce: Combine avocado dip, pepper sauce, and remaining ¼ cup sour cream. Spoon avocado sauce over hot crepes. Garnish with avocado slices and watercress, if desired. Makes 4 servings.

Beef Stroganoff Crepes

1 pound beef sirloin steak
1 tablespoon all-purpose flour
½ teaspoon salt
2 tablespoons butter **or** margarine
1 2½-ounce jar sliced mushrooms, drained
½ cup chopped onion
1 clove garlic, minced
2 tablespoons butter **or** margarine
2 tablespoons all-purpose flour
1 tablespoon tomato paste
¾ cup beef broth
½ cup dairy sour cream
2 tablespoons dry white wine
12 Basic Main-Dish Crepes (see recipe, page 204)

For filling: Partially freeze steak. Thinly slice steak into bite-size strips. Coat meat strips with mixture of the 1 tablespoon all-purpose flour and salt. In skillet quickly brown beef on both sides in 2 tablespoons butter or margarine. Add mushrooms, onion, and garlic. Cook till onion is crisp-tender. Remove mixture from skillet. Melt 2 tablespoons butter or margarine in skillet; blend in 2 tablespoons all-purpose flour and tomato paste. Add beef broth. Cook and stir till thickened and bubbly. Stir in dairy sour cream and dry white wine. Return meat mixture to pan.

To assemble: Spoon about 3 tablespoons filling along center of the unbrowned side of crepe. Fold two opposite edges to overlap atop filling. Place seam side down in a 13x9x2-inch baking dish. Repeat with remaining crepes and filling. Cover; bake in 375° oven 15 to 20 minutes or till heated through. Garnish individual servings with additional sour cream, if desired. Makes 6 servings.

Crepe-Style Manicotti

½ pound ground beef
½ cup chopped onion
1 small clove garlic, minced
1 8-ounce can tomatoes, cut up
1 6-ounce can tomato paste
½ cup water
1½ teaspoons dried basil, crushed
¾ teaspoon salt
½ teaspoon sugar
¼ teaspoon fennel seed, crushed
2 beaten eggs
3 cups ricotta cheese **or** cream-style cottage cheese
¼ cup grated Parmesan cheese
1 tablespoon dried parsley flakes
½ teaspoon salt
¼ teaspoon pepper
16 Basic Main-Dish Crepes (see recipe, page 204)
1 cup shredded mozzarella cheese

For sauce: Brown ground beef with onion and garlic. Drain. Add undrained tomatoes, tomato paste, water, basil, ¾ teaspoon salt, sugar, and fennel. Simmer, covered, about 15 minutes, stirring the mixture often.

For filling: Mix eggs, ricotta or cottage cheese, Parmesan, parsley, ½ teaspoon salt, and pepper.

To Assemble: Spoon about 3 tablespoons filling along center of the unbrowned side of crepe. Fold two opposite edges to overlap atop filling. Place seam side down in a 13x9x2-inch baking dish. Repeat with remaining crepes and filling. Spoon sauce over. Cover; bake in 375° oven for 25 minutes. Uncover; sprinkle with mozzarella. Bake till cheese melts. Makes 8 servings.

Lamb with Tarragon Sauce

1 pound lamb stew meat, cut into ½-inch cubes
1 cup chopped onion
1 cup chopped carrot
½ cup chopped celery
2 tablespoons snipped parsley
1½ teaspoons salt
1 teaspoon dried oregano, crushed
1¼ teaspoons dried tarragon, crushed
1 bay leaf
10 Basic Main-Dish Crepes (see recipe, page 204)
1 tablespoon butter
1 tablespoon all-purpose flour
1 teaspoon sugar
2 tablespoons dry sherry
1 beaten egg yolk

For filling: Combine lamb, onion, carrot, celery, parsley, salt, oregano, 1 teaspoon tarragon, and bay leaf. Add 3 cups water. Cover; simmer about 50 minutes or till meat is tender. Season to taste. Strain meat and vegetables, reserving ¾ cup cooking liquid; set liquid aside.

To assemble: Spoon about 3 tablespoons lamb-vegetable mixture down center of the unbrowned side of each crepe. Fold two opposite edges of each crepe to overlap atop filling. Place crepes seam side down in a 12x7½x2-inch baking dish. Cover; bake in 375° oven about 25 minutes or till hot.

For sauce: In a small saucepan melt butter or margarine; stir in flour, sugar, and remaining ¼ teaspoon tarragon. Stir in the reserved cooking liquid and sherry. Cook and stir till thickened and bubbly. Gradually stir about half of the hot mixture into beaten egg yolk; return to hot mixture. Cook and stir 1 to 2 minutes more. To serve, pour hot sauce over crepes. Serves 5.

dessert
crepes

Chocolate Eclair Crepes

⅓ cup sugar
1 tablespoon all-purpose flour
1 tablespoon cornstarch
¼ teaspoon salt
1½ cups milk
1 slightly beaten egg yolk
1 teaspoon vanilla
½ cup whipping cream
12 Fluffy All-Purpose Crepes (see recipe, page 204)
½ cup sugar
4 teaspoons cornstarch
½ cup water
1 1-ounce square unsweetened chocolate, chopped
Dash salt
1 tablespoon butter or margarine
½ teaspoon vanilla

For filling: In a saucepan combine ⅓ cup sugar, flour, 1 tablespoon cornstarch, and ¼ teaspoon salt. Slowly stir in milk. Cook and stir till bubbly; cook and stir 2 to 3 minutes more. Stir *half* into egg yolk; return to saucepan. Cook and stir just till bubbly. Stir in 1 teaspoon vanilla; cool. Beat smooth. Whip cream till soft peaks form; fold into filling.

To assemble: Spoon 3 tablespoons filling along center of the unbrowned side of each crepe. Fold two opposite edges to overlap atop filling. With wide spatula, transfer to baking sheet. Chill.

For glaze: In a small saucepan combine ½ cup sugar and 4 teaspoons cornstarch. Stir in water, chocolate, and dash salt. Cook and stir till thickened and bubbly. Remove from heat; stir in butter or margarine and ½ teaspoon vanilla. While hot, spread glaze over crepes. Chill. Makes 12 servings.

Crêpes Suzette
Pictured on page 200 —

¼ cup butter or margarine
¼ cup orange liqueur
¼ cup orange juice
3 tablespoons sugar
8 Basic Dessert Crepes (see recipe, page 204)
2 tablespoons brandy

For sauce: In a skillet or chafing dish combine butter or margarine, orange liqueur, orange juice, and sugar; cook and stir till bubbly.

To assemble: Fold a crepe in half, browned side out; fold in half again, forming a triangle. Repeat with remaining crepes; arrange in sauce in skillet or chafing dish. Simmer till sauce thickens slightly, spooning over crepes. In a small saucepan heat brandy over low heat just till hot. Ignite and pour over crepes and sauce. Serves 4.

Cherry-Topped Blintzes

Cheese Filling
12 Basic Dessert Crepes (see recipe, page 204)
2 tablespoons butter
Canned cherry pie filling
Dairy sour cream

To assemble: Spoon some Cheese Filling in center of the unbrowned side of crepe. Fold two opposite edges of crepe to overlap atop filling. Fold in remaining edges, forming a square packet; repeat with remaining crepes and filling. In a skillet cook filled crepes on both sides in butter till heated through. Serve crepes with warm pie filling and sour cream. Serves 6.

Cheese Filling: Combine 1 beaten *egg*, one 12-ounce carton *dry cottage cheese*, 2 tablespoons *sugar*, ½ teaspoon *vanilla*, and dash ground *cinnamon*. Beat till nearly smooth.

Orange-Chocolate Crepes

1 cup granulated sugar
¼ cup cornstarch
½ teaspoon salt
1½ teaspoons finely shredded orange peel (set aside)
1 cup orange juice
2 tablespoons butter or margarine
1 tablespoon lemon juice
12 Basic Dessert Crepes (see recipe, page 204)
1 1-ounce square unsweetened chocolate
2 tablespoons butter or margarine
1½ cups sifted powdered sugar
1 teaspoon vanilla
Boiling water

For filling: In a saucepan combine granulated sugar, cornstarch, and salt. Add orange juice. Cook and stir till thickened. Stir in 2 tablespoons butter or margarine, lemon juice, and orange peel; cover surface with plastic wrap. Cool without stirring.

To assemble: Spread about 2 tablespoons filling over the unbrowned side of crepe, leaving a ¼-inch rim around edge. Roll up jelly roll style. Place seam side down on waxed paper. Repeat with remaining crepes and filling.

For glaze: Melt chocolate and 2 tablespoons butter or margarine over low heat, stirring constantly. Remove from heat. Stir in powdered sugar and vanilla till crumbly. Stir in 3 tablespoons boiling water. Add about 1 tablespoon more boiling water, a teaspoon at a time, till glaze is of pouring consistency. Drizzle about 1 tablespoon glaze over each crepe; chill. Makes 12 servings.

Cherry-Topped Blintzes

Rich Cannoli Crepes

- ¾ cup sugar
- 3 tablespoons cornstarch
- ¾ cup milk
- 16 ounces ricotta cheese
- 1½ teaspoons vanilla
- ½ cup semisweet chocolate pieces, coarsely chopped
- 2 tablespoons finely chopped candied citron
- 12 Basic Dessert Crepes (see recipe, page 204)
  Sweetened whipped cream
- 2 tablespoons finely chopped pistachio nuts

For filling: In a saucepan mix sugar and cornstarch; stir in milk. Cook and stir till thickened; cook 1 minute more. Cover surface with clear plastic wrap or waxed paper; cool without stirring. With electric mixer beat ricotta and vanilla till creamy; stir in cornstarch mixture. Stir in chocolate and citron. Cover; chill.

To assemble: Spoon ¼ cup filling along center of the unbrowned side of crepe. Fold two opposite edges to overlap atop filling. Place seam side down in dessert dish. Repeat with remaining crepes and filling. Top with whipped cream and nuts. (If desired, tint nuts green with food coloring.) Makes 12 servings.

Lemon Meringue Crepes

- 1¾ cups sugar
- 3 tablespoons cornstarch
- 3 tablespoons all-purpose flour
  Dash salt
- 1½ cups water
- 2 egg yolks
- 1 egg
- 2 tablespoons butter
- ½ teaspoon finely shredded lemon peel
- ⅓ cup lemon juice
- 12 Basic Dessert Crepes (see recipe, page 204)
- 2 egg whites
- ½ teaspoon vanilla
- ¼ teaspoon cream of tartar

For filling: In a saucepan combine *1½ cups* of the sugar, cornstarch, flour, and salt; stir in water. Cook and stir over high heat till boiling. Reduce heat; cook and stir 2 minutes more. Slightly beat egg yolks and egg. Stir in *1 cup* hot mixture; immediately return to saucepan. Bring to boiling; cook 2 minutes, stirring constantly. Remove from heat. Add butter and lemon peel. Slowly stir in lemon juice; pour into bowl. Place clear plastic wrap or waxed paper directly on top of filling; smooth paper to touch side of bowl. Cool, then chill.

To assemble: Place 1 crepe, browned side down, on a foil-lined baking sheet. Spread with ¼ cup filling. Layer crepes, *browned side up*, and filling 4 more times, ending with filling. Top with a crepe. Repeat for second stack.

For topping: In a mixing bowl beat egg whites, vanilla, and cream of tartar with electric mixer till soft peaks form. Gradually add remaining ¼ cup sugar; beat till stiff peaks form. Spread or pipe egg white mixture on top of each crepe stack. Broil 4 or 5 inches from heat 1 to 2 minutes or till golden. Serve at once or chill. Serves 8.

Rhubarb-Strawberry Crepes

- 2 egg yolks
- ½ cup sifted powdered sugar
- ½ teaspoon vanilla
  Dash salt
- ½ cup whipping cream
- ⅔ cup granulated sugar
- 2 tablespoons cornstarch
- 2 cups sliced rhubarb
- 1 cup sliced strawberries
- ¼ cup water
- 12 Basic Dessert Crepes (see recipe, page 204)

For sauce: Beat together egg yolks, powdered sugar, vanilla, and salt till thick and light colored. Beat whipping cream till stiff peaks form; fold into yolk mixture. Chill.

For filling: In a saucepan stir together granulated sugar and cornstarch; stir in sliced rhubarb, sliced strawberries, and water. Cook and stir till mixture is thickened and bubbly. Reduce heat; cook 2 to 3 minutes longer.

To assemble: Spoon about 3 tablespoons filling along center of unbrowned side of crepe. Fold two opposite edges of crepe to overlap atop filling. Place seam side down in a 12x7½x2-inch baking dish. Repeat with remaining crepes and filling. Bake, covered, in 375° oven about 15 minutes or till heated through. Top each serving with chilled sauce. Makes 6 servings.

Beef- and Shrimp-Filled Wontons (see recipe, page 223)

WOK RECIPES

Cooking in a wok is as exciting as the results are great tasting. You can use your wok for several different methods of Oriental cooking; stir-frying entrées, deep- and shallow-fat-frying appetizers, simmering main dishes and soups, and steaming meat and vegetables. This section features all of them.

cooking in a wok

caring for your wok

A new wok must be seasoned before its first use. First, scrub your wok with cleanser or scouring pads to remove the rust-resistant coating applied during manufacturing. Then wipe the wok and heat it on the range to dry.

Season the wok by heating two tablespoons of cooking oil in the pan. Tilt and rotate the wok till the entire inner surface is coated. Cool the wok and dry it with paper toweling.

After each use, soak your wok in hot soapy water. Then use a bamboo brush or sponge to clean it. Rinse, hand-dry, and heat the wok on the range to dry excess water. Then rub a teaspoon of cooking oil over the inner surface.

skillet cooking

Although the wok is the traditional utensil for Oriental cooking, you can enjoy the fun of preparing Oriental foods even if you don't own one. Any recipe that's cooked in a wok also can be prepared in a skillet. Just be sure to choose a large heavy skillet with deep sides, and keep the food moving constantly. This technique helps ensure that all the ingredients are cooked as quickly and evenly as possible.

using a cleaver

Watching a skilled cook use a cleaver is fascinating. While it will take some practice, you can easily learn the smooth, rhythmic cleaver motion used to slice, chop, bias-slice, and roll-cut.

To hold cleaver and the food, grasp the cleaver blade between your thumb and index finger and wrap the remaining three fingers around the handle. With your other hand, hold the food with your fingertips curled under and your knuckles against the blade.

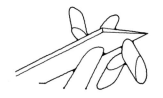

To bias-slice, make angle cuts at regular intervals (see sketch above).

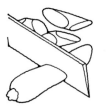

To roll-cut, make an angle cut and then give the food a quarter- to half-turn before angle-cutting again (see sketch above).

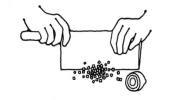

To chop, first slice and then move the cleaver in a seesaw motion till the food is chopped (see sketch above).

adjusting your wok

Heating your wok to the proper temperature is easy if you follow these guidelines.

For *gas* ranges, place the wide end of the ring stand *down* over the largest burner (see sketch above). Then place your wok in the stand and turn the heat to the highest setting. Heat the wok a few minutes. Then add cooking oil and allow it to heat a few minutes more.

For *electric* ranges, place the wide end of your ring stand *up* over the largest burner (see sketch above) and place the wok inside the stand. This allows the wok to sit closer to the electric coil. Then turn the heat to the highest setting and proceed as for a gas range.

stir-fried classics

Stir-Fried Shrimp with Vegetables

- 2 medium carrots
- 1 cup fresh mushrooms
- 1 pound fresh *or* frozen shrimp in shells
- ½ cup chicken broth
- 1 tablespoon cornstarch
- ¼ cup soy sauce
- 2 tablespoons cooking oil
- 1 clove garlic, minced
- 1 teaspoon grated gingerroot
- 1 cup thinly sliced cauliflower
- 2 cups chopped bok choy
- 1 cup fresh pea pods *or* one 6-ounce package frozen pea pods, thawed
- 1 cup fresh bean sprouts *or* ½ of a 16-ounce can bean sprouts

Thinly slice carrots and mushrooms. Thaw shrimp, if frozen. Shell and devein shrimp. Halve shrimp lengthwise. Blend chicken broth into cornstarch; stir in soy sauce and set aside.

Preheat wok or large skillet over high heat; add oil. Stir-fry garlic and gingerroot in hot oil for 30 seconds. Add cauliflower and carrots (see sketch in tip box); stir-fry 3 minutes. Add bok choy, pea pods, mushrooms, and bean sprouts; stir-fry 2 minutes more or till vegetables are crisp-tender (be sure to keep heat high throughout). Remove vegetables to bowl. (Add more oil to wok or skillet, if necessary.) Add shrimp to *hot* wok or skillet; stir-fry 7 to 8 minutes or till shrimp are done. Push shrimp away from center of wok or skillet.

Stir chicken broth mixture and add to center of wok or skillet (see sketch in tip box). Cook and stir till thickened and bubbly. Stir in vegetables; cover and cook 1 minute. Serve at once. Serves 4.

how to stir-fry

To stir-fry, use a long-handled spoon or spatula to frequently lift and turn the food with a folding motion, as shown.

Be sure to maintain high heat so food cooks quickly. Push food from the center of the wok or skillet. Then, pour in the thickening mixture, as shown.

Let it bubble slightly before stirring into food.

Stir-Fried Shrimp with Pineapple

- 1 pound fresh *or* frozen shrimp in shells
- 1 8¼-ounce can pineapple chunks
- 2 teaspoons cornstarch
- 3 tablespoons soy sauce
- 2 tablespoons cooking oil
- 1 teaspoon grated gingerroot
- 8 green onions, bias-sliced into 1½-inch lengths
- 1 8-ounce can water chestnuts, drained and sliced

Thaw shrimp, if frozen. Shell and devein shrimp. Halve shrimp lengthwise. Drain pineapple, reserving liquid. Blend reserved pineapple liquid into cornstarch; stir in soy sauce and set aside.

Preheat wok or large skillet over high heat; add oil. Stir-fry gingerroot in hot oil for 30 seconds. Add green onion; stir-fry 1 minute. Add water chestnuts; stir-fry 1 minute more. Remove green onion and water chestnuts. (Add more oil, if necessary.) Add shrimp to *hot* wok or skillet; stir-fry 7 to 8 minutes or till shrimp are done. Stir soy sauce mixture and stir into shrimp in wok or skillet. Cook and stir till thickened and bubbly. Stir in pineapple, green onion, and water chestnuts; cover and cook 2 minutes more. Serve at once. Makes 4 servings.

Sukiyaki

- ½ pound beef top round steak
- ½ teaspoon instant beef bouillon granules
- ¼ cup boiling water
- 3 tablespoons soy sauce
- 1 tablespoon sugar
- 2 tablespoons cooking oil
- 3 cups thinly sliced bok choy
- 1 cup green onions, bias sliced into 1-inch lengths
- ½ cup bias-sliced celery
- 8 ounces fresh tofu (bean curd), cubed
- 1 cup fresh bean sprouts *or* ½ of a 16-ounce can bean sprouts, drained
- ½ of an 8-ounce can bamboo shoots, drained
- ½ cup thinly sliced fresh mushrooms
- ½ of an 8-ounce can water chestnuts, drained and thinly sliced

Partially freeze beef. Slice beef very thinly across the grain into bite-size strips. Dissolve beef bouillon granules in boiling water; add soy sauce and sugar.

Preheat a wok or large skillet over high heat; add oil. Add bok choy, green onions, and celery; stir-fry 2 minutes. Remove bok choy, green onions, and celery. Add tofu, bean sprouts, bamboo shoots, mushrooms, and water chestnuts; stir-fry 1 minute. Remove vegetables. (Add more oil, if necessary.) Add the beef to *hot* wok or skillet; stir-fry 2 minutes or till meat is just browned. Stir beef bouillon mixture; stir into beef. Cook and stir till bubbly. Stir in vegetables. Cover and cook for 1 minute or till just heated through. Serve at once. Makes 2 or 3 servings.

Spicy Beef and Asparagus

- 1 pound beef top round steak
- 1 egg white
- 1 tablespoon cornstarch
- 1 teaspoon dry sherry
  Several dashes bottled hot pepper sauce
- 1 tablespoon soy sauce
- 1 tablespoon catsup
- 1 teaspoon red wine vinegar
- ½ teaspoon sugar
- 2 tablespoons cooking oil
- 1 clove garlic, minced
- ¾ pound fresh asparagus, cut into 1-inch lengths, *or* one 10-ounce package frozen cut asparagus, thawed
- 1 cup thinly sliced fresh mushrooms *or* one 4½-ounce can sliced mushrooms, drained
- ¼ cup thinly sliced green onion

Partially freeze meat; thinly slice meat across the grain into bite-size strips. In a bowl combine beef strips, egg white, cornstarch, dry sherry, hot pepper sauce, ½ teaspoon *salt*, and ½ teaspoon *pepper*. By hand, work the seasonings into the meat. Combine soy, catsup, vinegar, and sugar; set aside.

Preheat a wok or large skillet over high heat; add oil. Stir-fry garlic in hot oil for 30 seconds. Add asparagus, mushrooms, and green onion; stir-fry about 6 minutes or till asparagus is crisp-tender (less time is required if using frozen asparagus). Remove asparagus and mushrooms. (Add oil, if necessary.) Add *half* of the meat to *hot* wok or skillet; stir-fry 2 to 3 minutes or till meat is just browned. Remove meat. Stir-fry remaining meat 2 to 3 minutes. Return meat to wok or skillet. Stir soy sauce mixture; stir into beef. Cook and stir till bubbly. Stir in vegetables. Cover and cook for 1 minute or till just heated through. Serve at once. Serves 4 to 6.

Beef-Cucumber Stir-Fry

- 1 pound beef top round steak
- 2 medium cucumbers
- ¼ teaspoon instant beef bouillon granules
- ¼ cup boiling water
- 3 tablespoons soy sauce
- 2 tablespoons dry sherry
- 2 teaspoons cornstarch
- 2 tablespoons cooking oil
- 1 clove garlic, minced
- 8 green onions, bias sliced into 1-inch lengths
- ½ cup coarsely shredded carrot

Partially freeze beef. Slice beef very thinly across the grain into bite-size strips. Peel cucumbers; cut cucumbers into 1-inch-thick slices and seed. Dissolve bouillon in boiling water. Blend soy sauce and sherry into cornstarch; stir into beef bouillon. Set aside. Preheat a wok or large skillet over high heat; add oil. Stir-fry garlic in hot oil for 30 seconds. Add green onions and carrot; stir-fry 1½ minutes. Add cucumbers; stir-fry 30 seconds more. Remove onions, carrot, and cucumbers. (Add more oil, if necessary.) Add *half* of the beef to *hot* wok or skillet; stir-fry 2 to 3 minutes or till browned. Remove beef. Stir-fry remaining beef 2 to 3 minutes. Return all meat to wok or skillet. Stir bouillon mixture; stir into beef. Cook and stir till thickened and bubbly. Stir in onions, cucumbers, and carrot; cover and cook 2 minutes. Makes 4 to 6 servings.

Beef with Peanuts

- 1 **pound beef top round steak**
- 1 **teaspoon instant beef bouillon granules**
- ½ **cup boiling water**
- 2 **tablespoons soy sauce**
- 1 **tablespoon cornstarch**
- 2 **tablespoons cooking oil**
- ½ **cup raw peanuts**
- ½ **cup chopped onion**
- 1 **clove garlic, minced**
- 4 **cups chopped bok choy**
- 2 **cups fresh bean sprouts *or* one 16-ounce can bean sprouts, drained**

Partially freeze beef; slice thinly across the grain into bite-size strips. Dissolve bouillon granules in water. Blend soy sauce into cornstarch; stir in bouillon. Set aside.

Preheat a wok or large skillet over high heat; add cooking oil. Stir-fry peanuts over high heat in hot oil for 2 to 3 minutes or till lightly browned. Remove peanuts. Add onion and garlic; stir-fry 1 minute. Add bok choy; stir-fry 1 minute more. Add bean sprouts; stir-fry 1 minute more. Remove vegetables. (Add more oil, if necessary.) Add *half* of the beef to *hot* wok or skillet; stir-fry 2 to 3 minutes or till browned. Remove beef. Stir-fry remaining beef 2 to 3 minutes. Return all meat to wok or skillet. Stir soy sauce mixture; stir into beef. Cook and stir till thickened and bubbly. Stir in vegetables; cover and cook for 1 minute. Stir in peanuts. Serve at once. Makes 6 servings.

Stir-Fried Tomato and Beef

- 1 **pound beef top round steak**
- ½ **teaspoon instant beef bouillon granules**
- ⅓ **cup boiling water**
- ¼ **cup soy sauce**
- 1 **tablespoon cornstarch**
- 2 **tablespoons cooking oil**
- 1 **teaspoon grated gingerroot**
- 6 **green onions, bias sliced into 1-inch lengths**
- ½ **cup shredded carrot**
- 1 **large green pepper, cut into narrow strips**
- ½ **cup thinly sliced celery**
- 2 **tomatoes, cut into wedges**

Partially freeze beef; slice thinly across the grain into bite-size strips. Dissolve bouillon granules in water. Blend soy sauce into cornstarch; stir in bouillon. Set aside.

Preheat a wok or large skillet over high heat; add cooking oil. Stir-fry gingerroot in hot oil 30 seconds. Add green onions and carrot; stir-fry 2 minutes. Remove green onions and carrot. Add green pepper and celery; stir-fry 2 minutes. Remove green pepper and celery. (Add more oil, if necessary.) Add *half* of the beef to *hot* wok or skillet; stir-fry 2 to 3 minutes or till browned. Remove beef. Stir-fry remaining beef 2 to 3 minutes. Return all meat to wok or skillet. Stir soy sauce mixture; stir into beef. Cook and stir till thickened and bubbly. Stir in green onions, carrot, green pepper, celery, and tomatoes; cover and cook for 1 minute. Serve at once. Makes 4 servings.

Beef with Pea Pods

- 1 **pound beef top round steak**
- 2 **teaspoons cornstarch**
- 1 **teaspoon sugar**
- 2 **tablespoons soy sauce**
- 2 **tablespoons cooking oil**
- 1 **clove garlic, minced**
- ½ **teaspoon grated gingerroot**
- 2 **cups fresh pea pods *or* one 6-ounce package frozen pea pods, thawed**
- ½ **of an 8-ounce can (½ cup) water chestnuts, drained and thinly sliced**

Partially freeze beef; slice thinly across the grain into bite-size strips. In a small bowl mix cornstarch, sugar, ½ teaspoon *salt*, and ⅛ teaspoon *pepper*. Blend in soy sauce and ¼ cup *water*. Set aside.

Preheat a wok or large skillet over high heat; add cooking oil. Stir-fry garlic and gingerroot in hot oil for 30 seconds. Add pea pods and water chestnuts to wok. Stir-fry about 1 minute. Remove pea pods and water chestnuts from wok. (Add more oil, if necessary.) Add *half* of the beef to *hot* wok or skillet; stir-fry 2 to 3 minutes or till browned. Remove beef. Stir-fry remaining beef 2 to 3 minutes. Return all meat to wok or skillet. Stir soy mixture; stir into beef. Cook and stir till mixture is thickened and bubbly. Stir in pea pods and water chestnuts; cover and cook 1 minute. Serve at once. Makes 4 servings.

Stir-Fried Pork with Mandarin Oranges

- 1 pound boneless pork
- 2 tablespoons soy sauce
- 2 teaspoons cornstarch
- 1 teaspoon finely shredded orange peel
- ½ cup orange juice
- 2 tablespoons cooking oil
- 1 teaspoon grated gingerroot
- 2 cups fresh pea pods *or* one 6-ounce package frozen pea pods, thawed
- 1 11-ounce can mandarin orange sections, drained

Partially freeze pork; slice thinly into bite-size strips. In a small bowl blend soy sauce into cornstarch; stir in orange peel and orange juice. Set aside.

Preheat a wok or large skillet over high heat; add cooking oil. Stir-fry gingerroot in hot oil 30 seconds. Add pea pods; stir-fry 2 minutes for fresh pea pods (1 minute for thawed frozen pea pods). Remove pea pods. (Add more oil, if necessary.) Add *half* of the pork to *hot* wok or skillet; stir-fry 2 to 3 minutes. Remove from wok. Stir-fry remaining pork 2 to 3 minutes. Return all pork to wok or skillet. Stir soy sauce mixture; stir into pork. Cook and stir till thickened and bubbly. Stir in pea pods; cover and cook 1 minute more. Remove from heat; stir in drained oranges. Serve at once. Makes 4 servings.

Chicken and Pork Chow Mein

- ½ pound boneless pork shoulder
- 2 cups fine egg noodles
- ½ cup chicken broth
- 1 tablespoon cornstarch
- 3 tablespoons soy sauce
- 3 tablespoons cooking oil
- 1 teaspoon grated gingerroot
- 6 green onions, bias sliced into 1-inch lengths
- 3 cups chopped Chinese cabbage
- 1 4-ounce can sliced mushrooms, drained
- 1 whole large chicken breast, skinned, split, boned, and cut into 1-inch pieces

Partially freeze pork. Slice pork thinly into bite-size strips. Cook noodles according to package directions. Drain; rinse with cold water. Drain well. Blend chicken broth into cornstarch; stir in soy sauce. Set aside.

Preheat a wok or large skillet over high heat; add 2 *tablespoons* of the oil. Stir-fry gingerroot in hot oil 30 seconds. Add noodles; stir-fry 6 minutes. Remove noodles; keep warm. Add 1 *tablespoon* oil to wok. Add green onions; stir-fry 1 minute. Remove green onions. Add Chinese cabbage; stir-fry 2 minutes. Add mushrooms; stir-fry 1 minute more. Remove vegetables. Add chicken to *hot* wok or skillet; stir-fry 2 minutes. Remove chicken. (Add more oil, if necessary.) Add pork; stir-fry 2 minutes. Return chicken to wok. Stir soy mixture; stir into meat. Cook and stir till thickened and bubbly. Add the green onions, Chinese cabbage, and mushrooms; cover and cook 1 minute. Serve with noodles. Serves 4 to 6.

Pork with Celery and Tomatoes

- ½ pound boneless pork
- 1 teaspoon instant beef bouillon granules
- ⅓ cup boiling water
- 1 tablespoon soy sauce
- 1 tablespoon cornstarch
- ¼ teaspoon salt
- 2 tablespoons cooking oil
- 1 clove garlic, minced
- 1 teaspoon grated gingerroot
- 2 cups bias-sliced celery
- 4 green onions, bias sliced into 1-inch lengths
- 2 medium tomatoes, cut into thin wedges

Partially freeze pork; slice thinly into bite-size strips. Dissolve beef bouillon granules in boiling water. Blend soy sauce into cornstarch; stir in bouillon and salt. Set aside.

Preheat a wok or large skillet over high heat; add cooking oil. Stir-fry garlic and gingerroot in hot oil 30 seconds. Add celery and green onions; stir-fry 2 minutes or till crisp-tender. Remove celery and green onions. (Add more oil, if necessary.) Add pork to *hot* wok or skillet; stir-fry 3 minutes or till just browned. Stir bouillon mixture; stir into pork. Cook and stir till thickened and bubbly. Add celery, green onions, and tomatoes; cover and heat 1 minute. Serve at once. Makes 2 or 3 servings.

Peppery Crab with Asparagus

½ pound fresh crab meat, cooked and shelled, *or* one 6-ounce package frozen cooked crab meat
⅓ cup chicken broth
2 teaspoons cornstarch
2 tablespoons dry sherry
1 tablespoon soy sauce
1 teaspoon sugar
⅛ teaspoon crushed red pepper
2 tablespoons cooking oil
1 teaspoon grated gingerroot
¾ pound asparagus, bias sliced into 1-inch lengths (2 cups)
¼ cup sliced green onion

Thaw crab, if frozen. Cut crab into bite-size pieces. Blend chicken broth into cornstarch; stir in sherry, soy sauce, sugar, and crushed red pepper. Set aside.

Preheat a wok or large skillet over high heat; add oil. Stir-fry gingerroot in hot oil for 30 seconds. Add asparagus; stir-fry 3 minutes or till crisp-tender. Add green onion; stir-fry 1 minute more. Remove asparagus and green onion. (Add more oil, if necessary.) Add crab to *hot* wok or skillet; stir-fry 1½ minutes. Stir chicken broth mixture; stir into crab. Cook and stir till thickened and bubbly. Stir in asparagus and green onion; cover and cook 2 to 3 minutes. Serve at once. Makes 3 or 4 servings.

Chicken with Walnuts

1½ pounds whole chicken breasts, skinned, split, and boned
3 tablespoons soy sauce
2 teaspoons cornstarch
2 tablespoons dry sherry
1 teaspoon grated gingerroot
1 teaspoon sugar
½ teaspoon salt
½ teaspoon crushed red pepper
2 tablespoons cooking oil
2 medium green peppers, cut into ¾-inch pieces
4 green onions, bias sliced into 1-inch lengths
1 cup walnut halves

Cut chicken into 1-inch pieces. Set aside. In a small bowl blend soy sauce into cornstarch; stir in dry sherry, gingerroot, sugar, salt, and red pepper. Set aside.

Preheat a wok or large skillet over high heat; add cooking oil. Stir-fry green peppers and green onions in hot oil for 2 minutes or till crisp-tender. Remove from wok. Add walnuts to wok; stir-fry 1 to 2 minutes or till just golden. Remove from wok. (Add more oil, if necessary.) Add *half* of the chicken to *hot* wok or skillet; stir-fry 2 minutes. Remove from wok. Stir-fry remaining chicken 2 minutes. Return all chicken to wok or skillet. Stir soy mixture; stir into chicken. Cook and stir till thickened and bubbly. Stir in vegetables; cover and cook 1 minute more. Serve at once. Garnish with fresh kumquats and serve with hot cooked rice, if desired. Makes 4 to 6 servings.

Kung Bow Chicken

½ cup dried mushrooms
1 whole large chicken breast, skinned, split, and boned
1 teaspoon cornstarch
3 tablespoons soy sauce
1 tablespoon cooking oil
1 clove garlic, minced
1 large green pepper, cut into ½-inch pieces
½ cup bamboo shoots, cut in half lengthwise
2 tablespoons chopped peanuts
¼ teaspoon crushed red pepper

Soak mushrooms in enough warm water to cover for 30 minutes; squeeze to drain well. Chop mushrooms, discarding stems. Cut chicken into bite-size pieces. Blend 1 tablespoon cold *water* into cornstarch; stir in soy sauce. Set aside.

Preheat a wok or large skillet over high heat; add cooking oil. Stir-fry garlic in hot oil for 30 seconds. Add green pepper, bamboo shoots, peanuts, red pepper, and mushrooms. Stir-fry 2 minutes. Remove from wok. (Add more oil, if necessary.) Add chicken; stir-fry 2 minutes. Stir soy mixture; stir into chicken. Cook and stir till thickened and bubbly. Add green pepper, bamboo shoots, peanuts, red pepper, and mushrooms; cover and cook 1 minute. Serve at once. Makes 2 servings.

Chicken with Walnuts

fried
favorites

Paper-Wrapped Bundles

1 whole large chicken breast, skinned, split, and boned
1 tablespoon thinly sliced green onion
1 tablespoon dry sherry
1 tablespoon soy sauce
1 teaspoon sugar
1 teaspoon grated gingerroot
½ teaspoon salt
½ teaspoon dry mustard
 Few drops bottled hot pepper sauce
 Parchment paper, cut into 5-inch squares (about 32 squares)
½ of a 6-ounce package frozen pea pods, thawed and halved lengthwise, *or* 1 cup fresh pea pods, halved lengthwise
6 green onions, bias sliced into 1½-inch lengths
½ cup sliced bamboo shoots
 Cooking oil for deep-fat frying

Partially freeze chicken. Thinly slice into bite-size strips.

For marinade, in a small deep bowl combine the 1 tablespoon green onion, dry sherry, soy sauce, sugar, gingerroot, salt, dry mustard, and hot pepper sauce; mix well. Add chicken to marinade. Marinate at room temperature about 30 minutes, turning chicken twice; drain.

Position one parchment square with one point toward you. To fill, place a few pieces of pea pods, 1 piece of green onion, 1 piece of bamboo shoot, and 1 piece of chicken horizontally across and just below center of parchment square. Fold bottom point of parchment over filling. Crease paper to hold the fold; tuck point under filling. Fold in side corners, overlapping slightly, to form an envelope shape. Crease paper to hold the fold. Fold the remaining top corner down so the tip extends beyond the bottom of the bundle. Tuck the tip underneath the folded corners. Crease paper to hold the fold. Repeat with the remaining squares and filling.

Fry the parchment bundles, a few at a time, in deep hot oil (365°) for 1 to 1½ minutes. Drain on paper toweling. *Serve immediately.* To eat, unwrap the parchment using a fork or chopsticks. Makes about 32 bundles.

Filling variations: Use ½ pound fresh *or* frozen *shrimp*, shelled, deveined, and cut in half lengthwise; *or* ½ pound fresh *or* frozen *fish fillets*, cut into 1½x¼-inch pieces; *or* ½ pound boneless *beef sirloin*, partially frozen and cut into 2x¼-inch pieces. Add shrimp, fish, or beef to marinade in place of chicken.

Stuffed Fish

4 fresh *or* frozen fish fillets (1½ pounds)
2 slices boiled ham
1 egg
¼ cup chopped onion
1 tablespoon soy sauce
1 teaspoon cornstarch
1 teaspoon grated gingerroot
½ teaspoon sugar
⅛ teaspoon pepper
½ cup finely chopped fresh spinach
 Cooking oil for deep-fat frying

Thaw fish, if frozen. Skin fillets, if necessary. Cut fish into eight 3x2-inch pieces, patching as necessary to make even pieces. Cut slices of ham into quarters. In a shallow bowl combine egg, onion, soy sauce, cornstarch, gingerroot, sugar, and pepper; mix well. Dip fish pieces into egg mixture. Place one piece of ham on each fish piece. Spread 1 tablespoon of spinach over ham. Fold fish over to enclose filling; secure with wooden picks.

Fry fish rolls, a few at a time, in deep hot oil (365°) for 2 to 3 minutes or till golden. Using slotted spoon or wire strainer, remove and drain on paper toweling. Keep warm while frying remaining fish rolls. Makes 4 to 6 servings.

Sweet-Sour Pork

1 pound boneless pork
1 beaten egg
¼ cup cornstarch
¼ cup all-purpose flour
1¼ cups chicken broth
½ teaspoon salt
Cooking oil for deep-fat frying
1 large green pepper, diced
½ cup chopped carrot
1 clove garlic, minced
2 tablespoons cooking oil
½ cup sugar
⅓ cup red wine vinegar
2 teaspoons soy sauce
2 tablespoons cornstarch

Trim excess fat from pork; cut pork into 1-inch cubes. In a bowl combine egg, the ¼ cup cornstarch, flour, ¼ *cup* of the chicken broth, and salt; beat till smooth. Dip pork cubes in batter. Fry in deep hot oil (365°) for 5 to 6 minutes or till golden. Drain; keep warm. In a skillet cook green pepper, carrot, and garlic in the 2 tablespoons oil till vegetables are tender but not brown. Stir in the remaining 1 cup chicken broth, sugar, vinegar, and soy sauce. Bring to boiling; boil rapidly 1 minute. Slowly blend ¼ cup cold *water* into the 2 tablespoons cornstarch. Stir into vegetable mixture. Cook and stir till thickened and bubbly. Stir in pork cubes. Serve with hot cooked rice, if desired. Makes 4 to 6 servings.

eating with chopsticks

At your next Oriental dinner, impress guests with your chopsticks dexterity. It's easy with a little practice. Place one chopstick, about two-thirds of its length from the narrow tip, in the hollow between the base of your thumb and index finger. Let the chopstick rest on the end of your ring finger or little finger. Close the base of your thumb over the chopstick to hold it securely. In the same hand hold the second chopstick firmly between the tips of your thumb and index finger, with your middle finger resting on the first chopstick as shown. Hold the chopsticks about an inch apart and parallel to each other. To pick up food, move the top chopstick with your index and middle fingers while steadying it with your thumb. You move only the top chopstick, as indicated by the arrow; the bottom one remains stationary. Hold the chopsticks at an angle to the plate and pick up food with the narrow tips. While eating, occasionally tap the ends of the chopsticks to keep the tips even.

Korean Fried Beef Strips

1 pound beef flank steak *or* top round steak
2 tablespoons finely chopped onion *or* sliced green onion
2 tablespoons soy sauce
1 tablespoon cooking oil
½ teaspoon sugar
1 clove garlic, minced
⅛ teaspoon bottled hot pepper sauce
Cooking oil for deep-fat frying
Hot cooked rice
Soy Dipping Sauce

Partially freeze beef; thinly slice across the grain into bite-size strips. In a bowl combine onion, soy sauce, the 1 tablespoon oil, the sugar, garlic, and hot pepper sauce. Add beef strips, tossing to coat. Let stand 30 minutes at room temperature, stirring once or twice. Place some of the strips in a wire strainer or frying basket. Fry strips in deep hot oil (365°) for 30 to 45 seconds or just till browned. Drain on paper toweling. Keep fried strips warm in 250° oven. Repeat with remaining strips. Serve with rice and individual dishes of Soy Dipping Sauce. Makes 4 servings.

Soy Dipping Sauce: Combine 3 tablespoons *soy sauce;* 2 tablespoons *water;* 2 tablespoons *dry sherry;* 1 tablespoon sliced *green onion;* 2 teaspoons *sugar;* 1 teaspoon *sesame seed,* toasted; and a few dashes *bottled hot pepper sauce.*

Beef- and Shrimp-Filled Wontons

 1 beaten egg
 1 cup finely chopped bok choy **or** cabbage
 ¼ cup finely chopped green onion **or** leeks
 2 tablespoons soy sauce
 1 tablespoon grated gingerroot
 ¼ teaspoon sugar
 ⅛ teaspoon salt
 ½ pound ground beef **or** ground pork
 1 4½-ounce can shrimp, drained and chopped
40 wonton skins
    Cooking oil for deep-fat frying
    Sauces (see recipes, page 230)

For filling, in a large mixing bowl combine egg, bok choy or cabbage, green onion or leeks, soy sauce, gingerroot, sugar, salt, and dash *pepper*. Add ground beef or pork, and chopped shrimp; mix well.

Position a wonton skin with one point toward you. Spoon 2 teaspoonfuls of filling just off-center on skin. Fold bottom point of wonton skin over the filling; tuck point under filling. Roll once to cover filling, leaving about 1 inch unrolled at the top of the skin. Moisten the right-hand corner of skin with water. Grasp the right- and left-hand corners of skin; bring the corners toward you below the filling. Overlap the right-hand corner with the left-hand corner; press the wonton skin securely to seal. Fry wontons, a few at a time, in deep hot oil (365°) for 2 to 3 minutes or till golden. Drain on paper toweling. Serve warm with one or two sauces (see recipes, page 230). Makes about 40 wontons.

Chicken and Vegetable Egg Rolls

 ½ cup dried mushrooms
 1 whole large chicken breast, skinned, split, and boned
 1 clove garlic, minced
 1 tablespoon cooking oil
 1 16-ounce can bean sprouts, drained
 2 cups small spinach leaves
 ½ cup thinly sliced green onion
 ½ cup thinly sliced bamboo shoots
 2 tablespoons soy sauce
 2 teaspoons cornstarch
 1 teaspoon grated gingerroot
 ½ teaspoon sugar
 ¼ teaspoon salt
12 egg roll skins
    Cooking oil for deep-fat frying
    Sauces (see recipes, page 230)

Soak mushrooms in warm water for 30 minutes; drain and chop, discarding stems. Chop chicken. For filling, stir-fry chicken and garlic quickly in 1 tablespoon hot oil for about 2 minutes. Add vegetables; stir-fry about 3 minutes more. Blend soy into cornstarch; stir in gingerroot, sugar, and salt. Stir into chicken mixture; cook and stir till thickened. Cool.

Place egg roll skin with one point toward you. Spoon ¼ cup of filling diagonally across and just below center of skin. Fold bottom point of skin over filling; tuck point under filling. Fold side corners over, forming an envelope shape. Roll up toward remaining corner; moisten point and press firmly to seal. Repeat with remaining egg roll skins and filling.

Fry egg rolls, a few at a time, in deep hot oil (365°) for 2 to 3 minutes or till golden brown. Drain on paper toweling. Serve warm with one or two sauces (see recipes, page 230). Makes 12 egg rolls.

Pork and Shrimp Filling

 ½ pound ground pork
 1 clove garlic, minced
 1 tablespoon cooking oil
 2 cups finely chopped bok choy
 1 cup chopped fresh mushrooms
 ½ cup finely chopped onion
 ½ cup finely chopped celery
 ½ cup chopped water chestnuts
 ¼ cup shredded carrot
 1 4½-ounce can shrimp
 1 beaten egg
 2 tablespoons soy sauce
 1 tablespoon dry sherry
 ½ teaspoon sugar
40 wonton skins **or** 6 egg roll skins
    Cooking oil for deep-fat frying
    Sauces (see recipes, page 230)

For filling, in a skillet stir-fry pork and garlic quickly in 1 tablespoon hot oil till meat is browned. Drain off fat. Add vegetables; stir-fry 2 to 3 minutes more. Drain shrimp and chop. In a bowl combine shrimp, pork-vegetable mixture, egg, soy sauce, sherry, sugar, and ¼ teaspoon *salt*. Cool slightly.

Wrap wontons following directions in the Beef- and Shrimp-Filled Wontons recipe or the Chicken and Vegetable Egg Rolls recipe (for wrapping egg rolls). Fry wontons or egg rolls, a few at a time, in deep hot oil (365°) for 2 to 3 minutes or till golden brown. Using a slotted spoon or wire strainer, remove wontons or egg rolls. Drain on paper toweling. Serve with one or two sauces (see recipes, page 230). Makes 40 wontons or 6 egg rolls.

simmered specialties

Yosenabe

- 6 dried mushrooms
- 1 2-ounce package bean thread
- 4 ounces fresh *or* frozen rock cod *or* other fish
- 2 cups coarsely chopped Chinese cabbage
- 2 cups fresh spinach (6 ounces)
- 6 large shrimp in shells
- 1 cup shucked oysters
- 6 cherrystone clams in shells, washed
- 6 slices fish cake (kamaboko) (optional)
- 4 ounces fresh tofu (bean curd), cut into 1½-inch pieces
- 4 green onions, bias sliced into 1-inch lengths
- 4 cups instant dashi no moto

Cover dried mushrooms with warm water; soak 30 minutes. Cover bean thread with warm water; soak 15 minutes. Drain mushrooms and bean thread well and set aside. Thaw fish, if frozen. Put fish in colander or deep-frying basket; blanch by plunging into boiling water and cooking for 3 minutes. Immediately plunge into cold water; cool. Drain. Repeat blanching procedure with Chinese cabbage and spinach. In a large deep skillet or wok arrange mushrooms, bean thread, fish, Chinese cabbage, spinach, shrimp, oysters, clams, fish cake, tofu, and onions. Prepare dashi according to package directions. Heat dashi to boiling; pour over ingredients in skillet. Cover and cook 10 minutes. Serve in bowls. Makes 6 servings.

Savory Wonton Soup

- 1 beaten egg
- ¼ cup finely chopped onion
- ¼ cup finely chopped water chestnuts
- 1 tablespoon soy sauce
- 2 teaspoons grated gingerroot
- ½ teaspoon sugar
- ½ pound ground pork
- 1 4½-ounce can shrimp, drained and chopped
- 40 wonton skins
- 6 cups chicken broth
- 1 cup thinly sliced Chinese cabbage
- 1 cup thinly sliced fresh mushrooms
- 1 6-ounce package frozen pea pods, thawed and halved lengthwise
- ½ cup thinly sliced bamboo shoots
- 4 green onions, bias sliced into 1½-inch lengths

For wonton filling, in a bowl combine egg, finely chopped onion, water chestnuts, soy sauce, gingerroot, sugar, ¼ teaspoon *salt*, and ⅛ teaspoon *pepper*. Add ground pork and shrimp; mix well. Wrap wontons following directions in the recipe Beef- and Shrimp-Filled Wontons on page 223. (Use half of the wontons for the soup. Wrap, label, and freeze remaining wontons for up to 1 month.)

In a large saucepan or wok bring 8 cups *water* to boiling. Drop 20 wontons, one at a time, into boiling water. Simmer, uncovered, about 3 minutes. Remove from heat and rinse wontons with cold water; drain thoroughly. In same large saucepan or wok bring chicken broth to boiling. Add Chinese cabbage, mushrooms, pea pods, bamboo shoots, and the wontons. Simmer, uncovered, 4 to 5 minutes. Stir in green onions. Ladle soup into individual serving bowls. Makes 6 to 8 servings.

Egg Drop Soup

- 2 13¾-ounce cans chicken broth
- 1 tablespoon cornstarch
- 1 well-beaten egg
- 2 tablespoons sliced green onion

In a wok or saucepan slowly stir the chicken broth into cornstarch. Cook, stirring constantly, till slightly thickened. Slowly pour in the well-beaten egg; stir once gently. Remove from heat. Garnish with green onion. Makes 4 servings.

Crab and Spinach Soup

- 6 cups chicken broth
- ¼ cup finely chopped onion
- 2 tablespoons dry sherry
- 1 teaspoon grated gingerroot
- ½ teaspoon salt
- ⅛ teaspoon pepper
- 4 cups small fresh spinach leaves
- 1 7½-ounce can crab meat, drained, flaked, and cartilage removed

In a wok, large saucepan, or Dutch oven combine chicken broth, chopped onion, sherry, gingerroot, salt, and pepper. Bring to boiling. Add spinach leaves and crab. Return to boiling. Simmer, covered, 5 minutes. Makes 6 to 8 servings.

Yosenabe, Egg Drop Soup, and Savory Wonton Soup

Oriental Beef

1½ pounds beef stew meat
1 tablespoon cooking oil
1 cup water
½ cup chopped onion
½ cup dry white wine
¼ cup soy sauce
1 clove garlic, minced
2 teaspoons sugar
½ teaspoon ground ginger
1 16-ounce can tomato wedges
1 6-ounce package frozen pea pods
1 3-ounce can sliced mushrooms, drained
½ cup cold water
2 tablespoons cornstarch
Hot cooked rice (optional)

Cut the beef stew meat into 1-inch cubes. In large skillet or wok brown meat in hot oil. Remove from heat. Add the 1 cup water, onion, wine, soy sauce, garlic, sugar, and ginger. Cover and simmer 1½ hours. Add *undrained* tomatoes, frozen pea pods, and mushrooms. Bring to boiling; cook and stir, uncovered, 2 to 3 minutes or till pea pods are crisp-tender. Slowly blend the ½ cup cold water into cornstarch; stir into hot mixture. Cook and stir till thickened and bubbly. Serve over hot cooked rice, if desired. Makes 6 servings.

Braised Beef with Vegetables

8 dried lily buds (optional)
2 tablespoons soy sauce
2 teaspoons grated gingerroot
½ teaspoon five-spice powder
1 clove garlic, minced
1 pound beef round steak, cut into ¾-inch pieces
2 tablespoons cooking oil
4 teaspoons instant beef bouillon granules
1 cup bias-sliced carrots
1 8-ounce can bamboo shoots, drained and halved lengthwise
1 6-ounce package frozen pea pods, thawed
3 tablespoons cold water
3 tablespoons cornstarch
Hot cooked noodles *or* rice (optional)

In a small bowl soak lily buds in enough hot water to cover for 30 minutes; drain. Slice each lily bud into 1-inch lengths; discard tough stem ends.

For marinade, combine soy sauce, gingerroot, five-spice powder, and garlic; add to beef. Using your hands, mix the seasonings thoroughly into meat. Marinate the meat for 15 minutes at room temperature.

In a wok or large skillet cook meat in hot oil till browned. Drain excess fat. Combine bouillon granules and 2 cups hot *water;* stir to dissolve granules. Add the bouillon, lily buds, and carrots to beef. Bring to boiling; reduce heat. Simmer, covered, 35 to 40 minutes or till meat is tender. Add bamboo shoots and pea pods. Simmer 2 minutes more or till beef and vegetables are tender. Slowly blend the cold water into cornstarch; stir into hot mixture. Cook and stir till thickened and bubbly. Serve with hot cooked noodles or rice, if desired. Makes 4 to 6 servings.

Curried Beef

1 small onion, thinly sliced and separated into rings
2 cloves garlic, minced
2 tablespoons cooking oil
1 pound beef round steak, cut into ¾-inch pieces
1 cup water
2 tablespoons dry sherry
1 tablespoon instant beef bouillon granules
2 teaspoons curry powder
1 teaspoon sugar
1 teaspoon grated gingerroot
1 tablespoon cold water
1 tablespoon cornstarch
2 medium tomatoes, peeled, seeded, and chopped
Hot cooked rice (optional)

In a wok or large skillet cook onion and garlic in hot oil till onion is tender but not brown. Add beef and cook quickly till all sides are browned. Drain off excess fat. Stir in the 1 cup water, dry sherry, bouillon granules, curry powder, sugar, gingerroot, and dash *salt.* Bring to boiling. Simmer, covered, 35 to 40 minutes or till beef is tender. Slowly blend the 1 tablespoon cold water into cornstarch; stir into hot mixture. Cook and stir till thickened and bubbly. Stir in tomatoes; heat through. Serve over hot cooked rice, if desired. Makes 4 servings.

Lemon Squabs

2 12- to 14-ounce squabs *or* two
1-pound Cornish game hens
2 tablespoons dark soy sauce
½ cup cooking oil
⅓ cup water
2 tablespoons sugar
2 tablespoons lemon juice
1 teaspoon light soy sauce
½ teaspoon cognac *or* other
brandy
¼ teaspoon sesame oil
Halved lemon slices
Green onion brushes

Rub birds inside and out with dark soy sauce. In a wok or skillet brown birds on all sides in hot cooking oil about 10 minutes or till golden. Drain excess fat. Combine water, sugar, lemon juice, light soy sauce, cognac or other brandy, and sesame oil. Add to wok or skillet. Reduce heat; cover and simmer 45 to 50 minutes or till birds are tender. Remove birds; drain on paper toweling. Keep warm. Over high heat, boil pan juices about 5 minutes or till reduced to ¼ cup liquid. Using a sharp cleaver or knife, chop birds into bite-size sections, bones and all. Reassemble to original whole shape. Arrange on platter. Spoon pan juices over birds. Garnish with lemon and green onion. Makes 2 servings.

Serving suggestion: Serve the birds with shrimp or lobster chips from an Oriental shop. Fry chips in deep hot oil according to package directions. (Store unfried chips in a tightly sealed plastic bag.)

Wine-Basted Chicken

1 5- to 6-pound stewing chicken,
cut up, *or* two 3-pound
broiler-fryer chickens, cut up
4 cups water
1 cup dry white wine
4 stalks celery with leaves, cut up
1 small onion, cut up
2 star anise, crushed, *or* 1
teaspoon aniseed, crushed
½ teaspoon salt
Honey-Oyster Sauce *or* Sweet
Lemon Sauce

Place chicken in a wok, large kettle, or Dutch oven; add water, white wine, celery, onion, star anise or aniseed, and salt. Cover; bring to boiling. Simmer 2 to 2½ hours for stewing chicken or about 1 hour for broiler-fryers or till tender. Remove chicken; discard broth. Set chicken aside to cool. When chicken is cool enough to handle, remove meat, discarding bones and skin. Chill chicken thoroughly. Thinly slice chicken; arrange on serving platter. Pass Honey-Oyster Sauce or Sweet Lemon Sauce. Serves 6 to 8.

Honey-Oyster Sauce: In a small bowl combine ¼ cup *honey*, 2 tablespoons *oyster sauce*, 2 tablespoons *soy sauce*, 1 tablespoon *water*, and 1 teaspoon grated *gingerroot*. Let stand 30 minutes before serving.

Sweet Lemon Sauce: In a small bowl combine 3 tablespoons *catsup*, 2 tablespoons *brown sugar*, 1 teaspoon finely shredded *lemon peel*, 2 tablespoons *lemon juice*, 1 tablespoon *water*, 1 tablespoon *soy sauce*, and 1 teaspoon *vinegar*; mix well. Let stand 30 minutes before serving.

Duck with Dried Chestnuts

1 4- to 5-pound domestic
duckling *or* one 3- to
4-pound whole roasting
chicken
½ cup dried chestnuts
¼ cup finely chopped onion
2 tablespoons soy sauce
2 tablespoons dry sherry
1 tablespoon hot bean sauce
1 teaspoon sugar
1 teaspoon grated gingerroot
1 clove garlic, minced
2 green onions, bias sliced into
1-inch lengths

Rinse bird and pat dry; rub cavity with *salt*. Place duck or chicken in a wok, large kettle, or Dutch oven; add 1 cup *water*. Stir in chestnuts, onion, soy sauce, dry sherry, hot bean sauce, sugar, gingerroot, and garlic. Bring mixture to boiling. Simmer, covered, for 1¾ to 2 hours or till meat is tender; turn bird over the last 30 minutes of cooking. Using a sharp cleaver or knife, chop duck or chicken into bite-size sections, bones and all. Reassemble to original whole shape. (Or, carve whole bird.) Spoon excess fat from cooking sauce; pour some of the sauce over duck or chicken. Garnish with green onion. Makes 3 or 4 servings.

steamed delights

Steamed Pork and Vegetable Dumplings

    2   cups all-purpose flour
    2/3 cup boiling water
    1/4 cup cold water
    1/2 pound boneless pork
    1   green onion
    1   cup chopped cabbage
    1   tablespoon dry sherry
    1   tablespoon soy sauce
    1 1/2 teaspoons cornstarch
    1/2 teaspoon salt
    1/4 teaspoon sugar

In mixing bowl combine flour and boiling water, stirring constantly with fork or chopsticks. Add cold water; mix with hands until dough forms a ball (dough will be sticky). Cover; set aside.

With a sharp cleaver or knife, finely chop the pork and green onion. Combine pork, green onion, and cabbage. Stir together sherry, soy sauce, cornstarch, salt, and sugar; add to meat mixture and mix with hands. Set aside.

Divide dough in half. Return half of dough to covered bowl. On a well-floured surface roll other half to about a 1/16-inch thickness. Cut with a 2 1/2-inch round cutter. Place about 1 teaspoonful of meat mixture in the center of each dough circle. Lightly moisten edges of dough; bring dough up around filling and pinch together to seal. Position on a greased steamer rack (flatten bottom so edge stands upright). Repeat with remaining dough and filling. In a wok over high heat, bring water for steaming to boiling. Set steamer rack over boiling water. Cover steamer; steam about 15 minutes. Makes about 48.

steaming hints

You'll get equally good results with a metal steamer, a bamboo steamer set over a wok or skillet, or a steamer substitute. Just bring the water to boiling over high heat and make sure the water level is within 1 1/2 inches of the steamer rack. Then, reduce heat to maintain a gentle boil and place food in the steamer. Cover the steamer and steam till food is done. Add more boiling water if necessary, but avoid "peeking," as this lets steam escape.

Rice-Coated Beef Balls

    2/3 cup short grain rice
    1   slightly beaten egg
    1   small clove garlic, minced
    1   teaspoon salt
    1/2 teaspoon ground ginger
    1/4 teaspoon pepper
    1   pound lean ground beef
    1/2 cup finely chopped onion

Cover rice with water and set aside. In a mixing bowl combine egg, garlic, salt, ginger, and pepper; add ground beef and onion Mix well. Shape meat mixture into 24 meatballs. Drain rice; roll meatballs in rice till coated.

Over high heat, bring water for steaming to boiling. Position meatballs on a greased steamer rack leaving a space between them. Place steamer rack in a wok over boiling water. Cover; steam about 20 minutes or till done. Makes 6 servings.

Szechwan Pork-Stuffed Cucumbers

    4   large cucumbers
        Salt
    1   egg
    1/2 pound ground pork
    4   green onions, sliced
    1   small clove garlic, minced
    1/2 teaspoon salt
    1/4 teaspoon ground ginger
    1/4 teaspoon pepper

Peel cucumbers; halve *crosswise*. Slice a small piece from the end of each cucumber half so cucumbers will sit upright. Scoop out seeds and center of each cucumber half, leaving a 1/4-inch shell. Sprinkle shell generously with salt and set aside.

In a small mixing bowl beat egg with fork. Add pork, onions, garlic, the 1/2 teaspoon salt, ginger, and pepper; mix thoroughly. Stuff pork mixture into cucumber shells. Stand cucumbers, filled ends up, on a steamer rack (if cucumbers won't stand on a steamer rack, stand them in a heat-proof bowl that's at least 1 inch smaller than the steamer rack).

In a wok over high heat, bring water for steaming to boiling. Set steamer rack over boiling water (or, set bowl on steamer rack over boiling water). Cover steamer; steam about 25 minutes or till done. Makes 4 servings.

Szechwan Pork-Stuffed Cucumbers, Rice-Coated Beef Balls

Chinese Steamed Sponge Cake

Water
4 **egg yolks**
2 **tablespoons water**
½ **cup sugar**
½ **teaspoon vanilla**
¼ **teaspoon lemon extract**
4 **egg whites**
½ **cup sugar**
1 **cup all-purpose flour**
1 **teaspoon baking powder**
¼ **teaspoon salt**

In a wok over high heat, bring water for steaming to boiling. In a small mixer bowl beat egg yolks till thick and lemon colored (4 minutes); beat in the 2 tablespoons water. Gradually beat in the ½ cup sugar; beat in vanilla and lemon extract. Thoroughly wash beaters. In a large mixer bowl beat egg whites till soft peaks form; gradually add the ½ cup sugar, beating constantly till stiff peaks form. Fold yolks into whites. Stir together flour, baking powder, and salt; fold into egg mixture. Turn batter into a greased and floured 8x8x2-inch baking pan.

Place uncovered pan on steamer rack over boiling water. Cover the steamer with a dish towel; cover with steamer lid. Steam about 25 minutes or till done. Cut the cake into squares. Serve warm. Makes 9 servings.

Onion Rolls

2¾ **to 3¼ cups all-purpose flour**
1 **package active dry yeast**
1 **cup milk**
¼ **cup shortening**
1 **teaspoon salt**
2 **tablespoons butter *or*
     margarine, melted**
½ **cup thinly sliced green onion**

In a mixer bowl combine *1¼ cups* of the flour and the yeast. In a saucepan heat together milk, shortening, and salt just till warm (115-120°), stirring constantly. Add to dry mixture in mixer bowl. Beat at low speed of electric mixer for ½ minute, scraping sides of bowl constantly. Beat 3 minutes at high speed. By hand, stir in enough of the remaining flour to make a moderately stiff dough. Turn out onto a lightly floured surface and knead till smooth and elastic (8 to 10 minutes). Shape into a ball. Place dough in a lightly greased bowl; turn once to grease surface. Cover; let rise in warm place till double (about 1½ hours).

Punch dough down; turn out onto lightly floured surface. Divide dough in half. Cover; let rest for 10 minutes. Roll *half* of the dough into a 10x6-inch rectangle. Brush with *half* of the melted butter or margarine; sprinkle with *half* of the green onion. Roll up jelly-roll style, starting with long side. Cut into 10 rolls. Using one handle of a fork, press each roll firmly across the middle. Repeat with remaining dough, butter, and onion. Cover and let rise in warm place for 25 minutes. Meanwhile, in a wok over high heat, bring water for steaming to boiling. Place rolls on lightly greased steamer racks so sides don't touch. Set steamer racks over boiling water; cover. Steam rolls for 20 minutes. Makes 20.

Sweet and Sour Sauce

½ **cup packed brown sugar**
1 **tablespoon cornstarch**
⅓ **cup red wine vinegar**
⅓ **cup chicken broth**
¼ **cup finely chopped green
     pepper**
2 **tablespoons chopped
     pimiento**
1 **tablespoon soy sauce**
¼ **teaspoon garlic powder**
¼ **teaspoon ground ginger**

In a small saucepan combine brown sugar and cornstarch. Stir in the red wine vinegar, chicken broth, green pepper, pimiento, soy sauce, garlic powder, and ground ginger. Cook and stir till thickened and bubbly. Serve warm. Makes 1¼ cups sauce.

Chinese Mustard

¼ **cup water**
¼ **cup dry mustard**
2 **teaspoons cooking oil**
½ **teaspoon salt**

In a small saucepan bring water to boiling. Combine dry mustard, cooking oil, and salt. Stir boiling water into mustard mixture. Makes about ⅓ cup sauce.

Ginger Soy

½ **cup soy sauce**
¼ **cup water**
1½ **teaspoons ground ginger**

In a saucepan combine soy sauce, water, and ginger. Heat through. Serve warm. Makes ¾ cup sauce.

index

n-r

tips

Make your home special

Since 1922, millions of men and women have turned to **Better Homes and Gardens** magazine for help in making their homes more enjoyable places to be. You, too, can trust **Better Homes and Gardens** to provide you with the best in ideas, inspiration and information for better family living.

In every issue you'll find ideas on food and recipes, decorating and furnishings, crafts and hobbies, remodeling and building, gardening and outdoor living plus family money management, health, education, pets, car maintenance and more.

For information on how you can have **Better Homes and Gardens** delivered to your door, write to: Mr. Robert Austin, P.O. Box 4536, Des Moines, IA 50336.

Better Homes and Gardens ®

The Idea Magazine for Better Homes and Families